BROKEN JAR

365 Days on the Potter's Wheel

Jan Doke

PRESS

Why a <u>broken</u> jar?

Someone or something is molding all of us. Every single one of us is on some potter's wheel, and we are being shaped by the hands of this potter. Every Christian who desires continued growth must at some point stop and take account of what or who is shaping him or her. What is the shape we are becoming? Perhaps we are taking on a shape whose comeliness exceeds last year's shape; we are growing into a lovelier and more useful vessel for Christ. Going from one degree of glory to another is how we are designed to grow.

But what if we find instead that we are really no more beautiful or useful than we were last year—just a thicker, denser version – one more layer of the same old clay—lumpy in the same old places, marred by the same old signature irregularities. Or even more tragically, what if we are changing, in all this mad turning, into something harder to recognize as anything that is or could ever be very useful to our Master?

Part of the difference in the three possibilities lies, of course, in the identity of the one/One standing at the wheel into whose hands we have placed ourselves for all the twisting and turning, pressing and squeezing that is life. Is this designer one who knows better than we all the intriguing possibilities of the finished product? Does this potter into whose hands we have placed our orchestration know just the right touch that is needed here? ...and there? ... and down here on the underside? Is this potter trustworthy? Have we even gone to the trouble to check his credentials? And yet, what we have placed in his hands are our very lives.

If we are certain that we are indeed in the hands of the only worthy Potter, the Lord Jesus Christ, are we allowing Him to do as He pleases with us, the clay? Do we stiffen at or shrink from His touch, or do we trust Him to put pressure where it is needed to mold us to His liking? When we arrive at a shape *we* like, do we grow so proud and possessive of this present form that we disengage ourselves from the wheel to harden into an independent and "finished" pot to remain permanently fixed?

This book is for those jars who refuse to stay fixed. It is for those who are asking themselves hard questions about growing pains and comfortable stagnation. It is for those who wish to be transformed by the Potter from a showboat into an ark of testimony for Him. It is for those earthen vessels who know that to be *continually* molded by His hands—even broken and reformed, if need be—is the only way to keep *belonging* to Him and bearing His hallmark—the only way to continue glorifying the true Potter.

~ JANUARY 1 ~
FRAGRANT DREGS

"But we have this treasure in jars of clay to show that this all-surpassing power is from God and not from us." 2 Corinthians 4:7

"Whoever finds his life will lose it, whoever loses his life for my sake will find it." Matthew 8:39

What everyone else saw was a wicked woman breaking a jar of expensive perfume, procured questionably, upon the feet of Jesus, a pure man of whom she had certainly never known the likes. Desperation had delivered her to this crucial and shocking setting and situation where she found herself—out of her element, risking scorn and censure. But her way hadn't worked, so here she was—at the feet of Love and Purity—to offer the most extravagant of all gifts.

Like all the others there that day, she herself was a jar, and since birth she had been storing strong stuff inside. Little by little she had relinquished its contents hoping each ounce lost would be her last to surrender before she could call what remained really *hers*. Way down at the bottom, she had once kept her non-negotiables, her unsurrenderables – glorious components gilded with pride and esteem she had used so craftily to earn this personality, this lifestyle that once defined her and served her well. Beneath even these, so encrusted in the fabric of the vessel that it was almost impossible to distinguish between it and the clay itself dwelled the least optional possession of all— her claim to her freedom to *choose* her life. There it had dwelled securely out of reach, lying unconquerable in the dark, until now when in a strange kind of life-saving despair, she surrendered it all at Jesus' feet.

So many of us horde fragrant treasures for selfish means rather than offer them sacrificially, never once considering that they are only in our jar because they were graciously entrusted to us by our Potter to be used for Something greater than our glory and cherishing. If we can't even let Him have these things, then what are the chances that we will give Him the whole vessel?

The angels must surely sing a sweet song when an earthly vessel is upturned at the feet of Jesus to lavish Him with the fragrance of our gifts and talents. But I'm betting that their grandest chorus is reserved for those who find their jar empty, and so at last in victorious despair, shatter all that they have left—just an empty vessel—at the feet of the only One who knows how to rebuild it into the magnificent work of art it was always meant to be.

~ JANUARY 2 ~
BROKEN JAR

"… a woman who had lived a sinful life …brought an alabaster jar of perfume, and as she stood behind Him at his feet weeping, she began to wet his feet with

her tears. Then she wiped them with her hair, kissed them and poured perfume on them." Luke 7:37-38

From a whirlwind of restlessness, in a pit of despair
She searched for a beacon somewhere out there.
And waiting to revive her heart from its tomb
Loomed diamonds, leather, silk and perfume.
She pulled them close to her heart to enfold.
These, oh yes, these will bring rest to my soul.

But, alas, her entanglement in the trappings of this world
Failed to spark and kindle warmth in this frozen-hearted girl.
A spirit that is kindred, a sympathetic ear
Are all I need to sweeten the bitter journey I'm on down here,
So her heart lunged and gathered friends into her fold,
Faithful friends will surely bring rest unto my soul.

But even bosom buddies can't be near us every hour,
And she foundered, close to drowning, crying to an unseen power.
Her flesh cried out for flesh: It's a husband that I need!
We shall cleave to one another as the Bible has decreed.
A shoulder I can lean on, someone I can hold.
Oh, yes, a precious husband will bring rest unto my soul.

But spirits intertwined loosen time and time again
And threaten to unravel every now and then.
Someone to possess and carry on my family seed
Is what my soul is craving and is sure to meet my needs.
Children are Earth's brightest blessings, or so she'd long been told.
Ah, these flaxen-haired angels will deliver rest unto my soul!

But flesh is ever flesh, even in its rarest art,
And even children try the soul or leave and break the heart.
So onto her knees she fell, and with her alabaster jar
Strained her vision and found the Light and started journeying from afar.
She lavished upon the head of her Lord the last of her heart's perfume
And the shackles fell, and her weary soul arose from its shadowy tomb.
Now, she fixes her gaze upon His lovely heart of purest gold
And walks straight ahead holding His hand, and sweet rest abides in her soul.

~ JANUARY 3 ~
SHATTERED: THE WHOLE BALL OF WAX

"Therefore, I urge you, Brothers, in view of God's mercy, to offer your bodies as living sacrifices, holy and pleasing to God." Romans 12:1

What does it mean to shatter our very jar at Jesus' feet?

It means we offer the whole thing—not just what we *have* but what and who we *are*—for His total use, even though He might very well have to start by rebuilding it.

He gets the gold, the silver, the talents, the energy. He gets the temperament, the natural affinities, the fickle, enslaving emotions. He gets the relationships, the memories, the fears, the regrets, alas the very personality, if need be. He gets the sins, both those that are malnourished but still breathing, and those that are proudly or secretly well-nourished and even cherished.

We shatter our preconceived notions of what we think we're here for and every determination that has ever had its roots in our independent, personality-based spirit.

How? What does that mean?

Here's a good place to start: *"The weapons we fight with are not the weapons of the world. On the contrary, they have divine power to demolish strongholds. We demolish arguments and every pretension that sets itself up against the knowledge of God, and we take every thought captive to make it obedient to Christ." 2 Corinthians 10:4-5*

We intentionally and unconditionally surrender our own wisdom to God's wisdom. This means we quit pretending about our ability to handle sovereignty. We are just not up to it. We depend upon and defend the "knowledge of God" which, incidentally, means we must first study to learn what that *is*.

Our first defense against the arguments that compete with God is in our *thoughts*. We don't let them run wild. We "take them captive" and make them slaves to Christ. We realize the truth in what William James once said: "Sow a thought, reap an action; sow an action, reap a habit; sow a habit, reap a character; sow a character, reap a destiny." Everything—good and bad—that any of us has ever done started as a thought—just a thought that we chose either to trash or to sow. We must be vigilant to monitor very closely our *thoughts*.

And then He gathers with His own hand the shards of our surrendered vessel and takes the liberty that we never imagined we could grant. He molds us back again in a way that He alone can envision. At last we have abandoned into His careful keeping the just and fragrant returns of the most risky gamble God ever took, but really the only means by which He could enjoy a Father's knowledge of His children's love. Into His hands we have placed unlimited rights to our Self—the only real gift that was ever ours to give. And in return, His daily provision becomes our most prized possession.

~ JANUARY 4 ~
SILK OR SANDPAPER?
(Give Me Some More of That Stuff That I Hate)

"Endure hardship as discipline; God is treating you as sons." Hebrew 12:7

"Consider it pure joy, my brothers, whenever you face trials of many kinds because you know that the testing of your faith develops perseverance. Perseverance must finish its work so that you will be mature and complete, not lacking anything." James 1:2-4

"Blessed is the man who perseveres under trial, because when he has stood the test, he will receive the crown of life that God has promised to those who love Him." James 1:12

> Silk or sandpaper,
> Roses or thorns:
> Lungs of fresh air
> Or smothered.
> Oh, I long to stay tethered
> So tightly to God
> That I cannot tell one
> From the other.

One of the biggest problems I have with breaking my jar and giving it to God is that I think I already *know* what is good for me!

The poker-faced mirror reveals no sign of it, but I am cross-eyed. I shout, "Objection!" God answers calmly, "Overruled." I complain, "Too bitter!" He returns, "Eat it and smile." I muse, "Time for a break?" He replies, "Work an extra shift." I scream, "NO!" He counters, "YES!"

Proudly I prance across the stage to the rhythm of applauding admirers, but God sees me walking stupidly in front of an oncoming truck.

Sometimes I am crafty and well-practiced enough to manipulate getting what I want. The initial results feel silky smooth beyond my grandest expectations. But at the end of so many of those times I have been disappointed and have found that the price I paid was too great for the goods actually delivered. Taking the reins and driving fails to fulfill as I imagine when I set out on my journey. I really *don't* know what is good for me!

God has the power to be a tyrant who doles out and hordes at will, but instead He chooses to be a wise and loving Father who allows freedom of choice. The most basic choice He offers is whether I want to retain this freedom of choice or start each new day prayerfully signing my will over into His keeping.

Before us stretches a brand new calendar year, a perfect motivation to draw into our lungs a second wind, a new perspective, renewed courage to release our will in order to take hold of something better.

"Be alert. Be present. I'm about to do something brand new. It's bursting out. Don't you see it?" Isaiah 43:19 (*The Message*)

~ JANUARY 5 ~
GUARD RAILS AND ROAD BLOCKS

"O Lord, you have searched me and you know me. You know when I sit and when I rise; you perceive my thoughts from afar. You discern my going out and my lying down; You are familiar with all my ways. Before a word is on my tongue you know it completely, O Lord." Psalm 139:1-4

"Know ye that the Lord, He is God: It is He who made us and not we ourselves." Psalm 100:3 (KJV)

"Delight yourself in the Lord, and He will give you the desires of your heart." Psalm 37:4

Because He is my maker, He alone knows me through and through. With Him in control, there is no trial and error that otherwise haunts every move that I make.

Left alone in front of my deceptive mirror, I have no idea what it is I really want. I am color blind and have no depth perception. I seem to be going forward when really I am moving backward. I appear fit and well nourished when actually I am weak and starving. Sometimes I may feel like a million bucks, but God sees my penury. Too often to me God's silk feels like sandpaper, and His sandpaper feels like silk.

Still He gives me the option: I may blissfully continue believing the lies, stroking the feel of the satin while shunning the rudeness of the burlap; or I can ask Him to shatter my distorted funhouse looking glass, pick me up from the wreckage of the shards, and hold me up to the true Light that He is. Framed in His radiance, I am perfectly clothed for the day ahead whether the fabric shimmers or splinters at my touch. Daily surrender will become my delight, and the shattered glass will begin to resemble a broken jar of alabaster.

Dear Lord,

I surrender my asking you to give me the thing that isn't good for me. I now ask you to help me give to you fully the thing that will keep me from serving you best, no matter how I have cherished hopes in my heart of laying hold of it.

I know now that my thorns, my bruisings, and my disappointments are the guard rails on either side of the straight road that you are directing me to travel.

Oh, Lord, yes, I do need restraints, directions, a compass, and even road blocks and guard rails to crash into so that even if it must sometimes be in a bruised and bloody state, I will be jolted back to your true and best path.

Thank you.

In the Blessed Name of Jesus our Light, Amen.

~ JANUARY 6 ~
SPIRIT VS. FLESH

"Do not be overcome by evil, but overcome evil with good." Romans 12:21

"All a man's ways seem innocent to him, but motives are weighed by the Lord." Proverbs 16:2

"I consider that our present sufferings are not worth comparing to the glory that will be revealed in us." Romans 8:18

> Trudge into the tempest; neither cower, cover, nor hide.
> Beat your wings against the wind; sail against the tide.
>
> Shackle sure the muscled tongue; devastate the greed.
> Prance into the darkness; starve the nagging need.
>
> Run to catch the lightning. Jump to catch a star.
> Pan for the sun's gold. Declare a holy war.
>
> Plant a grappling hook in Heaven. Mine pure silver from the moon.
> Flail with vengeance till the death against the walls of your cocoon.

Another problem is that I feel that I have an excuse not to surrender: my problem is *different*; I am a victim of circumstance.

We hear it often and probably have, if not aloud, at least silently, applied it to ourselves. However, God has given us every reason to flail against this wall and reject it as an excuse for our actions, or lack thereof. Romans 12 warns us in clear and simple language; (seven out of the eleven words have only one syllable): "Do not be overcome by evil, but overcome evil with good." He calls us to walk on higher ground than our circumstances often serve up to us. Sometimes the call is to get up and move when we are longing to lie down and die. Other times the call is to stand still and wait when every muscle is twitching to come alive and run impulsively ahead of God.

The call is to quit living as victims trapped in the womb of our cocoons but rather to sprout wings and fly to ethereal realms as we were conceived to do. The discomfort of learning to flail against the world's gravity and the strained muscles from pressing against the weight of our circumstances are part of the high price of answering the call to faithfulness. The reward is sturdy wings. And for that, no price is too great.

~JANUARY 7~
HOLY VISIBILITY

"Weeping may remain for a night, but rejoicing comes in the morning." Psalm 30:5

"....but those who hope in the Lord will renew their strength. They will soar on wings like eagles; they will run and not grow weary, they will walk and not grow faint." Isaiah 40:31

Feeling victimized almost invariably leads to depression. Depression first of all paralyzes us, and then after it has us pinned down and captures our undivided attention, it lulls us into believing we are doomed to be forever the way we are now. How desperately we need the clarity of vision to see by faith the grace that is available to transform us!

God does see our needs, and He is moved by our troubles. He doesn't just sit on His throne with His magic telescope and laugh at us because we can't see that our whales are really His tadpoles. His compassion combined with our consecration has given us stubs of wings which can grow into the means of our spiritual propulsion above all storms. Our feet must still trudge through the mire of earthly struggle, but now our vision is given wings to glimpse the final victory.

Our eyes, by means of these faith wings, gain a holy visibility. Right now these wings might be mere sprouts and have only the capacity to lift us a little way above the ground turbulence, but in His own good time, when He knows that we are ready, they will lift us over every storm and circumstance. They will not be like the roller coaster ride that thrilled us on the top and then plunged us into a valley so deep that we couldn't see daylight.

God never meant for us to be strapped into a car that determines our highs and lows; He means for us to grow wings that take us to a higher view. Then even when the storm winds reach us way up there, we are still tethered to the security of living at an altitude that allows us to see some light beyond. Therefore, we can ride out the storm in eager anticipation of the calm just a little way ahead.

The next time depression threatens with its hypnotic crooning to tie you down, turn a deaf ear and listen instead to the lullaby of your Father.

"The Lord your God is with you,
He is mighty to save.
He will take great delight in you,
He will quiet you with His love,
He will rejoice over you with singing."
-Zephaniah 3:17

~JANUARY 8~
YOUR FATHER'S EYES

"A man of many companions may come to ruin, but there is a friend who sticks closer than a brother." Proverbs 18:24

If you had not offered that very first smile,
What might have become of me?
I might have lingered outside the garden
Not fully knowing God's sweet grace and pardon,
If you had decided that friendly that day was just too hard to be.

If you had not tangled your fingers in mine
And walked and talked with me
On those cold structured, stuck-in-my-faithlessness days,
I might never have learned unconditional praise
For the Father-God you beheld through the haze,
But you pointed 'till I too could see.

If you had not held on stubbornly
When our ship was tempest-tossed,
I would have missed the lessons divine
Of learning to wait for God's perfect time.
Then those in **my** *path might have missed the blessing*
That I had unwittingly lost.

If your childlike, true heart had not snuggled with mine,
Oh, what a treasure to miss!
The child in me sleeping may have slumbered right on
Never to awaken and sing Him her song,
A handmaiden's heart locked up in a frog,
If you had not given your kiss.

If you had not followed His Majesty's bidding
To offer me mercy and grace;
If you had not asked Him to make you a friend
To believe our hearts would hold hands in the end,
I would not see the beautiful eyes of my Father
When I look at you.

When my friend Andy inspired this poem, she was fifteen years my junior, only twenty-four years old. Yet, her intimacy with her Lord overcame her timidity and she boldly approached me about her concerns that I was keeping God in a box. My friendship with her inspired me to take another look at what I thought was just fine. Because she did it with the spirit of a cheerleader rather than a judge, my life will never be the same.

Never take lightly the blessing of helpers who run alongside you in the Only Race that Matters and whisper, or in crucial times, shout "Keep on running! I can see the finish line! I can hear the crowds screaming your name! They think you've already won! Don't you dare stop!"

~JANUARY 9~
LIMPING THROUGH OUR GETHSEMANES

"Immediately Jesus knew in His spirit that this was what they were thinking in their hearts, and He said to them, 'Why are you thinking these things? Which is easier to say,'Your sins are forgiven' or 'Get up, take your mat and walk'? But that you may know that the Son of Man has authority on earth to forgive sins'...He said to the paralytic ', I tell you, get up, take your mat, and go home.'" Mark 2:8-12

ARTIFICIAL RESUSITATION

How could I know I was drowning
In the shallows of myself,
Buoyed up by circumstance
And trophies on my shelf?

I'd rather drown in Jesus
And die with nothing more
Than be "safe" and dry and satisfied
On any other shore.

Sometimes it is so hard to believe that God is always trying to give us the highest joy and the most decisive victory. The difficulty in our understanding this lies in the fact that He does this not from our outside circumstances but from the inside out.

Once some friends lowered a paralytic through the roof. Jesus looked at the same emergency everyone else saw and then surprised them by saying, "Your sins are forgiven." When all the people were amazed at this, He asked, "What's the big deal? Which is harder—to heal a crippled man's legs or to forgive a soul's sins?"

Their answer should have been "To forgive sin!" We know it is harder— so hard that it required His blood and dying breath on a cross. In that instance, because of the situation which called for a witness of His kinship with His Father, He threw in the fleshly healing to boot, but His true emphasis has always been spiritual healing, which is slower, less showy, and more thorough than fixing the flesh. Remember what He says about becoming too attached to the flesh and overly concerned about its welfare? "If your right eye causes you to sin, gouge it

15

out and throw it away…If your right hand causes you to sin, cut it off and *throw it away!*" Isn't this Jesus' way of saying that our hands and our eyes are just the rearview mirrors and headlights of our vehicle, but the soul is the *engine* without which there would be no need for any of these added niceties?

Now we wish He would change us as He changed that crippled man. We wish He would quickly fix our fleshly flaws and fill our physical inventory orders. It would be easy enough for Him and would certainly relieve our stresses and aches. We wouldn't need to whine anymore, and we could frolic on through our picture-postcard lives.

~JANUARY 10~
GETTING SANE BY GOING CRAZY

"Now to Him who is able to do immeasurably more than all we ask or imagine, according to His power that is at work within us, to Him be the glory in the church and in Christ Jesus throughout all generations, for ever and ever! Amen." Ephesians 3:20-21

"We also rejoice in our sufferings because we know that suffering produces perseverance; perseverance, character; and character, hope. And hope does not disappoint us because God has poured out His love into our hearts by the Holy Spirit, whom He has given us." Romans 5:3-5

Once we face the true meaning of consecration and commit ourselves to the priority of an uninterrupted and uncompromised focus on Him, He quits settling for throwing us the peanuts of circumstantial remedy.

Therefore, funny things start happening. Before it's over with we might bemoan our birth, doubt our worth, and feel skeptical about our sanity. In fact, it begins to feel as if God is very far away from this scene—further than ever before right now when I need Him most. This isn't just an accident. God didn't switch on an automatic pilot that failed to operate properly when He went on break.

Really, He has taken us at our word. He is leading us into His joy like that crucified thief who was promised paradise that very day but who, at the moment of the promise, was suffering from a serious case of suffocation and blood loss. We have appeared through His roof asking for new legs. He could simply touch us and make us walk again, but He knows we would probably take those new legs and walk ourselves away from Him. Instead He leads us slowly with our stiff limp of agony through a place much like His own Gethsemane. That one cup just will not pass, no matter how we plead. We find ourselves more and more on our throbbing knees since our limp won't take us anywhere very fast anyway.

However, all this time what we can't see is that we are healing up from the inside out. Then when the time is right, we don't walk; we run. We leap! We shout for joy even more loudly than we cried for mercy. He has given us so much more than new legs; He has given us new eyes. Now even though the fog can't be cut with a chainsaw or all the electricity goes off, we can, with those eyes, still see the Light and follow It through to the safe side. He has not just fixed *things* up for us; He has fixed *us* up for *them*.

He has given us His joy—far deeper, calmer, and hardier than the kind we ordered—and we will never again insist upon having our way. He has offered us unconditional joy rooted deep inside that won't change every time someone rearranges the furniture. He has come to set up not a temporary, portable watch tower, but a permanent, immovable fortress.

~JANUARY 11~
WILD VISIONS

"Trust in the Lord with all your heart, and lean not on your own understanding. In all your ways acknowledge Him, and He will make your paths straight." Proverbs 3:5-6

Lean though we may with all of our might
Against the powerful gravity of time,
The snatches of heavenly we grab in this life
Are but a foretaste of the divine.

I wonder if I'll ever truly comprehend the nature
Of love that follows the Father's rhyme and reason.
I fear the machinations of my selfish comprehension
Might always reign as the grim determination of my seasons.

With a grateful heart and shameful, downcast eyes I kneel before you
So undeserving of Your hands that lovingly cradle my face,
Trembling anew as that very first time at Your majesty that condescended
To die and give Your robe to clothe naked sinners with such sweet grace.

O, Holy Spirit of God, drown out my garishly-colored visions,
And guide straight ahead with your perfect interceding!
O, Father, please keep dreaming each wild dream You have for me,
And lean hard with all Your might against my pleading.

Dear Heavenly Father,

Thank you for being faithful to maintain your wild visions for me. You are the God of our fathers of old who could see their heirs to come only as the sands of the seashore or the stars of the heavens, and yet here we are scattering the world. I lay down my claims to my tiny little plans and my insistence upon quick fixes and ask You to keep healing and growing me from the inside out so that I might be a strong vessel for You.

I pray through the power of Your resurrected Son. Amen.

~JANUARY 12~
LOVE SONGS FROM SOME PARABLES

"Love the Lord your God with all your heart..." Mark 12:30

As I sat in my car waiting my turn to get my oil changed, a man on the radio talked about how God sings us a love song. He described in all too familiar terms what it felt like to fall in love and be in love with his wife when they were young. He recalled open embraces in airports, holding hands as they walked, sitting across from each other in restaurants, picking at their food while gazing into each other's eyes and hanging onto each other's every word. In short, they were sharply focused on each other. He analyzed that they only could have arrived at such a level of focus by relinquishing their hold onto the rest of the world when they were together. They turned it all loose so they could grasp with both hands their togetherness. Then it was my turn, so I turned off the radio and went inside.

Had I heard the ending, I'm sure he would have finished the analogy with our necessity of somehow turning loose of the world so that we can truly focus on God, our true Love, upon Christ, our true Groom and Savior and the life He calls us to live in order to correctly interpret Him for the world. It occurred to me how possessive I am of some of my time that seems so sacred—how I am in love with some of the ways I spend that time—or maybe in love with the escape from having to spend it in the ways I don't want to. I thought that if God, through the Holy Spirit's whisper, were to say to me in those moments or some just prior to their beginning, "Jan, go do this or that—and I need you to do it now!" I might have trouble doing it, and have indeed *had* trouble doing it, and, okay, yes, have simply ignored or outshouted Him and just plain wouldn't even hear the request.

Jesus' Parable of the Sower speaks of the seed falling on the thorny soil. Jesus explained that thorny soil refers to hearts who are so distracted by and even invested in, the "cares of this life and the deceitfulness of wealth" that they don't have the nutrients—the time or energy or care—to nurture and nourish the seed that was dropped there by the Sower.

Is this in some way true for our heart's soil? Do we spend a little time in God's Word so that we can feel okay about investing most of our negotiable time in seeking pleasures of our own, pleasures that Ecclesiastes calls "a chasing after the wind"? How much of all that time would stand up and be counted as wheat or good fish were the Keeper of the Fisherman to come today and divide the good from the bad? How much would get burned up? We need the kind of focus that rivets us to the necessity of "redeeming our time" and "making the most of every opportunity" rather than protecting and hording time *as if this is the only life we are going to be given*. In so doing, we become the "imitators of God" spoken of in Ephesians 5. In so doing, we incline our hearts to hear God's love song.

~JANUARY 13~
GROWING IN THE LIKENESS OF A CHILD

"I tell you the truth, unless you change and become like little children, you will never enter the kingdom of heaven." Matthew 18:3

This is the response Jesus gives to His disciples after they have asked Him "Who is greatest in the kingdom of Heaven?" The question is so general that it is hard for a reader to decipher the exact motive in asking it. Apparently, however, Jesus sees that it has something to do with impure striving and vain competition. His answer is prefaced with words He reserved for commanding strict attention to what is coming next. "I tell you the truth…" He completely ignores their question and goes straight to the root of the problem prompting such a question. Was He stalling or skirting the issue or trying to keep them from finding out some secret that was none of their business? I don't think so. I think He perceives in them a sinister shift from their childlike ways when they first met Him that would cause them to throw down nets and get up from their tax collecting booths and follow Him. Maybe they are beginning to be caught up in the heady thrill of being finally chosen by a Rabbi—and a controversial one, at that—and are losing, as the church in Ephesus spoken of in Revelation 2, their "first love." So Jesus nips it in the bud by snatching their focus back where it belongs. He reminds them that discipleship is not about gaining a certain status but about becoming a certain kind of person, namely, a humble, childlike person. What does He mean by this?

When our grandson Bryson was four, he quietly whispered to his mother in church after studying a picture of Christ's cross on the screen at the front, "Momma, is that what my cross will look like?" Confused, she asked him, "What cross? What do you mean?" "The cross I will be put on," Bryson answered, matter of factly. Mom answered (*finally*, after letting her child suffer with such a belief for four years!), "Bryson, you don't *have* to be nailed to a cross. Jesus did it so we don't have to." He replied, "But I want to go to Heaven!" After a little more whispered explanation, Bryson nodded in understanding of a new insight into his future.

I wonder how long he would have thought all Christians must die on a cross to go to heaven had he not seen the cross in church that day. Apparently, he was happily resigned to this fate, living his life comfortably trusting whatever all that meant. And now seeing a picture of a cross, his curiosity about part of his future was stirred to see what new details he might learn. No complaints or flailing against the unfairness of it; just acceptance and a little curiosity.

Might this be along the lines of what Jesus meant that day? Might He have been reminding them, and us, that there are times when we are sorely tempted to grow (what an ironic word in this context!) discontented with quietly but persistently following in Jesus' footsteps by which means we change and, in turn, change our little corner of the world? Do we become tempted to want Christian living to be more about spectacular *doing* than about transformationally *being*?

19

Herein lies the danger of our losing the humble nature of Jesus in the shuffle. A child is not so sophisticated in his needs. Neither should we be.

~JANUARY 14~
SOUL MATES

"Though one may be overpowered, two can defend themselves, and a cord of three is not quickly broken." Ecclesiastes 4:12

There is something in you I want to hold
That I cannot see or touch,
And yet it is bigger and truer and "realer"
Than skin and bones and such.

I look in your eyes and Jesus is there
Thriving with joy in your soul!
He's peeking out of your sea-green eyes,
And it's His Spirit I want to hold.

I can squeeze your hand and touch your cheek,
Pat your head and smooth your hair,
But even when I hug all of you in my arms
I still long for the "Thing" that's not there.

You carry this precious treasure
In your vessel of mortal sod
Till it glimmers like crystal and beckons to me
To come closer and take hold of God.

The luxury is too deep for a human so shallow
To grasp in this temporal space.
I suppose its fulfillment awaits us in Heaven
Like beholding our Father's face.

There is Something in you I long to enfold
That I cannot touch or see.
It's warm and tender and moves close to my whisper
To breathe in the Jesus in me.

Since spiritual growth is fraught with necessary struggles, God made provisions for earthly help and encouragement. It could be that we have allowed His Spirit in us to fall asleep or be smothered or neglected in some other way. When we find in a friend that same Spirit alive and healthy and thriving, we are called back Home. In the company of one who shares not only the same Spirit but many of our heart's desires as well, we are able to grow deeper spiritual roots, and we find ourselves blossoming with spiritual fruit.

~JANUARY 15~
THE BLESSING OF FALLING UP

"Though one may be overpowered, two can defend themselves, and a cord of three is not quickly broken." Ecclesiastes 4:12

Indeed God does send us custom-made friends and loved ones. Spiritual soul mates who know us well and love us with deep commitment are an unparalleled blessing, but even in this blessing lies danger.

Sometimes it looks as if loved ones step out just at the wrong time. We are gasping for breath, and the one with our oxygen tank strapped on his back begins to shrink away or even walk out the back door. We begin to wonder about the quality of this life-buoy relationship that has kept us afloat so dependably for so long.

Even more to the point, we might begin to question the Lord who sent us this helper. Why must she be so distant, Lord? Why must I be misunderstood by one I have come to love and depend upon so much? If you had the wisdom, power, and compassion to create this relationship, then surely you have the power to keep it functioning properly or to fix it if it isn't. Can't you see that I need her sympathy? ARE YOU LISTENING?

All of these questions are like a ball and chain that hinder our faithful walk or a distracting specter that takes our eyes off what God means for us to be about at this moment. And then it finally happens. The storm of *this* loss blows us to our knees with our ears inclined toward His voice and our eyes riveted to His gaze in a way that the abandonment of fair weather friends could never have accomplished. A blinding flash startles us into looking up and realizing that our loved ones who resisted our total dependence upon them were being led by the same loving Hand of providence that now reaches down and lifts us up.

This has been no accident. Their shrinking away has allowed the Father's larger presence to enter in. Sometimes—probably more often than we would ever dream—loved ones have not stepped *out* just at the wrong time after all, but have moved *aside* just at the *right* time. We have fallen upward into that ethereal region where our curse is revealed to be our blessing. We are more than just saved for the moment; we are afforded a farsightedness for a future when another curse might tromp across our stage and swear to be just a curse. Next time we will know better.

Camouflaged within those very questions hide our answers. Sticking with God throughout painful and confusing times such as these will in due time reveal the perfect love He demonstrates for us in every situation over which we genuinely allow Him control. Crisis times such as these may be the loving voice of our Father warning us to open new eyes and His arms of wisdom picking us up to stand on higher and firmer ground to see at last a land we have never seen before. And that loved one who seems unsympathetic or cool in our darkest hour may be performing her life's most faithful service to us by listening and submitting to the Father of us both.

A true friend may aid God in stirring up a tornado that will uproot you from your quicksand and whirl you toward Heaven.

~JANUARY 16~
IDOLATRY'S SUBTLETY

"Faithful are the wounds of a friend." Proverbs 27:6

> *O, Lord, I must be just starving for Heaven—*
> *Running around with my feet off the ground*
> *In desperate pursuit of celestial fruit—*
> *Feeling such need for that thing that won't perish*
> *To cherish.*
>
> *I learn and forget it time and again:*
> *Even the sweetest, delectable ones*
> *Are marred with some tartness, and I come undone.*
> *From shared, perfect caring to pockets gone barren,*
> *Brought back to this place where I look up and beg*
> *To come Home.*

Yes, God does send us custom-made friends and loved ones. He is still the same God who created the special bonds between David and Jonathan; Paul, Barnabas, and Timothy; Ruth and Naomi; Jesus and John. He brings lives together for mutual comfort, spiritual upbuilding, and nurturing for kingdom purposes. He is the conceiver and designer of holy union whether it be found in friendship, kinship, or marriage.

But if we are in true alliance and constant partnership with Him in perfecting our walk, then, even though He plants the impetus that pushes another to throw us the lifeline or clear our air passages, He, in His faithfulness, can never allow him or her to *become* our lifeline or our oxygen. And the friend committed to the Father as the caretaker of our soul may stand uncharacteristically unsoftened and uncooperative to our usually artful, albeit unconscious, manipulation to administer a soothing but flimsy temporary poultice to our ailments.

Time and time again we strap on our blinders and expect man to be God. It may sound extreme, but really this is a form of idolatry. When we allocate undue power to things or to people, we, in effect, make them our idols. A mere person is just not up to standing in for God.

Blessed are you if you find yourself in the stubborn care of this God-driven soul mate who shatters all the friendship clichés and paradigms by faithfully sending you away unsatisfied to find a higher and more lasting Comfort. After you have suffered long enough from the crick in your neck from cocking your head in confusion and shock, bow it low in gratitude and thank the Lord for the gift of a someone so endowed with integrity—for one who stands immovable in the doorway from which you would escape God's sure and lifesaving surgery. A time might come when your Jonathan might more resemble Jonah's whale, but when it came to saving the true man, Jonah needed that fish as much as David needed Jonathan.

~JANUARY 17~
BEST FRIEND

"...His compassions never fail; they are new every morning; great is your faithfulness." Lamentations 3:23

"Enter through the narrow gate. For wide is the gate and broad is the road that leads to destruction, and many enter through it. But small is the gate and narrow the road that leads to life, and only a few find it." Matthew 7:13-14

God knows so well—and never forgets, as we sometimes do—that even the strongest and most devoted flesh is a creature given to fickleness. He wants us to depend upon only Him who can never be fickle and whose love for us is never affected by His moods, the weather, or his checkbook balance. There is an even more important fact to remember about humans' limitations compared to God's perfect faithfulness. This one requires ridiculously frequent reminders because besides being fickle creatures, we are also score-keeping creatures. Due to Christ's application of His blood to our lives, God's view of us and treatment of us in the present and in the future is not even affected by our past mistakes. "For I am convinced that neither death nor life, neither angels nor demons, neither the present or the future, or any power, neither height nor depth, nor anything else in all creation will be able to separate us from the love of God that is in Christ Jesus our Lord" (Romans 8:38-39).

It is true that we may choose to take *ourselves* out of His hands and thereby "gain" a more independent "control" of our circumstances, but as long as we stay there in the blessed hollow, He will be faithful to take us down all the best paths. Sufficiency in Christ always leads to brighter places than our myopic vision can see, abundantly richer dwelling places than any pseudo-deed we may long to be handed to us by even the best loyalty of our most cherished human companions.

He is our truest Friend and the best Friend of our true friends. His wounds are the most faithful of all. His great faithfulness calls for our highest trust. From our broken jars flows a trust—thick and reluctant at first, but later with more ease and fluidity— which surely must be a sweet aroma in the nostrils of God: He knows our learning to walk by faith is accomplished only on that narrow path that few will choose. Our trust in Him is the key we alone hold to complete the combination that creates and strengthens our *most* precious bond.

~JANUARY 18~
DON'T BE SURPRISED WHEN...

"Dear Friends, do not be surprised at the painful trial you are suffering, as though something strange were happening to you." 1 Peter 4:12

I never dreamed, I never knew I was so close to me and so far from you.
I always thought I was so strong. Nothing could cripple me. I was so wrong.

I never imagined I'd need to fall and cry for your mercy to stand up at all.
Then my heart was in mourning, grieved to the core. I asked to feel better; you gave so much more.

I asked you to blow the clouds from my view. From the clouds came a wind that blew me to you.
A little more crying, more seasons in pain. My spirit was in a drought; I needed the rain.

Who could have guessed conceived in black night so warm and so holy was born such bright light?
Who would have thought that darkness could bring such light to a blind man en route to a King?

In Christ there is one surprise after another. Sometimes we are surprised that after finding our way to Him, we could ever desire anything that would threaten to take us away from His side. We forget that we are so prone to wander in circles—that the old man keeps surfacing to try and bully the New Creation we have become. We are surprised that Satan does what God says He does: prowls around looking for someone to devour, for someone whom he can kill, rob, and destroy. We are surprised when we ask for God's help in fighting evil that He stands ready to give us a way out, to give us victory. We are surprised that when we read the Bible, we continue to learn new things, even though we have read that scripture a thousand times. We are surprised when God actually *works* in our lives; we talk about providence as though it were on the endangered species list. We are surprised when our prayers are answered. We are surprised when everything looks better after asking others to help us pray for help. We are surprised when what we could have sworn would destroy us makes us even stronger.

The Bible is filled with stories of people who reached their destination only after much traveling. We read of persecution and even unscheduled jail time for "innocent" people, and see time after time how they always end up being used for God's glory. He said He had overcome the world, and He said if we would abide in Him, He would abide in us. Why should we be surprised when our plans are waylaid? And why should we be surprised when His detours work out so much better than we could have imagined?

~JANUARY 19~
"HELP ME"

"I do believe; help me overcome my unbelief!" Mark 9:24

When our granddaughter Callie was three, she was full of energetic enthusiasm to learn. One of her favorite activities was to be read to, and since I so love to read, we made a good team. But as much as I love to read, I love to ask questions, and since reading and questioning so go hand-in-hand for us teacher-types, Callie got more than her share of inquisition. One of her most endearing qualities was her way of handling questions she wasn't quite sure how to answer. Rather than saying she just didn't know or taking a chance of getting it wrong by guessing, she would look up, knit her little brow, and say, "Help me" maybe ten or fifteen times in every book we read. When her dad was teaching her the Lord's Prayer, she stopped him and said, "Help me with temptation." None of us really knows where she learned this, but it revealed something delightful about her insides. Whereas "I don't know" might insinuate "...and I don't care," "Help me" leaves nothing to the imagination of the teacher. Callie had her mind open and was ready to learn. She didn't want to waste any time guessing; she went straight to what she saw as the best source to help her learn the answer.

This is what happens to the man in this story who brings his son possessed of an evil spirit to Jesus' disciples for healing. Having failed at healing the boy, the disciples bring him to Jesus, who uses the father's wording in His request as an opportunity to teach a valuable lesson to every generation since. The father says, "But if you can do anything, take pity on us and help us." Jesus replies, "If you can? Everything is possible to him who believes." The next verse tells us that this man "immediately" owns up to his imperfection here. "...he exclaimed, 'I do believe; help me overcome my unbelief.'" The man, like Callie, wastes no time on charades. He lays his cards on the table knowing he does not have a winning hand, but knowing also that the One before Him holds the rest of the deck. He seems to know there's no sense in trying to fool Jesus about how very hard it is for him not to be skeptical at this stage of the game. After all, his son has been in the grips of this terror that knocks him to the ground, throws him into seizures, and has finally robbed him of his speech. We aren't told the son's age, but we know from his dad's answer, "since childhood," that he is no longer a child; this has been happening for years. He looks Jesus straight in the eye, offers what he's got, and then honors Jesus by acknowledging that He is the only Source from which the balance is to be found.

And so must we. We must fall on our knees and confess that we love Him but probably not as much as we should, that we are hungry for Him, but probably not as hungry as we should be, that we trust Him, but probably not as much as we should, (you might even omit the "probably's"), and then ask Him to please accept our hunger to be more hungry, our desire to desire Him more, and our thirst to be even thirstier. We must ask that He accept and encourage and mold into something acceptable our hearts that are not satisfied with our complacency. "I believe; please help my unbelief." Jesus healed the man's son. He will honor our requests too.

~JANUARY 20~
SECOND THOUGHTS

"Satisfy me in the morning with your unfailing love that I might sing for joy all my days." Psalm 90:14

"...and after you have done everything, to stand." Ephesians 6:13

Anesthetize me, please, Lord, from all that I am losing.
Awaken me, Father, to the knowledge that my path follows your wise choosing.
Change your mind, I beg you, Father, about this path you've put me on.
Stand firm, my Guide, and do not relent from the road that will carry me Home.
Won't you please douse the flames that lap at my heart and make so possible this pain?
Oh, my Teacher and Guide, in spite of me, stir the ashes of desire once again.
Please quit withholding.
Please keep unfolding.
Why must you hurt me?
Please never desert me.
This rejection makes me feel worth less and less.
This struggle is gathering me into your nest.

Though the ideal Christian life is to be lived single-mindedly, sometimes the best we can do is debate our fleshly weakness or waywardness. Somehow, weakness gets in, the vision gets foggy, our feet become stuck in the miry clay. We were flying from one degree of glory to another, and then our flight slowed to a glide and our glide to a drift. It wasn't that we had a crash landing; it was just that we lost speed and altitude. Perhaps it was our own doing, or lack thereof; perhaps it was so that we could lay hold of a better gift: humility. Let us consider that at the beginning, the builders of the Tower of Babel might have had purer motives. Could there have been a point at which they could have stopped the building, and it would have been just another building that could have received God's favor?

But if it is God that clips our wings, let us never misjudge Him or think unkindly of Him for doing so. We should always be ready to speak in defense of our Savior and God, even if whom we are speaking to is ourselves.

~JANUARY 21~
HUNGER AND THIRST

"As the deer pants for streams of water, so my soul pants for you, O God. My soul thirsts for God, the living God. When can I go and meet with God?" Psalm 42:1-2

"O, Lord, You are my God. Earnestly I seek You. My soul thirsts for You. My body longs for You in a dry and weary land where there is no water…Because Your love is better than life, my lips will glorify You. I will praise You as long as I live, and in Your name will I lift up my hands. My soul will be satisfied as with the richest of foods." Psalm 63: 1, 3-5

We are driven by a force so powerful that it can be our best friend or our most dreaded foe. It can be the impetus that spreads our wings or clips them off into the quick and not only allows our descent but *propels* us in our downward spiral. This force is our passions.

There are many things I can take or leave. There are other things for which I am a hopeless sucker and even claim without much hesitation as my *cravings*. They are some sort of trademark I seem to need to distinguish myself from everyone else—a monogrammed security blanket in which I, without shame or embarrassment, cover myself.

Other passions require my best machinations to conceal them from the discovery of anyone but God. These I clothe in the best camouflage I can find.

And then there are the passions that God *alone* sees. Something inside of me refuses to allow even *myself* to come face to face with their danger and call them what they are lest I be uprooted from my false notions that I stand immune to certain diseases of humanity. Only through prayer and an intense desire to know might I defeat the fleshly desires that I hang onto with a white-knuckled death grip.

However, if I am ever to empty the jar completely upon the feet of Jesus and become his true vessel, I must see my passions for what they are and begin to allow God to transform them into what they need to be. I need to quit telling myself lies. My passion to hide myself under a pretty veneer must be defeated by my passion to see what scars the real woodwork. My seeing doesn't help or hinder God's *seeing*, but *until I am willing to see*, God's *power* to change me is held in check.

Today read Psalm 63, and ask God to purify your passions so that you might be released and God might be glorified.

~JANUARY 22~
TASTE BUDS FOR GLORY

"Blessed are those who hunger and thirst for righteousness, for they will be filled." Matthew 5:6 (NIV)

"Taste and see that the Lord is good." Psalm 34:8 (NIV)

Only Jesus would I see when the world would sell me futility,
Or offer idolatry's ecstasy. Only Jesus would I see.
Only Jesus would I see when temptation flaunts its goods at me;
When I flinch from pain protectively. Only Jesus would I see.
Only Jesus would I see—brighter than all my memories
That I clutch and hold so close to me. Only Jesus would I see.
Only Jesus would I see, not the fear that cautions my feet to flee,
Or the weariness that beckons me to my ease. Only Jesus would I see.
Only Jesus would I see when flesh offers love inconsistently,
Or my best passes by obliviously. Only Jesus would I see.
Only Jesus would I see when others outgrow their need for me,
And my heart starts to tremble silently. Only Jesus would I see.
Only Jesus would I see, not the turmoil arising in me;
Not my heart's instability. Only Jesus would I see.
Only Jesus would I see—not the bleak feelings inside of me
That point me to human frailty. Only Jesus would I see.
Only Jesus would I see; the sins that were mine on Calvary;
The blood, the unspeakable agony. Only Jesus would I see.
Only Jesus would I see—only His light shining radiantly;
Only His gaze fixed back on me; only His glory and majesty.
Only Jesus would I see, holding me close and comforting me.
I want to behold Him consistently. Only Jesus would I see.

God does not wrangle our free will from us. Others' prayers on our behalf can prompt God to deliver us to crucial crossroads, but the final say-so is ours alone. Our passions for things, people, relationships, and even success, apart from that which is hallowed for His use, will take us on spectacular odysseys, but we are bound ultimately to wind up dissatisfied and disappointed. Even when disappointment is long delayed, we can never settle into peace of mind, for alas, we keep worrying that what we finally have may not last. Fear is always our ultimate captor and stays up late to keep us company, even when all its cohorts have nodded off into harmless sleep.

Pray for *See* Fever. Pray that all other passions will pale into insignificance, or that, if you must be dealt with more sternly, they will quickly fail to satisfy so that you will successfully end up knocking on God's door with a sense of desperation—boisterously, frantically, *passionately*! For only when we taste the Lord and begin to find out that He is *good* can we begin to hunger and thirst for Him and His righteousness. Soon we will learn that everything apart from Him tastes like sawdust.

~JANUARY 23~
GETTTING A LITTLE TIPSY:
A CHALLENGE TO BECOME UNBALANCED
PART 1

"What good will it be for a man if he gains the whole world, yet forfeits his soul?"
Matthew 16:26

"Do not store up for yourselves treasures on earth where moth and rust destroy and where thieves break in and steal. But store up for yourselves treasures in Heaven where moth and rust do not destroy and where thieves do not break in and steal. For where your treasure is there will your heart be also." Matthew 6: 19-21

Many well-meaning Christians often make the misguided reference to "the real world." It's easy to get our specs on upside down and get a topsy-turvy view. The Bible tells us over and over that we are pilgrims on our way to our real home and that this world is just a campground. Jesus tells us He has gone ahead to prepare a place for us, and the book of Revelation gives more than a glimpse of what Heaven will be like.

The grandeur of the Rockies, the majesty of the Alps, and the thundering, azure immensity of the Pacific Ocean are thrilling to the senses, just as are enchiladas, Coca-Cola, and a starry night accented by a crescent moon that resembles the smile of God. However, the pleasure of partaking of these is always marred by something indigenous to this "real world." If the disappointment of unmet expectations or the distraction of unwelcome noise or physical discomfort doesn't confound the circumstances surrounding the immediate sensation, then there is one inevitability about these exciting moments that will get every one of us every time: they end. *Everything physical ends*. Of all the things we are given or earn or become, only our spirits will last forever.

Why, then, are we so dedicated to coddling the physical part of our nature as though we are making some sort of eternal investment? Without our even asking, the unspiritual forces of our world generously feed and pay homage to the desires of the flesh. We are tempted at every turn to jump recklessly into the arms of Mammon. Probably from God's point of view we should want to wrap ourselves in celestial cellophane, but instead we flirt with and sample a little more of the world's goods by our own initiative than are thrust upon us from just being inhabitants here.

Thus Jesus asks us everyday to reexamine which part of ourselves we are nourishing and which parts we are starving. We are all storing our treasures somewhere, and wherever that is, Jesus says, our hearts can be found also. We must be on guard daily that we do not indulge our flesh to the point of starving our souls.

~JANUARY 24 ~
A CHALLENGE TO BECOME UNBALANCED
PART 2

"To the Jews who had believed Him, Jesus said, 'If you hold to my teaching, you are really my disciples. Then you will know the truth, and the truth will set you free.'" John 8:30-31

"For our struggle is not against flesh and blood, but against the rulers, the authorities, the powers of this dark world and against the spiritual forces of evil in the heavenly realms." Ephesians 6:12

"Therefore, we do not lose heart. Though outwardly we are wasting away, yet inwardly we are being renewed day by day." 2 Corinthians 4:16

We all have different strengths and weaknesses stemming from both our backgrounds and our gifts. Some of us are genuinely unaffected by the same things that practically destroy others. However, we are all made of flesh and thus are "naturally" inclined to sin, First John tells us. That inclination to believe that our spirits are the fantasy and our flesh is the reality is the fallacy that can deal a killing blow to all that we were made to be about as the salt of the earth and the light of the world.

Ephesians 6:10-18 makes very clear that this is not some petty skirmish to be handled casually with one hand tied behind our backs. This is all-out war waged against our spirits, our immortal souls. Worthy engagement in this warfare requires constant vigilance and prayer so that we are never far from our true and most crucial focus—increasing the kingdom of Jesus Christ on earth. He alone can lead us through this darkness. If we do not seriously desire and pray for Him to reveal our weaknesses and our specific sinful tendencies, we cripple our spirits for the job they must be able to perform.

One way they are crippled is that *we can never repent of sins we do not see;* and since Jesus has become our mediator and intercessor, giving us every reason and opportunity to become aware of, as well as free from, our sins, we can "know the truth [about our sins], and the truth [about our sins] will set us free."

But we must look again—and more closely—at that verse to learn its secret. *"If you hold to my teaching, you are really my disciples. **Then** you will know the truth, and the truth will set you free."* Our freedom comes only after we have trusted Him enough to begin walking with him.

~JANUARY 25~
A CHALLENGE TO BECOME UNBALANCED
PART 3

"For you were once darkness, but now you are light in the Lord. Love as children of light (for the fruit of the light consists in all goodness, righteousness and truth) and find out what pleases the Lord. Have nothing to do with the fruitless deeds of darkness..." Ephesians 5:8-11

Another way our spirits suffer when we fail to acknowledge and become familiar with our sins is that we will keep marching stupidly into the same traps designed by the devil to discourage us; he wants us to believe that our spiritual nature is so much the underdog that it is not worth even tending to any longer. Sure, some of us keep playing the part and wearing the costume because we have also become cowards in our spiritual dissipation or because we need the crutch of appearances. We exert no effort, though, and our spiritual physique deteriorates as we place more and more stock in the things that meet the eye but in reality are "wasting away."

If we are fortunate enough to be shocked into getting a good look at ourselves and our real spiritual condition, it may be necessary to take extreme measures to work out the sags and cellulite and build back the muscles of godliness. Maybe then we will take off the blinders that allowed us to buy into the "well-balanced life" theory, a delicate and tasteful mix of the world and the spiritual. The cliché itself—a "well-balanced person"—has been touted for so long by such respectable people that most of us have likely worked to this end all our lives never realizing that such an idea is poison to the abundant life Jesus wants us to live. (Yes, I know the scriptures about moderation, but they were addressed to people who had no delusions about the necessity of single-mindedness concerning living unmistakably godly lives.)

The truth is that for some of us to empty our jars completely for the Lord's service and become a pleasing (and functional!) vessel for His use will require an extreme and a concentrated focus. This might be possible only by giving Him *every bit* of our luxury time, especially at first. Some of us honestly cannot afford to offer our flesh any options. We are the ones who tend to be so easily distracted and caught off-guard by our passionate or compulsive personalities or who are so naturally confident, and therefore impulsive, that we stray or even fall into a pit before we know what is happening to us. Then, finally, when some blessing (that we would swear is a curse) slows us down and shuts us up, something in the silence convicts us and convinces us: God is becoming smaller on our horizon. *Our spirits are shrinking, and our flesh is growing.* What we thought was *real* and was worthy of our thought, our time, and our money was not a wise investment after all. It was all a lie. We have awakened from the nightmare, and now we see that what is Real and Lasting was something we opted against at one or several of those crossroads some miles back.

~JANUARY 26~
A CHALLENGE TO BECOME UNBALANCED
PART 4

"But seek first His kingdom and His righteousness, and all these things will be given to you as well." Matthew 6:33

"Whoever finds His life shall lose it, and whoever loses His life for my sake will find it." Matthew 10:39

But praise be to God! He is still there at the crossroads waiting! And now that we are looking in His direction, just like the daddy in the prodigal son story, His arms are outstretched, and He is running in our direction. This time, though, we come asking Him to do something very foolish to our old way of thinking—and surely most of the "real" world will still think so: *We ask Him to make us unbalanced.*

So our prayers become more recklessly trusting and specific. We begin to see Him everywhere. He speaks to us in modern-day parables as we wash the road film off the car or weed the garden and prune the cucumbers. We might lose some interest in the music we once craved and those novels we used to stay up late reading are no longer worth buying. Certain movies fail to captivate, and our emotions gradually lose their once-dreadful power to oppress us. Old addictions beckon from afar, but because we are unbalanced people and have lost the "dignity" to feel ashamed, we enlist others to pray specifically.

And the demons start to keep their distance. Fears of the unknown future, and even death, develop into calmness and even anticipation of the days ahead held securely in the Hands of One whom no enemy, weather, or disease can waylay. We feel less and less intense about more and more issues, and we loosen out cramped-up grip on a lot of plans that once were not optional in the least. We love our friends and family more than before, but they are less crucial to our esteem and emotional stability.

The last shall be first. When we are weak, then we are strong. The more we lose, the more we gain. This really is a whole new world—the real world where all those strange paradoxes make perfectly good sense.

When so many who are bent on living for the moment are headed at warp speed for hell in Satan's hand basket, we discover that we can go special delivery to Heaven in God's. However, first we must jump in completely rather than pick and choose which parts of our life will go in and which parts we can't trust in anyone hands but our own. It seems that God is always calling for faith, as once more He asks us to hurdle off the cliff by leaping into His basket.

In other words, He wants us not just to polish the outside and stick on the right label. He wants the whole bottle so He can fill it with living water. At first, life here is more of a matter of recurring surprise than a matter of fact, but later we grow more comfortable as we understand a little more daily about true abundance, not just in the world to come, but in the present age.

~JANUARY 27~
CREATED FOR STARDOM

"O God, you are my God, earnestly I seek you; my soul thirsts for you, my body longs for you, in a dry and weary land where there is no water." Psalm 63:1

"Whoever finds his life will lose it, and whoever loses His life for my sake will find it."
Matthew 10:39

> *All of my beginnings are snuffed out prematurely—*
> *On their way to stardom but ultimately slain.*
> *All of my best efforts are but temporary measures*
> *All tied up with ribbon but left out in the rain.*
>
> *All of my bright passions are but fast-igniting driftwood,*
> *Quick to catch ablaze but cold, dead ashes after the flame.*
> *My vigorous pursuits may fill my granaries with plenty,*
> *But my perishing heart lies thirsting in a parched and sandy plain.*
>
> *But when I lay down my strivings and passion for everything but Jesus,*
> *When I pack up all my valuables and give the whole basket to God,*
> *Whatever becomes of my treasures and tears, ashes, blood, and glory*
> *His touch makes fertile promise and enriches His kingdom's sod.*
>
> *We're not born to be merely potters or poets; farmers, fishermen, or kings*
> *Unto ourselves for vanity's sake and trophies on our wall,*
> *But conceived for glory surpassing our vision to endure beyond earth's ages;*
> *Meant to be starlight but settling for dust— 'till we lay at His feet our all.*

If we are ever to fly the joyful flag of unconditional surrender, we must be honest about our feasts and famines. Are we indulging the flesh while starving the soul?

Right here, right now we can be remolded and recreated from scratch—reborn to become strong and useful vessels in His hands. First, however, we must be poured out, and maybe even broken.

~JANUARY 28~
THE LITTLE MAN INSIDE:
SEEKING OUT YOUR SYCAMORE

"A man was there by the name of Zacchaeus; he was a chief tax collector and was wealthy. He wanted to see who Jesus was, but being a short man, he could not because of the crowd. So he ran ahead and climbed a sycamore-fig tree to see him since Jesus was coming that way." Luke 19:2-4

For years the crowds had gathered and stared
As attractions would come and go.
The celebrated and infamous
Through the gates of Jericho.
Sometimes he'd go early and stand in the front,
So slight of stature was he.
Sometimes it was hardly worth his trouble
To bother with trying to see.
His heart had grown stingy as his pockets grew full,
His power undeterred by his size.
In matters of business he could more than compete
And had learned to be crafty and wise.

But this time the pull was too forceful:
Some said it was God's direct heir.
He cursed his plight in the thickening crowds,
Then he noticed a tree up there.
Jesus saw more than a slight, crooked man
Who against all odds still came.
He climbed up so he could see Jesus,
And nothing was ever the same.

There's a tree somewhere for all of us
Who engage in war against sin.
Our towering stature is merely façade:
There's a little man living within.
Living close to the dusty earth smothers;
Crowds stifle and hold us at bay.
Break out of the throngs and look upward,
For Jesus is coming your way.
Find your tree to climb up like Zacchaeus
If you would cease being blind.
Knock and the door will be opened:
Seek and you will find.

Although Jesus is always looking for us, sometimes we get too lost in the crowded conditions of life to see Him. Maybe it is solitude; maybe a spiritual mentor, but find some kind of a sycamore today to take you above the dusty earth so that you can see your Savior above all else.

~JANUARY 29~
WATER TO WINE

"Jesus answered, 'Everyone who drinks this water will be thirsty again, but whoever drinks the water I give him will never thirst. Indeed, the water I give him will become in him a spring of water welling up to eternal life." John 4:13

Dear Father,

I want to see Jesus. I know that before I can truly see Him, though, I will have to see the little man that I am. It is a fearful thing to ask, but Lord, I need to stay convinced of my littleness. Keep me aware of my unfinished state. I want to stare into the mirror and see less and less, because that is what is really there until I understand my need for you.

Sometimes, Father, my dependence upon you stares me in the face, and I see it with no delusion. These are the times that bring me to your feet with all the perfume I have, although the fragrance is weak and the consistency is watery. Never have you failed to take my jar and fill it with anything less than Yourself. Then, by and by, enamored of the attraction brought on by your sweet fragrance, I grow confused and believe that the sparkling contents are of my own making. Without acknowledgment of the origin of the aroma, soon the rich oil is depleted, and left behind is a diluted, insipid substance that quickly evaporates and leaves this vessel cracked, unsightly, and pretty much useless. But you are always standing by, faithfully waiting to turn the water that is I into the wine that is You.

I know that in Your faithfulness, You have also planted trees all along my path for a little man like me to scale and see you. I pray that I will understand well my bleak plight and so grasp the certain doom of staying earthbound that I will muster the energy to keep on climbing away from this dusty earth to more clearly view you and your ways.

And, Lord, thank you for what you do when I climb to a place where I can really see. Thank you that you dust me off and remind me that you will kindle in my small earthly frame a hot and powerful flame—Your Spirit—just as you did with small and miserly Zacchaeus, even against all odds. I know that only in your sufficiency can my poverty ever have meaning, and I believe that out on the limb staring at Jesus is the closest view of joy I have ever beheld.

Through the grace of Jesus, Amen.

~JANUARY 30~
OUT OF THE SLIMY PIT

"I waited patiently for the Lord; He turned to me and heard my cry. He lifted me out of the slimy pit, out of the mud and mire; He set my feet on a rock and gave me a firm place to stand. He put a new song in my mouth, a hymn of praise to our God." Psalm 40:1-3

I never dreamed, I never knew
I was so close to me and so far from You.
I always thought I was so strong.
Nothing could cripple me: I was so wrong.

I never imagined I'd need to fall
And cry for your mercy to stand up at all.
Then my heart was in mourning, grieved to the core.
I asked to feel better; You gave so much more.

I asked You to blow the clouds from my view;
From the clouds came a wind that blew me to You.
A little more crying, more seasons of pain.
My spirit was in a drought; I needed the rain.

Who would have ever guessed conceived in black night
So warm and so holy was born such bright light?
Who would have ever thought the darkness could bring
Such light to a stumbler en route to a King?

Jesus often taught in parables. He used all kinds of pictures and symbols to make His spiritual points to human listeners. But when Jesus spoke the Beatitudes to the multitudes, He wasn't being poetically ironic. When He told His disciples that the only way up was down, the only way to win was to lose, He couldn't have said it more literally.

Think about what *really* have been your blessings and what *really* have been your curses. Haven't the best blessings always been the surprises that you knew were *beyond* yourself, that were higher, brighter, and wiser, than you had it *in you* to be? Could that be because those were the times when you knew without a doubt that your life was not really in your own mortal, fallible hands but in the Hands of your Maker?

And once you got to that place of blessing, would you have traded the hard road that got you there for an easier one that might have led somewhere else? Would you have traded the waiting that settled you solidly into His hands for a quick fix that would have left you anchorlessly drifting?

Thank Him today for the hard times of waiting that proved to be the crucial darkroom for the blessed development of your faith.

~JANUARY 31~
THE DEEP AND THE WIDE

"O Lord, You have searched me and You know me...you perceive my thoughts from afar...you are familiar with all my ways. For You created my inmost being; You knit me together in my mother's womb...My frame was not hidden from You when I was made in the secret place. When I was woven together in the depth of the earth, Your eyes saw my unformed body. All the days ordained for me were written in your book before one of them came to be." Psalm 139:1,2,3,13,15-16.

"For with You is the fountain of life; in Your life we see light." Psalm 36:9

> "Deep and wide,
> Deep and wide;
> There's a fountain flowing
> Deep and wide."

Ponder the words. Children learn these words quickly; however, the fountain of God's love and power for us through His Spirit is tremendously hard even for adults to fathom.

His love for us is so deep. It can go down beneath the roots of our most severe neuroses. It is the sharp edge that hacks the life and power from those deadly roots. It resides beneath the roots of even our childhood and our fleshly heritage, cleaning out the foundational sod of our very existence. The fountain that is God's love and power flows clear and unhindered beneath the visible and earthly roots of our family in the flesh and mercifully grants us the fresh start to be different, to break old, even lifelong habits and form new ones. It is the substructure of everything we will ever stand upon and stand for until our last breath is gone and our bones are laid once again in the dust whence they were formed by His hand. Deep. Deeper than anything. Deeper than any habit. Deeper than any despair. Deeper than any desire.

And wide! I cannot run away from Him. He is as wide as the perimeters of the earth. He stands with one arm at my birth and the other at my death. I cannot fall out of His reach or wander out of His sight. He is the Good Shepherd whose rod and staff not only comfort but also prod me toward Home and whose ears are inclined me-ward. He hears David's psalms and my church congregation's hymns at the same time. His love is there for me when I reach for it and when I don't, when I can see every reason to rejoice and when I can find none. He whispers to me in the bleak midwinter and laughs with me on the Fourth of July.

The Alpha and the Omega. The Deep and the Wide.

~FEBRUARY 1~
READY FOR THE MASTER'S USE

"And I said, 'Here am I. Send me!'" Isaiah 6:8

When we reach for a hammer to beat something into place, the hammer just lies there faithfully in the shape it was forged waiting to be used. The surgeon, likewise, can rest assured that the scalpel placed in his hand to perform his crucial work will not squirm out of his grasp. In this respect, the fact that these tools are inanimate objects is advantageous. At least they don't change shapes in order to slide away or struggle out of our hands or scream, "No! I'll not be used! I do not enjoy having my head banged against nails!" Neither does the saw run when we reach for it or when it is picked up shout, "Have you no compassion? You're hurting my teeth!"

For everyone whose desire is to be a tool in the hands of the Master Craftsman or a lifesaving instrument for the Great Physician, the example of the lifeless tools that do not run and hide or scream and wiggle is one worth studying. The fact that they lie still enables them to be used, although, of course, they have no choice.

But Jesus said, "Are you not worth more than these birds of the air or the flowers of the field who are nourished and even glorified by no effort of their own?" If we are more important and useful to Him than sparrows and lilies that are living creatures, then we are infinitely more useful than the manmade dead lead of the tools hanging on the pegboard in our garages; our aid is more vital than instruments of a surgeon who mends mere flesh and revives only the outer man who eventually must waste away beyond even the finest surgeon's ability to repair.

What He can fashion with His tools immeasurably outclasses anything we can fashion with ours. He molds and hammers an infinite soul from clay and bones while we shape imperfect playthings from wood that rots and rock that crumbles. He sands and planes the rough, unsightly and fractious edges of strong-willed rebels into smooth, finely-contoured jars of sweet-smelling, healing incense. We come to Him in filthy rags, and He sends us back out in purple robes. Everything independently taken into our hands is ultimately reduced to ashes and soot; all that is given without reserve into His hands takes on a shine that age enhances. His gold is refined in well-tended fires until at last it is taken into eternal, heavenly realms never again to be bothered by tarnish and oxidation.

And the most humbling realization of this whole process is that in these amazing transformations, in these awesome works of art, He chooses to use *us*!

~FEBRUARY 2~
FORGED TO FIT HIS HANDS

"Do not offer the parts of your body to sin, as instruments of wickedness, but rather offer yourselves to God, as those who have been brought from death to

life; and offer the parts of your body to Him as instruments of righteousness." Romans 6:13

Left to our own devices, our restoration of a man is limited to bandaging superficial wounds. Heart surgery in a layman's hands would be as foolish as brain reconstruction with a kitchen knife. God alone has the vision and power to restore Life. Amazingly, however, He asks no less than that *we* be a part in His death-defying workmanship!

As His tool, my highest priority must always be to remain functional; as a living instrument in His hand, I must also remain resourceful for His kingdom's work. A dim, hazy focus, a starving spirit, and fattened flesh will dull my edges so that the sin God would use me to hack away at in another's life may only be painfully exposed and ruptured rather than surgically removed. Slovenliness will turn this vessel which could be vibrant with the Holy Spirit of Almighty God into dead weight to lie frigidly in His hands, affecting not only me but any others in my path of influence. I am called rather to be vigilant for His step in my direction; my ear must stay inclined toward Him as He calls for my employment; and I must be ever responsive to the Surgeon's touch as He nimbly moves me into a strategic position sometimes His eyes alone can see.

I am not a tool forged by human hands to be used for trivial purposes and then to be stashed silently away into storage nor even a surgeon's scalpel to lie mindlessly waiting to be picked up and given meaning. I am a living human being with life breathed into me by the only true and living God and formed in the image of the Eternal Founder and Father of the universe. I am more than cold steel or rotting wood. I am a spirit, and I have a will. I can run away and refuse to be used; I can leap off the pegboard when He enters the workshop.

He can use us only if we *will* be used. As you give this day into His hands, remember that you were bought at an extravagant price to stay strong and sharp, to be used regularly and often— and never hung upon a nail to rust.

~FEBRUARY 3~
STAYING FAITHFUL IN THE SURVIVAL TIMES
PART 1

"This is the word that came to Jeremiah from the Lord: 'Go down to the potter's house, and there I will give you my message.' So I went down to the potter's house. And I saw him working at the wheel. But the pot he was shaping from the clay was marred in his hands; so the potter formed it into another pot, shaping it as it seemed best to him." Jeremiah 6:1-4

In seasons of rest from our careers or demands which require a heavy load of mental attention, delighting ourselves in the Lord (Psalm 37:4) is so much easier because we are afforded the luxury of *focusing* on Him in a more exclusive way than usual. Even the struggles during these restful seasons grow more quickly and efficiently into blessings because we have time to drain the moat and clean out the debris without having to concentrate on just fighting off the alligators. In times like these we may eventually reach the point of feeling a stir of anticipation rather than apprehension or just all-out dread when we meet with problems or heartaches because we have learned the truth in what Paul said about being strong when we are weak by casting our burdens on the Lord. We just fasten our gaze on Jesus by a heartier diet of the Word and prayer, and sure enough, soon we gain a new perspective, and wisdom and deliverance are ours from a promised beneficence of the Holy Spirit.

However, sometimes I am so far from this season of rest that it feels like life has taken me by the tail and is swinging me around violently or has its rough hands around my neck and is threatening to shake my teeth clean out of my head. Those enlightened visions and mighty gusts of the Spirit fade into dim memory, and I cry out to the Father for a different kind of help. I am groping in the dark rather than growing in the light, dragging my feet on a muddy path rather than advancing on an incline where the sun gets brighter as I approach higher ground.

There is a little of this survival mode in practically every day of our lives, and in these times we find opportunity and even food for character development as we must seek God's help in our insufficiency. When the heart can find more glimmers to inspire than thorns to deflate, its buoyancy seems to carry blessings to others, but when just surviving continues for days, weeks, or months, it is hard to see how God is using us at all.

Pray to lie still in His hands. Watch for ways He might be reshaping you right now to be better used later. Pray to believe in His wisdom and skill as the Master Potter.

~FEBRUARY 4~
STAYING FAITHFUL IN THE SURVIVAL TIMES
PART 2

"The word of the Lord came to me: 'O house of Israel, can I not do with you as this potter does?' declares the Lord. 'Like clay in the hands of the potter, so are you in my hand, O house of Israel.'" Jeremiah 18:6

I do not mean to minimize the heartaches of life even in those less demanding and hectic times. Heartache is heartache; it's called that for a reason, and when we feel it, it hurts. Tears flow from the same pool of insecurity and need as at other times when we are called upon to wear many hats and be twelve places at once. However, digging down to expose the waterlogged roots to the sunshine or the thirsty soil to a nourishing stream is a job we can more readily get to when we are not tugged at by so many other hands.

Most of us spend the greatest part of our lives with at least *some* alligators in our moat, and with God's help we deal with the problems and distractions. We learn to give thanks that there is respite from the monster-slaying sometimes just at the time we thought we couldn't wield another slash.

Sometimes, though, the season of just hanging on and barely surviving continues much longer without any reprieve. Every day we bend low to ask Him for more strength and energy just to finish the day. Our voice sounds faint to our ears as we cast our petition Godward, and the vision we once had of ourselves as light and salt dwindles into a mirage in our mind's eye.

What is the secret to keeping a sweet spirit of faith in tomorrow when so many tomorrows entered into with hope have turned into todays I could hardly wait to become yesterdays? How can I be a strong and useful vessel in a needy world if all I am doing is surviving?

As fruitless as we may view these times, God likely sees them as more than just minimal survival. If we trust that it is He who has brought us this far, then we have to trust that He is still very awake and in control even now. These are the times when our faith must extend into thicker darkness than usual, when we would like to do marvelous things— or at least *visible* things—and witness our growth in stirring, dramatic ways, but instead God instructs us to go dip untheatrically in the pallid Jordan. Obviously this trial is different from our usual problems, or we would not have picked it out to label a trial. If it were easy to decode or even felt difficult yet rewarding, we would not call it minimal survival.

We must squint our spiritual eyes in an effort to focus in on something unintelligible to our normal scope of vision; our eyes have not been trained for this type of warfare. Maybe this is God's point exactly.

~FEBRUARY 5~
STAYING FAITHFUL IN THE SURVIVAL TIMES
PART 3

"The word of the Lord came to me: 'O, house of Israel, can I not do with you as this potter does?' declares the Lord. 'Like clay in the hands of the potter, so you are in my hand, O house of Israel.'" Jeremiah 18:6

"We also rejoice in our sufferings, because we know that suffering produces perseverance; perseverance, character; and character, hope. And hope does not disappoint us, because God has poured out His love into our hearts by the Holy Spirit, whom He has given us." Romans 5:3-5

Think back. Somewhere back there did you ask Him to stretch you beyond your comfort level, to use you at His will, to reveal to you your sins and vulnerable areas? Do the words "Mold me, Lord" ring a bell? Have you ever in one of your strong moments boldly approached God's throne and asked Him to sift the chaff from the wheat, or (Oh NO!) *perfect* you? But is *this* what I had in mind? Does it really have to look like *this*? This is really *hard! This* is wearing me out!

But think about it. What is the ultimate thing that God is always after? Isn't it our pure trust—unadulterated by sight and earthly hope of figuring out a way we can make things okay? We have to learn so many other lessons, of course, but aren't they all leading to the same end? It feels like we're barely hanging on because in this new area of perseverance, we are lightweights and amateurs.

No, just realizing this does not take away the stress, but it can cause us to take our eyes off the tops of our shoes and fix them on the interior of our souls. Understanding that God is being faithful to give us what we asked for (because *that* request was definitely His desire, too!) we can begin to search ourselves for new ways that, with God's certain aid, we can be something more—a more vibrant and versatile vessel—than we ever were before.

~FEBRUARY 6~
STAYING FAITHFUL IN THE SURVIVAL TIMES
PART 4

"And we, who with unveiled faces all reflect the Lord's glory, are being transformed into His likeness with ever increasing glory, which comes from the Lord, who is the Spirit." 2 Corinthians 3:18

"Therefore, we do not lose heart. Though outwardly we are wasting away, yet inwardly we are being renewed day by day. For our light and momentary troubles are achieving for us an eternal glory that far outweighs them all. So we fix our eyes not on what is seen but on what is unseen. For what is seen is temporary, but what is unseen is eternal." 2 Corinthians 4:16-18

Did I really believe God would just keep giving me exercises out of the same junior high textbook over and over again? If I have asked God to refine me and make me into a living sacrifice, then I must trust Him to know how to accomplish that task. After all, if I knew how to do that, why would *I* ever have needed to ask *Him* to begin with?

Will we really trust Him in all situations, or will we renege on the deal and ask Him to work with us another semester from that same old book because we are afraid that maybe He has mixed us up with someone else who could do this thing better or is more ready?

Once we admit that this is no mistake, we are ready to look with abler vision for the rough edges that He may want surrendered to His sandpaper. Maybe the rough edge is intolerance, maybe impatience, or stereotyping people. It could be that I sorely lack perseverance, or that I refuse to get involved with people or projects that really need the touch of my particular talents. It's even possible that my mind has gone unchallenged for a while, and He needs to sharpen it for His use, so the drudgery of boredom has set in to rob me of my happy but sterile complacency.

Thankfully, God is the Father and Divine Sculptor of all His children and very likely will use, if indeed He hasn't already, this unique time in your life to teach yet another of His children how to be an encourager. Be on the lookout. Scan the expanse of this dark sea for the encouragers—those glimmers that reflect the Sun off the shadowy surface, reminding yourself that *their* newly found light would be lessened in value without *your* newly found darkness. Then after you have shown them due honor for being faithful to lie still and silent in order to be equipped to feed you, thank the Father from whom radiated *their* gleam that gave *you* warmth and direction so needed in your dusky hours.

~FEBRUARY 7~
STAYING FAITHFUL IN SURVIVAL TIMES
PART 5

"Then the Lord said to Moses,' I will rain down bread from heaven for you. The people are to go out each day and gather enough for that day… The Israelites ate manna forty years until they came to a land that was settled; they ate manna until they reached the border of Canaan." Exodus 16:4, 34-35

"Therefore, do not worry about tomorrow, for tomorrow will worry about itself. Each day has enough trouble of its own." Matthew 6:34

"Give us this day our daily bread." Matthew 6:11 (KJV)

A final lesson worth learning in these survival times is one that God chose to teach the fickle and murmuring Israelites as they wandered for forty years through their wilderness. They were allowed to have their manna in daily rations, not in wholesale amounts. Is it possible that God is asking us at this time not to seek His will for our whole lives but just His will for this day?

I have noticed that the slayer of my peace of mind and perfect trust is not what I am going through at this moment, but what I am dreading happening tomorrow or later on this morning. We should rather thank Him that we are standing up and moving ahead at this very moment and be grateful that He is faithful to care for us right now. The grumblers led by Moses probably would have liked the security of receiving shipments in crates, but God saw that as a temptation to become independent from Him, so He gave them their manna daily. The time and circumstances are different, but apparently the lesson is the same.

Thomas Carlyle said, "Our main business is not to see what dimly lies at a distance, but to do what clearly lies at hand."[1] Could it be that worrying about tomorrow is just a way to rationalize not doing what lies clearly at hand today?

God still wants us to remember that anything less than total trust in Him is too much of a burden for us to carry. Our hands and pockets are just too small for all we will need on this journey.

~FEBRUARY 8~
A BREATH ON THE CHEEK:
SOUVENIRS OF GOD'S PRESENCE

"'But Lord,' said Martha, the sister of the dead man, 'by this time there is a bad odor, for he has been there four days.' Then Jesus said, 'Did I not tell you that if you believed, you would see the glory of God?'" John 11:39-40

In George Orwell's famed *Animal Farm*, the intelligent but lazy donkey, Benjamin, is having a conversation with Boxer, the slow-witted but industrious horse. When Boxer praises the blessings of having a tail with which to swish the flies away, Benjamin replies cynically that he'd *rather* have the blessing of having no flies to deal with at all. [2]

I heard a story recently about a Christian sister who was awakened one night by a soft breath on her cheek. At first she feared it was a dangerous intruder and willed herself not to open her eyes and alarm him. The breath came again but this time was followed immediately by the certain scent of smoke. She rushed upstairs and found a lamp cord smoldering in the newly-remodeled attic bedroom of her two sons. She was able to put out the fire and prevent certain disaster in such a closed-in place with only one exit. She testifies with certainty that the Lord woke her just in time to deliver her sons into safety.

The first question I asked myself was "Why couldn't God just as easily have extinguished the fire Himself rather than waking the mother to do it?" According to Benjamin the donkey's philosophy, an even better question is "Why couldn't God just have never allowed the fire to begin with?"

It's another parable—a concise, compact lesson to point out the truth about the bigger picture. All through my life, fires have persisted in breaking out. Sometimes the inferno was begun by my own irresponsible behavior in allowing the cords to frazzle or by my reckless behavior in leaving flammable material too close to the heat. Other times, however, flames have licked ominously at my would-be peace from no fault of my own. Had Someone blown on my cheek in the middle of the night when the fire first erupted, it would have been so easy for me to recognize the Rescue and fall to my knees in gratitude. But when we meet with other fiery trials whose embers smolder longer and painfully parch our serenity, the same truth is so much harder to see. We lose our focus and begin to believe God does not see our plight. It is hard to see the reason for His hesitation in coming, just as it was so hard for Mary and Martha to understand Jesus's hesitation in coming to rescue their dying brother. I suppose they could just as easily asked why Lazarus had to get sick at all.

But without the fire that required a wake up call to bring about the delivery of the sons, and without Lazarus's sickness that brought about the death that Jesus canceled, neither the mother nor the sisters would have a testimony about the God of Right Here, Right Now who watches, listens, and rescues so that we, too, can see the glory of God.

~FEBRUARY 9~
THE GOD OF RIGHT HERE, RIGHT NOW

"As Jesus was getting into the boat, the man who had been demon-possessed begged to go with Him. Jesus did not let him, but said, 'Go home to your family and tell them how much the Lord has done for you, and how He has had mercy on you.' So the man went away and began to tell in the Decapolis how much Jesus had done for him. And all the people were amazed." Mark 5:18-20

Why can't we just stay close to the safety of Jesus after each close call from which He rescues us? Now that we've seen Him and know His wonders are our reality, couldn't we just keep holding His hand so tightly that no ill could possibly befall us again? Why doesn't He just keep the fires from breaking out?

It seems that no matter how tenaciously we hold to Him, trouble still happens. The demon-possessed man wanted to go with Jesus in the boat, but Jesus made him go away from Him and into a place where untrained eyes could behold in amazement an unmistakable miracle. Jesus was taking a chance by bidding him go when he wanted to stay; the man could have *forgotten* the blessing he had received and thus strayed from his faithfulness to Jesus. But if he had stayed with Jesus, what would have happened to the people of Decapolis?

The trick is to *remember* the troubles from which we have already been delivered.

We are told to give thanks for what seem to be our hardships and trials and to trust the Divine Creator and Supreme Lover of our souls. We are told that God means our "trouble" to be used for our good and that He can surely, with our submission and trust, reveal to us the inimitable blessing of His deliverance.

In fact, His deliverance *is* the blessing.

First, it is the blessing for us. It is the impetus for our greater faith for the next time smoke fills the room or flames shoot up. No fire, no rescue. No rescue, no awe. No awe, no gratitude.

And right here, it becomes the blessing for others. No gratitude, no witness. No witness, no testimony. No testimony, no recognition of God in our lives today. God would still be alive and working, but someone or something else would be receiving the credit, the *glory*. Moreover, whatever or whoever would get the credit would not be able to promise delivery every single time just in the nick of time. So the one rescued might be grateful for *this* time, but she could hold no real hope for any of her *future* catastrophes.

Every rescuer other than the Ruler of the Universe is just a temporary and coincidental hero. He can make no guarantees about tomorrow's disasters. He *may* or may *not* be at the right place at the right time. Only Jehovah is the God of Right Here, Right Now for *every* one of us *every* time.

~FEBRUARY 10~
NO TROUBLE, NO DELIVERANCE

"He bound his son Isaac and laid him on the altar on top of the wood. Then he reached out his hand and took the knife to slay his son, but the angel of the Lord called out to him from heaven...Abraham looked up and there in the thicket he saw a ram caught by the horns. He went over and took the ram and sacrificed it as a burnt offering instead of his son." Genesis 22:9-10; 13

"To them God has chosen to make known among the Gentiles the glorious riches of His mystery, which is Christ in you, the hope of glory." Colossians 1:27

"My purpose is that they may be encouraged in heart and united in love, so that they may have the full riches of complete understanding, in order that they may know the mystery of God, namely Christ, in whom are hidden all the treasures of wisdom and knowledge." Colossians 2:2-3

Life on this earth with no recognition of God is a hopeless affair.

We are not asked to make up tall tales in order to manipulate the world into believing in a make-believe God we have created as an "opiate," as Karl Marx believed[3] We are simply asked to go and tell what we know to those whose eyes have not been trained to see. If we have seen no deliverance, we know nothing to tell.

God is indeed the God of Abraham and the God of Jacob, but He longs to show me He is the God of *Jan*. He wants to run to *my* rescue and provide a lamb in *my* thicket for the salvation of *my* child. He wants me to know He is not just stuck in a time warp on the pages of a book, but alive and near me, watching and listening and waiting for me to call on Him. He wants me to know we do not live lives of coincidence but of providence. And when he meets me in the anteroom of my crisis to turn certain death into blazing, unmistakable glory, He wants me to tell others so that they can be expecting Him to meet them in theirs, too.

Of course He has delivered us once and for all from the power of eternal death, but death is so foreign to us, the living, that He condescends in His mercy to show us in other ways just a slice of what that amazing rescue really means.

Every time He breathes on our cheek and wakes us up to His presence in our lives, we should praise Him for the smoke in our attic.

~FEBRUARY 11~
CHOOSING THE BEST FROM THE BETTER

"Rejoice in the Lord always. I will say it again: Rejoice! ...Do not be anxious about anything, but in everything, by prayer and petition, with thanksgiving, present your requests to God. And the peace of God which transcends all understanding, will guard your hearts and your minds in Christ Jesus." Philippians 4:4,6-7

A lot is being said about spiritual pride these days. It is true that our Christian progress can indeed be corrupted into a trophy, and priggishness can tarnish the shine God desires in our spirits. We are to reflect Him, and we should be vigilant so that nothing distorts that pure image. It is a cunning trick of our Enemy to fill us so full of ourselves that everything else is squeezed out. For a Christian, there could be no greater temptation toward pride and self-filling than to reach the point of walking more in step with God than in step with the world.

However, there must be a distinction made between being filled with a damning pride in this area and being overcome with rejoicing over that filling with "the peace of God which transcends all understanding." Fear seems to breed fear, and it is not unreasonable to predict that if we too greatly fear becoming spiritually arrogant, our focus on positives chameleoning into negatives will lead us down a dangerous path not just for ourselves but for others in our providential path of testimony.

For instance, many Christians, who when asked if they consider themselves saints will laugh and, with false modesty, answer with a resounding "No!" and asked if they believe they will spend eternity in Heaven with God and Jesus, will say they are not sure.

Is it spiritually smug to be confident that Christ has really done for us what He said He would? Shouldn't anything less than confidence in this area set off warning signals and red flashing danger lights? If we are not sure we are Heaven-bound, then do we think that Jesus was lying about that place He went to prepare for us in His Father's house, or have we decided that we do not qualify as one of the group to which He was speaking when He said those words? (If the latter is the case, then an unsure answer is sadly but certainly appropriate.) However, since you are one who would choose to read about being broken at the feet of Christ, it is more likely that the only reason you would answer that you are not a saint and plan to be raised to immortality is that you fear that answer might indicate spiritual arrogance. If we fear this, then it follows, for the same reason, that we would also fear recognizing and acknowledging growth.

We are told twice in the same scripture to "Rejoice in the Lord always." God does not want us to fear others' possible misjudgment of us as spiritually arrogant to the point of being ashamed of the power He is having in our lives.

~FEBRUARY 12~
PARTICIPATING IN THE DIVINE NATURE

"...though by this time, you ought to be teachers, you need someone to teach you the elementary truths of God's word all over again. You need milk, not solid food! Anyone who lives on milk, being still an infant, is not acquainted with the teaching about righteousness. But solid food is for the mature, who by constant use have trained themselves to distinguish good from evil." Hebrews 5:12-14

"His divine power has given us everything we need for life and godliness through our knowledge of Him who has called us by His own glory and goodness. Through these He has given us His very great and precious promises, so that through them you may participate in the divine nature and escape the corruption in the world caused by evil desires. For this very reason, make every effort to add to your faith goodness; and to goodness, knowledge; and to knowledge, self-control; and to self-control, perseverance; and to perseverance, godliness; and to godliness, brotherly kindness; and to brotherly kindness, love." 2 Peter 1:3-7

When Paul spoke of "fighting the good fight" and "finishing the race," he did not sound like growing teeth for the meat was some badge of false glory to be hidden. A firm intention to keep our growth a secret will many times result in the tragedy of keeping Jesus a secret. Are we to let our light shine or hide it under a bushel? After all, it is not as though we ever claim that the light is of our own making. We are not the generator, but we are called to be faithful reflectors. Grace is our only hope, and the longer we live as Christians, the more we know how much we need it. The only way to grace is through Christ, and to forget this would surely be our death. But not allowing ourselves to feel the peace and satisfaction of walking with an ever-sharper focus on the Lord would rob us of life- the abundant life that Jesus died to give us.

The knowledge that arrangements have been made for us to "participate in the divine nature" should provoke our unbounded joy. We should be leaping over pews and shouting at people in cars next to ours at signal lights. Our tongues should be knocking our teeth out, and our feet should be doing the Fred Flintstone shuffle. *Divine* (like God!) nature! And look! It says we can *"escape the corruption of the world"!* He explains what needs to happen in order for us to be able to participate in a fulfilling manner: we are to make "every effort" to add the better to the good and then the best to the better.

~FEBRUARY 13~
GUARDING OUR HEARTS AGAINST CHILDISH THINGS

"When I was a child, I talked like a child, I thought like a child, I reasoned like a child. When I became a man, I put away childish things." 1 Corinthians 13:11

"Above all else, guard your heart, for it is the wellspring of life. Put away perversity from your mouth; keep corrupt talk from your lips; let your eyes look straight ahead, fix your gaze directly before you. Make level paths for your feet, and take only ways that are firm. Do not swerve to the right or to the left; keep your foot from evil." Proverbs 4:23-27

"Let us not become weary in doing good, for at the proper time, we will reap a harvest if we do not give up." Galatians 6:9

Now that we are no longer ashamed to admit that we are walking in a more consistently upright manner, we begin to look for signposts to yet higher ground and, like the hymnist, long to "scale the utmost heights."[4] As we advance in our Christian journey and grow taller in our Christlike stature with God's Spirit dwelling more firmly in our stead, it is expected that we should manage to put away some of our childish things. Our stride grows longer and more even. We reach a stretch where our crossroads are less often choices between good and evil and more often choices between the better and the best. To one who desires above all else to be a true servant, however, the decisions are nevertheless still crucial; indeed, the prayers for preparation for the next step should be as intense as those for the strength of choosing between the more clear-cut obedience and disobedience, good and evil. Understanding that not to grow means to die on the vine, I must never lose my passion to continue growing in the Lord. The growth that happens from infancy through adolescence is so dramatic that no one can miss seeing it, whereas the growth that occurs from that point on into and through adulthood happens more subtly. However, everyone agrees that to stop growing — to die — before having the chance to go through adulthood is a tragic thing. There are always more tears at those funerals. The spiritual equivalent would be an even worse tragedy.

At this time of slower and subtler growth, we must guard our hearts against both spiritual complacency and spiritual weariness, being faithful to deny the fleshly whimsies of appetite which our Enemy might whisper to us we can finally, at this level, "afford" or "handle responsibly." By this kind of vigilance, we allow God to develop in us a hunger for solid food that will nourish and strengthen our spirits into a greater and more useful level of maturity for His kingdom.

~FEBRUARY 14~
GUARDING OUR HEARTS AGAINST SKEPTICISM

"Do not be wise in your own eyes; fear the Lord and shun evil." Proverbs 3:7

"He called a little child and had him stand among them. And He said, 'I tell you the truth, unless you change and become like little children, you will never enter the kingdom of heaven. Therefore, whoever humbles himself like this child is the greatest in the kingdom of heaven.'" Matthew 18:2-4

"I am sending you out like sheep among wolves. Therefore, be as shrewd as snakes and as innocent as doves." Matthew 10:16

Before we put away all things we consider childish, we must take a close look at what Jesus meant here when He warned us against being anything BUT a child. Obviously there is some aspect of childlikeness we absolutely must possess if we want to enter the kingdom of heaven.

I believe what Jesus meant here, to a great extent, has to do with a trusting heart. Just living life—without even trying—we learn skepticism. People prove insincere, don't keep their promises, tell us lies, and just generally let us down and disappoint us. The longer we live, the more this happens to us. Before we know it, we can be face to face with a scary result: a skeptical, untrusting, and hard heart. Even though we might want to believe that our hearts are soft and trusting toward God and only hard and skeptical about people, we need to realize that there is a grave danger in allowing our hearts to act the same way all the time to both God and man, especially when the people we become hard to and skeptical about are fellow Christians.

How do we honor Jesus' command to be as "shrewd as snakes" if we are going to have to be at the same time "like little children"? How are we supposed to handle someone's repeated untrustworthiness both shrewdly and childishly? To me these are hard questions, but their answers deserve our wrestling before the Lord to learn.

And what I have learned is that there is no easy answer. There is only very close vigilance and regular prayerful attention to our proneness to allow disappointment in others to grow stealthily and dangerously into a generally untrusting and hardened heart, not just toward people, but toward God as well. For, I am learning that by allowing an arrogant spirit of character-judging to creep in, our hearts and minds become easy victims of a corroded and corrupted trust in God's power to *change* people.

Perhaps it's supposed to work something like this: as we grow in our knowledge of God's Word and stay in relationship with our Lord, we learn to be shrewd discerners between worldly and Christlike behavior; but we pray earnestly never to lose faith in God—that Someone High and Mighty and Unseen—to be able to, at any moment, swoop down like a childhood hero and take a heart by storm.

~FEBRUARY 15~
BELIEVING IN OUR CHILDHOOD HERO

"While they were stoning him, Stephen prayed, 'Lord, do not hold this sin against them.' When he said this, he fell asleep. And Saul was there, giving approval to his death." Acts 7:59-8:1

"Meanwhile Saul was still breathing out murderous threats against the Lord's disciples. He went to the high priest and asked him for letters to the synagogues in Damascus, so that if he found any there who belonged to the Way, whether men or women, he might take them as prisoners to Jerusalem. As he neared Damascus on his journey, suddenly a light from heaven flashed around him. He fell to the ground and heard a voice say to him, 'Saul, Saul, why do you persecute me?'... Now get up and go into the city, and you will be told what you must do." Acts 9:1-6

"...The Lord said to Ananias, 'Go! This man is my chosen instrument to carry my name before the Gentiles and their kings, and before the people of Israel.'" Acts 9:15

"But whatever was to my profit, I now consider loss for the sake of Christ. What is more, I consider everything a loss compared to the surpassing greatness of knowing Christ Jesus my Lord, for whose sake I have lost all things. I consider them rubbish, that I might gain Christ and be found in Him...I want to know Christ and the power of his resurrection and the fellowship of sharing in His sufferings, becoming like Him in His death, and so, somehow, to attain to the resurrection of the dead." Philippians 3:7-11

Flashes of light in oceans of ebony;
Glimmers of glory in caverns of black.
We see God's face gleam with pride parental
As He pats us on the back.

Then we flounder and falter helplessly;
The writing of our doom is on the wall.
But watching in love at the bottom of the pit,
He waits to cushion our fall.

Hearken back to your childhood, and take hold of those grandiose visions that once were so real to you. Saul, the murderer of Christians, became Paul, the great missionary apostle when Jesus swooped down on the road to Damascus. It's not a fairy tale.

Jesus, our Hero, asks us to climb up in His lap like those little children He welcomed and trust Him to do "immeasurably more than all we ask or imagine."

~FEBRUARY 16~
RECOGNIZING CRUCIAL JUNCTURES

"Watch and pray so that you will not fall into temptation. The spirit is willing, but the body is weak." Matthew 26:41

"Enter through the narrow gate. For wide is the gate and broad is the road that leads to destruction, and many enter through it. But small is the gate and narrow the road that leads to life and only a few find it." Matthew 7:13-14

Just as aging physically does not necessarily mean maturing emotionally and intellectually, neither does growing into a white-haired "religious person" necessarily mean growing more like Christ. Because God doubtless desires that I continue growing in likeness to His Son, and since growth usually occurs as a result of my decisions, I am certain to continue to arrive at as many crossroads in this part of my journey as in the first part.

The crossroads are there, no doubt, but they are so subtle that we might not recognize one for what it is until we are a few miles or a few hundred miles down the road. Sometimes they are camouflaged by Satan, who would be thrilled for us to continue complacently in our decent but deadly ruts. The subtlety of crucial junctures is ominous to our growth and, over a period of time, can lead to our spiritual decline. If we fear to follow Him onto the roads less taken, our growth will surely be stunted. Even in the most basic character development, it is wise to remember what William Danforth warned: "Lines of least resistance make crooked rivers and crooked men."[5] Without constant vigilance for a more mature prostration of our wills to His, eventually our spirits may stagnate, wither, and likely even atrophy and die on a broad yet crowded expressway.

How crucial it must be, then, for our eyes to be trained to *recognize* the crossroads! It would be nice if all of them were marked by bells clanging, whistles blowing, and maybe even some of those gates that fall down in front of us to block our entry until the time is right, like the ones that keep us from driving our cars into the path of a train or plunging into a river over which a bridge is out. Unfortunately, a maturing Christian who above all wants to keep God above all attracts Satan's more serious attention and cannot be allowed such luxuries as these noisy warnings. But God has equipped His children with all we need to train our eyes for the little subtleties, and though we are not to be *fearful* just because the devil has us in his sights, we must remain sharply and singly *focused* on the Father of Light. Not even the good and the better should take our eyes off the best. Learning to distinguish the best from the rest is crucial.

~FEBRUARY 17~
GAINING THE MIND OF CHRIST

"And I will ask the Father and He will give you another Counselor to be with you forever—the Spirit of Truth...the Counselor, the Holy Spirit, whom the Father will send in my name, will teach you all things and will remind you of everything I have said to you...He will guide you into all truth." John 14:16-17, 26; 16:13

"The man without the Spirit does not accept the things that come from the Spirit of God, for they are foolishness to him, and he cannot understand them because they are spiritually discerned. The spiritual man makes judgments about all things, but he himself is not subject to any man's judgment: 'For who has known the mind of the Lord that he may instruct Him?' But we have the mind of Christ." 1 Corinthians 2:14-16

In 1 Corinthians 2:14-15, Paul begins by telling us about things that can be only spiritually discerned and ends by bestowing this wonderfully comforting pronouncement: *"But you have the mind of Christ."* God forbid that we fall out of that targeted hope. The secret of gaining the mind of Christ, however, is explained earlier in verses 7-9 of the same chapter: *"...we speak of God's secret wisdom, a wisdom that has been hidden and that God destined for our glory before time began. None of the rulers of this age understood it, for if they had, they would not have crucified the Lord of glory. However, as it is written: 'No eye has seen, no ear has heard, no mind has conceived what God has prepared for those who love him'...but God has revealed it to us through His spirit."*

Without this priceless gift of His Spirit, I would be nothing but a bundle of tendencies gathered from those who have influenced my life, not just positively, but also negatively. We would each be a different combination of tendencies and together would almost certainly prove explosively chaotic.

But with His Spirit living in me and producing His fruit, my tendencies are either divinely restrained, because I have submitted the whole vessel to His use, or they blend in a way as to become assets to His kingdom. With His Spirit dwelling in us, together we become His body, salt and light left to preserve and show the way out of this dying world into the timeless and incorruptible Home of the Soul.

~FEBRUARY 18~
NOURISHING THE MIND OF CHRIST

"All men are like grass, and all their glory is like the flowers of the field. The grass withers and the flowers fall...but the word of our God stands forever." Isaiah 40:6-8

For our spiritual nature to thrive, we must nourish it in part, by feeding on the Word. Here is one place we can so innocently neglect to choose the best of all the good options. Instead of getting hooked on books *about* the Word, we need to stay mainly *in* the Word. So many good books are at my disposal that it is easy for me to fall into the trap of reading six at a time and having a stack of ten more waiting in the wings. We must remember that while man's words may be good for pointing us to the Source, they are not the Source. We have to be careful not to be beguiled into believing that strong and regular doses of them can replace our need to feed on the words from the very mouth and heart of our true Father.

Good books, like most things, are not evil in themselves, but when our desire for more and more human wisdom becomes a passion that throws us into a whirl-wind blowing us away from, rather than closer to, God, we are bound to become weaker, and the Accuser licks his lips and rubs his hands together in delight. We have chosen the good and maybe even the better, but to his delight, we have, in that choice left the *Best* untouched.

It may be a slower and less dramatic demise than that of an earlier stage of growth, but still we are made less effective and propelled a little further away from the only Heart that has any saving power for our souls and the souls that we will touch.

~FEBRUARY 19~
HIDDEN WORDS

"I have hidden your Word in my heart that I might not sin against you." Psalm 119:11

"If your law had not been my delight, I would have perished in my affliction. I will never forget your precepts, for by them you have preserved my life." Psalm 119:92-93

"Your word is a lamp to my feet and a light to my path." Psalm 119:105

Even better than merely reading the Word is *memorizing* the Word.

Psalm 119 is the longest chapter in the Bible. It is a 176-verse acrostic poem, by far the most elaborate poem in the Bible, all the verses of each of its stanzas beginning with the same letter of the Hebrew alphabet. Another distinction aside from its highly elaborate literary style is its singular focus on the Word of God.

I especially love verse eleven because of the ways God has proven it to me over and over again.

However, I will confess that when I began taking scripture memory seriously, I suffered through a lot of frustration: it seemed that as soon as I would start on a new one, I would "lose" the one I learned last week. I wanted it to work cumulatively as it did in school when I memorized a long poem for a class recitation. Part of the reason I have always enjoyed memorizing poetry is to share it with others—as a sort of literary conversation, the way art enthusiasts might enjoy walking through a gallery together. But so many times when I have wanted to rattle off a scripture for someone, it has seemed indeed "hidden." Then I began to realize that these times of forgetting weren't really the crucial times when I or someone else might really be depending upon that particular scripture for spiritual strength, and conversely, that when one of those crucial instances *did* arise, the words would miraculously come out of hiding right on cue.

When the psalmist spoke of his reasons for memorizing God's words, he revealed his reason was of dire importance—that he might not sin. Maybe God knows that if I could recite scripture after scripture flawlessly, as I have at times learned to recite poetry, it might become more about my talents that I want you to notice than God's eternal wisdom. I have learned now that when I commit scriptures to memory, even if it isn't next week, and even if I can't dazzle you in an offhanded way, God will always find a way to make me glad I have those words hidden away ready to use for *His* purposes.

~FEBRUARY 20~
AVAILABLE FOR INTIMACY

"Many will say to me on that day, 'Lord, Lord, did we not prophesy in your name and in your name, drive out demons and perform many miracles?' Then I will tell them plainly, 'I never knew you...'" Matthew 7:22-23

"Martha, Martha, you are worried and upset about many things, but only one thing is needed. Mary has chosen what is better, and it will not be taken away from her." Luke 10:41-42

"Be still and know that I am God." Psalm 46:10

Bible study and scripture memory are hearty nourishment for the mind of Christ, but it is possible to know the Word in a scholastic way and never really know the Author intimately. If only our minds are changed, we are still ill-equipped for the thorny path we may need to take in order to be faithful to His purposes for our growth. We must also have hearts that know Him intimately enough to trust that He is with us every step of the way. If we do not know His companionship and learn to trust that it is there, even when we cannot see around the next bend, we will finally despair and turn back to the easy and familiar path. Here again, so many good options parade before us.

There are hungry people to feed, the sick and imprisoned to visit, the lost to teach, and Jesus told us to care for all of these. However, He told us also that we could do all these things, and He still might never have "known" us. What a terrible boat to miss!

What Martha did when she fed the stomachs was good, but what Mary did when she sat at Jesus' feet and fed her spirit was better. Both have lived on in the story, but it was Mary's choice at this simple and subtle crossroads in her life that immortalized the story.

Nothing should be allowed to come between us and our communion with our Father in prayer. For some of us, being still and quiet is the supreme sacrifice, just as was the costly nard Mary poured so lavishly on the feet of Jesus. Music is a soothing retreat for our spirits, especially music that praises God, but like good deeds and good books, music, too, can rob us of valuable time alone in stillness and quietness with the Father who wants our undivided attention. Ask yourself in every activity: "Am I available to God right now if He wants to speak to me?"

There is something disconcerting and even hurtful when the one to whom I am showing my heart is preoccupied with something else. A glaze comes over his eyes, and I am tempted to look around and see whom he is looking at behind me. I feel as though I am not being looked *into* but rather looked *through*. I wonder if God feels this way when we make Him the background music instead of the lead singer or the props instead of the star. The rapturous melody that transports me into praise and worship might, if not held in check, ironically carry me away from a path He may want me to take.

~FEBRUARY 21~
THE GREATEST OF THESE

"Be still and know that I am God." Psalm 46:10

"The Lord who delivered me from the paw of the lion and the paw of the bear will deliver me from the hand of this Philistine." 1 Samuel 17:37

"Therefore, since we are surrounded by such a great cloud of witnesses, let us throw off everything that hinders and the sin that so easily entangles, and let us run with perseverance that race marked out for us. Let us fix our eyes on Jesus, the author and perfecter of our faith, who for the joy set before Him endured the cross, scorning its shame, and sat down at the right hand of the throne of God. Consider Him who endured such opposition from sinful men that you will not grow weary and lose heart." Hebrews 12:1-3

"And now these three remain: faith, hope and love. But the greatest of these is love." 1 Corinthians 13:13

We need focused, face-to-face time with Him—time to meditate on Him and remember what He is doing for us and in us.

We need listening time to gain encouragement from the cheering "great cloud of witnesses."

We need the empathy and inspiration that God in His wisdom makes available to us from the often lonely shepherd-author of the Psalms, outwardly outclassed, outnumbered, and overpowered as he stands looking down at the dead lion and bear, and later, with a little leather sling and four surplus rocks, over the once scoffing but now dead giant Goliath whose surly and taunting tongue lies stilled in his now detached head.

Not even the rapture of hearing a concert from a choir of angels could replace my need to fall at His feet in deep gratitude as I remember how He has been *my* Father, the Lover of *my* soul, the Prince of *my* peace, and *my own* personal Great Physician and Redeemer whose body was scarred for *me*.

God made allowances for our difficulties in discerning between the good the better, and the best. He gave us some pointed examples to remind us of the challenge before us. In 1 Corinthians 13, where His paragon for love is spelled out specifically lest we have any excuses for coloring it in paler hues, He speaks of some "good" things like prophecies and knowledge, of some "better" things, like faith and hope, but He points out plainly the one thing that is *best*.

~FEBRUARY 22~
WATER FROM A HARD ROCK

"He brought water out of a hard rock. He gave you manna to eat in the desert, something your fathers had never known, to humble and to test you so that in the end it might go well with you." Deuteronomy 8:15-16

We can't get very far into the Bible without realizing that there always have been and always will be forks in the road where we will need to understand that one may not be just as good as the other. It is at these times before we take another step that we need to be skilled in using the Divine Compass of His Word. There is, after all, more than one spirit that is longing to own us, and if we are not familiar with the Holy One, then how are we to recognize which spirit is His? If I have not spent time with my face turned into His breezes, how am I to know from which direction blow the winds of that which inspires me?

His path may not be as well illuminated as the wide thoroughfare or the stones worn as smooth and easy on our step; we might even fear that upon this wilderness route of blind curves and thorny tangles, we could become lost.

But we can remember the beginning when we would have *sworn* we were losing something very valuable when we gave up control of our world only to find to our delight that we gained something *better, brighter, and sturdier*. This is the same Divine Finger that beckons us to take another step further from the beaten path and closer to His lonely desert. We will see then that even though this desert is lonely, it is blessed in a way nothing but this kind of hard rock could show us: it is blessed with *His* manna and with *His* water. There can be no doubt in a desert this hard that any of these provisions came from ourselves.

Only when we dare to lose more of ourselves in finding more of Him will we learn supremely what it means to choose the very best.

~FEBRUARY 23~
STRUGGLING TOWARD GOD

"So I find this law at work: When I want to do good, evil is right there with me. For in my inner being I delight in God's law; but I see another law at work in the members of my body, waging war against the law of my mind and making me a prisoner of the law of sin at work within my members. What a wretched man I am! Who will rescue me from this body of death? Thanks be to God—through Jesus Christ our Lord!" Romans 7:21-25

Chains that would bind me like weeds in my garden appear like a specter, imposing and grim. One day they are nowhere in sight in my life; my horizon is free and uncluttered with fetters. Then in the first rays of the next day's sunlight, I'm blinded by the glinting of a strong, unrelenting presence.

Chains of the shameful face of hopelessness, chains of grim habit, chains of false pride. Chains of deep passion for things of no substance; chains of impatience for faith to be sight. Chains of remembrance that hinder forgiveness; chains of forgetfulness of blessings bestowed that hinder gratitude. Chains of "security" borne on false winds, and its three devilish offspring, jealousy, fear, and manipulation, both hidden and brash, squeezing and cutting the soul 'till it bleeds—sapping the strength I so desperately need for the all-encompassing, uncompromising, regenerating struggle toward You.

Oh, God, how I long to continue desiring the highest volition, the struggling toward You! How I pray for the need to be ever-acute, the throb to enthrall me, the pain ever-pungent. How I fling all my weight against all that would bind me in an effort not just to break *free* but *into* that space just behind You, Your jetstream compelling—struggling, ever struggling toward You.

~FEBRUARY 24~
LEARNING TO TRUST

"Trust in the Lord with all your heart and lean not on your own understanding..."
Proverbs 3:5

"For the foolishness of God is wiser than man's wisdom, and the weakness of God is stronger than man's strength." 1 Corinthians 1:25

"Now, if we are His children, then we are heirs—heirs of God and co-heirs with Christ if indeed we share in His sufferings in order that we may also share in His glory." Romans 8:17

Seemingly, one of the ironies of this life is that the concept of responsible independence, the thing we most need to learn when we are very young, is the very thing God wants us to unlearn as we grow more mature in our faith. It becomes less of an irony when we recognize that dependency upon our parents or any human being at all, is not at all the same thing as dependency upon God. And when we take it a step further and realize that indeed there is no way for us ever to grow into a healthy dependence upon God, who is wholly spiritual and entirely Holy, *except* to gain our independence from all earthly creatures and things, then we see that it is no irony at all; it is entirely logical.

But still, it is difficult, as logical as we may learn to see it. Though we are spiritual, the fact that "we" are captured in earthly flesh tempts all of us to cry out for a harmonious life in this world, which is the stage we are given to play out this act of our existence. We want to depend upon certain things: a body that is healthy, families and friends to take love from us and return it to us somewhat mutually, and things just to work out pretty much the way we have them planned.

But what if they always did? Wouldn't that just reinforce our insistence that they continue to do so? Wouldn't we be more likely to find completion and fulfillment in working our petty little earthly plans with no need whatsoever for any Bigger Plans, much less to "share in His glory"?

~FEBRUARY 25~
GRACE THAT IS SUFFICIENT:
LEARNING TO DELIGHT IN OUR WEAKNESSES

"Three times I pleaded with the Lord to take it away from me. But He said, 'My grace is sufficient for you, for my power is made perfect in weakness.' Therefore, I will boast all the more gladly about my weaknesses, so that Christ's power may rest on me. That is why, for Christ's sake, I delight in weaknesses, in insults, in hardships, in persecutions, in difficulties. For when I am weak, then I am strong." 2 Corinthians 12:8-10

My glassy sea suddenly is billowed by gusts.
My boat is upended; I'm learning to trust.
The scales of prudence tip away from what's just.
Unfairness prevails; I'm learning to trust.
My finely-oiled engine falls victim to rust,
So I limp away powerless, learning to trust.
My ironclad certainties erode into dust.
Starved and defenseless, I'm learning to trust.

Though time and again I am butchered by pride,
I keep buying the ticket for the ill-fated ride.
It's easier to live with the wounds and the scars
Than to cast my reliance on self to the stars.
But before things are easy, they're hard, so I must
Be tutored by a Father, who longs for my trust.

Now assured of my frailty, I surrender this lust
And shove all my brilliance face down in the dust.
Not knowing quite how, only sure that I must.
Gaining power from weakness…learning to trust.

~FEBRUARY 26~
PRAYING OUR OUGHTS INTO WANTS

"We know that the law is spiritual; but I am unspiritual, sold as a slave to sin. I do not understand what to do. For what I want to do, I do not do, but what I hate, I do. And if I do what I do not want to do, I agree that the law is good. As it is, it is no longer I myself who do it, but it is sin living in me. I know that nothing good lives in me, that is in my sinful nature. For I have the desire to do what is good, but I cannot carry it out. For what I do is not the good I want to do; no, the evil that I

do not want to do—this I keep on doing. Now if I do what I do not want to do, it is no longer I who do it, but it is sin living in me that does it." Romans 7:14-20

I do, but "I" don't. I transgress, but it is not "I." I disagree, but "I" agree. It is so hard to see these passages in Paul's letter to the Romans as anything but double-talk, and taken out of their proper context, they are oxymoronic, para-doxical, and just plain confusing. What's going on here is anything but simple to explain, for it is the deepest-reaching root of our spiritual dilemma. It is the core problem of everyone who abandons the tangible world she can see to enter into the unseen spiritual world that hovers all around us.

Paul wrote another letter, probably a couple of years earlier, to the Corinthians, which states the problem in more general, but less confusing terms: *"So we fix our eyes not on what is seen, but on what is unseen. For what is seen is temporary, but what is unseen in eternal" (2 Corinthians 4:18).* It has to do with trying to remember to use our new glasses for these more mature eyes rather than continuing to pull out the old ones that will no longer show us life in a realistic light. If we keep using worldly spectacles to see spiritual truth, the image will be distorted every time. Here are some things I know:

- In all things, both secular and spiritual, before something is easy, it's hard.
- Practice makes us better, and not just in a worldly sense.
- Some things are harder than others, and that varies from person to person.
- It helps to *pray* for my "oughta's" to become my "wanta's."

~FEBRUARY 27~
DEEP-WATER FAITH

"Deep calls to deep in the roar of your waterfalls; all your waves and breakers have swept over me." Psalm 42:7

"When He had finished speaking, He said to Simon, 'Put out into deep water, and let down the nets for a catch.'" Luke 5:4

"Without faith it is impossible to please God, because anyone who comes to Him must believe that He exists and that He rewards those who earnestly seek him." Hebrews 11:6

It wasn't that he had recently earned his black belt that stirred up David's spunk to take on the brutish Goliath that day when his older brothers wimped out. Joshua and Caleb's loud, unlikely cheers to cross over the Jordan and whip the giants in the land of the gargantuan grape clusters weren't spurred on by a good day at the chariot track. Abraham didn't just up and leave his homeland because of wanderlust, nor was Noah inspired to undertake the building of an ark by an interesting article on zoo keepers that he picked up in the dentist's waiting room. It probably wasn't his desire to land a job with P.T. Barnum that drove Daniel into the lions' den anymore than it was Shadrach and friends' experimentation to invent Babylon's first sauna that motivated them to try out the fiery furnace.

They didn't look in the mirror or at their SAT scores or personality profile in order to size themselves up as competent. They seemed to ask simply, "Is this a thing that needs to be done?" It wasn't that there was nothing to fear. Maybe, instead, they just believed that there was something greater to be feared if they refused to allow God these opportunities. Though there was not yet a New Testament for them to read, maybe they knew that "without faith it is impossible to please God."

Or, better yet, maybe it wasn't any kind of fear at all. Maybe it was love. Maybe it was trust in the One whom they loved most perfectly.

Whatever it was that caused it, this desire to please God overshadowed a fear that would have rendered the natural man immobile and ineffective when God called him to action and purpose.

Let us dare this day to love God with a holy reverence that takes Him at His word. Let us believe that in pleasing our Father as good sons and daughters, His hand will reward us infinitely better than we, by our own meager, earthbound limitations, can reward ourselves.

~FEBRUARY 28~
LAUNCHING OUT FROM OURSELVES

"For you did not receive a spirit which makes you a slave again to fear, but you received the spirit of sonship. And by Him, we cry, 'Abba, Father.'" Romans 8:15

"For God did not give us a spirit of timidity, but a spirit of power, of love, and of self-discipline." 2 Timothy 1:7

Doing something over and over again is something more than repetition; it's practice. The more we practice a thing, the better we get at it.

Unfortunately, it isn't just the good habits we improve through practice but the bad ones as well. We continually need to ask ourselves if we are practicing the bad habits of walking by sight and fighting our own battles. If practicing a thing makes perfect, then we had best look carefully at what we are perfecting, for it is by means of this same discipline of practice that both the thief and the artist sharpens his skill.

We know that "the fear of the Lord is the beginning of wisdom" (Proverbs 1:7), but this is an awe-fear that puts every other thing we would fear into perspective. It tells us that nothing besides God is worthy of our fear. It leads us ultimately to understand that if He is with us, nothing else can stand against us. Scripture also tells us that "God did not give us a spirit of fear" but that through Christ "we can do [stand] all things" (Philippians 4:13), and that we will not just scrape by but be "more than conquerors" (Romans 8:37).

We know also that "perfect love casts out" that counterfeit fear (1John 4:18). Could the reverse also be true? *Could perfect fear cast out love?*

Is the perfecting of our fear to launch out into the deep waters of active faith casting out the love that we could be perfecting? Even the *shallows* of faith reflect that God shows His power when He uses us (within the realm of our inclinations) or in the ways we have been developed through and with our particular talents. The *deep* waters of faith reflect something even more intriguing: God demonstrates His power *mightily* when He takes a committed, faithfully-praying servant laying herself down as putty in God's hands and does something *unpredictable* and *uncharacteristic* with that personality.

Today be brave enough to ask God to launch you out of the shallows of your comfort zone into the rich depths of *His* sufficiency. It will affect you in a joyfully unforgettable way.

~FEBRUARY 29~
GOD'S RESOURCEFUL SERENDIPITY

"You have not come to a mountain that can be touched and is burning with fire; to darkness, gloom and storm; to a trumpet blast or to such a voice speaking words that those who heard it begged that no further word would be spoken to them because they could not bear what was commanded: 'If even an animal touches the mountain, it must be stoned.' The sight was so terrifying that Moses said, 'I am trembling with fear.' But you have come to Mount Zion, to the heavenly Jerusalem, the city of the living God. You have come to thousands upon thousands of angels in joyful assembly, to the church of the firstborn, whose names are written in heaven. You have come to God the Judge of all men, to the spirits of righteous men made perfect, to Jesus the mediator of a new covenant, and to the sprinkled blood that speaks a better word than the blood of Abel." Hebrews 12:18-24

Now that we have come to Mount Zion, can we launch out of our comfortable trenches (even if they are good trenches) every now and then and let God show us and others this *mighty* power of going beyond human expectation?

For instance, maybe you've never been very good at mustering up the faith to give generously. Perhaps you fear that an emergency might arise and, well, it just wouldn't be prudent not to be prepared. Or maybe you've never been able to organize your life or discipline your schedule to fit in a daily appointment with God for prayer, study, and silent meditation. Usually the reasons we give ourselves for failing to draw nearer to God in these and other sacrificial ways is that it goes too much against the grain of our nature and personality to be an early riser, a silent sitter, or a dangerous spender.

But when we bring to this drawing board the power of God in conjunction with a willingness to practice extravagant faith, we come up with pictures of people like David, Esther, Joshua, Noah, and Abraham—those who focused on the fact that something needed to be done rather than focusing on their fear or their natural inclinations. They realized that their personalities were incidental foliage, mere periphery around the taproot of a character shaped by a stronger faith in God than in themselves. For even the strongest of human characteristics without a core root to God's power would not be enough to conquer furnaces of fire, teeth of hungry lions, or a worldwide flood. Why do we believe He has any other agenda for modern man? Darkness and evil still abound, and God and godliness are still required to turn hearts and nations to the Light.

In one of long-time Texas preacher Joe Baisden's many wise sermons, he said, "If all you see in the world today is what you can see with your eyes, you have reason to be fearful." These are modern words like the ones from "the great cloud of witnesses" spoken of in Hebrews. They encourage us to look with our faith eyes rather than our natural eyes so limited by things like the mirror, our personalities, and our experiences in life thus far.

Once I read a simple but extremely visual line of encouragement to move forward in blind faith: "Start spinning and God will give you the thread."[6]

~MARCH 1~
SAILING ON THE SEA OF GOD'S VISION

"Love the Lord your God with all your heart and with all your soul and with all your mind and with all your strength." Mark 12:30

Sometimes we blame God for our own refusal to retreat from our deep and deadly ruts of natural inclination. We might ask why God doesn't *make* us this way or that way, why *He* doesn't do something to propel us or plant some impetus inside us to change our direction. But isn't this asking Him to do our part *and* His? Isn't this a covenant relationship we have entered into?

It is true that in His covenant with Abraham, He did promise that He would, indeed, in a huge respect do both our parts. He already knew we couldn't obey the law perfectly, so He promised that His atoning blood would one day satisfy the part our sinful nature could not. When we enter into death and atoning blood at baptism (Romans 6:3-4), and arise clothed in Christ (Galatians 3:27), then "we are no longer under law, but under grace" (Romans 6:14). Ephesians 2: 8 explains that it is "through grace, by *faith*" we have been saved. Ours is a covenant of faith, not perfect works.

So what is our part in this covenant? It is to live lives of faith in Him—not lives of *sight*, but lives of *faith!* Oswald Chambers in *My Utmost for His Highest* writes, "Man has to go out of himself in his covenant with God as God goes out of Himself in His covenant with man."[1] God is waiting to bless our trust in Him, to buoy us up in the deep waters of dire faith—and even more so when the loudest natural voice in natural man screams to flail against the tide that would take us out on the sea of God's grand and glorious vision—but we go out anyway, away from the safety of the shallows where our toes can dig into the warm, secure sand of our limited vision. We have to lean against the heavy gravity of our natural fears and stop waiting to be inspired to start "spinning." We have to *be* in the deep waters for Him to save us there.

One of the songs we sing regularly at our church is "I will bless the Lord and give Him glory." Once those words seemed odd to me because I was accustomed to thinking and singing about God's blessing *us* rather than the other way around. But I have grown to love those words and their message. God's blessings to us are a past and continuing reality whose translucent beginning in the manger became radiantly transparent in the resurrection. Singing of God's blessing us is a reminder to us of an indisputable truth; singing of our blessing God is a rededication to go against the worldly flow, a recommitment to exercise our spiritual muscles.

What a blessing we must be to God when with the free will He has given us, we decide to allow Him to use us for His possibilities!

~MARCH 2~
FANNING FLICKER INTO FLAME

"Now we have this treasure in jars of clay to show that this all-surpassing power is from God and not from us." 2 Corinthians 4:7

"For our light and momentary troubles are achieving for us an eternal glory that far outweighs them all." 2 Corinthians 4:17

"Now to Him who is able to do immeasurably more than all we ask or imagine, according to His power that is at work within us..." Ephesians 3:20

Dull and unbecoming with no grace or brilliant hue,
A seed is dropped into the soil and waited on to do
A task impossible for one with no apparent power;
But caressed by sun and kissed by dew, it blossoms into a flower.
With fiery garnet plume and all bedecked in an emerald gown,
Its glory hardly resembles the husk once rough, unsightly, and brown.

Left alone to light the world, our lanterns have no spark.
Our fuse is dry and cold and powerless to light the dark.
But touched just once by the Finger of the Keeper of the Flame,
The reluctant wick sparks into a blaze that will never be the same.

The hide we walk around in is no better than a tomb.
Like the unsown seed, impoverished, we lie powerless and doomed.

But planted by the Master Gardener, life breaks through,
And our carcasses take on sweet fragrance and a bright and brilliant hue.
Christ fans our flicker into hot flame and floods our trickle with power,
And the grace that warms the soil of His Spirit embraces her newly-born flower.

If it's the love behind the gift that really counts with us, then isn't it the same with God who sees perfectly into the heart that motivates actions? The opportunity He gets to use us is the gift we give, but the motive behind that gift, which must be the very best blessing to Him, is our trust that triggers us to give.

When we grow out of ourselves into a deeper dependence upon God's power, then, and only then, will we be focused to see that help—that wonderful revelation of His reality in the here and now of our lives—when it comes. Then, and only then, will we be driven to our knees in gratitude and abounding love. Only when we dare travel beyond our strength to places that require our trust in Him will we, like Daniel and David, become witnesses and partakers in the possibilities of the Almighty God.

~MARCH 3~
ONLY *THEN* WILL YOU KNOW

"'Lord, if it's you,' Peter replied, 'tell me to come to you on the water.' 'Come,' He said. Then Peter got down out of the boat, walked on the water and came toward Jesus. But when he saw the wind, he was afraid and beginning to sink, cried out, 'Lord, save me!'" Matthew 14:28-30

"To the Jews who had believed Him, Jesus said, 'If you hold to my teaching, you are really my disciples. Then you will know the truth, and the truth will set you free." John 8:31-32

Dear Jan,
I see your flailing arms and hear your fretful cry.
Behold the birds, how they fly surrounded by nothing but air and sky!
I've also given *you* wings, but you are just too attached to the sod.
Come up and soar with me. I long to carry you.
Love,
God

Dear Jan,
I'm not ignoring you and all you beg to know.
But you want to see the end of every road before you'll go.
When you've trusted my Spirit, I've kept my word on every path you've trod.
You don't need to understand it all. Rest in your faith!
Love,
God

65

Dear Daughter,
You'll think nothing of this someday if you'll trust me to keep your treasure.
Don't squirm as I fit your head for your crown and fashion your heart to my pleasure.
Don't stand so amazed, disheartened, dismayed, when your boat rocks on stormy waters.
You're a pilgrim, my child, getting closer to Home every day. Hold on tight!
Love,
Your Father

~MARCH 4~
WAITING FOR A SIGN

"Put on the full armor of God so that you can take your stand against the devil's schemes. For our struggle is not against flesh and blood, but against the rulers, against the authorities, against the powers of this dark world and against the spiritual forces of evil in the heavenly realms...take up the shield of faith with which you can extinguish all the flaming arrows of the evil one." Ephesians 6:10-12, 16

Sentinel

Cloaked in the clouds that his father fashioned;
Hijacking beams of Heaven's own sun,
The prince of this world knits his schemes
To dishearten, beguile, and destroy.

But whispering "Look upward!" another stands near,
A sinewy spirit on call for command
From the faithful Keeper of Promises who waits
For a sign of our faith to unbridle His joy.

Many who say they *do* believe in God and heaven say they do *not* believe in the devil and hell. And others who say they do believe in Satan and hell don't talk or live like they do. But the Bible makes it very clear that Satan and hell are both real and not to be scoffed at or ignored. Jesus was tempted, and we also have been and will be again. However, the Bible makes it clear how we are to fight. One of our pieces of armor is our faith. It is called our *shield*, and with it we can put out Satan's burning arrows he enjoys shooting at us.

Do you know what those look like in your life? If you don't have at least some idea what those arrows look like, it's pretty certain that your spiritual eyes are slipping and your spiritual muscles are getting flabby. Building ourselves up in the faith takes purposefulness and time. Meanwhile, ask a trusted Christian that you respect to help you recognize your weak areas.

~MARCH 5~
FULFILLING THE LAW OF CHRIST

"Carry each other's burdens, and in this way you will fulfill the law of Christ."
Galatians 6:2

"Do not store up for yourselves treasures on earth, where moth and rust destroy, and where thieves break in and steal. But store up for yourselves treasures in Heaven where moth and rust do not destroy and where thieves do not break in and steal." Matthew 6:19-20

Sometimes the treasures we store up on earth are not the kind that you can see but are every bit as real and threatening to our spiritual health as the kind that fills our purses and clutter up our homes and garages. We are wise to study our desires, habits, and inclinations to know our weaknesses before they overtake us and render us useless in the work of the Kingdom—and maybe even eventually numb our desire for spirituality altogether. It is easier to see when the treasures *are* those material things, and because of their visibility to others who might put pressure on us to get a spiritual grip, probably a little easier to control than the invisible kind.

Sometimes our treasure is the thrill of impressing others with our abilities and accomplishments. Knowing that we do something well often isn't enough; we feel a strong desire for others to know it, too. Sometimes the desire, when we look at it closely, turns out to be better described as a *need*. Something hungry in us is fed by the *approval* of others. We are fed with even more satisfaction by their *appreciation*; and sometimes we feel the need to be glutted luxuriously by their *admiration*. The need varies in each person depending upon the degree of their hunger. And if a person's esteem is in starvation mode, this need might feel very much like a desperate lusting. Vanity, whose literal definition is "emptiness," is an earthly treasure very hard to see but an ominous one for Christians, who are given the very spirit of the one Living God to fill us. We simply have no business being empty when we have all of heaven at our disposal.

My daughter-in-law is a remarkable young woman. More than once, she has walked fifteen to twenty miles (literally!) in the morning, come home in time to fix lunch for her kids, and still done a full-day's work. And this was when she was six months pregnant! But her physical prowess is not what makes her remarkable. When training for a three-day, sixty mile charity walk, one lady in Leslie's group could not keep up with the others, so Leslie chose to walk with her many times rather than at the front. Later during the actual event, Leslie became ill. Though she had the desire and determination to continue anyway, for the sake of her concerned family, she quit after the first day. She had the perfect opportunity to impress and even inspire admiration from many, but again, she laid that earthly treasure aside in consideration of others. The slower walker was burdened with her inability to keep up; Leslie's family was burdened with concern for her health.

Because she chose to bear these burdens for us, she achieved a higher victory: she fulfilled the law of Christ. I couldn't admire her more if she had come in first place.

~MARCH 6~
A STEWARDSHIP OF GAZE-SETTING

"For where your treasure is, there your heart will be also." Matthew 6:21

Is it because we have two eyes that we tend to believe that we can clearly focus on two things at a time? Try it. Look across the room and try to focus on two things at the same time. Maybe the two things you chose were too far apart. Try it again, this time with two objects that are closer together.

I don't know about you, but it doesn't work for me, even when the items are close together. I can focus on one and see the other one out of the corner of my eye, and I can reverse the process and focus on the other one and see the first one in a fuzzy fashion out of my peripheral vision, but I cannot *focus clearly* on two things at a time.

This makes me think of something Jesus said: "No one can serve two masters. Either he will hate the one and love the other, or he will be devoted to one and despise the other" (Matthew 6:24). He tells us in the next verse that He is talking about money here. In this verse, money equals the master because money is the thing the man is serving. It is my guess that he is serving the thing he is focusing on, and he is very likely focusing on the thing he sees as the home of his treasure. *"For where your treasure is, there will your heart be also."* It is hard to know whether the cycle more rightly begins with the fixation of our eyes upon something which travels through them, consuming our heart until we worship it as our master, or if we, by our own or some outward discipline, become slaves to something and then watch it carefully to learn how best to serve it. Either way, our hearts and our gaze are umbilically connected to where our treasure lies hidden, and we serve best the master we are most convinced will best reward us.

If I could, I would change the editors' italicized heading in my Bible that reads "Do Not Worry" to read "Focus on God," or "Seek First His Kingdom," for near the end of this "section," the crux of the whole matter is finally revealed to us: *"But seek his kingdom first, and these things will be given to you as well."* The announcement not to worry wasn't the main point; it was just a means to the end, something that we needed to understand before we could take in the real issue.

I believe Jesus was telling us that if we let anything take one of our eyes off our Pattern, whether it be worry about daily needs or gaining goods to store up for some pseudo-security, then the other eye will not really see it either. My vision of Jesus and what it takes in my personal life to become like Him cannot afford to be hazy or something I just glimpse from the corner of one of my eyes.

~MARCH 7~
BEING WEIRD FOR GOD

"For the grace of God that brings salvation has appeared to all men. It teaches us to say 'No' to ungodliness and worldly passions, and to live self-controlled, upright, and godly lives in this present age, while we wait for the blessed hope— the glorious appearing of our great God and Savior, Jesus Christ, who gave himself for us to redeem us from all wickedness and to purify for Himself a people that are His very own, eager to do what is good." Titus 2:11-14

"For I consider that our present sufferings are not worth comparing with the glory that will be revealed in us." Romans 8:18

It might seem scary at first to think of all that could happen if you take your focus off some of the crucial things in your life in order to think single-mindedly about what is required personally of you in order to grow spiritually on a daily basis. It may seem like a pretty flimsy limb to climb out onto, but that is just what God asks us to do *in every aspect of our lives*. Let me clarify that: *God* doesn't see it as a limb, but He knows that to us, perception is everything. I suppose somehow in all His omnipotence He could find a way to show us what it really is, that it isn't a flimsy limb at all. He doesn't, though, at least not at first. He asks us to go out on His limb in giving our money, and He asks us to go out on the same limb with the giving of our time and talents when we don't think we have enough of either to accomplish much of the big things He asks. (Remember Moses when God told him to deliver His children from the Egyptian Pharaoh?)

But here is something even more drastic: He asks us to go out on a limb in the way we live our lives every day. He asks us to dare to be "a people that are His very own." The King James Version says "a *peculiar* people set apart." God asks us to be *weird* for Him, and to most of us, that is more like a dead twig than a limb onto which, if we dare to venture, we are sure to be doomed to a fast, hard fall. After all, if we are honest, most of the money and worry we spend can be chalked up to our pitiful need to be accepted and to fit in, to blend well. I suppose this is because once again we find it easier and more natural to focus on building relationships with *earthly* beings than with our Father, who is a wholly *Spiritual* Being.

But He knows we can do it, and He knows that "our present struggles" to conquer our fear of climbing out on that limb are "not worth comparing to the glory that will be revealed in us."

~MARCH 8~
PRESSED DOWN, SHAKEN TOGETHER, RUNNING OVER

"Give and it will be given to you. A good measure, pressed down, shaken together, and running over will be poured into your lap. For with the measure you use, it will be measured to you." Luke 6:38

The picture this verse brings to my mind is pouring a five-gallon sack of flour into a canister and then banging it on the counter top to get the air out so the last little bit will fit.

Luke 6:38 has always sounded like an encouragement to go out on God's limb in the giving of our money. Most of my life I looked at that word "giving" and saw dollar signs after it. It reminds me of my Uncle Roy whose monetary generosity began amazing me when I was just a young child. He could not outgive God, even though it looked like he really tried to all his life. The more he gave to worthy causes, the more God blessed him with more to give.

But now I believe that scripture is referring to anything and everything we give— to every limb experience to which we surrender our "better" earthly judgment. The scripture promises that God will richly reward our giving "pressed down, shaken together and running over…" just as He did with Uncle Roy; but it doesn't refer only to rewarding our gifts of money.

The real point He wants us to get is that for every limb-climbing venture we brave, closing our eyes and ears to our cumbersome and weighty doubts, He will reward us with a new measure of faith. He doesn't ask us to learn a lot of new tricks or totter on a strange, new brink every time. There is really only one limb, and regardless of whether we go out on it in regards to giving Him our money, time, talents, or social acceptance, we are driven out there by the same courageous heart—the heart that had rather be on a limb close to the One it loves than far away from Him, "safely" on the ground.

And then finally, with our seasoned focus steadily trained upon Him and His powerful and faithful love for us, I believe we will begin to see clearly, as God sees, that with Him, there is no such thing as a flimsy limb.

~MARCH 9~
UNWORTHY BUT NOT WORTHLESS

"For the grace of God that brings salvation has appeared to all men. It teaches us to say "No" to ungodliness and worldly passions, and to live self-controlled, upright, and godly lives in this present age, while we wait for the blessed hope—the glorious appearing of our great God and Savior, Jesus Christ, who gave Himself for us to redeem us from all wickedness and to purify for Himself a people that are His very own, eager to do what is good." Titus 2:11-14

Dear Father,

I come before You filled with hope because I know that regardless of how *unworthy* I am of Your unspeakably rich and deep, all-encompassing love, I am not *worthless*. I know I am not worthless because You decided that the blood of Your perfect precious Jesus was not too great a price to pay for my spending eternity in Your presence. Oh, thank You, Father! I am humbled and brought low again just to think of it, but my heart beats in wild expectation of the world to come—the real Home of my soul that has been prepared and is waiting until the time I will be allowed to wake up to Your face and in Your arms.

Sometimes, though, I am tempted to feel worthless in my unworthiness. I know that the devil rubs his hands together in delight when he sees my temptation to despair of my state and think it is irreparable.

Oh, God, I so need daily to be redeemed from myself! My spirit needs to be set free daily, at least, from the demands of the rest of me that isn't living on spiritual oxygen but menially surviving on the stale dregs of carnal vision and fretful striving. I want the spirit of You—the image You created of Yourself in me—in order to break the bonds and infect the rest of me until all that would hinder my holiness would surrender.

Oh, Father, you know me so well! You know that I, like a child who is strangely blessed by touching the hot stove, needed to go through a hard lesson in order to learn the ill-effects of jumping to wrong conclusions. I have deprived myself and others of so much joy that You want to give us. I seem to see everything through my eyes only. Will I ever learn not to do this? Oh, yes, for You will teach me. When we, Your wayward children sometimes so bent on destruction, find ourselves far down a path of our own choosing, You are faithful to hearken to our cries for help. You faithfully shine Your light on the signposts we have ignored. Thank You, Lord, that this goes for us also who are miles down the road before we stop and look up as well as those who took Your hand on step one. Thank You for reminding us that when we say "no" to ungodliness, You will fill us again, and that when we rebuke Satan, he will flee.

With You, the hope is endless!

~MARCH 10~
THE BLESSING OF KNOWING OUR IGNORANCE

"Do nothing out of selfish ambition or vain conceit, but in humility, consider others better than yourselves." Philippians 2:3

"Your Word is a lamp to my feet and a light to my path." Psalm 119:105

Omniscient Teacher,

Please keep teaching me. Don't despair of my slow learning. Please keep shedding more light on my dark areas. Illuminate the sheets that appear blank or obscure until I can read the Truth in my life.

I give bad advice, add two and two and get three, believe too strongly in theory and project in others' lives only what has become the sum of *my* life. How quickly I run ahead and act upon hasty, unfounded shreds of facts, upon what is reflected from my mirror only; and how smug I am—so certain that because I understand myself, I am capable of predicting the behavior and motives of everyone else. I get all enmeshed with the one person that I am and start believing that we are all just like I am. I am so sure of it sometimes that I make unfair judgments based on my very limited view when I need to discern in a godly manner.

Please help me to remember that there are endless nooks and crannies in all lives, paths and passages that I cannot see. I long for the mind of Christ to know when to speak and question and when to rest silently in the mystery of the complexity of so many different kinds of people and just leave it in Your hands. Help me to see my limitations and not be overly analytical or caught up in the false security of prideful conceit, thinking I know more than I do. I need to be more assured of my ignorance so that I can stop this starting at the end and ending at the beginning.

You are my Hope. Your Word is a light unto my path and the perfect blueprint of the mind of Christ. You are the Great Redeemer, even of me. Thank You for all You are doing for me through Jesus. Amen.

~MARCH 11~
MEMORIES FOR A RAINY DAY

"O God, you are my God, earnestly I seek you; my soul thirsts for you; my body longs for you, in a dry and weary land where there is no water.
I have seen you in the sanctuary and beheld your power and your glory.
Because your love is better than life, my lips will glorify you.
I will praise you as long as I live, and in your name I will lift up my hands.
My soul will be satisfied as with the richest of foods; with singing lips my mouth will praise you.
On my bed I remember you; I think of you through the watches of the night.
Because you are my help, I will sing in the shadow of your wings.
My soul clings to you; your right hand upholds me.
They who seek my life will be destroyed; they will go down to the depths of the earth.
They will be given over to the sword and become food for jackals.
But the king will rejoice in God; all who swear by God's name will praise him,
While the mouths of liars will be silenced." Psalm 63

David penned this beautiful psalm declaring his satisfaction in the Lord while fleeing deadly enemies in the desert of Judah. He begins by desperately pleading with God to show Himself. He compares his extreme need of his body and his soul to that of needing water to sustain life for another minute in the *"dry and weary land"* where there is none.

Next he goes into memory mode and reminds himself of what it was like when God *did* make Himself visible to him. *"I have seen you in the sanctuary and beheld your power and your glory."* A sanctuary is a place of safety, the antithesis of where David finds himself now—a dry and weary desert where there is no water or refuge—just plenty of enemies.

That vivid memory reminds him of how wonderful God's love is (*"better than life"!*) and causes him to praise him with his lips and hands and to promise to do this as long as he lives.

And now comes my favorite line: *"My soul will be satisfied as with the richest of foods."* He compares his soul's satisfaction with God to his taste buds'satisfaction with regal fare. I get excited over the preparation and anticipation of good food, and I am not even a king. Imagine the kinds of delicacies David was served! What powerful and lovely imagery—a comparison you can taste!

He continues letting the memory of God's glory in the sanctuary strengthen and inspire him even throughout his nights of wakeful and vigilant sleep. The memory mode seems to come to full fruition with his singing *"in the shadow of [God's] wings"* and a realization that his soul which clings to God is rewarded by being upheld by God's *"right hand."* He concludes with a resounding victory cry, certain that his God will defeat his enemies and bring them to shame.

It isn't just beautiful poetry; it's a sermon: When in your dungeon, remember the God of your sanctuary.

~MARCH 12~
CELEBRATING DIVERSITY

"Now the body is not made of one part but of many. If the foot should say, 'Because I am not a hand, I do not belong to the body,' it would not for that reason cease to be part of the body. And if the ear should say, 'Because I am not an eye, I do not belong to the body,' it would not for that reason cease to be a part of the body. If the whole body were an eye, where would the hearing be? If the whole body were an ear, where would the sense of smell be? But in fact, God has arranged the parts in the body, every one of them, just as He wanted them to be. If they were all one part, where would the body be?" 1 Corinthians 12:14-19

One of the reasons it is dangerous to compare ourselves with others is that God designed us in different ways. When I look at lovely Christians whom I admire, sometimes they do life so differently than I do that I have a hard time believing they could look at my life and like me or respect me as a Christian.

But I know that just as God put His qualities of calmness and soothing in some and benevolence and organization in others, He probably put passion and energy (maybe even silliness and hyperactivity!) in yet others. Couldn't it be that our temperaments and personalities and natures are gifts, too, just like teaching, preaching, cooking, singing, and balancing the books?

Our God is so many faceted that surely it would take all kinds of personality traits to show every detail of His nature. Could it really be that God might want me to embrace a part of my nature that I have spent years trying to eradicate? Is it possible that the pain (necessarily attached to passion) that sometimes looks very much like an indicator of foolishness is really my cross to bear in my choice to follow Him and be faithful to portray the qualities God assigned to the nature He created in me? Since we all have a cross but are assigned such different tasks, shouldn't our sacrifices look different also?

What you and I love about each other is the *God* we see in each other.

~MARCH 13~
HEAVEN'S SYMPHONY:
MY HOLY SPIRIT LOVES YOUR HOLY SPIRIT

"Now the body is not made of one part but of many. If the foot should say, 'Because I am not a hand, I do not belong to the body,' it would not for that reason cease to be part of the body. And if the ear should say, 'Because I am not an eye, I do not belong to the body,' it would not for that reason cease to be a part of the body. If the whole body were an eye, where would the hearing be? If the whole body were an ear, where would the sense of smell be? But in fact, God has arranged the parts in the body, every one of them, just as He wanted them to be. If they were all one part, where would the body be?" 1 Corinthians 12:14-19

I can't resist the nature of God I see in you. My spirit lunges for it. I want to stare at it and hold it in my hands. It is beyond the shadow of a doubt the most beautiful thing I have ever seen. Far above my wildest dreams of adventure (and I DO love adventure!) loom my dreams of the God I find in you. When the part of God you radiate must move out of my reach, the part of God in me is lonely for it. When the picture you paint with such grace and clarity of our Father-God walking beside you in the garden floats into my eager eyes; when your quiet confidence strolls up and touches my hand-wringing, panic-stricken chaos; when the song of your worshipful heart falls upon my ears, my passion that I have so often found exasperating suddenly takes on new and exciting possibilities. Your nature gives more meaning to my nature!

It wasn't by accident that God made us to look and act and process life in different ways; all the same instruments make for monotony. The piercing blasts from my trumpet find more depth and melody when your saxophone plays along. The flutes need the percussion to beat out a rhythm and give meaning to the rests.

But just as the musician would think it ridiculous to refuse to play the music because owning the instrument costs sacrifices such as money, time, practice, and upkeep, we should realize that the part we play in the symphony is worth some sacrifice—some money for the benevolent, some time for the hospitable, some disappointment for the passionate.

~MARCH 14~
IGNITING A HOLY FIRE

"Now we see but a poor reflection as in a mirror; then we shall see face to face. Now I know in part; then I shall know fully, even as I am known." 1 Corinthians 13:12

We long to know why we are never comfortable in our spiritual journey for very long at a time. We want to see the sense it all makes while we are going through it. We wish we could know with one hundred percent certainty all the time that what we will harvest for God is worth what we are spending on the crop. But instead, we squint and crane our necks only to see "a poor reflection," or as the King James version so mysteriously phrases it, *"through a glass darkly."*

We long to see the big, complete picture of God, but instead we see little segments of Him different days in different ways from the few who will allow Him to fill and overflow from their vessels. What we are waiting for is the wedding.

I believe all Christians long desperately for the wedding of all the beautiful facets that make up the splendor and majesty of God. Right now about the closest we can come on earth to living that out is fellowshipping *our* stamp of God with *others'* stamp of God. We are imperfect humans marred by a world steeped in sin, so none of us bears perfectly and faithfully the true image of God in *all* His glory and holiness.

But when we supply enough Heavenly oxygen, sparks of Him burn through our humanity, and those who love God and are journeying devotedly to our real Home hearken delightedly to the stirrings of God in other Christians. Wouldn't it be tragic if no one recognized this light emitting from His spirit?

In not looking quite like the others around you or growing weary of not living emotionally or mentally in sync with your family or friends, are you allowing the discomfort to block a particular prism of His light to shine through you? Isn't it possible that what God fashioned in you is there to be a testimony of His nature? You may not even know that what has been growing and taking on a glorious luster in your life due to your faithfulness is a part of the nature of *God* that He wishes the world to see and fall in love with.

We must tell each other what we see! If we decide that we cannot afford to be who He has assigned us to be, we are depriving not just ourselves but others of some blessing He meant to give. We must encourage each other to nurture whatever gifts God has planted in us. We must plead with each other to spend ourselves in Sparks of the true and living God bouncing around in you and me. If we stand close enough together, they can combine and start a fire, a conflagration of such magnitude that it *could* warm and light the whole world!

~MARCH 15~
A HEART THAT KNOWS GOD

"...If anyone would come after me, he must deny himself and take up his cross daily and follow me. For whoever wants to save his life will lose it, but whoever loses his life for me will save it." Luke 9:23-24

From the musical storage closet inside me the sweet, rich voice of Twila Paris saunters into my consciousness: "A heart that knows You is a heart that can wait, die to the dearest desires."[2] The voice and the melody are so soothing that I almost miss the severity of the message: "Die to the deepest desires." This sounds dreadfully like pulling myself up by my own bootstraps. Just *weakening* my desire requires taxing calisthenics. *Dying* to my desires calls for something more extreme than the rigorous, bone-bending of a contortionist. But dying to my *dearest* desires lies blatantly beyond the bounds of my imagination, and the sum of my experiences has taught me that visualization always precedes actualization. I am at a total loss to accomplish anything I cannot first see with my mind's eye. It is akin to the futility of trying to describe purple or orange to a person who has been blind from birth. For an even more pointed comparison: dying to my dearest desires is like going blind on purpose.

Why not just kill the dearest *desires* rather than make *ourselves* die to them? Wouldn't that be less severe and more realistic?

Less severe? Surely. More realistic? Never. How could it happen? My deepest desires wouldn't die a natural death; their passion to live is too strong. The pulse of passion is consistent and potent. It is the carrot that dangles beyond the expanse of duty that I must traverse. It is the pot of gleaming gold that waits at the end of a lot of trails less enchanting and alluring than the rainbow. If the desires will not die naturally, then what of me is there left to be their executioner? Is there a contrary and inconsistent part of my will that stands aside from the rest and polices its action? No, there is *no* part of me fit to be depended upon to kill my dearest desires.

The next most logical idea would be just to ask *God* to kill the wrong desires, and maybe some that are not even wrong, just inferior to the ones He wishes to be my dearest. But this idea is no better than the first. God would never have needed to spend so much time telling us about resisting temptation if all we had to do is to ask Him to remove it. "Deliver us from evil," He modeled, not "Take evil from us."

The song goes on to answer the hard question: "A heart that knows You is a heart that can still celebrate, following love through the fire." That is what we have to do. We have to believe in the great love our Father has for us. We have to believe that it is a love worth following through any fire, even the one that is burning into cinders and then ashes our deepest desires.

Psalm 37:4 is one of my favorite pieces of encouragement, and it is in this hard place of laying down the only life we can imagine that we need these words most: *"Delight yourself in the Lord, and He will give you the desires of your heart."*

~MARCH 16~
THE VICTORIOUS DEATH

"...and anyone who does not take his cross and follow me is not worthy of me. Whoever finds his life will lose it, and whoever loses his life for my sake will find it." Matthew 10:38-39

"Therefore, if anyone is in Christ, he is a new creation; the old has gone, the new has come!" 2 Corinthians 5:17

Becoming a new creation is not merely taking off the old costume; it is laying down the old *life*. Do you daily offer your whole self to be used in any way God wants to?

Likely most of us venture out with a need and desire to know God, but along the way, we decide we had rather know about something *else* a little better first, so we pull an arm or leg back in, throw over it the garb of pseudo-godliness to deceive others (but more importantly, ourselves), and thus delay our full knowledge a little bit longer.

We need to remember that a new creature, like a new baby, is not perfect in the virtue that it does everything right but only in its vulnerability and its pliability to be molded and formed by the ones upon whom he is dependent. As he grows, however, he is expected to do more and more right because he is being nurtured and enabled by the very ones who keep raising their expectations of him. Also, his awareness is heightened, so he not only conforms out of fear or in order to please, but because more and more he understands the "why's" of his parents' thinking. More and more he is taking on the mind of an adult.

If we continue to pull ourselves back and deceive ourselves about this, we will continue to be like a baby whose vision and awareness are never heightened past infancy. The secret of growth in both the baby and the Christian lies in the trust in each new stage of growth. At every crucial crossroad where we look both directions; at every moment of decision when we lift our arm to decide which way to throw its weight or our foot to decide which path to start down, we make a decision of whether we trust God to show and enable us in this new, unpracticed, and yes, *unvisualized* stage of growth. Sometimes we say, "No, I *need* to see where I'm going!" but hopefully, more often we ask Him to place His will and mind over ours and take us with Him. There is only one way for a heart to know God, and that is for the mind of man, which cannot visualize surrendering his will, to be overtaken and overshadowed by the mind of Christ.

There is a humorous story about a cow, a chicken, and a pig discussing their sacrifices for the farmer's breakfast. I'm sure God is pleased when we sacrifice for His kingdom our "milk" and "eggs", but how He must wholeheartedly *rejoice* when we reach the point of believing that like the pig, we give nothing if we don't give our lives.

It is not too much to ask that we die to our dearest desires if that death will bring us into the life of the dearest desires of a higher mind with a more glorious view.

~MARCH 17~
IMPATIENT FOR HEAVEN

"Let us not become weary in doing good, for at the proper time we will reap a harvest if we do not give up." Galatians 6:9

Dear Conceiver and Giver of All Good Gifts,

My cup overflows with gratitude for the blessings you lavish upon me, a flippant and blasé child so much of the time. I am so tempted, though, to pull those blessings close to me and fall in love with them. I get impatient for Heaven. Through seasons of pleasure whose gentle winds blow sweet fellowship and warm my heart and cause it to overflow, I realize You are giving me a foretaste of Heaven. Oh, how very hard it is for me to accept these times as I know I must—a *foretaste* and not the real thing.

Greed is easier to recognize when it comes in the form of material lusting and covetousness. I am weak many times in these areas, but I am not deceived about my weakness and about the dangers that lie at hand. It has taken me so long to see that greed can come in other forms, too. I have asked you to reveal my sins to me, so once again I see that you have been trying to get through to me in my pain. I am so slow to see, but thank you for your forbearance in teaching me.

I have felt anxious and worried about losing my place in the hearts and lives of those I love most. I have foolishly dwelled on memories and grieved that I seem to be losing control over a present that would be as gratifying as the past. I have longed for some things to stay the same that I now see need to change in order for me and others to serve you faithfully. You have heard me crying, "Lord, please keep me beloved in the heart of this friend that now must leave" when what I really meant was "Please don't let anyone take my place!" Yet, in the same prayer, I have asked for us both to be used unselfishly in your kingdom. I fear this is doubletalk.

Lord, I acknowledge in shame my childishness in this place where I should stand as an adult. I know you have given me guidance and strength to grow up and put away many childish things, but I have cherished some things above my desire to be your handmaiden. I have tried to hold on to the things you never meant to be claimed as *rights*. I have seized blessed refreshment for the crucial forward journey, fastened my gaze on the feast, and lost sight of the purpose of the pilgrimage. Does it ever make You want to quit providing the oasis?

Oh, Father, take my feet and move me on down the road to do the things you created me to do, to reach the people you have placed in my path ahead. I relinquish my grip on heavenly pleasures and leave them for Heaven, where I know I shall lack for nothing. I ask for your Spirit to remind me to wait for Heaven's rewards so that I will not be distracted or preoccupied and miss seeing the duties You desire for me to fulfill on earth.

I come to Your throne only because I am covered in the blood of your Son. Amen.

~MARCH 18~
CAMPFIRE SONGS

"Shout for joy to the Lord, all the earth...Enter his gates with thanksgiving and his courts with praise." Psalm 100:1, 4

Often I hear myself and others refer to something as being "heavenly." What we mean is that its quality is so much superior to the norm that we think it is other-worldly or "out of this world." Becoming spoiled to these luxuries is ridiculously easy; it happens like gravity, with no effort on our part whatsoever. Without thinking, we lean in the direction of what feels or tastes heavenly to us. I have noticed that the longer I love and the better I know myself, the more I tend to waltz casually and effortlessly toward the people and activities upon whom I have placed the "heavenly" stamp.

Being magnetically drawn to what we consider heaven*ly* seems only natural and harmless enough—maybe even our just desserts for our discomfort as aliens in this strange country. After all, we are campers whose tents are wearing out and whose feet are sometimes sore. But just as the other kind of dessert can become addictive with harmful side effects, so can this kind. The trouble with falling in love with heavenly pleasures is that *this is not Heaven*, and *gifts* from God are not *God* Himself.

But on the other hand, it is no less than blasphemous to grow blasé about the blessings God gives us along the way on our journey. And what blessings He gives! No one does it better than God. He uses a bucket, not a salt shaker, when He blesses the earth with glory for our lives with rich tender relationships to touch, move, and change our hearts. Finding a mate to love and grow old with, sharing the same memories, children, and grandchildren are providential treasures. Watching our children's eyes widen and spirits stretch as they grow and learn, fall in love, and start the same cycle over again with their children are surely blessings conceived in the mind of God to delight His children in no small fashion. The abounding and varied glories of nature and the exhilaration of frolicking and adventuring in its bosom and, much to our delight, recovering precious remnants of youthfulness we had forgotten; the joy of a newly-found friend and the comfort of old soul mates, whose kindred spirits harmonize so naturally with ours in laughter and song; the many-faceted diamond of sibling love; the swelling of a Nana's heart when a grandchild writes her a love poem; witnessing the gracefully deepening laugh lines crinkle in our parents' and grandparents' silver-wreathed faces.

These are the providence of a good and gracious Father who wanted to sweep us off our feet with His gifts of love. To take any of these for granted would be a slap across His face.

Today wherever you are when you brush up against your heavenlies, rather than being like the hog gorging himself with acorns under a tree without ever looking up to see where they came from, how about looking up and breaking out into "Praise God from whom all blessings flow; Praise Him, all creatures here below. Praise Him above, ye heavenly hosts. Praise Father, Son, and Holy Ghost."[3] I'll bet before you finish, it will cease to be a solo.

~MARCH 19~
LOVING DISRACTIONS

"They exchanged the truth for a lie and worshipped and served created things rather than the creator." Romans 1:25

Recently our Bible class teacher asked these very pointed and personal questions: What is it in your life without which you would fall apart? What is it that when it isn't working well, you aren't either? A hush louder than the sonic boom shook the room, and eyes searched the tops of our best Sunday shoes for the next few seconds. No hands went up.

I suspect that a roomful of hearts stood bumper to bumper at a secret crossroads looking wistfully in a direction they had never dared to venture before. Silent tongues belied our deafening answers to those piercing questions.

What if our attachments to things or people become so strong that we feel lost without them? Attachments to things are obviously foolish, and even if we do allow it to happen sometimes, we know better and learn valuable lessons for preparation against the next time such temptations come knocking. Our pulpit minister admonishes us often about becoming too attached to things by reminding us that we are to *use things* and *love people,* not vice versa.

But it is possible to become too attached to people. Most suicides happen as a result of broken relationships. If that seems a rather extreme example for Christians who know better, keep reading. How often do you hear someone speak of a "broken heart?" Have you ever known of someone who was never able to get on with life after the death of a loved one? Yet we would all agree that if God has seen fit to keep giving life and breath to someone, He means for him to keep using it. I wonder if most of us transgress here, even if not so extremely.

I taught high school freshmen for most of my twenty-five-year teaching career and often had to comfort young people who could not pull their eyes and minds away from a wound inflicted by someone they loved. We live and learn, and as adults we become better able to distinguish between problems that are real and those that are imaginary, or at worst, temporary, due to our moods and circumstances. But sometimes our growth gets stunted and we, too, find it very difficult to focus on what we are really here to do and to become. Instead we are distracted by our compulsion to keep trains of lesser importance moving efficiently down their tracks. We grow preoccupied with our strong need to keep something "heavenly" feeling heavenly.

When something we considered heavenly ceases to deliver the heavenly qualities we have grown so accustomed to, suddenly we are jolted into realizing that our expectations were too high; this, after all, is *not* Heaven, and furthermore, nothing here is *purely* heavenly.

God gives us foretastes of Heaven in order to draw our eyes to the Provider of all good gifts, so that we will long most of all for a relationship with Him. When the boy gives the girl a ring, if her love is drawn away from the giver and toward the object, the gesture becomes a mockery and defeats his purpose in giving it.

~MARCH 20~
THE BLESSING OF LETTING GO

"Love the Lord your God with all your heart and with all your soul and with all your mind and with all your strength." Mark 12:30

"Let us fix our eyes on Jesus..." Hebrews 12:2

When God gives us gifts, do we fall in love with the gift at His expense? Are our affections transferred from the Giver to the gift? If God sees that our being in love with the gift *deters* our spiritual growth rather than *enhances* it, He could well decide that we are better off without it. We might see that as cruel, but He is just being a good and faithful Parent to us. We become agitated, uncomfortable with the changes, disillusioned with the ones responsible for the changes, doubtful of our continued worth, unsure that tomorrow will dawn with sunny promise, unsure what we should believe in anymore. And when all these things start happening, what are the chances that we are focusing on the life God has planned for us to live this day? In the whirlwind of this distracting confusion, can we really "be still and know that He is God"? Or will we find out when we get still that something, someone, or some circumstance was really god?

So what should we do to ensure that we don't have to go through such a providential ripping from our lives? Should we give up eagerness and enthusiasm about mortal pleasure? Should we keep our distance from everyone to avoid disappointment or becoming overly attached? That would turn us into joyless cynics, not to mention the damage it would do to others who need our encouragement and love. We would cease to resemble Christ, in whom we are told to "rejoice always." How then do we find the balance between the numbness and loving the gift above the Giver?

The answer to this problem is the same as the answer to all the others. We must go back and listen to what Jesus said that we must remember above all else: "Love the Lord your God with all your heart, soul, mind and strength." It sounds so easy because it can be said so quickly. But if we put this true first thing first, and do it with all our might, we will find that, just as He promised, things will begin to show up that we thought we had lost because we were seeking not those things anymore, but His kingdom. When we *fix* our eyes on Jesus instead of just letting them glance His way or skim across the thought of Him, our hearts are enabled to be filled with the Light we see there. When we stop and go at His will, then He is able to pour Himself into these vessels He has created us to be. Then perhaps He will give us what we struggled to hold on to because it is no longer our focus; it is no longer a threat to our relationship with Him.

~MARCH 21~
TO YOU, WITH LOVE FROM THE FATHER OF LIGHTS

"Therefore, I tell you do not worry about your life...Look at the birds of the air; they do not sow or reap or store away in barns, and yet your heavenly Father feeds them Are you not more valuable than they? Who of you by worrying can add a single hour to his life?" Matthew 6:25-27

"Every good and perfect gift comes from the Father of Lights." James 1:17

In my slow, painful process of acquiring some patience in waiting for Heaven, I have uncovered a collection of ironies that at first embarrassed me and later delighted me. First, I have seen that despite my many years as a grammar teacher, I still sometimes don't know the difference between an adjective and a noun. "Heavenly" is merely a modifier of the real thing, the noun, Heaven. The first is merely the shadow of the substance to come, a wisp of the cluster, a winsome glimpse of the enchanting mural, a delicate tendril of the bounty, a fine but slippery filament of the entrancing tapestry.

The second irony is that now I thank God more, not less, for my earthly blessings. I find myself more humbly appreciative than ever before for the sights and sounds of the seasons as they wax and wane in and out of my life, for the comfort and security of my husband's return to me day after day, for the brighter, warmer flame of Jesus burning in my children's eyes as they advance into adulthood and parenthood confident in the Hand that takes them there, for the dear, unmistakable glow of welcoming love in the eyes of my cherished friends, for the poignant enchantment of my grandchildren, and for the charming kaleidoscope of faces and personalities who honor me with their presence in twenty-eight prayed-over desks.

By fixing our eyes on the Giver, we are blessed with a deeper capacity to appreciate the gift. We finally, shamefully see (but it is better to see something shamefully and late than not at all!) the real reason for our disappointments. We had taken our gifts for granted, quit falling to our knees in gratitude, and started demanding. We had demanded that the people and circumstances of this imperfect world provide us with incessant heavenly feelings.

If we really believe that God is directing our lives, then when we demand something of circumstances or people, we effectively abandon our faith in the Father who knows about and provides for *all* of our needs. Our frustration toward others translates as either frustration with or disbelief in a God of providence. There is really no other choice. When we finally come face to face with this truth, we are helpless to do anything except to fall at His feet and ask forgiveness, giving ourselves with all of our wishes and demands completely into His wise and tender care.

~MARCH 22~
HOW TO REMAIN A FAITHFUL SHEEP

"For it is by grace you have been saved, through faith—and this not from your-selves, it is the gift of God—nott by works so that no one can boast." Ephesians 2:8-9

"Then the King will say to those on His right, 'Come, you who are blessed by my Father; take your inheritance, the kingdom prepared for you since the creation of the world...I tell you the truth, whatever you did for one of the least of these brothers of mine, you did for me." Then He will say to those on His left, 'Depart from me, you who are cursed, into the eternal fire prepared for the devil and his angels...I tell you the truth, whatever you did not do for one of the least of these, you did not do for me.' Then they will go away to eternal punishment." Matthew 25:34, 40-41, 45-46.

The New Testament is replete with reminders that what saves us from eternal death is grace (that is, a *gift*) through faith (that is, *believing*) that He is the Son of God and that His pure blood shed on Calvary is sufficient to cover our sins and therefore present us as spotless before God Almighty. Nothing we can *do* can ever cleanse us—only that precious blood.

But then we run up against Jesus' parable of the Sheep and the Goats. And, lo! It's all about what people *did* or did not *do* that Jesus seems to be using as a criteria into Sheepdom or Goatdom.

How do we rectify this apparent contradiction?

In Mark 9 Jesus and three of his apostles, Peter, James, and John, spend the first half of the chapter on the Mount of Transfiguration involved in Amazing Things featuring Moses and Elijah resurrected from the dead and no less than the very voice of God coming from a cloud and speaking directly to them. Meanwhile, we learn from the second half of the chapter the other nine apostles, left behind, uninvited to go with Jesus and the other three, are trying, but failing, to heal a demon-possessed boy. Jesus walks up just in time to witness these nine arguing with some Pharisees who apparently have been watching this whole fiasco with the unhealed boy. First Jesus questions them about arguing with Pharisees and then chastises them, calling them an "unbelieving generation."

Why didn't these nine have enough faith this time? Could it be that having been left behind, their already weakened (jealous, envious) spirits were susceptible to these Pharisees' jeers, and because they were no longer acting (living, doing, being, *working)* like Christ but rather like the world, they were no longer spiritual enough to *believe* spiritually? Could it be that when they fell back into embracing the world in their reactions (envy, jealousy), the jeering Pharisees were able to infect them with their unbelief?

"If you do not stand firm in your faith, you will not stand at all." Isaiah 7:9

~MARCH 23~
IF YOU HOLD TO MY TEACHINGS, *THEN*...

"For it is by grace you have been saved, through faith—and this not from yourself, it is a gift of God—so that no one can boast." Ephesians 2:8-9

"Consider Abraham: 'He believed God, and it was credited to him as righteousness.'" Galatians 3:6 (quoting Genesis 15:6)

"To the Jews who had believed Him, Jesus said, 'If you hold to my teaching, you are really my disciples. Then you will know the truth, and the truth shall set you free.'" John 8:31-32

Jesus was teaching to these who were learning to walk in His ways what the nine "left out" apostles in Mark 9 had apparently forgotten: knowing the truth and thus being set free only happens after we are "holding to" His teachings.

He is saying that we can't wait until we know it all for sure before we start following Him. We have to turn loose of our sight and our ways and follow Him and His ways wherever He is going—wherever His ways take us—before we will be rewarded with freedom.

Yes, we are indeed saved by grace, but it is through faith (believing), which can only come when we are following Him—*doing* as He does.

Faith is indeed the avenue to His grace; righteousness is indeed credited to us because of our faith. However, the faith—the *believing*—can only really come when we are *acting (working)* like sheep and following Jesus. We have to put all the scriptures together to get the full picture.

Is your faith weak these days? Is your joy in Christ somewhat subdued? Go back through the process Jesus explained to those Jews we read about in John 8. Check yourself, and enlist your best accountability partner to help, to see if there is an area you have hung back from truly following Him in His ways. Could it be that your joy is quieted by some subtle shackles that are keeping you from being set free? Is it a lack of mercy? Too much dabbling in the world's goods, the world's thinking? More concern for blending with the masses than being a "peculiar people"? Storing up treasures down here at the expense of your eternal bank account? Holding a grudge rather than forgiving?

Jesus knew that just listening would never convince us; the words are just too outlandish. He knew that the only way we could ever know that joy comes from dying, and freedom comes from serving was for us to jump in and do it. It's the same reason you learned to swim *in* the water and not on the side of the pool.

~MARCH 24~
WHAT IT TAKES TO SEE GOD

"Joshua told the people, 'Consecrate yourselves, for tomorrow the Lord will do amazing things among you.'" Joshua 3:5

The Israelites, camped on the east side of the Jordan, are finally on the threshold of receiving their Promised Land. Tomorrow God will stop the Jordan at flood stage and allow the priests carrying the Ark of the Lord to lead the people across to their Home. General Joshua stands before the people and calls for their consecration.

This type of consecration, including washing—not just their bodies but all their garments—and abstaining from sexual intercourse, was called for earlier among the people (Exodus 19) before their meeting with God at Sinai. When I read what Joshua told the people, I did a double take. I was just sure I had misread it. Surely it must have meant "so that" God will do amazing things among you, not "for." "For" means "because." It seemed more probable that Joshua would be telling them that they needed to get their act together and purify themselves *so that* God would work amazingly among them, not *because* God would work amazingly among them. Why was it "for" and not "so that"?

Do you think that God ever does amazing things that we don't even notice? I am always so impressed with God all over again every time I find a perfectly symmetrical wildflower growing right out in the middle of nowhere where there is pretty much *no one* to see it. I happened to find it only because I, by design, had put myself out there for the very purpose of being secluded from the multi-tudes, even from people-tude altogether. And there it was. Perfection. The colors, brilliant; the form, flawless. Yet it was not being flaunted and, in fact, because its life span is very short, would very likely be seen by no other eyes but mine. I just stood there and let it soak in that there are certainly millions of others that *no* eye has seen. God is always at work, and His work is always done perfectly, even when no one is checking on Him to make sure.

Then there are those times when the Creator speaks His will into reality in the form of answered prayer or angelic intervention, and again, no one notices—not because it happens in the middle of nowhere, but because we forget we prayed for it, or we give ourselves or others some sort of ridiculous credit for a feat or a circumstance we should know we haven't the power to perform or arrange.

Or, *we are not looking at things from a spiritual point of view.* We mindlessly let the world become "too much with us," as the poet Wordsworth put it, and fail to recognize the Hand of God.[4]

Joshua knew that even in the desert, people tend to see with earthly eyes rather than faith eyes. He wanted to be sure they knew that when the priests' feet touched the water's edge, it wasn't just a coincidental blockage that caused the water upstream to stop flowing and "pile up in a heap" so that they could reach the Jericho side.

Let us consecrate ourselves today, washing whatever "garments" are unclean and abstaining from anything that would take our eyes off the "amazing things" God will do among us. Let us prepare our eyes so that we will not make lame excuses for the breathtaking Glory of Almighty God working among us.

~MARCH 25~
THE WAY WE CHANGE THE WORLD

"Blessed are the pure in heart, for they shall see God." Matthew 5:8

"The eye is the lamp of the body. If your eyes are good, your whole body will be full of light. But if your eyes are bad, your whole body will be full of darkness…No one can serve two masters. Either he will hate the one and love the other, or he will be devoted to one and despise the other." Matthew 6:22-24

Years passed, and another "Joshua", Jesus, stood among a different multitude with the same message of consecration. He knew that the passing of many generations with their mistakes and the wealth of wisdom that comes with mistakes had not succeeded in convincing their offspring that there are no shortcuts to knowing God. He knew that it is altogether possible, yea likely, that people can look at a world where God is doing "amazing things" among His people and still not see them for what they are. He knew that multitudes could look at miracles and call them commonplace, and with no realization of God and thus no gratitude to Him, they could continue on their unenlightened path either consciously or unconsciously denying God. He knew that by denying God's power, they would remain shackled to the world and its meager possibilities and thus never be set free to experience the joy of living by the provisions of a kind and bountiful Jehovah-Jireh, the God Who Provides.

And so He told them the Truth about what it would take to see God. He talked about their hearts and their eyes. He said what they needed was to be "pure in *heart*," washed clean, consecrated, so that when they saw God, they would recognize Him, believe Him, be grateful to Him, be dependent upon Him.

Now we, His followers, take up His challenge daily to be *pure* in heart. When we shop for pure anything—pure water, pure cotton, pure sugar—we expect that there not be anything mixed in with the water, cotton, or sugar. A pure heart, then, is an undivided heart—a heart that seeks to please God unmixed with a seeking to please someone or some society or some lower standard than God's—one that is not trying to serve "two masters."

Then He explained to them about their *eyes* being the key to what happened inside them. He called the eye "the lamp of the body" and explained that how their eyes saw things was going to make a great deal of difference in whether they were full of light or full of darkness.

As our hearts become more and more undivided—*pure*—our vision to see and appreciate the Holy grows more and more acute so that when God acts, we notice! The more we notice God at work, the more we testify to that. This testimonial aspect of our lives is what Jesus referred to when he called us "the light of the world."

It starts with a heart that is being made pure by what it is allowed to *know* and to *serve* as its master. This purity of heart lends a light to the eyes to allow them to "see God" and to point Him out to others.

In this way, we change the world.

~MARCH 26~
BEATITUDE:
LAMPS THAT ILLUMINE GODLINESS

"Blessed are the pure in heart, for they will see God." Matthew 5:8

"The eye is the lamp of the body. If your eyes are good, your whole body will be full of light. But if your eyes are bad, your whole body will be full of darkness." Matthew 6:22-23

"You are the light of the world." Matthew 5:14

"The teachers of the law and the Pharisees brought in a woman caught in adultery. Jesus said to them 'If any one of you is without sin, let him be the first to throw a stone at her.'... Jesus straightened up and asked her, 'Woman, where are they? Has no one condemned you?" 'No one, sir,' she said. 'Then neither do I condemn you," Jesus declared. 'Go now and leave your life of sin." John 8:3, 7, 9-11

"Blessed are the pure in heart,
For they shall see God."
Others of us with other hearts
Will behold Him, no doubt, finally—
When the fetters of life are loosened
And the boxes we live in are gone—
But they will see Him *every day*
In faces we all have known.
Many times today on this very earth,

In this plain, vanilla sod,
They will look with the eyes of Jesus,
And, lo! They will find Him...
God!

If our eyes are good our bodies will be "full of light," Jesus says. Not only do "good" eyes glorify God by helping us bear witness to His marvelous works, but also they help us better discern His reflection— His image— in others.

Someone looks at a man and sees only his warts, his bulges, his bumbling ways, his unpolished tongue while another looks at the same man and is drawn to his acts of mercy, his generosity, his humility. What makes the difference?

Jesus knew that we would need to know about this woman caught in adultery. We would need to see that some aspects of God's nature are more quickly noticed than others. Sometimes the reason we are slow to notice some godly aspects of people is that they are so rare. Sometimes it is because we don't want to believe things like humility and a readiness to forgive are as important as the aspects we already have under control.

~MARCH 27~
A FEAR TO BE CHERISHED

"Guard my life, for I am devoted to you. You are my God; save your servant who trusts in you...Teach me your way, O Lord, and I will walk in your truth; give me an undivided heart that I may fear your name. I will praise you, O Lord my God, with all my heart. I will glorify your name forever. For great is your love toward me; you have delivered me from the depths of the grave. The arrogant are attacking me, O God; a band of ruthless men seeks my life— men without regard for you." Psalm 86:11-14

Psalm 86 is believed by most to be written by David as a prayer for God's help to deliver him from his enemies who do not fear or respect David's God. It is an odd mixture of sentiments upon first glance and merits the extra thought required to harvest all of its bounty.

David identifies himself as the Lord's servant in both the beginning and ending stanzas of this highly-organized, five-stanza poem. The Hebrew term for "devoted to you," used twenty-six times in the Psalms is *hasid,* and refers to the godly who are set apart by God to be devoted to Him. David, then, in saying "You are my God" is not saying that he has chosen God but that God has chosen him to be His servant. (1 Samuel 13:14, 15:28; 16:12; 2 Samuel 7:8). David, then, approaches God with the expectation that the God who chose him will surely save him.

Then in his process of requesting that God deliver him, he asks for an undivided heart for the interesting reason of *fearing* His name. Fear is not something we usually ask for, but this is what David wants. He seems to be saying that a life that is merely delivered from the enemy outside itself is not worth delivering. What good would it be if God delivered David from his enemies but left him prey to his own sinfulness? David wants to know and walk in God's way and truth and have a heart fully devoted to God (fear His name) so that he will be someone *worth* delivering, someone who will stay alive *in order to* bring greater glory to his King whom he serves.

Have we ever run to God for deliverance from someone or something—a scary situation, a financial or emotional crisis, illness or death—just so we can go on walking around on this planet doing very little good for anyone and bringing very little glory to God? Jesus came to save us not just *from* something, but *for* something.

"For we are God's workmanship created in Christ Jesus to do good works, which God prepared in advance for us to do." Ephesians 2:10.

We are created for good works. When we are created "in Christ Jesus" (Romans 6:3-4), we are *hasid,* and thus, like David, may "approach His throne of grace with confidence (boldly—KJV)" (Hebrews 4:16). However may we, like David, never forget that the second half of the scripture,"so that we may receive mercy and find grace to help us in our time of need," begs us to go forward from the place of deliverance cherishing the kind of fear that makes us better dispensers of mercy, better reflectors of God's glory.

~MARCH 28~
THE WELLSPRING OF LIFE

"My son, pay attention to what I say; listen closely to my words. Do not let them out of your sight; keep them within your heart; for they are life to those who find them and health to a man's whole body. Above all else, guard your heart, for it is the wellspring of life." Proverbs 4:20-23

Solomon exhorts his son to listen to wisdom so that he might find life. Of all the advice he offers, he underlines guarding the heart as the most important. He calls the heart the "wellspring of life." He compares the heart to water, which is the source of maintaining life. Just as pure water breeds health to the life of the body, a pure heart breeds health to the life of the soul. Unguarded, the source of life could become polluted and thus destructive and even deadly. Thus, Solomon pleads with his son to guard it well.

The verses that follow could be interpreted in two ways: maybe they are just a continuation of the list begun with listening to his father's words and guarding his heart; I believe they are *ways* to guard the heart.

- *"Put away perversity from your mouth; keep corrupt talk far from your lips."*

Jesus said "Out of the overflow of the heart, the mouth speaks" (Matthew 12:34), which seems to indicate that Solomon had his cart before his horse. Jesus said it starts in the heart and then travels out through the mouth. But really one does not exclude the other; they are both right because it is a vicious circle. What is in our hearts often does spew out of our mouths betraying the heart's contents. But also, when we say something long enough, we can become calloused even to what once was very offensive to us. The shocking or even scandalous, with enough repetition, can become ho-hum and commonplace. It happens with both the ears and the mouth. Paul reminded the Corinthians of this concept when he said, "Don't be misled: 'Bad company corrupts good character'" (1 Corinthians 15:33). The bad "company" may be our very words we perhaps spoke flippantly at first or to fit in, never really meaning to let them take root and corrode our purity.

Solomon's list continues:

- *"Let your eyes look straight ahead; fix your gaze directly before you."*
- *"Make level paths for your feet, and take only ways that are firm."*
- *"Do not swerve to the right or the left; keep your foot from evil."*

In this Christian age, these proverbs might look like this: "But one thing I do: Forgetting what is behind and straining toward what is ahead, I press on toward the goal to win the prize for which God has called me heavenward in Christ Jesus" (Philippians 3:13-14).

We must guard our hearts from the cesspool of the world in order to purify the cesspool of the world.

Lives are waiting to be changed, hearts are waiting to be healed, and it all begins with the one heart you and I have been given to guard.

~MARCH 29~
GUARDING OUR WELLS PETER STYLE

"Above all else, guard your heart, for it is the wellspring of life." Proverbs 4:23

Have you ever thought about how unspeakably blessed we are to have the benefit of being able to read the very words of those who were Jesus' *talmidim*, close followers? Those who walked, ate, and slept with him testify to us each time we open our New Testaments.

In Jesus' lifetime, Peter became notorious for his impulsiveness. Sometimes this manifested itself admirably such as in bailing out of a perfectly good boat into the Sea of Galilee to take Jesus up on a challenge to go for a walk with him right then and there. Other times it came forth in shame; he vowed one minute that he would never betray Jesus, and the next minute he was denying he ever knew him. But Peter's grieving heart was healed and strengthened when Jesus, after his resurrection, confirmed his belief in Peter on the shore at breakfast (John 21). Eventually Peter was given another opportunity to stand and deliver to the enemies of The Way, and this time, he did so to the point of giving his own life for the memory of his Lord rather than to deny Him. Peter, therefore, should be an excellent source of knowledge in how to guard our hearts, the "wellsprings" of life.

In Peter's first letter, addressed to Jewish and Gentile believers scattered throughout Asia Minor, he is totally fixated on holiness. Everything he says in this letter comes down to living lives that shine with the unmistakable sheen of a holiness that can come by no less than the transforming power of "this new birth into a living hope through the resurrection of Jesus Christ from the dead and into an inheritance that can never perish, spoil, or fade—kept in heaven for you" (1 Peter 1:3-4).

Enter into this new day with the words of Peter on your heart screaming passionately, as only Peter could, about the how's and why's of holy living:

"Therefore, prepare your minds for action; be self-controlled; set your hope fully on the grace to be given to you when Jesus Christ is revealed. As obedient children, do not conform to the evil desires you had when you lived in ignorance. But just as he who called you is holy, so be holy in all you do; for it is written: 'Be holy because I am holy.' Since you call on a Father who judges each man impartially, live your lives as strangers here in reverent fear. For you know that it is not with perishable things such as silver or gold that you were redeemed from the empty way of life handed down to you from your forefathers but with the precious blood of Christ, a lamb without blemish or defect. He was chosen before the creation of the world, but was revealed in these last times for your sake. Through Him you believe in God, who raised Him from the dead and glorified Him and so your faith and hope are in God. Now that you have purified yourselves by obeying the truth so that you have sincere love for your brothers, love one another deeply from the heart. For you have been born again, not of perishable seed, but of imperishable, through the living and enduring word of God. For 'All men are like grass, and all their glory is like the flowers of the field; the grass withers and the flowers fall, but the word of the Lord stands forever.' And this is the word that was preached to you".

~MARCH 30~
GUARDING OUR WELLS PAUL STYLE

"Since, then, you have been raised with Christ, set your hearts on things above, where Christ is seated at the right hand of God. Set your minds on things above, not on earthly things. For you died, and your life is now hidden with Christ in God. When Christ, who is your life, appears, then you also will appear with him in glory." Colossians 3:1-4

"We demolish arguments and every pretension that sets itself up against the knowledge of God, and we take captive every thought to make it obedient to Christ." 2 Corinthians 10:5

Paul's apostleship came about in a different way but was every bit as strong and transforming as the others who wrote to encourage those of us who would be coming later and needing to know how to guard our hearts in this age. Paul was a voracious missionary for Christ. His missionary journeys took him to every ear he could bend. He was indomitable, being cowed by neither the most scholarly intellectuals who worshipped a multitude of pagan gods and goddesses nor by kings, governors, and emperors.

In his letter to the Colossians, Paul, like Peter, appeals to our new nature in Christ and exhorts us to do something that requires the stern discipline of repeated practice because our old nature was once so entrenched in doing the opposite. He first tells us to "set our hearts" on something we can't see rather than on all the delectable-sounding goods the world peddles. From a natural point of view, this seems like such a futile thing to ask since we know how hard our hearts pull us. It can be so bad that sometimes we just have to set our *minds* against our hearts because we don't know how to get down deeply enough inside ourselves to change our "wanters." He seems to realize this as soon as he says it because immediately he follows with "Set your *minds* on things above." He is saying, "If you can't make your heart cooperate yet, just look at this thing logically: when you "buried" that old man, obviously it was a dead body. Christ, though he is invisible, came in to be your new life. Someday he will appear in glory and you will be right there alive with Him!" Paul was telling us the way to guard our *hearts* has to be to guard our *minds*.

He reiterates this in his second letter to the Corinthians. He is speaking of how to wage war against the standards of the world with these new divine weapons we have. He says we can win by taking "captive every thought to make it obedient to Christ." My first objection to this was that I couldn't see how we could be expected to reach way out there and "catch" the thought *before* it is a thought.

I think he is speaking here of what we do with the thoughts that come to us when we first have them. Do we *sow* them (plant, water, fertilize, cultivate the soil around them), or do we cast them away from all nourishment, starving them so that they never grow from that seed into fruit?

We can't chastise ourselves for the things that come into our minds: that is called temptation, and even Jesus had to deal with temptation. What we *are* responsible for are the things in our mind that our hearts get "set on."

~MARCH 31~
NO OTHER GODS

"You shall have no other gods before me." Exodus 20:3

In Genesis 22 God told Abraham to go up on a mountain and sacrifice (*kill*) his beloved son Isaac, for whom he had waited until he was a hundred years old. Abraham obeyed and was about to plunge the knife into his son when God stopped him and directed him to get a ram out of a nearby thicket and sacrifice it instead. Although the first commandment was not yet written, what might God have been trying to teach Abraham about His exclusive claim to being God?

Can you think of anything that could be a threat of rivalry to God's position in your life?

John 1 describes Jesus as the Word become flesh that God, His Father, sent into the world to make His dwelling among us. John says, "From the fullness of His grace we have all received one blessing after another" (John 1:16). In verse 29, John tells of John the Baptist's saying, "Look, the Lamb of God who takes away the sin of the world." In these corresponding stories, think about the following characters: the Father, the Son, the Sacrifice. In the Genesis story, God and the Father were *different* characters. God saved the Father (Abraham) from having to kill his long-awaited, beloved son. However, in John's story, God is the *same person* as the Father. In other words, rather than following instructions from a higher authority, in the New Testament story, God the Father took the initiative to sacrifice His own Son, this time not stopping before the killing blow.

Think about what such an extreme action as this suggests about the necessity for this sacrifice and God's desire to rescue the *rest* of His children.

It's hard to miss the message that for some reason, *this* sacrifice was crucial. This time no ordinary ram in the thicket would suffice. But why?

Obviously, the rest of His children, though stained and misguided by lesser gods, were precious to the Father. Abraham passed the test of the first commandment having never read the textbook. We have the Notes for the test written in sixty-six different ways.

God knew that His family would not have been complete without us. We will not be complete with any other gods.

"How great is the love the Father has lavished upon us, that we should be called the children of God!" 1 John 3:1

~APRIL 1~
HOW <u>NOT</u> TO GUARD YOUR HEART

"Above all, love each other deeply because love covers over a multitude of sins." 1 Peter 4:8

"A man's wisdom gives him patience; it is to his glory to overlook an offense."
Proverbs 19:11

I thought when you said in your Word, "Guard your heart, for it is the wellspring
of life,
You meant I should guard it from bleeding to death, from the pain that can slice
like a knife.
I thought it was wise to invest in protecting such a precious tool from abuse;
I thought I should build a fortress of stone to preserve it well for your use.

So somehow I've done it little by little; I've wisely constructed the fort.
I've collected the bricks of numbness and apathy, isolation, and the sort.
They've been mortared together with lack of involvement, and logic and
distance and such,
And lacquered over with learning to do rather well without needing to touch.

After all, it was touching that I had desired in my deepest, most vulnerable heart,
So since there was none, wasn't it only prudent to cut out that part?
But cutting out the parts that hurt has cut out the parts that delight.
Now the sensitive skin that can scream in pain lies undisturbed and quiet;
Unmoved by the rustling of real desire, pacified and still—
A lot less susceptible to the ache of neglect, but also a lot less real.

Solomon said, "What a man desires is unfailing love" (Proverbs 19:22), but
a few verses later explains that "Many a man claims to have unfailing love, but a
faithful man, who can find?" (Proverbs 20:6). I do believe that unfailing love is
the deepest desire of every human, but alas, no human can love perfectly all the
time. It is so tempting to play it safe and just give up the gamble of loving. But a
wise leader once said, "The ship in the port is safe, but that is not what ships were
built for."[1] So if the answer isn't quitting or numbing (with alcohol, drugs, suicide,
or chronic bitterness) the parts that can feel, then what shall we do?

We must realize, like the psalmist, that only the love of God can completely
satisfy and quit placing God-sized jobs on humanity. Here is the way he puts it:
*"Satisfy us in the morning with your unfailing love, that we may sing for joy and
be glad all our days" (Psalm 90:14).* It is a verse worth hiding in your heart if you
plan to keep your ship on the high seas.

~APRIL 2~
NEW CREATION:
YELLOW BUTTERFLIES AND BLUE HYDRANGEAS

*"See how the lilies of the field grow...Yet I tell you that even Solomon in all his
splendor was not dressed like one of these. If that is how God clothes the grass of*

the field, which is here today and tomorrow thrown into the fire, will he not much more clothe you...?" Matthew 6:28-30

"Because of the Lord's great love, we are not consumed, for His compassions never fail. They are new every morning; great is Your faithfulness." Lamentations 3:23

"...if anyone is in Christ Jesus, he is a new creation; the old has gone, the new has come!" 2 Corinthians 5:17

Dear Merciful Restorer of Lost Glory,

When I consider the parable of springtime that you so vociferously and garishly parade before me every year, I am aghast that I can ever forget the truth of your wonderful restoring nature. It has always been easy for me to be thrilled with blue hydrangeas that crowd together on a lushly verdant bush that was until a few weeks ago dry, brittle, brown, and well, I hate to say it, Lord—just downright unsightly. And that thing about butterflies bursting forth brilliantly from a crusty little box that belies any splendor whatever has fascinated me as long as I can remember. But there is so much in all this You have been saying that I am ashamed to say I have not had the ears to hear or the eyes to see.

We, not the lilies or the grass or the hydrangeas or the butterflies, are your crowning creation, made in your own image. You are so much more anxious to restore *us* to that image than these other lovely props of nature. Yet, sometimes when I look upon an unsightly life, I am sorely tempted to cross her off as a lost cause—too far gone. I have looked upon his dry husk and judged him an unlikely prospect for new life. How many tomatoes must materialize from a vine; how many crocuses must burst through the snow; how many caterpillars must turn into butterflies before we finally get the message that You will turn a sinner— *any* sinner— who comes into You into a new creation, too? Furthermore, that new creation can be used to bear much more fruit.

Lord, I am so enamored of Your handiwork in nature. Flowers, stars, the moon, sunsets, birds, berries, the forest, the mountains, the ocean—I drink it in and lick it up. I want to romp around in it, write poetry about it, and gather it up and bring it all in the house with me at night.

Please forgive me for not seeing your children in such a favorable light, for not loving and cherishing the cornucopia of splendor and variety you display in *humanity,* for not honoring Your power to transform *us* just as You do nature. I pray through the life-giving blood of Jesus. Amen

"The most pathetic person in the world is someone who has sight but no vision."-Helen Keller

~APRIL 3~
THE THINGS WE DON'T SAY:
THE COST OF REMAINING SILENT

"A word fitly spoken is like apples of gold in settings of silver." Proverbs 25:11

PICKET FENCE

If matter never disappears but only changes form,
What happens to unspoken words?
Do they melt into creamed corn?
Maybe they harden and their points get sharpened,
Their appearance making us wince.
Maybe then we whitewash them,
Hook them together, and plant them between us
And neither of us ever knows
Whence came this stout picket fence.

"Sticks and stones may break my bones, but words will never hurt me." There's never been a less truthful sentiment spoken. Anyone who has lived for three years or more knows the truth about words: they can cut like shrapnel. That's the *cursed* thing about words.

The *blessed* thing about words is that they can also encourage, comfort, and heal. Words are, to some of us, the greatest gift of love. We would trade off many a high-dollar possession for some deeply felt words of love. But this isn't big news to anyone, and there's no sense in wasting our time belaboring these facts.

What I fear *isn't* talked about enough is the effect that the *lack* of words can have. For those who desperately need to hear or to read words of affirmation, encouragement, and love, the absence of them can be devastating. I know that this problem of needing words and not receiving them is widespread because I have spoken with so many troubled women whose husbands are "men of few words." Many use this phrase as though it is a sign of wisdom, and even the Bible praises us for being "quick to listen and slow to speak" (James 1:19), but later in the same book we are told, "Anyone then who knows the good he ought to do and doesn't do it, sins" (James 4:17).

It's true that some people are just oblivious to the need to speak because they don't need words so much and therefore, can't imagine how anyone else could. Please be aware that what you *don't* say can hurt you and others just as much as what you *do* say.

Children are growing into dysfunctional, insecure adults because of things that may not be true but that they *perceive* as true. To many, not to hear that they are loved is exactly the same as not being loved. We are told to do unto others as we would be done unto. Sometimes we need to take this a step further because the specifics of that may not be appropriate, according to our differing natures and needs. What we need to ask is, "What is it that I hope will never be *withheld* from me by those I love?" Then try to see what that is in others, and do not fail to give what is needed. Silence can hurt.

~APRIL 4~
"HE WILL REJOICE OVER YOU WITH SINGING"

"Is there no balm in Gilead?" Jeremiah 8:22

When love's fixed coverlet retreats from my touch and I am dismayed in that
lonely place,
I question again if I truly have been focusing faithfully on your face.
I wonder if I, and not You, after all, created this treacherous overflow
That yearns and aches and sighs and waits and hangs onto threads that always
go.

But when I take the path you show and refuse to go my own way;
When I refuse to shrink from Heavenly blows, deeper and deeper the knowledge
grows
That the pain I bear to trust and stay will be lost in the balm of Heaven someday.

When what I am needing to find when in love is direct return, one-for-one,
Dear Father, the odds against my winning just make me want to break and run.
But when I consider that I am your child whose bidding down here is just to
obey,
Then I remember my prayers: "Use me, Lord, as your vessel," so I decide to
stay.

Oh, when I take the path you show and refuse to depart from your way;
When I refuse to shrink from Heavenly blows, some small, tender root is nour-
ished and grows.
Assurance sets in and I know that though it takes pain to trust and stay,
A balm sufficient for all my wounds awaits me in the glory of your face
someday.

"I consider that our present sufferings are not worth comparing to the glory that will be revealed in us." Romans 8:18

But for *now* we can take comfort in knowing this: *"The Lord your God is with you, He is mighty to save. He will take great delight in you, He will quiet you with His love, He will rejoice over you with singing" (Zephaniah 3:17).*

~APRIL 5~
JOB'S DREAM, OUR REALITY

"If only there were someone to arbitrate between us to lay his hand upon us both, someone to remove God's rod from me, so that his terror would frighten me no more. Then I would speak up without fear of him, but as it now stands with me, I cannot." Job 9:33-35.

"Before this faith came, we were held prisoners by the law, locked up until faith should be revealed." Galatians 3:23

"For there is one God and one mediator between God and men, the man Jesus Christ." 1 Timothy 2:5

The "us" referred to in Job is God and himself. Job stands condemned by his friends who never consider that God might be working in less obvious ways than man's feeble mind could explain. Job, knowing himself better than his friends do, cries out for a true mediator, one who could wisely and objectively listen to both sides of the story, and respond justly. With about the same amount of hope that we might wish for a magic genie in a bottle, he wishes for someone who could speak both his language of humanity and God's language of holiness. Instead of finding the accompaniment of the intercessor he so desperately needs to alleviate his agony of body, heart, and soul, he must stand alone in the courtroom of God.

Job's Dream has become our Blessed Reality! Some have lived lives so darkened by emptiness and the Enemy's lies—so shut off from the true life-giving and life-saving Light of knowing Jesus— that we can imagine Job's desolation. Others cannot remember not knowing the presence and availability of Christ, and for us, Job's dilemma is incomprehensible. If we are not reminded, we might forget that, unlike Job, we have knowledge of our high priest who "being in very nature, God, did not consider equality with God something to be grasped, but made himself nothing, taking the very nature of a servant, being made in human likeness…humbled himself and became obedient to death" (Philippians 2) all so that we might be represented to a Holy God by a Worthy Defense Attorney.

For the very reason of our blessed ignorance, we should never go for very long without studying the Old Testament. Woe to us if we ever take for granted so great a salvation, so bountiful a blessing as the crucified and risen Savior who "always lives to intercede for [us]" (Hebrews 7:25) Let us never fail to give thanks that whether we are living in high cotton with healthy kids and livestock a'plenty or sitting broken among the ashes, the gospel screams to us in a thousand voices the glorious reality of a great High Priest who always has one of his hands on us and the other on God. It's a dream come true.

~APRIL 6~
JOB'S DILEMMA, OUR ASSURANCE

"After Job had prayed for his friends, the Lord made him prosperous again and gave him twice as much as he had before." Job 42:10

Job was restored what he had lost
In the same currency as before:
Children for children,
Livestock for livestock
Prosperity and health
For prosperity and health.

And now today when suffering comes,
Will God appear and restore it again:
Joy for tear?
Pleasure for pain?
When the game with Satan is over?

Ah! Thanks be to God for the Gift
That Job was born too soon to comprehend!
Now when we suffer and lose all we own,
He fills our eyes with vision unknown
To eyes saturated with meager sight—
And He gives us not more of what we had
That soon enough will be gone again,
But fills our blessed emptiness
With the eternal fullness of Jesus Christ.

Before Christ came to fulfill the law, the emphasis was on externals. God's rewards and punishments were usually something immediate and tangible. Then Jesus came and taught us about the roots. "You have heard it said... but I say unto you..." "Eye for eye and tooth for tooth" became "pray for those who persecute you." Animal sacrifices and circumcision of the flesh gave way to the cleansing blood of the spotless Lamb of God. He came to heal us from the inside-out, to help us grow from being "whitewashed sepulchres" to being holy vessels for Him. The temple made of stone gave way to the temple made of sanctified hearts.

Isn't it wonderful to know, when life takes us by storm, that there is a safe haven waiting? Isn't it blessed to remember that "our present sufferings are not worth comparing with the *glory* that will be revealed in us" (Romans 8:18) and that "neither death nor life, neither angels nor demons, neither the present nor the future, nor any powers, neither height not depth, nor anything else in all creation will be able to separate us from the love of God that is in Christ Jesus our Lord" (Romans 8:38)?

~APRIL 7~
OUR FIRST-PERSON GOD

"Then you will call upon me and come and pray to me, and I will listen to you. You will seek me and find me when you seek me with all your heart. I will be found by you, declares the Lord..." Jeremiah 29:11-14

Since ours is a love relationship with our Father, I greatly suspect that He feels pretty much the way we do about communication with those we love. We want direct communication— ideally face to face, but at least voice to ear. The Bible leaves no doubt that God is a jealous God; I find seventeen references to His jealousy in my inexhaustive, back-of-the-Bible concordance alone. Even though God's jealousy, unlike our earthly kind, is purely motivated by His knowledge that nothing less than His love will satisfy our deepest longings, by definition, jealousy desires to be cherished by the object of its love. God surely desires our love and thus the kind of loving two-way communication that we desire in our closest relationships.

To be discussed in the third person or to be talked about behind our backs hurts. We feel betrayed. We had much rather one we love come to us and talk *to* us rather than to go to someone else and talk *about* us.

At the end of Job's story, in chapter 42, God tells Eliphaz, Zophar, and Bildad that He is angry with them for what they have said about Him and instructs them to sacrifice a burnt offering. Then He says that He will withhold punishing them according to their foolishness only after Job prays for them. The words these guys spoke about God honestly don't look so bad. Some of the things they say are true and would be good advice in many circumstances. Besides that, at the beginning of chapter 38 when God responds to Job's words to Him, God doesn't sound as though Job's words are abounding in wisdom. "Who is this that darkens my counsel with words without knowledge? Brace yourself like a man; I shall question you, and you shall answer me." What, then, is the difference between their words and Job's? Could it be that God honors Job while He is angry at the three counselors because while all they do is to talk *about* God, Job talks *to* God?

So many times in the Psalms, David begins writing *about* God, in third person, but before too long, he is writing *to* God, in first person. The Twenty-Third Psalm begins "The Lord is my shepherd...*He* makes me lie down...*He* guides me...*He* restores my soul...", but by the time he has reached the fourth verse, he has begun speaking thusly: "...for *You* are with me...*Your* rod and staff....*You* prepare a table...*You* anoint my head..." David and Job had the kind of hearts that so loved their Deliverer that they couldn't talk for very long *about* Him before they just naturally fell into talking *to* Him.

Testimony about God, in third person, is what good missionary work is all about, no doubt. We are admonished to tell, to teach, to preach ABOUT our God and our Savior, Jesus. However, if we find ourselves *stuck* in the third person, we shouldn't be surprised if someday Jesus responds to us as He warns us about in Matthew 7:23 and Matthew 25:12: "Away from me. I never *knew* you."

~APRIL 8~
JOYFUL IN HOPE

"Never be lacking in zeal, but keep your spiritual fervor, serving the Lord. Be joyful in hope, patient in affliction, faithful in prayer." Romans 12:12

In the past hour and a half, all twenty-five of Johnnie May's remaining teeth had been pulled, her gums stitched from stem to stern, and a complete set of dentures installed in her mouth. As we discussed her pain, she admitted to feeling more than a little discomfort from all this oral trauma, but she hastened to remind me that this kind of pain was much easier to live with than the toothaches and abscesses she had suffered that brought her to this point. A woman of unimpressive educational background and insignificant worldly means, she opened her beleaguered mouth that day and lavished upon me rare wisdom from her priceless experience. She saw this whole ordeal as another parable handed down directly from the Father of lights in order to illuminate her way through her minefield of a life.

As for pain, we are all going to have some regardless of the path we choose. Whether we choose to walk the lonely, narrow path and cling to the truth sacrificially or take the broad, crowded path of self-centeredness, we are going to come upon trouble. There is no antitoxin for pain; there are just different attitudes toward it. There is no avoiding it; there are only choices of how to go through it. The thing all pain has in common is that it hurts; the thing that distinguishes one kind from another is what awaits us on the other shore. Johnnie's toothaches were not only almost unbearable because of what was happening to her nerve endings but because of what was happening in her heart. Her teeth were rotten and abscessed, and her consciousness that their condition, left alone, would only worsen served to multiply the agony. With every physical twinge, there was the heartsick pang of hopelessness. There can be no worse pain than pain without hope. The kind of pain she felt after twenty-five extractions, a mouth full of stitches, and dentures pressed down on top of all that was definitely nothing enviable, but it was pain with hope. Now, the future held promise. In fact, she would prefer a *thousand* stitches with healing power to those few abscesses doomed to further decay. She knew what she spoke was true because she had lived another level of the parable only a few years earlier. Her former life racked with drug addiction and its resulting dreadful desperation was that hopeless toothache; her new life in Christ was the painful but hopeful adjustment to her temporarily uncomfortable but beautiful new dentures.

What she was explaining was what Paul wrote to the Romans about being "joyful in hope." We have an eternal inheritance that cannot be stolen or spoiled. That is the hope that keeps us going through whatever it takes to lay hold of what lies on the other shore. When we lose our focus on that, pain feels like despair, but when we keep clearly focused on that hope, we can go through having all our teeth pulled (or knocked!) out,whether literally or figuratively, without falling into despair. It is pain with a wonderful purpose. It is the bright smile of a mouth full of gleaming new teeth.

"We are hard pressed on every side, but not crushed; perplexed but not in despair; persecuted but not abandoned; struck down but not destroyed" (2Corinthians 4:7-9).

~APRIL 9~
SPIRITUAL GUTS

"Then we will no longer be infants, tossed back and forth by the waves, and blown here and there by every wind of teaching and by the cunning and craftiness of men in their deceitful scheming. Instead, speaking the truth in love, we will in all things grow up into him who is the Head, that is, Christ." Ephesians 4:14-15

"For God has not given us a spirit of timidity, but of power and love and discipline." 2 Timothy 1:7 (NASB)

To survive this life, we are always being called upon to gird up our loins and do some things we'd rather not— things distasteful, exhausting, or even dangerous. We can't live a very valiant life if we don't learn from an early age that courage, which is facing the thing we are afraid of, is going to be required of us from time to time.

As Christians we are called on to stand for Something, for Someone, that the world describes as fantasy, imagination, ridiculous. The life we set out to live when we die to ourselves and take up our cross is, to the world, a foolhardy exercise in futility. To do it right requires spiritual guts.

For one thing, it really is not so farfetched to think that in the not-too-distant-future we could be called upon to deny Christ or be tortured or even killed. Most of us feel fairly safe from such persecution, but when you look at morality—or the lack thereof— and how it has plummeted in the past couple of decades; when you pick up an old magazine or watch an old movie and notice how our heroes have changed, how what once was the moral of the story is now the thing the story is mocking and ridiculing; when you look at how all things godly are under attack in all places public, the idea that ridicule can turn into illegality is not such a bounding leap. Are we ready? Have we nourished our souls on the Truth, that which is unseen and eternal, so that we won't need to stop and ask ourselves if this is Something worth giving up our lives for?

But more immediately, spiritual guts are necessary so that we can stand for the Truth when others do not, so that we can speak the Truth when someone we like and desire fellowship with is speaking something less. Is it tempting when this happens to say nothing, just to blend, to talk ourselves into believing that our silence will be interpreted as dissent without our having to make a scene that might embarrass us or someone else? What if our silence isn't even noticed? What if our silence is interpreted as agreement? Do we care?

Paul wanted Timothy and the Christians in Ephesus to understand how to avoid this trap. He told them when they found themselves at odds with the crowds' beliefs, not to wimp out since God did not give them a spirit of fear or timidity, but to "speak the truth in love."

It takes spiritual guts to realize that what we stand for and what we will not stand for matters. As the light of the world, we are always being given opportunities to shine. God called us to this mission. It is our foremost purpose. The highest priority is saving the lost. We don't have to *fight* about it; we can, and must, do it in love.

~APRIL 10~
DANCING WITH OUR DELIVERER

"For you know that it was not with perishable things such as silver or gold that you were redeemed from the empty way of life handed down to you from your forefathers, but with the precious blood of Christ, a lamb without blemish or defect." 1 Peter 1:18

"For in Christ all the fullness of the Deity lives in bodily form, and you have been given fullness in Christ, who is the head over every power and authority." Colossians 2:9-10

As I sat in the rehab center week after week listening to her story of a life wrecked by addiction to sex and drugs beginning at age twelve, it was almost unimaginable that she had seen so much heartache and trouble in such a short time. She was only twenty-seven and could have authored a dozen books chronicling her deadly spiral down to where she now had landed. The phrase that kept coming to my mind as I listened was "this empty way of life." It wasn't that she hadn't had a few new ideas along the way to try to change her state; it's just that each one was another form of emptiness. It was just another chapter of the same book, another verse to the same old song. Hollow. Blank. Hopeless. Empty.

Her story might be more extreme than yours or mine, but it isn't so different, really. All of us were redeemed from an empty way of life, whether the emptiness was in the shape of addiction to some lethal substance or selfishness; whether it wore the gaudy trappings of illicit sex or the dull sackcloth of a bitter, unforgiving spirit. Everyone is enslaved to something. Make no mistake, we will serve a master. That service will either be characterized by joy and delight motivated by hope which is afforded us by a good and kind master, or by dread and despair brought about by hopelessness handed down from a master who comes only to steal, kill, and destroy.

As the weeks passed and she became excited about being rid of the curses of addiction, we looked at a story Jesus told once about someone else who had banished one evil spirit only to find a little while later that it had returned and brought with it seven more. "And the final condition of that man [was] worse than the first" (Matthew 12:43-45). If we just kick a bad habit without finding Jesus in the healing process, we are apt to think more highly of ourselves than we ought and invite in the demons of conceit, arrogance, misplaced credit, and pride. Instead of fighting one demon, we find our house riddled with them. We must stay focused on Him who heals and cleans us. We must dance with the one who "brung" us.

Getting our act together, our ducks in a row, and our house swept is not good enough. It might be a clean house now, but it is still empty. "Clean" living and high morals are not enough to fill up the emptiness. Life in a void, even a clean one, is not much of a life. We will still be hungry. "For God was pleased to have all His *fullness* dwell in Him, and through Him to reconcile to himself all things, whether on earth or things in heaven, by making peace though His blood shed on the cross" (Colossians 1:19). In order to be full, we must be filled with God and His spirit. It is what we were made for.

~APRIL 11~
PRACTICE MAKES PERFECT:
GUARDING AGAINST HYPOCRISY

"...Be on your guard against the yeast of the Pharisees, which is hypocrisy. There is nothing concealed that will not be disclosed, or hidden that will not be made known." Luke 12:2-3

Yeast is one of the pictures Jesus used often to point out the dangers of a little becoming a lot, of a small "innocent" thing growing into some hideous, monstrous evil, or of a disease-like vice in one person or group of people infecting another person or even another whole group of people. Hypocrisy is the disease at hand, and the Pharisees are the carriers. Jesus wants His followers to know that it is deadly and that it can stealthily attach itself to any of us who are not on guard against it.

When you think about it, carriers of hypocrisy, in one form or another, are the only people to whom Jesus ever spoke in strong, even harsh, language. Jesus was notoriously magnanimous with other sinners, saving an adulteress from a stoning and bringing the tax collector Zacchaeus down from the tree so that he could have lunch at his house. On more than one occasion He warned the Pharisees that even the prostitutes and the tax collectors would enter the Kingdom before they would.

What makes this sin stand out so much from the rest? Why is hypocrisy spoken of as such diabolical yeast? Having lived long enough to have fallen into its trap more than I like to admit, I have come to believe there are two reasons.

First, hypocrisy starts out as a lie that we tell others and grows into a lie we tell ourselves. Secondly, the more we practice deception, as with all things we practice, the better we get at it. The combination of these dangers makes for a deadly concoction that we can consume in larger and larger doses without feeling its effect.

If we are not on guard, we might, in our attempt to look good, pretend to be something we are not; we might cast stones at others for the very thing we are neck-deep into ourselves. We might become so busy pointing out specks in others' eyes that we don't even take the time anymore to look into the mirror at the junk in our own.

And thus, pretty soon the façade we are selling to others we begin to buy into ourselves.

If we can get by with hiding from others some "little" bad habit we are ashamed of but not ready to dispense with, and we do it long enough, we do not simply succeed in keeping our secret; we succeed in actually changing who we *are*. We become *good* at deception; our consciences grow less sensitive to truth and more hardened to dishonesty. By repeatedly participating in fraud, we lose an innocence that we cannot regain. We learn something that we cannot unlearn. According to the Psalmist, we even endanger our communication with God. "If I had cherished sin in my heart, the Lord would not have listened…" (Psalm 66:18) Choosing to protect our image by sacrificing honesty is "cherishing sin."

May we keep a constant inventory of our character to discover if we have been caught off guard against the ominous yeast of hypocrisy. If our heart can still detect it, it is not too late to let God cleanse it.

~APRIL 12~
A HOLY TERROR

"Do not be afraid of those who kill the body but cannot kill the soul. Rather be afraid of the One who can destroy both body and soul in hell." Matthew 10:28

The context of this scripture is Jesus' sending out of the Twelve to the lost sheep of Israel to prepare them for the kingdom of heaven. They are to heal the sick, raise the dead, and drive out demons. It is from this discourse that we glean some of Jesus' most-quoted sayings: "…shake the dust from your feet," "Freely you have received, freely give," …be as shrewd as snakes and as innocent as doves," "A student is not above his teacher," and "…anyone who does not take his cross and follow me is not worthy of me. Whoever finds his life will lose it, and whoever loses his life for my sake will find it."

About midway through this speech, in His effort to prepare them for the persecution that must certainly come if they do their job well, He tells them, "Do not be afraid of those who kill the body but cannot kill the soul. Rather be afraid of the One who can destroy both body and soul in hell." Usually talk of hell's destruction brings Satan to mind, but the "One" Jesus speaks of here is not Satan, but God.

Now obviously this is not the kind of fear that would paralyze or distance us from fear's source, for immediately after these words, He speaks words of comfort, reminding them that they are worth more than the flocks and flocks of individual sparrows who cannot fall to the ground apart from the will of their Father. He goes on to say, "Even the very hairs of your head are all numbered."

This type of fear is rather a "holy" terror which could in our language best be translated as an undivided, unflinching *focus* produced by purposeful prioritizing. He is reminding them that eternity must remain their goal, of course, but at the same time He is underlining for them the Thing we must all never allow ourselves to forget concerning that eternity, Something that many people don't want to face: the place (or condition, if you prefer not to see geography as deep enough to contain it) where the body and soul are destroyed is *Hell. Hell really exists.*

Even those closest to Jesus on this earth needed to be reminded that there is a hell that awaits those who choose not to be in a saving relationship with Him. Jesus doesn't euphemize the terrible truth or allow it to become background fuzziness to His best friends. He doesn't seem to think it might put them off or cause them to turn away from Him or their mission. He tells them this not to discourage them but rather to encourage them. He wants them to fear God in this way because He knows that the proper fear of God will keep them, and us, fearless of everything and everyone else.

For Christians, death is no longer a problem we focus on; the soul is. Our bodies can be destroyed at any time in numberless ways that we cannot predict. If we focus on this part of death, we will be paralyzed by fear and will be ineffective Christians. We need to make peace with the fact that our bodies are mortal and get over our fear of losing them. We should only fear losing our contact with and our love for God. This is the fear that makes us fearless. Furthermore, we should remind those we love, as Jesus did.

One in the hand is *not* better than two in the bush if the bush is God's hand.

~APRIL 13~
WHAT BAFFLES THE ANGELS

"Even angels long to look into these things." 1 Peter 1:12

What on earth could possibly be a mystery to heavenly beings? We have only to look back a few verses to find out.

"Though you have not seen Him, you love Him; and even though you do not see Him now, you believe in Him and are filled with an inexpressible and glorious joy, for you are receiving the goal of your faith, the salvation of your souls" (1 Peter 1:8-9).

Angels, having always lived by sight, are amazed that we live only by faith! I can certainly understand their fascination. Faith-walking is not for wimps. Is it just me, or do you sometimes, when you're against a wall, just long to quit straining to see the unseen, quit lunging out past the edges of *terra firma*, and instead, just brace yourself for the worst? Especially in troubles, it sometimes just feels exhausting to maintain a high level of expectation.

And yet, that is what we as Christians are called upon to do. We are called to see the unseeable, to believe the unbelievable, to stake our very lives on the idea that all things really are working together for good. We are expected to turn our backs on all the world offers as solace and consolation in favor of a promise that whatever befalls us, it will all be worth it in the end. We are to reject all means of deadening any necessary pain in order to be the spiritual creatures that can bring glory to our Master so that a lost world can *see* Him and thereby gain the only Hope there is. Jesus never pulled any punches here; He said in order for us to live, we must die. Faith-walking, unlike faith-talking, requires us to take up a cross and follow Him into places any rational thinker would dig his heels in and refuse to go. We are told to "lean not on our own understanding" (Proverbs 3:5), but rather to walk across a narrow wire above an invisible net.

Isaiah puts it this way: "If you do not stand firm in your faith, you will not stand at all" (Isaiah 7:9). Something less might seem to be doing the trick, but there's always a rub. Even if the world's contrivances and ways manage to keep us pacified and safe throughout a goodly-numbered lifetime of years, at last we stand at the end of this life, and eternity of one kind or the other yawns before us with certainty. You don't have to sit beside very many deathbeds to realize the folly of possessions, fame, and accomplishment. Those things don't remove the terror of the question mark after the words, "What now?"

Though this kind of walk takes extreme courage and spiritual energy, we are told that we *must*, for indeed, we are *saved* by faith. It can be done! There is an entire chapter in Hebrews dedicated to those who did this very thing. They are our "great cloud of witnesses" cheering us on.

This is not Heaven, and we are not angels. Anything less than faith-walking will not buoy us up in this sea of sin we are tossed upon. But this will not last forever. Paul encourages us: "I consider that our present sufferings are not worth comparing with the glory that will be revealed in us" (Romans 8:18).

~APRIL 14~
IGNORANCE IS BLISS

"For I resolved to know nothing while I was with you except Jesus Christ and Him crucified." 1 Corinthians 2:2

By this Paul probably means he is dedicating himself fully to teaching and preaching Jesus— the pure gospel—with no frills such as persuasive words or dog and pony shows. He was trying to demonstrate the *Spirit's* power, so that his listeners would place their faith in God's power rather than men's wisdom.

I'm not sure God expects us literally to be ignorant of everything else except Him; we are to navigate through this world with the aim of changing it, bringing others to a realization that there is a better world and a better way. We must interact with people in order for that to happen.

But there is just so much room for expertise in one human brain. We can only be authorities on a limited number of subjects. Often I find myself feeling embarrassed and even ashamed when I am the only one in the room who doesn't "get it." Names are dropped, phrases are thrown around, seemingly commonplace information, factual and fictional, rise up as the center of attention, and often I find myself out of the loop. If you teach high school freshmen, you get to experience a more honest opinion at these times than you would if you interact only with adults, who are aware of social rules that "require" a bit of reserve rather than shock or open curiosity about how anyone on the *planet* could manage to be so utterly *stupid* as not to *know about* these people, these movies, these songs. It's not that I don't have my own areas of interest or even partial authority; it's just that in the competition for my time, my heart, and my mind, some of the more popular items lose out.

We are not guaranteed a certain number of years in this life. Jesus was given only thirty-three. I know that He learned carpentry from Joseph, and, being a good listener, I am sure He knew *something* about a lot of things, but when you listen to what He talked about, it was the kingdom of God. Paul made tents for a living and knew enough about philosophy and geography to give him common ground with and exposure to people over his world, but all of his travels and all of his conversations led up to Christ and Him crucified. He determined that he would seek to be an authority on nothing more or less than This One Thing. And I seriously doubt that when others were speaking about something he knew nothing at all about, he felt ashamed or inferior that he had not spent his limited hours and days learning about it rather than about God and His will.

About what do people consider you to be an authority? What do you pride yourself upon knowing *well*? How many hours or years have you spent gaining the knowledge that makes you an authority? We might be using up our last hours on trivial pursuits rather than fighting the good fight and finishing the race.

It is not only true that what we don't know can't hurt us; what we don't know might actually *help* us. Who we are and *whose* we are are not only revealed by what we know but also by what we *don't* know.

~APRIL 15~
A MOVEABLE FAMINE

"...I remind you to fan into flame the gift of God which is in you..." 2 Timothy *1:6*

"...and do not give the devil a foothold..." Ephesians 4:27

"Put on the full armor of God so that you can take your stand against the devil's schemes....take up the shield of faith with which you can extinguish all the flaming arrows of the evil one." Ephesians 6:11, 16

"The devil's schemes," "the flaming arrows of the evil one." These are serious accusations which pull no punches about coloring the devil in all his brash and blatant hues. The context of the armor of God passage is a warning that our most real and constant battle is not against someone, or even a lot of someones, put together as we are. As Christians we are in all-out war against "the rulers, the authorities, the powers of this dark world and against the spiritual forces of evil in the heavenly realms." We are also told that "the day of evil" will come to each of us; Paul doesn't say "in case" or "if" the day of evil comes. He says "so that *when* the day of evil comes, you may be able to stand your ground" (Ephesians 6:13).

Days of evil come to us many times without much warning. We are standing firm and walking in the light when suddenly we find ourselves at a crossroads. Actually, what we come upon is a little detour from the path we were heretofore traversing. It might not even look like a detour at all; it might very well look like just an optional path—

no better, no worse— just different.

But what it really is is temptation. If it were dressed in the attire of our particular weakness, we would know it for what it is and flee. However, sometimes because we have been walking so ably for so long, or because we have never had a particular weakness for this specific sin, we might assent to it with little thought of danger. We may decide, since we feel strong in this area, to go ahead and read a book or watch a movie which we know is covered with the Enemy's fingerprints. Being strong against one type of sin doesn't guarantee safety against his wiles. He is crafty and he seeks, like a lion, to devour us (1 Peter 5:8).

We forget that the devil wants in, and he doesn't care which door he uses— the front, back, or side. Once we invite him in, even into a room in which we feel very safe, he then can more easily distract us long enough to get free run of the house. He can move into a room that is not ready for him— into one of our weak areas where we are less fortified.

Oddly, we seem to know the converse is true. We understand that when we "fan into flame" God's gifts, we become better able to serve Him in a myriad of ways, not just in the way we did the fanning. We know, for instance, that we are told to study the Word diligently for better reasons than just becoming better at studying the Word.

Whether we call the portal a foothold or a chink in the armor, giving the devil any leeway can begin to starve the Christian, and thus the world, of the feast of God's glory. Just as nourishing the Holy Spirit on one front brings about delightfully surprising advances on other fronts, giving the devil entrance into one room can, and usually does, invite him into other rooms. Stand guard over your entire house.

~APRIL 16~
A HAND OVER THE MOUTH

"The Lord said to Job, 'Will the one who contends with the Almighty correct Him? Let him who accuses God answer Him!' Then Job answered the Lord, 'I am unworthy—how can I reply to you? I put my hand over my mouth.'" Job 40:1-4

"If you have played the fool and exalted yourself, or if you have planned evil, clap your hand over your mouth." Proverbs 30:32

The first time I encountered Job's words, "I put my hand over my mouth" was in a musical composition by Michael Card.[2] Thinking it was his own paraphrase of Job's moment of holy embarrassment, I went to the source and found that it indeed was a direct quote from Job 40:4. I was fascinated by the aptness of the picture. It seemed to me to be the perfect description of one who found himself in the unusual circumstance of being dressed down in a conversation with the Almighty. I remembered doing the same thing on so many occasions—times when I had forgotten to do something I said I would do for someone; times when I had let something sharp or acrid spew from my mouth to douse someone I loved with its poison; times of foolishness that had immediately produced a regret whose response was an immediate and heartfelt slapping of a hand over my mouth. This gesture had always seemed so ordinary, so earthly, so...modern, somehow, like some cultural, faddish idiom that we do from human to human, but not quite regal, sacred, formal, or *ecclesiastical* enough to do while looking at and addressing God.

And then it hit me that although God did use this opportunity to admonish Job by asking Him a long series of rhetorical questions that illustrated Job's (and our) dire inability to grasp even the simplest of God's ways, He also, in the end, took Job's side against his seemingly more enlightened friends and "blessed the latter part of Job's life more than the first." It seems that God was more pleased with Job's face-to-face relationship that asked Him some heart-wrenching questions than He was with the more remote relationship the others had with Him that too easily handed out pat answers and sterile philosophies.

It led me to ask myself some questions: Is my relationship to God that close? Is it that *real*? Is it one of vulnerable humility or proud arrival? Am I so sancti-fied—so set aside for His use—that I sense His presence that strongly? Do I see Him sitting there across the table from me or feel Him walking beside me as I go about my life's business to the extent that I might ever so sense my regrettable actions or *thoughts* that I, too, would— with God as my only audience— literally, as did Job, put my hand over my mouth in shame? Is my conscience still tender enough to recognize *from a heavenly standpoint* when I have "played the fool and exalted [myself]" or "planned evil," as Solomon warns?

Let us pray that we will be as sensitive to *God's* eyes on us as we are to so many lesser eyes that cause us so often to put our hands over our mouths.

~APRIL 17~
THE WORD PLANTED IN US

"My dear brothers, take note of this: Everyone should be quick to listen, slow to speak and slow to become angry, for man's anger does not bring about the righteous life that God desires. Therefore, get rid of all moral filth and the evil that is so prevalent and humbly accept the word planted in you, which can save you."
James 1:19-21

John tells us that Jesus was the Word incarnate sent down from the Father to dwell among us. Jesus tells us that His physical departure from us in this place in no way meant that we were being left as orphans but that He was leaving His Spirit, the Counselor and Comforter within us "as a deposit." This is the "word planted in you" that James is speaking of here. It is interesting that he says that the way we are enabled to live out God's holiness (eager listening and sluggish speech and anger) as well as the way we rid ourselves of immorality is to "humbly accept the word planted in you" that brings about salvation. Rather than urging us to seize it or even to obey it, he uses the verb "accept." He seems to be trying to get us to see that if we truly *accept* as fact that the word has indeed been planted in us, just as Jesus promised, we will naturally see to it that it, like any planted thing, receives the proper care and nourishment to thrive.

The life of my brother-in-law Dennis exemplifies this scripture eloquently. His nature shouts that supernatural life is, indeed, a thing that can be laid hold of. It is nearly impossible to make Dennis mad. When confronted or questioned by those who disagree with his viewpoint, Dennis responds with a noticeable absence of defensiveness. When approached by someone challenging his beliefs or even questioning his actions, Dennis's face breaks out into an ironic smile that disarms his opponents who are fired up and ready to argue. Having spent years as a missionary, he knows the importance of maintaining relationships; thus, he refuses to take personally rebuttal or even harshness. This probably didn't come naturally to him, as it does not to most of us, but having accepted that the word of the Lord is indeed planted in him, he has trained himself to nurture it. When his earthly nature has tempted him to protect his dignity or nourish a need to be right and to win, he has resisted and chosen, instead, to feed God's word planted within him. As a result, he walks around with a friendly smile, a gentle voice, and a kind, unruffled spirit that diffuses hatefulness before it can escalate and invites the approach of others.

Let us remember, as we eagerly embrace the Comforter-Spirit, that He is also a *Counselor*-Spirit. Let us not neglect to receive God's counsel in the way we speak with those we are trying to reach for Him. James's advice about how to listen and respond is concise and easily memorized: *"quick to listen, slow to speak, and slow to become angry."* If everyone reading this would just dedicate this day to living out these three pieces of advice, there's no telling how much comfort the Counselor could distribute to a needy world.

~APRIL 18~
THE QUESTION BEHIND THE QUESTION

"What a man desires is unfailing love..." Proverbs 19:22

"The tongue has the power of life and death, and those who love it will eat its fruit." Proverbs 18:21

"The heart of the discerning acquires knowledge; the ears of the wise seek it out." Proverbs 18:15

There is a lot of talk about the tongue and the lips in Proverbs 18. What Solomon is concerned about here is the way we use our words. He says that the tongue has "the power of life and death," no small arsenal, and we all hold it right here in our mouths. How, then, do we ensure its proper use? How do we keep under control such a potentially destructive firearm? How can we be sure that our words work powerfully to bring about life rather than death? His answer is discernment.

We need to employ a good amount of discernment when we listen. It is my guess that someone you love has recently asked you a question that wasn't the *real* question. Maybe it wasn't a question at all; maybe it was a statement whose end punctuation sounded to the casual ear very much like a period or maybe even an exclamation mark. However, the ear empowered by a discerning heart recognizes that even though the voice might have fallen so as to suggest closure, the voice of the heart rose into a question mark just hanging there in the air waiting for the real answer.

Solomon says what we all desire is unfailing love. If this is true, we are all in some respect vulnerable to every one we love and from whom we desire returned love. In various degrees of consciousness, because we are human, we, from time to time, ask each other about that love we desire: Have time and circumstances, laziness and stupidity, ignorance and negligence taken too great a toll? Is your love for me still intact, or has it failed? Do you still respect me? Are you proud of me? Do you still delight in me?

But most of the time we don't ask directly. Usually we ask these questions by asking something else, or even by making a statement, which though uncalled for by grammar, requires, for the heart's sake, an answer. "Is your arm broken? My mailbox is starving!" "Hey, Mom, did you notice that I cleaned the kitchen?" "Would you like to see my high school yearbook?" "You forgot to kiss me goodbye." "Do you miss me when we're apart?"

When you ask someone if she will forgive you for making the same old dumb mistake yet again, of course you are hoping the answer is "yes," but, honestly, is just a simple "yes" sufficient to answer your real, deeper question? If we can discern what our heart desires at times like these, we should employ the "Golden Rule" and go the extra mile to respond likewise to those subtle questions beneath the questions others ask of us. Listen with your heart, not just your ears.

"A word fitly spoken is like apples of gold in settings of silver." Proverbs 25:11

~APRIL 19~
THE TROUBLE WITH ENVY

"Therefore, rid yourselves of all malice and all deceit, hypocrisy, envy, and slander of every kind. Like newborn babies, crave pure spiritual milk, so that by it, you may grow up in your salvation, now that you have tasted that the Lord is good." 1 Peter 2:2

Envy seems an unlikely partner of such outlaws as malice, deceit, hypocrisy, and slander. It seems so much more passive and benign, somehow paler than the blackness of its counterparts in this and other scriptures. And yet, there it is, with no apology or defense attached, handed down to us by spiritual fathers such as Peter, James, and Paul. And although the word "covet" is used, envy is also condemned in the tenth commandment.

What we might see when we picture envy is simply a longing that causes us to look up dreamily into the sky away from a less desirable reality. This seems harmless enough. But if the longing for what someone else has goes unchecked too long, apparently our "pure spiritual milk" becomes soured and somehow has the dangerous power to stunt our growth in salvation. How does something so seemingly harmless turn into something so malignant?

John reports Jesus as saying "A new command I give you: Love one another. As I have loved you, so you must love one another. By this all men will know that you are my disciples, if you love one another" (John 13:34-35). Matthew reports Jesus as saying "Do not store up for yourselves treasures on earth where moth and rust destroy and where thieves break in and steal. But store up for yourselves treasures in heaven...For where your treasure is, there your heart will be also" (Matthew 6:19-21). Together these sayings of Jesus give us a hint at the reason envy is blacklisted.

For one thing, when we see others as competitors who have won the thing that we have always wanted, we might be tempted to grow less generous with our love. Maybe we subconsciously decide that if they have the *Thing*, they don't need our love to boot, that no one deserves to have all that and our hearts too. Sometimes we are distracted by the "unfairness" of it all. Of course, these are catty thoughts, and no one wants to claim them, but the Enemy uses everything he can grasp a straw of against us. He wants to hurt the testimony of Christians by turning our focus upon ourselves. Who needs a brotherhood of selfishness and bitterness? The world offers that already. By peddling to the world a false picture of Christianity, we offend our Heavenly Father.

But perhaps even a worse offense is that of finding our sufficiency in what the world has to offer. Granted, it isn't always worldly goods that motivate our envy, but even envying others' situations, relationships, and peacefulness are out of order for us who should be relying on God to supply us with what He knows we need. In light of all we have received from His bounty, we need to beware of calling Him unfair, aloud or in our hearts, or accusing Him of shorting us. We say with our grumbling that He is not an all-wise Father, or that if He is, He is an unkind or unfair one.

Envy is one of those thoughts we should take captive "to make it obedient to Christ" (2 Corinthians 10:5). We must stay vigilant to recognize it before it burrows into our hearts and works its offense against the Lord of our lives.

~APRIL 20~
SUPERSTITION- A SNARE TO SINGLE-MINDEDNESS

"Come near to God and He will come near to you. Wash your hands, you sinners, and purify your hearts, you double-minded." James 4:8

In the scientific enlightenment of these modern times, most of us readily scoff at such fears as walking around the house wearing only one shoe or opening an umbrella inside. However, ask ten intelligent Christians how they feel about Friday the Thirteenth or breaking a mirror, and the odds are that half will wince as though there is some sort of unspoken hierarchy of superstitions.

An even larger percentage of us is affected by memories of past occurrences which, if we are honest, we must admit are just superstition dressed in enlightenment's clothing. My nephew has been plagued with an unusually large number of "unlucky" events on his birthday. He has come to expect his birthday to be a letdown, if not downright tragic. The anticipation that should accompany celebrating the day of his birth has been overshadowed by apprehension.

The prophet Jeremiah, known as the "weeping prophet," lived a most unenviable life serving God. Being a prophet of doom to Judah, an air of tribulation surrounded him from the beginning of his ministry. He was the would-be victim of murderous plots by those who were sick of hearing his doomsday threats, regardless of the fact that he was faithfully speaking for Almighty God. So much was his life beleaguered with ill will that our language has adopted his name as a perfect descriptor of one who is dreaded because of the message he bears. At one point Jeremiah cries out, "O Lord, you deceived me, and I was deceived; you overpowered me and prevailed. I am ridiculed all day long; everyone mocks me... All my friends are waiting for me to slip, saying 'Perhaps he will be deceived; then we will prevail on him and take revenge on him.'" (Jeremiah 20:7.10). However, he soon rallies: "But the Lord is with me like a mighty warrior; so my persecutors will stumble and not prevail...Sing to the Lord! He rescues the life of the needy from the hands of the wicked." (vv. 11, 13)

Jeremiah was the perfect example of one who seemed to have every reason to expect the worst, for history to continue repeating itself every morning when he got out of bed. Though he had moments of weakness, wondering why he was ever allowed to be born to see such trouble and sorrow, he is *most* famous for the words penned in Lamentations 3:22-26: "Because of the Lord's great love, we are not consumed, for his compassions never fail. They are new every morning; great is your faithfulness. I say to myself, 'The Lord is my portion; therefore, I will wait for Him.' The Lord is good to those whose hope is in Him, to the one who seeks Him; it is good to wait quietly for the salvation of the Lord."

We must resist the temptation to be double-minded, believing on one hand that "the Lord is good to those whose hope is in Him" and on the other hand that we are doomed if a black cat crosses the street in front of us. We must celebrate *every* birthday we are given knowing that we have lived another year *only* because of another 365 mornings of His compassion, not because we were lucky enough to avoid breaking mirrors or walking under ladders.

~APRIL 21~
CROSSWORD LANGUAGE

"Speak to one another with psalms, hymns, and spiritual songs." Ephesians 5:19

Recently a dear friend of thirty years came for a visit. She had not been here long before she discovered one of my crossword puzzle books and adopted it as her own for the length of her visit. Since we went for many years without seeing each other, a lot of trivial details of our lives had gone undiscussed, our mutual love of crossword puzzles being one of them. Soon we were talking to each other in "crossword language," and laughing at how well we could communicate in this rather oblique and specialized "foreign" tongue which would have left any "non-crossword" person squinting her eyes and scratching her head. It's a kind of code, and learning it does not come easily; unless you have spent many hours on crossword puzzles, you just don't get it. It takes much time in the books to learn this language in which "titular," "Asta," "ogle," "snit," and "neap" are garden variety, everyday words.

I was reminded about how a similar code of communication had kicked in for us a couple of years ago when we were reunited the first time in twenty-six years. We both drove to our rendezvous spot wondering how this visit would go. Would we be enough of the same two people to be able to lock arms and get back into step with each other? Would we still have enough in common to be able to fill the weekend with conversation?

It took only a moment in her presence to know how silly all that concern had been. There she was, still Susie, taking me in with those familiar loving, brown eyes and charming me with her cute voice and witty ways. After we untwined from a long hug, we just looked at each other and laughed out loud for a solid five minutes. No words, just sustained, tear-bringing, delightful laughter. But then we *did* begin talking, and haven't stopped since. My heart had been bonded to hers long ago in Germany when we were part of a small American church struggling with the trials of culture shock, homesickness, and members coming and going at warp speed. We were strangers on foreign soil from different parts of the country, but we shared a common Father who, through His Word, had taught us a common language. Even though we were apart all those years, we were growing closer together, more alike, because of our commitment to learning the same language from the same Teacher.

This is the way it is supposed to be with Christians. The language we speak from poring over the Word should enable us to communicate clearly to one another our common hope and the shared inheritance awaiting us. Our common language should call us higher and point us upward. Hearing it fall from another's tongue should cause us to feel such a kinship to its speakers that we rush to them as we do through our own front door. Whenever one Christian meets another, it should be like a homecoming. The world will look on, listen, squint its eyes, and scratch its head. (This part happens all the time when unsavvy outsiders encounter street talk.) However, an outsider encountering Christians speaking their language eloquently will desire to learn this language that creates such an intriguing and unbreakable bond between people who have grown up on opposite sides of the country or even the world. Jesus put it this way: "All men will know that you are my disciples if you love one another" (John 13:35.).

~APRIL 22~
NO TWO WAYS ABOUT IT: THE WAY

"Whoever believes in the Son has eternal life, but whoever rejects the Son will not see life, for God's wrath remains on him." John 3:36

"Salvation is found in no one else, for there is no other name under heaven given to men by which we must be saved." Acts 4:12

"Jesus answered, 'I am the way and the truth and the life. No one comes to the Father except through me." John 14:6

Jesus is offering comfort to His disciples with the news that He is on His way to prepare a place for them so that they can be where He is someday. He tells them that they know the way to this place, but Thomas retorts, "Lord, we don't know where you are going, so how can we know the way?" (John 14:5) The answer Jesus gives here might seem rather ephemeral and cryptic, but actually He is giving them the most literal answer there is to their questions...and to ours.

Job, who probably lived during the time of the book of Genesis, asked a similar question in a sigh: "If only there were someone to arbitrate between us, to lay a hand upon us both, someone to remove God's rod from me so that His terror would frighten me no more" (Job 9:33-34). Isaiah promised that the Answer was on the way: "For unto us a child is born, to us a son is given, and the government will be on His shoulders. And He will be called Wonderful Counselor, Mighty God, Everlasting Father, Prince of Peace...He will reign on David's throne establishing and upholding it with justice and righteousness from that time on and forever" (Isaiah 9:6-7). Jesus would later unroll Isaiah's scroll and read more of his words: "The Spirit of the Sovereign Lord is on me, because He has anointed me to preach good news to the poor. He has sent me to bind up the brokenhearted, to proclaim freedom for the captives, and release from darkness for the prisoners, to proclaim the year of the Lord's favor..." (Isaiah 61: 1-2, Luke 4:18-19). "Then He rolled up the scroll, gave it back to the attendant and sat down. The eyes of everyone in the synagogue were fastened to Him, and he began by saying to them, 'Today this scripture is fulfilled in your hearing'" (Luke 4:20-21). He was the ultimate ram in the thicket that saved Abraham's son and ours, "sacrificed once to take away the sins of many people" for "without the shedding of blood there is no forgiveness" (Hebrews 9:27, 22). He is "the Lamb of God who takes away the sin of the world" (John 1:29).

Some claim that we can go to God by other means—Mohammed or Buddha, Mother Earth, or energy fields— and in the name of open-mindedness and non-judgmentalism, many well-meaning but misguided believers in Christ defend them. Jesus makes it clear, however, that this simply is not the case. There are things worse than being called judgmental or close-minded, and we need to settle once and for all time the matter of whether we will stand for the Truth and lead others through the Open Door or leave them blissfully ignorant on the outside "where there will be weeping and gnashing of the teeth" (Matthew 8:12, 13:42). There are no two ways about this.

~APRIL 23~
NO TWO WAYS ABOUT IT: THE TRUTH

"Come near to God and He will come near to you. Wash your hands, you sinners, and purify your hearts, you double-minded." James 4:8

"Jesus answered, 'I am the way and the truth and the life." John 14:6

In the context of Jesus' instruction here, he is readying his disciples to hear all about the most elaborate gift they will ever receive this side of Heaven, a gift so expensive that it cost nothing less than His life's blood shed through unspeak-able torture: the "Holy Spirit," "the Counselor," "the Comforter," the "Spirit of truth." He wants them to know that the Way Home is their undivided, undiluted, uncompromising belief in Him, the Promised Messiah of God, the Truth that will prove counter-cultural to the world they inhabit. He has told them over and over that if they really believe in Him, they will obey and follow Him. His way was and is the only Truth.

Jesus' half brother James later wrote bluntly about the core of the problem Jesus is seeking to help His disciples avoid. He writes in James 1:6, "If any of you lacks wisdom, he should ask God, who gives generously to all without finding fault, and it will be given to him. But when he asks, he must believe and not doubt, because he who doubts is like a wave of the sea, blown and tossed by the wind. That man should not think he will receive anything from the Lord; he is a double-minded man, unstable in all he does."

We are enlightened to this Truth when we give up our spirit to take on His. We die to ourselves and our false, worldly notions and live by means of His Spirit of Truth. This mystery is described beautifully in Romans 6:2-4: "...We died to sin; how can we live in it any longer? Or don't you know that all of us who were baptized into Christ were baptized into his death? We were therefore buried with him through baptism into death in order that, just as Christ was raised from the dead through the glory of the Father, we too may live a new life."

Sometimes, however, we believe something so strongly that we think it is the truth, even though it may be contrary to what Jesus taught and lived. Conflicted by the two "truths," we follow Him half-heartedly or from afar. Jesus readied his disciples for this by saying, "On that day (see Acts 2:36-41) you will realize that I am in my Father, and you are in me, and I am in you. Whoever has my commands and obeys them, he is the one who loves me. He who loves me will be loved by my Father, and I too will love him and show myself to him" (John 14:20-21). We must be honest about the fact that this is a limiting statement, not one open to many different, individual "truths."

We can follow Him only if He shows Himself to us, and there are no two ways about how this happens. It happens through His Spirit, the "Spirit of truth" (v. 17). If we wish to follow Jesus Home, we can't create our own road map. He is the Way; we are not. Without His Spirit doing its work in us, our minds will not be singly His. Our doubt will cause us to be "double-minded and unstable" in all we do.

~APRIL 24~
NO TWO WAYS ABOUT IT: THE LIFE

"Jesus answered, 'I am the way and the truth and the life. No one comes to the Father except though me.'" John 14:6

In light of what most of us were taught growing up, Jesus' message is just one paradox after another: *"Blessed are the poor in spirit, for theirs is the kingdom of Heaven" (Matthew 5:3). "Blessed are those who are persecuted because of righ-*

teousness, for theirs is the kingdom of Heaven" (Matthew 5:10). "Blessed are you when people insult you, persecute you and falsely say all kinds of evil against you because of me. Rejoice and be glad because great is your reward in Heaven…" (Matthew 5:11-12). *"Whoever finds his life will lose it, and whoever loses his life for my sake will find it" (Matthew 10:39). "For whoever wants to save his life will lose it, but whoever loses his life for me will find it" (Matthew 16:25). "I tell you the truth, unless you change and become like little children, you will never enter the kingdom of Heaven. Therefore, whoever humbles himself like this child is the greatest in the kingdom of heaven" (Matthew 18:3-4). "If anyone wants to be first, he must be the very last, and the servant of all" (Mark 9:35). "Whoever wants to become great among you must be your servant, and whoever wants to be first must be slave of all" (Mark 10:43-44).*

"…the greatest among you should be like the youngest, and the one who rules like the one who serves" (Luke 22:26). "Indeed, there are those who are last who will be first, and first who will be last" (Luke 13:30).

Down is up, "foolish" is wise, last is first, servant is master. This is how Jesus calls us to look at life. It will not happen accidentally. None of us will just fall into this way of seeing things. The flashy-dashy razzle-dazzle of this world slaps us in the face at every turn. The opposite of Jesus' lifestyle is hyped via every media known to man.

But Jesus doesn't ask us to do something He didn't do. The life He lived in the time He lived it was every bit as counter-cultural as the life He expects His disciples to live today. It takes courage, stamina, perseverance, self-control, and self-denial.

But mostly it takes faith— faith to remember the "later-on's": *"…our present sufferings are not worth comparing with the glory that will be revealed in us"…."* (Romans 8:18); *"For our light and momentary troubles are achieving for us an eternal glory that far outweighs them all. So we fix our eyes not on what is seen, but on what is unseen. For what is seen is temporary, but what is unseen in eternal" (2 Corinthians 4:17-18). "But rejoice that you participate in the sufferings of Christ, so that you may be overjoyed when His glory is revealed" (1 Peter 4:13.) "And if the Spirit of Him who raised Jesus from the dead is living in you, he who raised Christ from the dead will also give life to your mortal bodies through His Spirit, who lives in you" (Romans 8:11).*

~APRIL 25~
PROCRASTINATION: THE DEVIL'S PLAYGROUND

"I… delight to see how orderly you are and how firm your faith is in Christ." Colossians 2:5

"Be very careful, then, how you live— not as unwise but as wise, making the most of every opportunity, because the days are evil. Therefore, do not be foolish, but understand what the Lord's will is." Ephesians 5:15-16

If good intentions pave the road to hell and idleness is the devil's workshop, then surely procrastination must be the devil's playground.

It happens time and time again that a bright young mind leaves home and sets out to college only to meet with a failure that baffles everyone who knows what a sharp mind this one has. More likely than not, the enemy is procrastination. For lack of planning ahead and getting the job done in a timely manner, he, now without parental plodding for the first time in his life, finds himself buried too deeply beneath too much to get done in too short a time. He is overwhelmed, and likely, rather than trying to learn the new skills it will take to shovel his way out, grows depressed and maybe even hopeless. A mind God created to be used for His glory is dimmed by despair, parents grow anxious and distressed, and through it all, time keeps marching on bringing with it more and more to be done that is left undone due to the paralysis that sets in with depression and hopelessness.

It isn't just a logistical or organizational problem; it's a spiritual one. Orderliness is vital if we are to use our lives to fight the war against evil. Living sloppy lives doesn't just cause us to get behind in our schoolwork or the routine chores that every adult must tackle; it hinders our ability to live soberly and calmly enough to exercise the readiness needed to stand for Jesus against the devil's schemes. Living an orderly life helps us "stand our ground" in our struggle, not against flesh and blood, but against "the powers of this dark world and ... the spiritual forces of evil in the heavenly realms" (Ephesians 6:12). In this famous passage, Paul describes this armor metaphorically by listing the various items of battle regalia: "the belt of truth," "the breastplate of righteousness," "the shield of faith," "the helmet of salvation," the sword of the spirit", and prayer. But right smack dab in the middle of all these is "with your feet fitted with the *readiness* that comes from the gospel of peace" (Ephesians 6:10-18). Readiness is part of the "full armor of God" listed right there with truth, righteousness, and the Word of God, and readiness is impossible in a life driven by panic or paralyzed by hopelessness.

Teaching our children from an early age the spiritual dangers of habitually putting things off could result in helping them know the joy of making the most of every opportunity. If, however, you are in the *midst* of suffering the consequences of procrastination, take courage in these words: *"...we rejoice also in our sufferings, because we know that suffering produces perseverance; perseverance, character; and character, hope. And hope does not disappoint us, because God has poured out his love into our hearts by the Holy Spirit, whom He has given us." Romans 5:3-5*

~APRIL 26~
NEAT, BUT NOT TOO NEAT

"Stand firm, then, with your feet fitted with the readiness that comes from the gospel of peace." Ephesians 6:15

"Do nothing out of selfish ambition or vain conceit, but in humility consider others better than yourselves. Each of you should look not only to your own interests, but also to the interests of others. Philippians 2:3-4

Scripture does encourage us to live orderly lives and to take care of our business in a way that allows us to be ready to take on holy assignments without being bogged down in unmet obligations. However, there is another side to the coin of readiness about which we should always be vigilant.

Some of us tend to protect our neat, orderly lives *too* much. Maybe we have gotten to this point from a wildly-swinging pendulum that took us out of sloppiness and procrastination, or maybe this is simply our personality type. Regardless of the reason, an obsession with orderliness and predictability can be dangerous, even deadly, to our service as a disciple of Jesus.

People are the focal point of the message of the gospel. Jesus came to save the lost. It isn't hard to see that lostness abounds. Evil is running amok. This is why Jesus warns us plainly about avoiding the broad road which many take and sacrificing all to take the narrow road which "only a few find" (Matthew 7:13-14).

But people clutter up our lives. When we start letting people get into our lives, there's no telling what might happen. We might be on our way out the door with a well-planned agenda when the phone rings bearing news of someone in need of this very chunk of time we have so eagerly anticipated using for our well-defined purposes. This was at least part of the problem with the ones who passed by the hurt stranger in Jesus' Good Samaritan parable. Jesus' strategically-chosen protagonist, a Samaritan, was honored for stopping his own life to take care of the life of a stranger. Geographically, this was a deadly road to travel; in a distance of seventeen miles, it plunged from 2,500 feet above sea level to about 800 feet below sea level. The rocky, desert landscape also provided hiding places for robbers to attack the few, lonely travelers who ventured out on it. It is almost certain that the Samaritan had his own important plans for the day; there's no other reason he would go down this particular road otherwise. Yet, he chose to lay down his plans and pick up some new ones. His feet were ready to do the right thing.

This is what laying down our lives means. Dying to ourselves doesn't always have to be a literal thing. It means being willing to put aside our own lives in order to throw out the lifeline to another. If we are bogged down in loose ends of our own, then our feet are not ready. However, if we are tethered too tightly to our own schedules, neither will our feet be ready to jump at the chance to help someone else. We will be sluggish about letting go of our own agendas.

"This is how we know what love is: Jesus Christ laid down His life for us. And we ought to lay down our lives for our brothers." 1 John 3:16

~APRIL 27~
LIFTED OUT OF THE NILE

"For we have this treasure in jars of clay to show that this all-surpassing power is from God and not from us." 2 Corinthians 4:7

Moses was one of the Israelite babies that the Egyptians ordered to be killed, but Providence caused his mother to sail him down the Nile in hopes that he would be saved. Sure enough, the Pharaoh's daughter rescued him and kept him safe until God commissioned him to rescue the rest of the Israelites and lead them to their Promised Land.

Moses was saved not just *from* something, but *for* something. He was saved for his encounter with God—saved to stand before the Cleansing Fire that would consume all but what he needed to set the Israelites free from Pharaoh's grasp.

Notice what *we* have been saved for.

"For it is for freedom that you have been set free." Galatians 5:1

"Go and make disciples of all nations, baptizing them in the name of the Father and of the Son and of the Holy Spirit, and teaching them to obey everything I have commanded you. And surely I am with you always, even to the very end of the age." Matthew 28:19-20

It was not for pride, not for a well-ordered, predictable life, and not even just to escape hell, but for *freedom* and what that means to God's creation that is meant to glorify God.

Thank God today for the one or ones who were sent to the edge of the Nile to lift you out. Thank Him for wanting you to be saved from those waters badly enough that He prompted someone to reach down and pull you out. Then thank him or her for paying attention to that prompting and obeying Him.

And remember as you go out into your Egypt today that you were not just saved *from* the crocodiles or *from* drowning; you were saved *for* something. With this gratitude to motivate you, be vigilant about any opportunities that float up to your door.

~APRIL 28~
CREATED FOR THE HIGH SEAS

"Do not store up for yourselves treasure on earth where moth and rust destroy and where thieves break in and steal. But store up for yourselves treasures in Heaven where moth and rust do not destroy and where thieves do not break in and steal. For where your treasure is, there your heart will be also." Matthew 6:19-21

All of Jesus' parables ultimately get down to this: What do we value most?

Jesus said, *"Where your treasure is, there your heart will be also."* We can tell where our heart is by what we are most invested in— where we spend most of our time, our thoughts, our money. Consider this carefully: What do you value *most?*

Some will soon realize that what they value most are things. Others might be making progress on this material level. However, if we try to console ourselves by looking at our relatively vanity-free, bare-essential clothing and possessions, could our "treasure" be in something less tangible, more subtle? Could our "treasure" be our *identity?*

Jesus also said, *"...anyone who does not take up his cross and follow me is not worthy of me. Whoever finds his life will lose it, and whoever loses his life for my sake will find it" (Matthew 10:37-39).* Jesus' cross was His tool to be used to help accomplish the world's redemption. Our crosses are our unique jobs God gave us to advance Christ's cause. What do you see right now as your "life" that you might be hanging onto rather than laying down to take up the life of Jesus (your "cross") and follow Him?

Think about what identifies you (how people see you, the picture you have been painting about yourself for the world to see). Of which part of your identity are you most proud? Do you have any identifying characteristics that are *unholy?* Do you have any identifying characteristics that, if not downright unholy, are *distracting* to the glory of God that He wants your life to demonstrate? Is it a scary thing to think about stepping away from protecting any unholy, worldly, or distracting aspects of your identity in order to take on His identity? In other words, do you fear losing all you have built and having nothing to replace it with? Does the thought of erasing what you, in some worldly way might have considered a work of art, make you sad?

We know from John 3:16 that it is crucial to God that the "world" He loves be given a chance to know and believe in the "only begotten Son" He sent as our ransom.

Can we, then, afford to allow ourselves to be too lazy to study, too scared to confront others, or too stubborn and untrusting to turn loose of our own image to let God create His in us? We are really not given the option of staying safely moored in the harbor; we must launch out onto the high seas.

"I tell you the truth," Jesus replied, *"no one who has left home or brothers or sisters or mother or father or children or fields for me and the gospel will fail to receive a hundred times as much in this present age... and in the age to come, eternal life" (Mark 10:29-30).* According to this scripture, is there anything you are holding onto that Jesus would excuse as being more important than Himself or His gospel?

~APRIL 29~
"HELLO. I'D LIKE YOU TO MEET MY FATHER"

"Do your best to present yourself to God as one approved, a workman who does not need to be ashamed and who correctly handles the word of truth." 2 Timothy 2:15

It really helps to know the One we're introducing.

What if you were engaged, and every time you tried to share with your fiancé stories of your childhood experiences or your exciting adventures before you met, he brushed them off with something like this: "Oh, I don't care about all *that*. I am just so in love with you *now*!"? Would this communicate true love?

When we don't avidly study who God is, what He has done through the ages, how He lovingly prepared for our redemption through the Messiah, do we not communicate this same sad message to Him?

Can we *love* someone (or Someone) we don't even *know*?

Isn't it the *knowing* that makes the loving so precious? When someone avows to love us with only a surface knowledge of us, doesn't it make us suspicious, or cause us to wonder if the love will hold when deeper knowledge of us comes? Maybe it's curiosity; maybe it's mystery; maybe it's fascination, but can we be sure that it's truly *love*?

"To the Jews who had believed Him, Jesus said, *'If you hold to my teaching, you are really my disciples. Then you will know the truth, and the truth will set you free" (John 8:31-32).* The order here indicates that we are set free only *after* we are holding to His teaching. It seems, then, that studying alone will not suffice. We must begin to *follow* Jesus— to "hold to His teaching"— in order to know Him and the truth that He is. Then, as we begin to know that we are being set free, we truly have something to share with others in captivity. It is something more than a passing fascination or infatuation; it is a knowledge of Him who saves us.

James 1:5 tells us how to start: *"If any of you lacks wisdom, he should ask God, who gives generously to all without finding fault, and it will be given to him."*

We must pray for wisdom

- as we study the word of truth, to handle it correctly in teaching others;
- as we ponder our lives to recognize and realize how God has been caring for us personally and drawing us to Him through people and circumstances.

But, of course, this will take a protected quiet time (preferably not at bedtime when we are too tired to study or ponder). A glance at our calendars proves that there are events we prioritize enough to protect by scheduling. Considering the One we're getting to know and the freedom to be gained for ourselves and others in chains, could there possibly be anything more important to protect?

124

~APRIL 30~
WHEN YOU KNOW THE BRIDGE IS OUT

"Therefore, go and make disciples of all nations, baptizing them in the name of the Father and of the Son and of the Holy Spirit, and teaching them to obey everything I have commanded you. And surely I am with you always, even to the very end of the age." Matthew 28:19-20

"Go into all the world and preach the good news to all creation. Whoever believes and is baptized will be saved, but whoever does not believe will be condemned." Mark 16:16

The Great Commission is the last of Jesus' recorded words on this earth. In Acts 1:2, Luke refers to these "instructions" Jesus gave to His apostles through the Holy Spirit. Acts 1:4 reports Jesus' words: *"Do not leave Jerusalem, but wait for the gift my Father promised, which you have heard me speak about. For John baptized with water, but you will be baptized with the Holy Spirit."*

Acts 2 records the fulfillment of this gift Jesus talked about. Peter has just addressed the crowd about this Jesus whom they crucified being the promised Messiah. *"When the people heard this, they were cut to the heart and said to Peter and the other apostles, 'Brothers, what shall we do?' Peter replied, 'Repent and be baptized, every one of you, for the forgiveness of your sins. And you will receive the gift of the Holy Spirit." (Acts 2:37-38).* The rest of Acts recounts story after story of individuals responding to the gospel message in just this way, with Paul's conversion story appearing three times (chapters 9, 22, 26). Paul's letters bear out the same message (1Corinthians 12:13, Romans 6:3-4, Galatians 3:26-29, Colossians 2:11-12) as well as Peter's (1Peter 2:20-21). 1 Peter 4:17 also points out that the gospel is not just good news to be heard, but something to be "obeyed."

We may get this gospel message across in several different ways, but it is crucial that we get it across. We can't let the devil allow us to believe that we are being legalistic or narrow-minded and judgmental. If we had learned that a bridge was out on a road, would we be worried about offending someone by warning him about this and trying to stop him from taking this road? No, that's absurd. We would know that we were really rescuing him from grave danger.

God has designed you to do some things better than others. Pray for awareness of your best style of evangelism. It might be one of the following:

- Relational — friendship evangelism;
- Evidential — showing through the Word and the world why God is real and what He says is true;
- Testimonial — telling your own faith stories;
- Invitational — inviting others to go with you to church and other Christian events; or

- Confrontational— bravely, confidently, and lovingly sitting down with a Bible between you and someone else and shining the Gospel light on a dark life.

~MAY 1~
BEING A MIRACULOUS SIGN

"This is a wicked generation. It asks for a miraculous sign..." Luke 11:29

Though style may be optional, that we become rescuers is not. If we have been rescued, gratitude should prompt the kind of desire to obey our Savior and Master that compels us to throw out the only lifeline there is, remembering all the time that it is He who is the lifeline and we are only the "thrower-outer's" of it.

Jesus performed many miracles in His short ministry, but His main purpose was to point the people to the Answer to all of their needs, not just the one He was taking care of right then. Remember how indignant the people became when instead of healing a man's *legs* first, Jesus chose to proclaim that his *sins* were forgiven? He asked the question, "Which is harder, to heal a man's legs, or to forgive sin?" In the end, He did both. His point was that we are shallow and foolish seekers who ask for a limb to be bound up while ignoring a dying root. After healing someone, Jesus didn't ask all of them to go out and heal other legs or eyes or stomachs. Jesus no doubt wanted the recipients of His miracles not to go out and *do* miracles, but to go out and *be* miracles. This way, when someone saw a life victorious over lust, greed, worry, envy, pride and the like, they, too, would want to be healed in *those* ways. They would want to know and follow this Great Physician. Following the Great Physician is the crux of all matters and the desired product of all miracles.

There is an ongoing controversy in these latter days about whether or not people are still endowed with the ability to perform the kinds of miracles Jesus and some of His followers performed. However, there is nothing debatable about whether or not His followers should *be* miracles. We are told to be a "peculiar people," "sanctified," "a people that are his very own," "a holy priesthood," and "a royal priesthood," just to list a few descriptors of the picture of a Christian. We've been redeemed by the blood of the perfect Lamb of God. We have been raised to walk in newness of life. In short, we should look *different*. The world should look at us and scratch their heads.

When people watch you live, do they notice that you are not acting, reacting, and responding the way you "should" be, meaning the way the World usually does?

Are you a living testimony to the power of the resurrection of Jesus?

This is a "wicked generation"— a skeptical generation, people who begin losing hope from an early age and harden as they grow older and try everything under the sun to quench their desires and to give their lives some kind of meaning.

Most of them, having failed to find it, pass on to the next generation their skepticism and hopelessness. We are God's primary sign to this wicked generation.

God wants to make something *supernatural* of us. Is your life a miracle?

~MAY 2~
A POINTLESS KIND OF DISCIPLINE

"Every good and perfect gift is from above, coming down from the Father of the heavenly lights..." James 1:17

In learning to live the disciplined life that Christianity calls for, there is a danger that our ability to follow the rules well might ironically lead us *away* from a closeness to God and into a strange new kind of worldliness. Our lives could take on a kind of formulaic nature that loses intimacy with the Life, the Truth, the Way.

While it is true that Jesus calls us to a different, even a "peculiar" lifestyle, He does it not just so that we will become machines that are predictable, yet mechanical.

He could have easily created a universe, or several, full of robots that would obey His every command. The problem with that plan was that the robots would be heartless. Their glitches might be minimal compared to our transgression, but their ability to need, to love, to function in a Father-child relationship would be absolutely zero. While He calls us to live holy lives, He does it for deeper, nobler reasons than that we will become disciplined. Being merely disciplined might produce a great amount of satisfaction, but in the long run, it cannot bring about the joy that we are taught about in so many New Testament scriptures. Likewise, doing a lot of good works for the wrong reason reaps a kind of reward that might take us a long way with earthly beings whose vision is limited to eyesight, but to the Father of the "heavenly lights," it takes us nowhere. *"Many will say to me on that day, 'Lord, Lord, did we not prophesy in your name and in your name drive out demons and perform many miracles?' Then I will tell them plainly, 'I never knew you. Away from me, you evildoers!'" (Matthew 7:22-23)* He calls them "evildoers," even though they have done some of the very works others did who received His blessings. "Evildoers" is not just *neutral*, meaning their works availed them nothing, but it is blatantly *negative*, meaning that their good works were part of their undoing.

In light of Jesus' negative response to these good works, how are we to understand what the scriptures mean that teach that He "rewards," and that there are "good and perfect" gifts sent from above? How are we to be good workers that God will bless and not curse?

James 4:10 says *"Humble yourselves before the Lord, and He will lift you up."* It is one of thirty-six scriptures that speak of God's desire for humbleness in His people. It is the quality that helps us to remember every time we manage to do some good work, that it was God who pursued us and prepared for us a way back to Him. Surely any honest observer realizes that the circumstances of our lives that have brought us to a place where we can even *know* of God were none of our own doing. If we chase the rabbit backward far enough, it takes us to a place of our own ignorance and helplessness, a place where someone (or Someone) else had to be the Doer and we only the do-ee.

~MAY 3~
A DISCIPLINE WITH MEANING

"Not everyone who says to me 'Lord, Lord' will enter the kingdom of heaven, but only he who does the will of my Father who is in heaven. Many will say to me on that day, 'Lord, Lord, did we not prophesy in your name and in you name drive out demons and perform many miracles?' Then I will tell them plainly, 'I never knew you. Away from me, you evildoers!'" Matthew 7:21-23

"And without faith, it is impossible to please God, because anyone who comes to him must believe that He exists and that He rewards those who earnestly seek Him." Hebrews 11:6

We know we are to be people who do good works in the name of Jesus, but apparently not all who do these are rewarded. In fact, some are plainly cursed by Jesus and called "evildoers." How, then, are we to be sure that living a life of goodness is the kind of goodness that Jesus desires— the kind that blesses and does not curse us on that last day?

Part of what we have to remember is how we got to the point of even *wanting* to live for Jesus. Philippians 2:13 reminds us of why we need to remain humble even after we seem to have gotten some of the hard things of living this life under control: *"...for it is God who works in you to will and to act according to His good purpose."* Humility is definitely one of the keys to pleasing God.

Hebrews tells us about another one. It is all about faith, of course, as everything in Hebrew 11 is, but it is more than just the *believing* part of faith. The last part of this famous scripture talks about the circumstances under which God rewards us. It says *"He rewards those who earnestly seek Him."* These seekers are not after the rewards of a *good* life or even the rewards of the *disciplined* life, although they are significant. They earnestly seek *Him*. They are after the Giver rather than the gift.

The answer, then, is that Jesus is not looking for just a certain lifestyle or even a certain kind of person. He is looking to reward those whose main aim is to find *Him*. This must be why when his disciples questioned Him shortly before His death about where He was going, He reassured them with this answer: *"I am the way, and the truth, and the life. No one comes to the Father except through me"* *(John 14:6)*. He said to others, "I never knew you!"

It's all about *knowing*, not about *doing*. Of course, the knowing will bring about the doing, but it is not the doing that saves us in the end. It's the knowing.

And knowing requires time. Even though we may find many shortcuts to doing things, there are no shortcuts to knowing people (or People.) Knowing God, as with people, requires talking and listening, giving and taking. Knowing is hardly ever accomplished on the run. It happens purposefully, not accidentally. This is why what children most need from their parents is not to be sent off with an open-ended credit card but to be chosen to receive lots of their quality time. This is also likely why God moved the psalmist to write in Psalm 46:10: "Be still and know that I am God." Give me your undivided attention. Listen to Me; gaze upon Me. The rewards are inestimable.

~MAY 4~
THE COVERLET OF LOVE

"Above all, love each other deeply, because love covers over a multitude of sins."
1 Peter 4:8

In one scripture, we read about some lulled into paralysis by smooth sailing down deeply chiseled, timeworn trenches. Having grown accustomed to the first principles of Christianity, these, clinging tenaciously to the status quo, refused to grow up from milk-sippers into meat-eaters. The Hebrews writer tells them, "By now some of you should be teachers." In another scripture, James warns his readers about jumping into teaching positions presumptuously, lest they be judged more strictly. Obviously, teaching is such a serious and vital assignment and so rife with both possibility and liability that it not a job to be taken on lightly. Certainly, this flies in the face of the careless quip that teaching is something people do because they can do nothing else.

At fourteen, my life was up for grabs. My parents' marriage was shipwrecked for the second time, my mother had moved to another town, my sister was married and gone, and alone I stood in my well-worn ruts of social acceptability and scholastic mediocrity which occasionally swooped down into survival status. Because of my overly adventuresome and curious nature, I teetered on the brink of trouble but somehow managed to throw my weight to the right most of the time. Now as I entered high school, I paused at an ominous fork in the road, Robert Frost's poster child for "The Road Not Taken," looking first down one path and then the other. God seized the opportunity to mine something new in me, and He used as his shovel Mrs. Brittain, my freshman English teacher.

Most teachers for the past few years had pretty much come across to me with the "Wuan hwuanh wa" voices of all adults in the Peanuts cartoons, but Mrs. Brittain captured my attention on day one with her sharp wit and energetic, creative unpredictability. When she assigned an essay, I wrote with all I had and was rewarded with, right next to my A+, the words, *"Excellent! You are an author!"* Me? Nu-huh. I was a borderline *hoodlum*! She carefully nurtured and cajoled my tentatively budding intellect which up to this point had been buried deeply beneath a fear of failure covered by a coat of rambunctiousness. But she didn't stop there. She made it her business to find my eyes with her knowing smile and between classes and after school, even offered some much-needed, motherly counseling. She never expected or accepted anything less than what she knew I was able to produce. Rather than letting her pity for my plight tempt her to slather me in praise for pseudo-quality work, she took the harder, higher road and pushed and challenged and coaxed me higher and higher, so that when the praise came, I was afforded the deep satisfaction of *true* esteem. She squinted her eyes, saw some possibility, capitalized upon it, won my respect, and changed the rest of my life.

Two years ago, I retired from teaching. Most of those years I was a *freshman English teacher*. I was invited a few times to move up and teach seniors, but I remembered Mrs. Brittain and stayed put at those crossroads where I knew many a child would pause and look for a beckoning sign before proceeding down the path less taken.

Love really does cover a multitude of sins, not only in the present but into the future.

~MAY 5~
THE TEACHER

"Not many of you should presume to be teachers, my brothers, because you know that we who teach will be judged more strictly." James 3:1

The melody so artfully composed
That it echoes a crystal ring;
The lyrics so lovingly chosen,
All that remains is to sing.
Yet...
She stands off balance on her pedestal of awe
And questions her baffling lot;
Her security slips as she comes face to face
With this person she really is not.
But this is the self that is called for now,
As theory gives way to hard fact.
Still constant's the struggle in her day as she juggles,
Keeping her two worlds intact.
She knows she's only a vessel of clay,
But she's towering in their eyes;
And she molds with her hands seeming castles of sand,
But the substance is only disguise.
She's a victim of reaping what others have sown
In these lives set before her to keep.
But one day she's startled by a tantamount truth:
She's sowing what others will reap.

She's sowing confidence, truth, and respect,
And patience with her voice and her hands.
The soil she works may lie barren for seasons
Before it at last understands.
She knows she must strike while the iron is still hot
And make hay in the morning sun,
And instill there the lust for the laughter of life
Before lives have been too far begun.
How can she know whom she takes by the hand,
Paupers, prisoners, or kings?
She thanks God that judgment can only be His
And offers them all the same wings.
She passes her knowledge from her torch to theirs,
Endeavoring not to pass on her fears.
She can only pray that the knowledge will grow
To be wisdom in some riper years.
Real, but a little bit moreso,
With magic stored up in her hat,
And so hallowed to some who adore her
That she graces the desk where she sat.
So she tunes up her voice, and she sings them her song.
Then the audience so soon disappears.
She goes backstage for a summer,
And remembers with bittersweet tears.

Lovingly dedicated to my mentor, Patricia Brittain,
and to my daughter, Emily Gillmore

~MAY 6~
CELLMATES WITH A SOULMATE

"He leads forth the prisoners with singing." Psalm 68:6

"The Lord sets prisoners free." Psalm 146:7

"Who shall separate us from the love of Christ? Shall trouble or hardship or persecution or famine or nakedness or danger or sword? ...No, in all these things we are more than conquerors through Him who loved us." Romans 8:35, 37

Cellmates

I can think of nothing so lovely right now
As being cellmates with a Soulmate.
Punish me with years on end shut away

From the rest of the world that aren't my kind.
Lock up me up tight with a similar heart
That races and throbs just the same as my own.
Hand me my bed sheets, and usher me in
To be locked in with Him who created me,
Pronounce me confined with just that One;
Slam the iron door and throw away the key.

A few years ago when a new Christian friend had to serve some time in jail as a consequence of events of her old life, I noticed that her face seemed more and more radiant each time I would visit her. There she was locked up with her new faith and her Bible. Her outward circumstances were deplorable; her life had effectively been put on hold, she was shackled away from even the most rudimentary freedom, and yet, she was gaining spiritual ground every day that she lingered in confinement.

Prison would not be the ideal place to find inspiration from our surroundings; the folks we would meet would not likely be friends on whom we could depend; the food would definitely leave something to be desired by our palates and stomachs. However, it could afford us some uninterrupted time alone with the Almighty and thereby feed our souls on the richest of fare. And also, it could teach us a valuable lesson about how to better spend our time once we gain our freedom from that place.

How long has it been since you shut yourself up with God? I mean just took yourself away from all other distractions, isolated yourself from life's "luxuries," and just purposely soaked in all the God you could hold? If you have never done this, you have a treat in store for you when you finally do. You will learn all kinds of things when you do this— not just about your Lord but about yourself.

~MAY 7~
SHUT IN WITH GOD

"Be still and know that I am God." Psalm 46:10

We shouldn't have to go to jail to learn the value of times of spiritual retreat. When we decide to sequester ourselves from the rest of the world and give God our undivided attention, we learn all kinds of things. For one thing, we learn to *hear* Him. Without the nervous expectation of a phone ringing or someone knocking on the door, and without the pull of the duties that usually surround us, we can begin to make better sense of God's Word. We can reread some of those old stories we have forgotten or never finished. We finally have the time to use our concordances and cross-references to search out a subject thoroughly. We begin to see some things with amazing clarity that have always been mysterious or cloudy. God is so multifaceted that when we spend years giving Him just small doses of our time, He can seem pretty confusing. In just a few minutes, it is impossible to

hear the whole story about much of anything, much less the deep things of the spirit that took God sixty-six books to describe. The most thrilling adventures of my life (and I have had some adventures!) have been being led by the Spirit wildly through God's Word. Suddenly lots of loose threads come together in a fascinating revelation to bring me peace or to create in me a new excitement about this Word that really is "alive and active." I have been delightfully reminded how it, unlike any other bunch of bound pages, has the power to usher me into the presence of Majesty and Hope.

Another thing that happens is that we are brought face to face with ourselves. We might be roused to the sad truth that we have grown way too dependent upon the luxurious trappings of the world— the noise that sometimes confounds our spiritual quests, the meaningless activities that fritter away our time or wear us out physically until there is no energy left for spiritual exercise. In this case, we might finally gain the motivation needed to fight harder to eliminate some of them. On the other hand, we might find to our delight that we do not miss these subtle adversaries; we might finally see them for what they are and laugh at ourselves for letting such imposters fool us thus far. When we go back into our lives, we will now more easily see through their façade and be able to weed them from our lives.

There is one thing we will learn for sure: God will be waiting to meet us there. When we purposely set out to lock ourselves in with God, He will show up. He will have arrived before us and, in this blessed imprisonment, He will be faithful to dispense to us the freedom that comes only from being bound to Him.

"You will seek me and find me when you seek me with all your heart. I will be found by you," declares the Lord, "and I will bring you back from captivity." Jeremiah 29:13-14

~MAY 8~
SPIRITUAL LIABILITIES

"Whoever digs a pit may fall into it; whoever breaks into a wall may be bitten by a snake.

Whoever quarries stones may be injured by them; whoever splits logs may be endangered by them." Ecclesiastes 10:8-9

Ecclesiastes is all about the futility of trying to live in lifeless pursuits. The teacher speaks of the vanity, or emptiness, of a life built on unrealistic expectations. He teaches about everything having its own season and about the folly of riches and instant gratification. He says that wisdom is indeed better than folly, but even wisdom is not enough to base one's life on. In fact, he says, *everything* is vanity except fearing God and keeping His commandments.

Some of the teachings of Ecclesiastes, however, are a bit cryptic. We have to read carefully to pick up on the writer's tone in order to understand if he is being literal or figurative, solemn or sardonic. These scriptures are an example of verbal irony, a type of mild sarcasm. What is his point?

Consider these scriptures in light of some other ones that are much less obscure.

"Do not be deceived: God cannot be mocked. A man reaps what he sows. The one who sows to please his sinful nature, from that nature will reap destruction; the one who sows to please the Spirit, from the Spirit will reap eternal life. Let us not become weary in doing good, for at the proper time we will reap a harvest if we do not give up. Therefore, as we have opportunity, let us do good to all people, especially to those who belong to the family of believers." Galatians 6:7-10

Liabilities are not limited to the foolish and selfish things we choose to do. Even the good, industrious, helpful, unselfish deeds we do have possible liabilities. The Ecclesiastes passage begs a question: How often do I pass up doing something good for someone because there is a *possibility* that I might suffer a little bit? Solomon's tone seems to suggest that the possibility exists, but that it is very slight. It is like saying that anyone who washes dishes could be punctured by a fork, or anyone who carries an umbrella could be struck by lightning. Some of the excuses we give might sound good enough to elicit true grace from the one we are turning down; some of our excuses might even be enough, if said enough times, to convince even ourselves.

But Galatians reminds us that there is a Higher Court listening. There is One who is never fooled when our excuses are just the skin of a lie. Let us pray for the scales to be taken from our eyes so that we can take an honest look at our motives and weigh our small liabilities against the Divine assets.

~MAY 9~
TRYING TO BYPASS CHARACTER

"Blessed are the poor in spirit, for theirs is the kingdom of heaven.
Blessed are those who mourn, for they will be comforted.
Blessed are the meek, for they will inherit the earth.
Blessed are those who hunger and thirst for righteousness, for they will be filled.
Blessed are the merciful, for they will be shown mercy.
Blessed are the pure in heart, for they will see God.
Blessed are the peacemakers, for they will be called the sons of God.
Blessed are those who are persecuted because of righteousness, for theirs is the kingdom of heaven.
Blessed are you when people insult you, persecute you and falsely say all kinds of evil against you because of me. Rejoice and be glad, because great is your reward in heaven, for in the same way they persecuted the prophets who were before you." Matthew 5:3-12

Joe Baisden, my preacher for the biggest chunk of my adult life, used to say "You can't arrive without traveling." Think about what the "traveling" suggests: long hours behind the wheel, or even worse, in the back seat captured in an eight-year-old body; the kind of weariness that sighs with longing with every mile marker; cramping legs and aching back longing to stretch. Think about what it meant to Abraham: journeying for miles with an aging father and no clear destination; wondering for decades if that promise God made about his offspring was just in his imagination; wrestling with his conscience about giving in and sleeping with his wife's handmaiden; struggling with fear of the Egyptians and giving in to the temptation to save his own skin at his wife's expense; living with the guilt of giving in and getting caught.

But God knows the assignments He has for us. If we will lie still on His anvil, He will develop our character according to those assignments. It's no good trying to figure out why our friend doesn't struggle with the same problems we do. Each of our vehicles looks different, and the roads we will be sent down will be the ones ours was built to travel. Each stone of the old temple was cut exactly for the place it would be set and so must we be in this new one. If we rail against God and rebel, we may "arrive" by some unnatural means, but where we are will not be used to God's glory. It will prove to be a barren place that affords us little meaning.

We must pray for the strength to trust God in all the twists and turns on the highway or the wilderness He leads us through. A slow journey with Him will prove better than an early arrival at the wrong place. Grass grows quickly, but it takes a lifetime to grow an oak.

"It may be hard for an egg to turn into a bird: it would be a jolly sight harder for it to learn to fly while remaining an egg. We are like eggs at present. And you cannot go on indefinitely being just an ordinary, decent egg. We must be hatched or go bad." C. S. Lewis. [2]

~MAY 10~
TRUE VALUE

"I tell you, use worldly wealth to gain friends for yourselves, so that when it is gone you will be welcomed into eternal dwellings... No servant can serve two masters. Either he will hate the one and love the other, or he will be devoted to one and despise the other, you cannot serve both God and money." Luke 16:9, 13

By far the hardest of all Jesus' parables for me to understand was The Shrewd Manager. At first glace, the manger seems to handle his job-loss problem in a crooked way, and Jesus seems to *commend* Him for his trickery. But upon further study, the truth is that the manager actually sacrifices his own dishonest gain. By choosing to turn away from greed, he secures for himself the trust needed to gain employment again.

Jesus tells this parable within the earshot of the Pharisees "who loved money," (Luke 16:14) and as they "sneered" at Jesus, He said to them, *"You are the ones who justify yourselves in the eyes of men, but God knows your hearts. What is highly valued among men is detestable in God's sight" (Luke 16:15).* Why "detestable"? That's a strong word.

Greed is something most of us know at least a little about. It might not be in the form of money, but greed threatens to nudge its way into most of our lives in some way. Actually, greed itself doesn't just march in; it is ushered in by the Enemy. Because it can be masked to seem so innocuous, he claims it as one of his sharpest and deadliest tools to cut his way into our lives and get a strong foothold there. The Pharisees had managed to justify themselves in the eyes of men, and so they "sneered" at Jesus who was upsetting their peaceful standing with their public. Maybe even they had bought their own lie.

Timothy said *"...the **love** of money is the root of all kinds of evil,"* not money itself. It is a neutral, inanimate tool— neither good nor bad in itself— to be given over into the hands of whomever we decide is our "master." The problem is that we can become desensitized to how we use our money, and our "getting" can become a hobby. Sometimes just the *hunt* is the thrill, and we find ourselves with too many of the same things or with stuff we had forgotten we even bought. We become collectors at the expense of someone needier whom we might have the opportunity to help.

Greed can be used against us by Satan more easily than some vices because, like the Pharisees, we can sometimes justify it in the eyes of men. Someone won't necessarily run to us in a drastic effort to snatch us from the fire. It will be up to us to blow the whistle on our own greedy tendencies and habits. It is a terrifying thing to fall into the hands of an evil master, but we will if we grow too attached to our earthly treasures we are laying up, and, like the rich, young ruler, will turn away from Jesus sorrowfully. We will have chosen a different master to whom to be devoted.

Jesus finished this parable by saying, *"...whoever is dishonest with little will also be dishonest with much. So if you have not been trustworthy in handling worldly wealth, who will trust you with true riches?"*

"The real value of a thing is the price it will bring in eternity." John Wesley3

~MAY 11~
BETTER THAN SILVER AND GOLD

"Now, a man crippled from birth was being carried to the temple gate called Beautiful, where he was put every day to beg from those going into the temple courts. When he saw Peter and John about to enter, he asked them for money... Then Peter said, "Silver or gold I do not have, but what I have I give you. In the name of Jesus Christ of Nazareth, walk...He jumped to his feet and began to walk.

Then he went with them into the temple courts, walking and jumping and praising God." Acts 3:2-8

This man asked for money apparently because he was unable to work due to his handicap. Had he received the thing he asked for from Peter and John he would have been fed for a day or two, but he would have still been lame and disabled. But—and this is just me wondering; the story doesn't indicate this at all—I wonder if after a few days of hard work, the man might have missed the days of panhandling at the gate for a meal or two at a time.

The story is a microcosm of our lives as the children of God. We ask for one thing, and God in His wisdom gives us another. We want to be rid of our hunger for a day or two and God wants to rid us of our disability forever. But many times we think we have asked for bread and been given a stone or for a fish and been given a snake. In our nearsightedness, we can't grasp the value of the higher gift. We shake our heads and sigh and think what God is saying is "Wait."

Sometimes He is saying just that, and that is a valid answer, but other times He is not saying that at all. What He is saying is, "No. I will not give you the stone or the snake or the silver or the gold or the house or the college or the job or physical healing you are asking for. But what I do have I will give you." Then He will reach down and give us our legs again. We may not see them as legs— our way to walk away from this begging for just another kind of penury, another kind of handicap. Frankly, we may see His answer as cruelty, as more than we bargained for when we asked. We might not think we even remember how to *use* legs after being handicapped for so long. All we really wanted was a temporary measure. Again.

When God offers us something hard as the answer to our prayers, it helps to think of it in the perspective C.S. Lewis gives us: "We are half-hearted creatures, fooling about with drink and sex and ambition when infinite joy is offered us, like an ignorant child who wants to go on making mud pies in a slum because he cannot imagine what is meant by the offer of a holiday at the sea. We are far too easily pleased." [4]

~MAY 12~
CHERISHING A DEATH WISH

"If I had cherished sin in my heart, the Lord would not have listened." Psalm 66:18

This psalmist is excited. He has been praising God ecstatically throughout this psalm. He starts out by calling on the whole earth to sing of God's glory, awesome deeds, and remarkable power. He recalls how the Lord has turned the sea into dry land in order to deliver His people. He goes on to praise God for the wise testing He has put His people through so that they would be "refined like silver." Then he thanks Him for throwing them into prison and laying burdens upon them, for letting "men ride over [their] heads," for taking them "through fire and water," but all of it so that He could finally bring them to a "place of abundance." Then toward the end, he gets personal and speaks of his coming with burnt offerings and fulfilling his vows to this faithful God who has done wonderful things for him. He thanks God for hearing his prayer and not withholding His love from him. But he knows that it might have been different. He is certain that had his heart not been pure, God would not have heard his voice in prayer.

He speaks of *cherishing* sin. That sounds rather oxymoronish, doesn't it? The word "sin" conjures up deeds of darkness, filthy living, death, and destruction. How could all that be something anyone would *cherish in his heart?*

We don't like to admit it, but sometimes we cherish sin. Before you get too defensive, ask yourself a few questions. Is there anything that you feel is keeping you from a closer, fuller relationship with God? Are you allowing anything to come between you and your Master? In fact, *is* God your real master, or is something or someone else? It might be a thing, or lots of things; it might be a desire; maybe it's an attitude. A bitter, grudging, non-forgiving spirit toward someone? Or pride? "Needing" to maintain a certain image you have worked hard to obtain? Companions? Is the acceptance of someone or a group of someones more important than God's pleasure with you?

"Then the dragon was enraged at the woman and went off to make war against the rest of her offspring— those who obey God's commandments and hold to the testimony of Jesus" (Revelation 12:17). That's us. Our enemy doesn't just sit around idly. He is mad that he can't have God's power, and so he "prowls around like a roaring lion seeking whom he may devour" (1 Peter 5:8). Satan is wily and has lots of tricks up his sleeve. We are caught off guard, and he sneaks some by us from time to time. Without close and regular checks, he can dig in and become like an infestation. This is how sin-cherishing happens.

Peter and Paul knew it could happen and they warned the new churches in their letters*: "Therefore, dear friends, be on your guard so that you may not be carried away by the error of lawless men and fall from your secure position" (2 Peter 3:17). "So if you think you are standing firm, be careful that you don't fall" (1Corinthians 10:12).*

But we have weapons: the belt of truth, the breastplate of righteousness, feet fitted with readiness, the shield of faith, the helmet of salvation, the sword of the spirit (God's Word), and all kinds of prayer. The armor of God is more than sufficient to protect us. *"Put on the full armor of God so that you can take your stand against the devil's schemes." Ephesians 6:11*

~MAY 13~
A DEADLY CYCLE

"In those days Israel had no king; everyone did as he saw fit." Judges 17:6; 21:25

A good one-word description of the book of Judges is "cycles." It wasn't that God wanted them to have a king and they refused, thus falling into political and spiritual anarchy. They had all the political structure they needed in the judges God raised up to guide and advise them. The problem was that they had many *"kings"* — as many as they had people— but they had no *King*. Each person served his own agenda and desires. Everyone did what was right in his *own* eyes. Without the only real King as authority over their opinions and as guide over their directions, they were enslaved to many deadly masters, kowtowing in every direction to every whim. Thus, in a period of approximately three hundred years, the Israelites, who so relished their free-agent status, found themselves under the oppression of seven different enemies. It happened in a cyclical fashion, and it was always the same: sin, servitude, supplication (repentance), salvation, silence... and thus, back again to sin. The "salvation" step happened when God would use one of his Judges to deliver them as a result of their supplication that occurred after their servitude had broken their rebellious spirit. But alas, instead of staying in the salvation phase and making God their King instead of themselves, they invariably forgot who really delivered them, began to believe it was their own bright thinking, and thus fell into the deadliness of silence toward God, which did then and does now lead back to sin.

That this is exactly what happens to us now, as well as in the time of the Judges, might take some hard pondering for some, but for the ladies I work with at a drug and alcohol rehabilitation center, it is a no-brainer. When they hear about the cycles of Judges, they pretty much all at one time clearly assert from all sides of the room, "It's the same with us today." They are all somewhere between phase two and phase four. They have no doubt that sin got them into this bondage, and still in the midst of their brokenness, they know they cannot afford to be silent in the face of such an able Deliverer.

But shouldn't we all be this way? Must we suffer at the hand of ignorance and naïveté just because we are not locked off from the freedom of society with others? Must we be at the extremity of such obvious captivity as drug addiction to see that without a sold-out dependence upon and service to our true Master and rightful King, we are *all* in danger of some sort of bondage?

Is there something that enslaves you— materialism, your habits, your agenda, your schedule, your lifestyle, an undisciplined tongue, food, laziness, procrastination? Lay it before God in supplication. Let Him give you salvation from it. And when He does, remember your Deliverer with such gratitude that you will never grow silent and fall back into the shackles of sin.

~MAY 14~
OBSESSED WITH HAPPINESS

"I consider that our present sufferings are not worth comparing with the glory that will be revealed in us." Romans 8:18

Wishing to Want

I'm sitting here wishing to want what I should,
Trying to long for the things that are good,
Hoping to cling with my heart to the best,
And loosen my grip on all of the rest.
I'm willing my mind to serve in a way
That forgets about self and requires no pay;
No thanks, adoration, or strokes to my pride.
I'm craving to wake up and find that I've died.
Deeply desiring a heart that's compelled
To desire what it should with a passion unquelled;
Trying to long for what You see as good,
I'm sitting here wishing to want what I should.

One of the biggest obstacles to our holding to His teachings and in following closely enough to be truly set free is our obsession with happiness. Jesus repeats the same message so many times in so many ways: we can't focus on two things at once; we can't be double-minded; we must die to ourselves; we must take up our cross; we can't serve two masters. Yet, we find ourselves in states of conflict and anxiety so often because there seems to be this deeply-ingrained belief that we should constantly be in pursuit of happiness. Sometimes Jesus' teachings don't seem tailor made for my immediate happiness. Yet, He has told us the first will be last, the last will be first, and that these times on earth, whether happy or sad, are all fleeting. In His very paradoxical beatitudes, Jesus tries to convince us of this thing about blessedness that so goes against the grain of our thinking in this fallen existence.

He says we are to be the light of the world. Look at the things that give light. Just as there is no Life without the shedding of blood, there is no light without the shedding of fuel. In order for us to give off light, part of us must burn away. We run up against so many brick walls and are hurt, bruised, almost crushed due to our obsession with happiness rather than with burning up and shedding light for His glory. Even our daily devotional times can be used for only a happy retreat from the world— an end in itself— rather than a means of refueling in order to be reburned.

God is calling us higher, to grow in fearlessness, and to put away the childishness of being obsessed with happiness rather than being obsessed with showing the dark world the light of Jesus, not just in profound words but in productive and yes, even exemplary, living that burns a light.

~MAY 15~
THE WAY THAT I FEEL

"...I consider everything a loss compared to the surpassing greatness of knowing Christ Jesus my Lord, for whose sake I have lost all things." Philippians 3:8

Oh, Father, I wish I truly could say
That all I desire in this world is your will,
But it is not true, for I'm begging you now
To make special arrangements for the way that I feel.

I want you to take this hurting away.
I want you to give me a heart free from cares.
But something keeps saying that if you did that,
You'd have to pull up the good wheat with the tares.

Like the ones you prayed for who crucified you
Were ignorant and blind to what they were doing,
I suspect that I have no clue what I'm asking
Or what my nearsighted heart is pursuing.

I long for the day when I truly can say
That all I desire in this world is your will,
But now I'm caught shamefully between Heaven and Hell,
Frozen in time by the way that I feel.

So many times when I thought for sure
That I'd chained up my will and left you with the key,
My ghost slithered out as alive as before:
I'm afraid that I'm doomed always to be me.

Oh, Lord, I'm selfish and stubborn and vile
To worship at the shrine of the way that I feel,
But I will keep hoping that the bright day will dawn
When all I desire in this world is your will.

~MAY 16~
PEACEMAKERS OR PEACEFAKERS?

"Do not hate your brother in your heart. Rebuke your neighbor frankly so you will not share in his guilt." Leviticus 19:17

"Blessed are the peacemakers, for they will be called sons of God." Matthew 5:9

Most of us are more familiar with the New Testament scripture about being a peacemaker, found in Jesus' Beatitudes, than with the Old Testament one from Leviticus.

Paul echoes Jesus' words in his letter to the Romans: "If it is possible, as far as it depends upon you, live at peace with everyone" (Romans 12:18). Peter agrees as he echoes Psalm 34: "Whoever would love life and see good days...must seek peace and pursue it" (1 Peter 3:11). And these are just a smattering of the whole of what is said in the Bible about the virtues of peace.

Because of this plethora of scriptures pointing us toward living a peaceful life, we might have picked up a stereotype worth examining. There is more to this "peace" than might meet the eye, and this scripture in Leviticus can be a great help in uncovering some of its less obvious aspects. When I first saw this scripture, I was intrigued and more than a little bit curious. The second part *could* just mean that if we know a brother's sin and don't help him see it, we could be held partially responsible. But if this is the case, why is it in the context of not hating him in your heart? It sounds very much like a personal matter. Rebuking doesn't *sound* like peacemaking, so perhaps we could just chalk up the seeming contradiction of both commands by saying that the former is the Old Testament way of thinking akin to "an eye for an eye, a tooth for a tooth." After all, we know that Jesus nixed that way of thinking in Matthew 5:38 when He set out to teach us about the higher law of love.

But as we continue our study, we see that such an argument will not hold up. For in the New Testament, in fact, right there in the same book with Jesus' Beatitudes, He further instructs His disciples in this way: "If your brother sins against you, go and show him his fault just between the two of you" (Matthew 18:15). Obviously, then, Jesus, whose every word was right and in harmony with all His other words, meant that sometimes, in order to achieve real peace, something more *active* must happen. Sometimes peace *can* be achieved by quiet and passive means; we *can* overlook sins against us. Other times, however, true peace that will allow us not to "hate our brother in our heart" must be something that we "seek" and "pursue," in the words of Peter and the psalmist. And the way we must do that is to confront our brother or sister whom we need to forgive. In this light, the warning in Leviticus not only lines up with the teachings of our Rabbi, but makes a lot of sense in its own context: *whatever our brother has done to us cannot be worse than our hating him for it.*

Jesus *meant* it when He said "Blessed are the peacemakers," or He would not have attached it to such a beautiful reward. But He referred to peace in the truest and strictest sense of the word—real, deep peace—from the *heart*— even if it means going to some trouble to achieve it. Otherwise, we are not peacemakers, but peacefakers.

~MAY 17~
TAKING WORDS WITH YOU

"Do not be quick with your mouth, do not be hasty in your heart to utter anything before God. God is in heaven, and you are on earth, so let your words be few. As a dream comes when there are many cares, so the speech of a fool when there are many words." Ecclesiastes 5:2-3

"Return, O Israel, to the Lord your God. Your sins have been your downfall. Take words with you and return to the Lord. Say to Him: 'Forgive all our sins and receive us graciously, that we may offer the fruit of our lips.'" Hosea 14:1-2

In Ecclesiastes 3:7, Solomon advises that there is "a time to be silent and a time to speak." Two chapters later we hear him tell of one of those times when silence is wiser than speaking. This passage about letting our words be few is clearly in the context of making vows, and how it is a fool who hastily makes them to God when he finds himself in a tight spot.

The prophet Hosea, however, clearly calls Israel to a time of speaking. They have spurned God time and time again, and now he tells them that returning to Him penitently is their only hope. The sacrifice he advises this time is nothing less than *words*, "the fruit of [their] lips." Although animal sacrifices played a vital role in preparing us for the True Lamb of God by teaching us that there is no forgiveness of sin without the shedding of blood, David knew that animal sacrifices alone would never be enough: "You do not delight in burnt offerings. The sacrifices of God are a broken spirit; a broken and contrite heart you will not despise" (Psalm 51:17).

For a time some of the aspects of communication with God were less direct—through patriarchs, priests, and prophets—but when Jesus died and the curtain of the temple was torn from *top to bottom* (heaven to earth), God invited us into the Holy of Holies to commune with Him in all ways, *directly*. We are *living* sacrifices to Him *now* (Romans 12:1), and can live unto Him effectively only by remaining in Him (John 15:3)—abiding in Him, feeding on Him, *communing* with Him. We were created to be in relationship with God. Every one of us knows that the lifeblood of any relationship is communication. For lack of it, families are ship-wrecked at the hands of rebellion, unfaithfulness, and divorce.

I have loved from a child Proverbs 25:11: "A word fitly spoken is like apples of gold in settings of silver" (KJV). When I was older and came across Revelation 5:8, I nodded and smiled at the similar figure of speech of God's scribes so separated by time yet so united by their Love. Listen to John as he describes His vision of the twenty-four elders falling down before the Lamb: "Each one had a harp, and they were holding golden bowls full of incense, which are *the prayers of the saints*." When one Christian asks another how her prayer life is going, she is really asking, in the highest sense of the question, "How's your love life?" Let us not become so busy working *for* our Lord that we no longer take time to commune *with* Him. Our words are His perfume.

~MAY 18~
EASY PREY

"Be controlled and alert. Your enemy the devil prowls around like a roaring lion looking for someone to devour. Resist him, standing firm in the faith..." 1 Peter 5:8-9

If I were Satan, what would I feel about me, and what would I be doing in regards to me? In what ways might I catch his attention as easy prey?

Am I living a sloppy Christian life? Am I all talk and no action? Or am I a bundle of fruitless action *"for the Lord"* with no communication *with* the Lord? Where do I run first when I detect weakness in myself? Is it perhaps to worldly distractions that will help me deny the problems that might need to be fixed? What do I do when trouble befalls me? Do I fall into vain worry and assume the worst? What about when someone wrongs me? Do I criticize and complain to others rather than lovingly confronting or forgiving?

What makes me laugh? Is my laughter at the expense of others or provoked by coarse and vulgar "humor?" Where do I stand on the holiness scale, or is that a characteristic I want nothing to do with because it "offends" some of those I am trying to impress? Whom am I trying to impress? Whom or what do I love most?

Jesus, in a discussion with Jews who claimed Abraham as their father, said, "You belong to your father the devil, and you want to carry out your father's desire" (John 8:44). Would even these be prey for the devil, or would he protect those who were doing his bidding?

Maybe for a while you will thrive in your sin, but there is no love or loyalty in the devil. "He was a murderer from the beginning," Jesus told these same people. Satan cannot save his own, even if he wanted to. In the end, it is he who will be devoured. He and all of his will be cast into a lake of fire.

The scriptures tell us what to do if we recognize by these or similar questions that we are becoming easy prey: "Submit yourselves to God. (*Believe His Word over your own feelings.*) Resist the devil, and he will flee from you. (*Stand up against wrong. Don't be a spiritual wimp.*). Come near to God, and he will come near to you. (*Protect your private time with God. Fight for it if you have to.*) Wash your hands...purify your heart. Groan, mourn and wail. (*Train your conscience by God's Word, and then listen to it when it convicts you. Ask Him to reveal your sins to you.*) Change your laughter to mourning and your joy to gloom. (*Take your sins seriously. They are no laughing matter.*) Humble yourselves before the Lord and He will lift you up" (James 4:7-10).

~MAY 19~
NOT-SO-EASY PREY

"Finally, be strong in the Lord and in His mighty power. Put on the full armor of God so that you can take your stand against the devil's schemes. For our struggle is not against flesh and blood but against the rulers, against the authorities, against the powers of this dark world and against the spiritual forces of evil in the heavenly realms." Ephesians 6:10-12

Perhaps we are not easy prey. Our lives are not sloppy but self-controlled and upright, as God desires. In this case, we become not easy prey, but *crucial* prey for Satan. We won't be easily led by him, but because of the salt and light we shed upon this world for his Enemy, our Heavenly Father, he must try to catch us off guard and destroy our influence.

Ironically, to be sought out by the enemy is good news. It indicates that we are a worthy adversary and a sharp weapon in God's hands. Now that we have gotten his attention by our energy for God's cause, perhaps, as Jesus told Peter, he would like to "sift us as wheat" (Luke 22:31).

But we shouldn't be paralyzed by fear. With God on our side, who can stand against us? In fact, we should be all we can to be his active enemy, and therefore, God's active friend. Now, though, we must be more vigilant! Here are some good questions for the not-so-easy prey:

Since he is unsuccessful at killing my spirit, how might he be coming at me physically? Are there stumbling blocks that could weaken me physically and thus destroy my energy and activity for God? Are any of my cravings abnormally strong, so strong that they seem "other-worldly"? Am I so drawn by a temptation that sometimes I feel as though I am under a spell—so strong that I work hard to keep this temptation a secret lest someone hold me accountable and I must renounce it?

Or from a different angle, is my "righteousness" causing me to be rough and unkind?

Here are some prescriptions: "Be on your guard. Stand firm in the faith. Be men (and women) of courage; be strong. Do everything in love" (1 Corinthians 16:13). "Therefore put on the full armor of God so that when the day of evil comes, you may be able to stand your ground and after you have done everything, to stand. Stand firm, then, with the belt of truth buckled around your waist, with the breastplate of righteousness in place, and with your feet fitted with the readiness that comes from the gospel of peace. In addition to this, take up the shield of faith with which you can extinguish all the flaming arrows of the evil one. Take the helmet of salvation and the sword of the spirit which is the Word of God, and pray in the spirit on all occasions and with all kinds of prayers and requests. With all this in mind, be alert and always keep on praying for all the saints" (Ephesians 6:13-18).

Whether we are easy prey or hard to capture, we are all at war. There is no middle ground. Being uncommitted to God's way is a definite commitment to the Enemy's.

~MAY 20~
NO EASY TASK AFTER ALL

"Come, my children, listen to me; I will teach you the fear of the Lord. Whoever of you loves life and desires to see many good days, keep your tongue from evil and your lips from speaking lies. Turn from evil and do good; seek peace and pursue it." Psalm 34:11-14

This scripture has become very familiar to me within the last year due to a song I have memorized that incorporates its exact words. It was not until the past twenty-four hours that I have come face to face with the difficulty of being the kind of person it describes. On one hand we are told to "seek peace and pursue it," but on the other hand, we are told to keep our "lips from speaking lies." This all seemed very harmonious until something happened that changed my mind about this seemingly non-controversial and mellow advice.

In a conversation with my friend, my subconscious came to a realization that she needed to hear me say something to help her be able to feel at peace with her feelings. Her feelings were not exactly in line with mine— in fact, my feelings were a little hurt— but I could see where she was coming from. She needed to go, and there was little time, so in order to end the conversation peacefully, I said I understood. I see this at this point as an attempt to seek peace, like the psalmist advises. But was that the truth? Was it the unadulterated, unvarnished, naked truth? Of course it wasn't. It stopped short of being totally honest, and later as I wrote to explain myself more fully, she caught my inconsistency, and I was not just embarrassed but somewhat spiritually shocked at the ease with which I stepped over into Enemy territory.

How can we, in situations like this one— which are very common, by the way— do this thing right? How do we both "seek peace and pursue it" and still keep our "lips from speaking lies"? It seems like it must end up being a *choice* we must make between the two.

In our look at the difference between being a peacemaker and a peacefaker (using this very text), we saw that sometimes confrontation is the only honest way to make true peace. Sometimes anything less is imitation and therefore will fail in bringing about the "many good days" we desire to see. But does this thing still apply in situations like mine with my friend where there is a time issue that stresses me into making a decision quickly about whether I will speak the whole truth and throw her day into some emotional unrest or "seek peace" by saying something less than the truth? I'm pretty sure that what I decide about this will affect what I decide about a lot of other hard and uncomfortable biblical issues. If I erase a little here, why can't I erase a little there and there and there?

No, there can be no fudging. I am going to have to choose both. The answer comes in a different spirit of speaking the truth— one that is both honest and peace offering, one that is free from manipulation and attack. It is all going to have to start with a closer look at the way Jesus communicated with those who loved Him.

~MAY 21~
FOOLS RUSH IN WHERE WISE MEN FEAR TO TREAD

"Come, my children, listen to me; I will teach you the fear of the Lord. Whoever of you loves life and desires to see many good days, keep your tongue from evil and your lips from speaking lies. Turn from evil and do good; seek peace and pursue it." Psalm 34:11-14

This dilemma of seeking peace while speaking only the truth is common enough to demand the serious follower of Christ to take it up and wrestle with it. Feeling the need to say *something* in a time when closure seems to be called for can get us into trouble if there truly is no peaceful closure at that point. It is, at best, a stop-gap measure that usually only delays an inevitable confrontation, or worse, an unspoken festering bitterness.

One of the words that others have sometimes used to describe me is "quick." Whether it was referring to a quickness of feet, reflex, or wit, I have always liked the feeling it gave me to be described that way. Perhaps the very desire to continue that legacy— to nurture that trademark— is one of the hidden motivations to be ever-ready with a word. Being the first to raise my hand in class, knowing the answer to the riddle before anyone else, buzzing in first in "Jeopardy" have always held a certain irresistible appeal to me, even though I will admit that I have been chagrined by answering incorrectly more times than not because of this chancy haste. Truly, for some of us, it takes more energy to hold back than it does to move forward.

However, being quick is not all it's cracked up to be. It may be a solid virtue for an athlete on the playing field and medical personnel when life hangs treacherously in the balance, but when it comes to the tongue, it can be as much a thing of folly and vanity as hundreds of thousands of dollars thrown away on cosmetic surgery. James gives very clear instructions on this issue, and he admonishes *everyone* to take note of it. "My dear brothers, take note of this: Everyone should be quick to listen, *slow to speak*, and slow to become angry..." (James 1:19). Closure may *feel* like a temptingly neat and tidy way to end a conversation, but if it is fake closure, we are more likely than not to reap its whirlwind. James tells us this because he knows that unless a hard decision or commitment is bathed first in prayer, it will likely go wrong. He spends most of his one and only letter speaking of the importance of praying—when we are sick, when we're in trouble, when we seek wisdom.

So when faced with a situation in which time constraints might tempt us to rush into falseness just for the sake of closure, or to speak truthfully but to risk sounding harsh or being misunderstood, there is a third wiser, more Biblical option: We can forfeit the tidiness of closure and the vanity of quickness for the wisdom of waiting. We can gently ask for a postponement of the end of the conversation. The patience to finish a thing right by taking it before the True Judge will be well worth the wait. *"Be patient, then, brothers, until the Lord's coming" (James 5:7.)* Invite the Lord, and He will come.

~MAY 22~
A MERRY HEART

"A merry heart doeth good like medicine..." Proverbs 17:22 (KJV)

Proverbs 31 is an acrostic poem describing the ideal wife. According to verse 30, which sums up all the specific details aforementioned, she is "a woman who fears the Lord" and is to be praised and rewarded. In verse 25, after King Lemuel has painted a whole truckload of concrete accolades, he adds as commentary one of my favorite images of this lady: *"She is clothed with strength and dignity; she can laugh at the days to come."* There are lots of different types of laughter, some admirable and others not so much, but the laughter described here is of the purest and most delightful sort. Unlike vain laughter that is solely for drawing attention to the laugh-er or cruel laughter done totally at the expense of a laugh-ee, this laughter is inspired by and centered upon unselfishness. This laughter is a beautiful gift. To the Proverbs 31 woman, it is a gift sent from God as a reward of mirthful levity for her godly diligence. It is a reward to those around her, too, because it communicates the vital message that once we have done our best, we can rest in the goodness of the Lord to bless us.

Blessed are we who have someone in our lives possessed of such a gift. My sister-in-law Cynthia is a great bounty to the Doke family because of her beautiful consistency of hearty, comforting laughter. Even when I am sleeping in the back room late at night, I always have to giggle a little when I hear Cynthia come in the front door. Whoever lets her in gets not only a warm hug but a good dose of hearty laughter. Who knows how she can find anything funny at that time of the night after traveling for three hours up a boring freeway in the wee hours, but there's always something for Cynthia to bubble over about. Whatever her present situation, however heavy her load, she has the unselfish grace to abandon herself and lend to you and only you her ears and her big, expressive blue eyes, sparkling with life and sparking with energy. Her laughter is never mean-spirited but is always preceded or followed by words of kindness and encouragement designed especially with you in mind. She is Robert Browning come to proclaim, "God's in His Heaven, all's right with the world!"[1] There is no way, this side of heaven, to assess the benefit each of us has gained from Cynthia's indomitably merry heart.

Sometimes in light of all the grand accomplishments others seem to be making to salting the earth with the love of Jesus, it might be hard to imagine being very valuable. Maybe we don't feel very smart or talented; maybe we don't have the health to do mission work or the wealth to support those who do, but maybe we do have a cheerful heart that can reach out with a warm smile or joyful laughter. Maybe our gift, like Cynthia's, is encouragement. Barnabas was such a fellow. Acts 4:36 says that his name was really "Joseph," but the apostles called him "Barnabas" because it meant "Son of Encouragement." He was a priceless asset to the apostles and worked in unique ways critical to the cause of Christ. If you are a Cynthia / Barnabas, know that you are invaluable to the world around you. If you know a Cynthia / Barnabas, send him or her some flowers or write a note today, and return a little of what has been given to you.

~MAY 23~
"WITH ALL YOUR HEART"

"'You will seek me and find me when you seek me with all your heart. I will be found by you,' declares the Lord, 'and will bring you back from captivity." Jeremiah 29:13-14

First Kings 10 and 2 Chronicles 9 record the story of the queen of Sheba visiting King Solomon. Because she had heard about his fame and his "relation of the name of the Lord," she came "to test him with hard questions" and to talk with him about "all that was on her mind." After many questions and much surveying of his kingdom, her response was one of overwhelming fascination, for what she had found had far exceeded the reports she had heard. Indeed, she had come because she could not believe anyone could be such a wonderful king until she saw it with her own eyes. It is doubtful that she came merely out of curiosity but probably because she, too, was a monarch and wanted to learn more about how to do her job in an exceptional manner. She was an earnest seeker, willing to do whatever it took to learn what she needed to know.

Are we seeking the ways of our King and Mentor as we go about being his priests and ambassadors? Jesus came to show us how to live the life God desires. Not long before He left this place to return to Our Father, He explained that not only did He expect us to do what He had been doing, but because of the Holy Spirit He would leave behind, to do "even greater things than these." But the Holy Spirit does not thrive in us without a regular diet of God's Word. If you find yourself frustrated with difficulty in understanding a scripture, do you give up or search harder? According to His prophet Jeremiah, He wants us to search, like the Queen of Sheba, with *all* our hearts.

In our world of electronic communication and automatic gadgetry, we have little practice in waiting. Technology does such a good job for us that when accomplishing something takes longer than a few minutes, we are sorely tempted to decide it isn't worth the time and trouble. But God Almighty is a deep and many-faceted

Lord and will not be thoroughly applied to our lives with any kind of effectiveness by shortcuts. Some of Jesus' contemporaries wanted to take a shortcut, too. Rather than spending time with Him and listening to Him, they wanted miraculous sign after miraculous sign before they would repent. His answer? He called them a "wicked and adulterous generation," and then He reminded them of the Queen of Sheba: "The Queen of the South will rise at the judgment with this generation to condemn it; for she came to the ends of the earth to listen to Solomon's wisdom, and now one greater than Solomon is here" (Matthew 12:42).

According to the eighteenth-century English poet Wordsworth, "The world is too much with us."[2] Well, Mr. Wordsworth, things aren't any different in twenty-first-century America. The gravity of sin lies upon us like lead. If we are to change this world, we need desperately to know Him well enough to duplicate Him. We are going to have to spend the time it takes to do it with all our hearts. Only then will He be found.

~MAY 24~
A BED TOO SHORT AND A BLANKET TOO NARROW

"I will make justice the measuring line and righteousness the plumb line; hail will sweep away your refuge, the lie, and water will overflow your hiding place."
Isaiah 28:17

In a recent reading of Isaiah, I came upon this chapter filled with beautiful but terrifying poetry. Isaiah is pleading with a stiff-necked Israel on behalf of the Lord, warning them of their impending captivity if they continue to honor their idols and superstitions over God. Already having described for them the "glorious crown" and "beautiful wreath" reserved for the remnant of His people, he now speaks to them in no uncertain terms about the alternative. They have become dangerously relaxed in a false refuge, believing that they have somehow made some sort of covenant with the grave that will exempt them from death. The lines of poetry flow rhythmically along employing images of floods and plumb lines, and suddenly a pronouncement is made that jarred my senses, rocketing me from the days of Isaiah into my right here, right now world: *"The understanding of this message will bring sheer terror. The bed is too short to stretch out on, the blanket too narrow to wrap around you"* (v. 20).

Having done my share of traveling—riding long distances in cramped vehicles and being laid over in crowded airports—I can identify with the discomfort of not being able to stretch out when in sore need of rest. And being a cold-natured person, the image of a blanket too small to bring any warm relief is all too familiar. Sleeping is a delicate thing with me, requiring near perfect conditions for the task to be accomplished; I have always been more than a little envious of those who can sleep anywhere. Had I been in Isaiah's original audience, *this* metaphor would be *just* the one *I* would have needed to hear to jolt me into some serious reconsideration.

Though I am not a member of his original audience, I am under his tutelage, even still. The Word of God, after all, is the Word of God. Though I do not adhere to some strange, pagan belief involving a covenant with death, could there be other beliefs that I do adhere to that might also be a bed too short and a blanket too narrow?

Do I believe that the things I can buy with money will improve the quality of my life?

Do I believe that flesh and blood have more relevant answers to my problems than God's Word?

Do I believe that just because I botched a thing up last time, I am sure to do it again?

Do I believe that just because someone's sister or brother or mother or father was a certain kind of person, that he/she is that kind of a person, too?

Do I believe that how a person feels about me is what makes me who I am?

Study your resting place, your security. Are there beds you are trying to rest upon that will not bring you true rest? Are there blankets you are trying to warm up in that hold no real warmth?

~MAY 25~
ANYTHING WORTH DOING

"Let us not become weary in doing good, for at the proper time we will reap a harvest if we do not give up. Therefore, as we have opportunity, let us do good to all people, especially to those who belong to the family of believers." Galatians 6:9-10

I think it's funny how we are so prone to believe little aphorisms as long as they have some catchiness to them. Give a string of words some rhythm or rhyme, and we seem to feel good about passing them on as a reasonable place to hang our hats and hopes. Many of these we repeat for years (or our whole lives) without once ever seeking to find out their origin or to ask if, aside from the way they sound, they really have any value at all. Take, for instance, "head over heels in love." Isn't the head *always* above the heels? Shouldn't we really be saying "heels over head in love"? Or "Absence makes the heart grow fonder." Well, sometimes that's true, but most of the time it isn't. Most of the time absence makes the heart grow forgetful.

One of these worth studying from a spiritual standpoint is "Anything worth doing is worth doing well." I can see why we would buy this one if we mean by "well" the best that we can do, but that is not how we usually end up translating this into practical living. The way we usually translate "well" in this saying is "perfectly" or "thoroughly." And therein lies the rub. If we decide that we should do only those deeds or get involved in things that we can do with some expertise, most of us limit ourselves to the point of sacrificing a lot of good energy and some valuable service that God could use for His glory and towards the world's redemption. Of course we should seek to get in touch with our special talents so that we can bless others thereby, but what about those times when something is needed to be done, and no one with that particular talent seems to be around? Isn't it better to do what we can in the time that we have to do it and trust God to take up the slack than to bow out because we aren't talented in that area and couldn't do the job perfectly?

Consider this scripture: "Whatever you do, work at it with all your heart, as working for the Lord and not for men, since you know that you will receive an inheritance from the Lord. It is the Lord you are serving" (Colossians 3:23-24). This might be considered an argument against my premise that everything worth doing is not necessarily worth doing well, but I disagree. This scripture is in the context of slaves' attitudes toward their masters; it is encouraging them to remember that God is their real master and to trust Him to be the final Judge of everyone's actions. If He is our Master, would He say, "Good job for not trying since you couldn't do it perfectly!" or would He praise us for being faithful to do the best job we could ("with all your heart") with the little we had? We only have to go to Matthew 25:14-30 to know how Jesus sees this. A talent back then was a unit of coinage, and the one who used his two was commended just as the one who was given five. The parables of the mustard seed and the yeast both teach how abundance can come from smallness (Matthew 13:31-33).

Everything worth our doing must not necessarily be done well. The One who took a few fish and fed a multitude and changed water to wine can certainly stretch our two cents' worth into something fit for His kingdom.

~MAY 26~
FAITHFUL LIKE HIS FATHER

"I remember my affliction and my wandering, the bitterness and the gall. I well remember them, and my soul is downcast within me. Yet, this I call to mind and therefore I have hope: Because of the Lord's great love we are not consumed, for His compassions never fail. They are new every morning; great is your faithful-ness." Lamentations 3:19-23

Today is my wedding anniversary. I have been married to my dear Larry for 36 years today. In a word association test, the word "Larry" would immediately evoke from me the word "faithful." Although in all contexts it is a praiseworthy trait, the word itself is rather general and vague. Sometimes faithfulness connotes an honored promise to be exclusively mine. Other times it means dependable or devoted. Larry is all of these and more. This particular passage speaks of the faith-fulness of God to offer compassion to us when we need it. My favorite part is the specific note as to how often and regularly He meets us offering us a brand new slate: "His compassions never fail. *They are new every morning."*

Most of my life I had known only the very last part of this passage, having somehow dissected it from its whole context. When you look at why Jeremiah is thankful for the fresh mercy every single morning, it makes this tender avowal even more precious. Regret over his "affliction and wandering" is bitter within him. I can only assume, since it's placed next to "wandering," that the affliction must mean some sort of besetting sin that continues to creep into his life. Because he cannot forget all he has done, he is depressed ("my soul is downcast within me.") Then he remembers that his Lord is full of mercy and therefore is filled with renewed hope and even rejoicing.

Larry is that kind of faithful, too. It doesn't matter how I have acted or what I have said in my grouchy exhaustion the night before; he offers me a sweet kiss and smile the next morning. I am awarded a new slate to write on, a brand new day filled with all kind of possibilities rather than the stale one I deserve that would be hindered by oozing wounds and unsightly scars from yesterday. He is not perfect, but this one thing more than makes up for his weaknesses.

The reason he is like this is not due to a poor memory; it's all in the family. He has sat at His Father's feet all His life, and He's just doing like His Father does. (And it didn't hurt any that his earthly father did the same thing!)

Is there someone who needs us to give him or her another chance, a new start?

Whether married or single, the lesson of compassion is targeted for all of us. We all need it, and we all need to give it. Let us go into this new day with a prayer on our lips to be faithful dispensers of God's mercy and grace.

"Give, and it will be given unto you. A good measure, pressed down, shaken together and running over, will be poured into your lap. For with the measure you use, it will be measured to you." Luke 6:38

~MAY 27~
THE FLAG IN THE DISTANCE

"For the trumpet will sound, the dead will be raised imperishable, and we will all be changed. For the perishable must clothe itself with the imperishable and the mortal with immortality." I Corinthians 15:52-53

What an exciting chapter this is! Obviously, some have tried to convince the Corinthians that there is no resurrection from the dead, so Paul recounts for them the inheritance of death through the first Adam and the inheritance of resurrection from the dead from the second Adam, Christ. Next, Paul goes into the details of this resurrection as it will affect them (and us.) At this point, I can just picture Paul as he composes this letter. He is leaning forward, eyes afire with the vision of how it will be. As he rubs his hands together in anticipation of the picture he is about to paint, I can just hear him deciding that what started out a burden—a crucial attempt to snatch them from the Enemy's groping hands— is quickly turning into a treat for him, for indeed, this is his favorite story.

Verse 35 begins a detailed description using eye-popping, ear-splitting imagery of the resurrection body that we will inherit. He can't talk to them face to face, and there are no phones yet to allow him to use his physical voice, so he must pack his written words full of images— many different kinds to fit the different personalities that would be reading the letter. He is following his Rabbi, Jesus, who in His parables, employed every kind of occupational image available so as not to leave someone in a fog as to what He was trying to say.

The body he describes is one that excites us more and more the older we get. "The body that is sown is perishable, it is raised imperishable; it is sown in dishonor, it is raised in glory; it is sown in weakness, it is raised in power; it is sown a natural body, it is raised a spiritual body" (Vv. 42-44).

Just this morning I decided to challenge my fifty-six-year-old body to the 10k run (6.2 miles) that I have done once or twice a year for the past five years. This time it was different. This time those last two miles were really hard. I just kept my eye on the flag flying at the gas station where I had left my car. After reading this passage in light of this reminder that I am living inside a body that is on the decline, I have decided that most of these Corinthians must have been senior citizens, and Paul knew ending this letter with a promise of a much-improved post-resurrection body would be a most effective motivator for them to stand firm and not go back to their former, easier way of life. He's like the wise parents who somewhere around western Arizona pass around the slick, colorful Disneyland brochures in order to rally their edgy kids who have ridden cooped up in the back seat of a car all the way from Texas: He's reminding them why they are on this journey.

Senior citizens or not, we all need reminding. If it's not arthritis, it's a busted knee, a pimply face, or a broken heart. If you haven't read 1 Corinthians 15 lately, read it now. It could be just the medicine you need.

"Therefore, my dear brothers, stand firm. Let nothing move you. Always give yourselves fully to the work of the Lord because you know that your labor in the Lord is not in vain." 1 Corinthians 15:58

~MAY 28~
PARABLES FROM THE GARDEN

"But if you do not do what is right, sin is crouching at your door. It desires to have you, but you must master it." Genesis 4:7

A few years ago I became interested in growing flowers. No, that is not true. I became *obsessed* with growing flowers. I could not go to town without coming home with a trunkful of flowers. I bought lots of books on gardening, looked at the pretty pictures, and began plowing up our yard piece by piece. I talked my husband into building me a pretty little fence around my garden plot, and then I set out to fill every square inch with every kind of color and fragrance in the horticultural world. Never having had any experience in this sort of thing, my hobby was a fast, furious, and somewhat reckless venture into the unknown. I knew what I wanted. I had a vision, and I couldn't wait to bring it to reality.

But little by little I learned things. Mostly I learned that gardening is a parable replete with lessons about Christian living. Just walking into my garden was like tuning into a Heavenly radio station.

The weeds (sin) come without invitation and thrive with no work whatsoever, whereas the flowers (righteousness) come only with sacrificial care and lots of hard, consistent work. If you don't stay at the weeds, they will take over all the work you have done to create beauty. And if you don't get them out at the root, you can't even get back in the house before they are full grown again. Flowers need good soil, water, and fertilizer; weeds go gangbusters on nothing but time. When you try to stay ahead of the weeds so that your beauty can live and thrive, there are demons on guard just waiting to waylay you: extreme heat, fire ants, poison ivy, even an occasional snake. When you leave, you must find someone to care for your flowers. On the other hand, your weeds do just fine without anyone looking after them; in fact, they love it when you leave. They thrive when you are not paying attention. Sometimes it looks as though you have been successful in raising a beautiful, full-bodied plant; the foliage is full, green, and waxy, but alas, it stops short of bearing fruit. Among all the showy leaves no bud appears, or if one does, an insect or disease will do it in before it can grow to maturity. When I brought a plant home, more times than not I would plant it in the shade when it was a sun lover or vice versa.

I don't know how much money I spent those first few years, but I know that only about one-half percent of what I spent turned glorious. I learned that weeds and death, just like the sin God warned Cain about in Genesis 4, crouched at my door. They desired to have my garden and pretty much got it due to my lack of mastery over them. Oh, it wasn't that I didn't spend time working at it; I was just ignorantly ill-prepared for reality.

I wonder how much more successful I would have been if I had actually *read* those gardening books.

~MAY 29~
THE FRAGRANCE OF CHRIST

"But thanks be to God, who always leads us in triumphal procession in Christ and through us spreads everywhere the fragrance of the knowledge of Him. For we are to God the aroma of Christ among those who are being saved..." 2 Corinthians 2:14-15

One of the lessons I learned in my gardening craze was that often the vivid and showy blossoms are not the most fragrant. One of my few successes is my hydrangea bush that grows faithfully with little effort on my part right outside my front door. Each spring huge perfect pink blossoms resembling rubber swimming

155

caps from my childhood issue forth. They are every gardener's visual dream, but their fragrance is a disappointment. In fact, besides roses, most brilliantly-colored flowers lack a fragrance to match, whereas modest and unassuming blooms such as jasmine, plumeria, and freesia, shed forth bountifully their perfume. There's something about this message of nature that is comforting and encouraging.

Our sense of smell is so closely attached to our memory that just a vague whiff of a certain perfume can immediately transport me to my grandmother's house as a three-year old, my first date, or my wedding night. I can hug a person wearing a certain fragrance, and I am swept away into another world from my past. Perhaps this is why God chose to have Paul use this particular imagery in his letter to the saints in Corinth.

When we know Christ, we smell like Him to other believers. The world is filled with many disgusting odors; deceit, greed, lust, murder, disease, and abuse are just a few. Too much uninterrupted lingering in its stench without retreating into a wholesome spiritual atmosphere where we can soak up more knowledge of Christ can eventually corrupt our ability to distinguish the real from the false, the reality from the nightmare. Just a few sentences before this one, Paul has reminded them of the importance of forgiving each other "in order that Satan might not outwit us. For we are not unaware of his schemes" (2 Corinthians 2:11). An unforgiving spirit is another of the foul—even poisonous—odors of the Christ-less life.

Maybe the world has crowded in too closely and left its stench in our nostrils so strongly that all we can think about are the burdens and the limitations of earthly existence. Then we get a whiff of someone who has been soaking in the knowledge of Him, and we are swept back into His reality. Oftentimes the carriers of this tantalizing aroma are no more of centerpiece significance than the honeysuckle that stops many a runner in his tracks for an encore whiff. Nonetheless, they are critical reminders of what is true and real and lasting.

And not only are we traveling bouquets to other struggling believers; our lovely scent also reaches up to the Heavenlies!

"And when He had taken it, the four living creatures and the twenty-four elders fell down before the lamb. Each one had a harp and they were holding golden bowls full of incense which are the prayers of the saints." Revelation 5:8

~MAY 30~
THE SMELL OF DEATH

"But thanks be to God, who always leads us in triumphal procession in Christ and through us spreads everywhere the fragrance of the knowledge of him. For we are to God the aroma of Christ among those who are being saved and those who are perishing. To the one we are the smell of death; to the other, the fragrance of life." 2 Corinthians 2:15-16

According to the first part of this passage, we are the "aroma of Christ" to everyone, whether he or she is a believer or an infidel. Christ is *complete, unadulterated* goodness; there is nothing vile, putrid or rotting about Him. He is, in fact, the very definition, the epitome of goodness. Aroma, therefore, in *this* sense is an objective absolute, not a subjective, experiential thing. What *goes out* from Him is always aromatic.

The second part of the passage deals with how He is *received*. This is the subjective part. It isn't just about personal taste, or in this case, personal smell, as in the difference in the way a pizza with anchovies smells to an anchovy-lover and the way it smells to one who hates fish. This has to do with what the very thought, the very smell, of Jesus Christ does to the insides of one who has accepted and joyfully surrendered to the fact that He, indeed, is Lord of both the universe and his or her individual life and to one who is in rebellion to that fact. The difference here isn't just a difference in individual taste; it is the difference between a swimmer who dives into a pool and a non-swimmer who falls into the same pool. To the first, it is an act of the will that brings refreshment and rejuvenation; to the second it is an act of terror, which, without intervention, will bring death.

The imagery here comes from Roman culture. A general would lead his victorious troops along with their captives in a parade-type procession while the public would cheer and burn sweet-smelling spices in the streets. Everyone smelled the same spices burning, but the context greatly affected the spirit in which the smell was received. To the victors, it was the sweet smell of success; to the captives, it was the apprehensive and dreadful stench of the dungeon.

And we walk around emitting this smell to the one as well as to the other. Since Satan is by Jesus' own words the prince of this world (John 12:31), does the thought that you are the smell of death more often than the fragrance of life bring about a sense of dread? It might until you consider this one thing: unlike the captives of the Roman soldiers who had little hope at that point, the captives we are placed among to shed forth this fragrance are just as we were. We walk among them smelling this way with a purpose. We have a story of victory to tell them, not so that we can gloat about what we have that they don't, but so that we can hold out to them *Hope* in the person of Christ the Cornerstone, not Christ the stumbling block.

And this is their hope: *"From one man he made every nation of men, that they should inhabit the whole earth; and He determined the times set for them and the exact places where they should live. He did this so that men would seek Him and perhaps reach out for Him and find Him, though He is not far from each of us"* (Acts 17:26-27).

~MAY 31~
MAIL THAT BEARS HIS STAMP

"You yourselves are our letter, written on our hearts, known and read by everybody. You show that you are a letter from Christ, the result of our ministry, written

not with ink but with the Spirit of the living God, not on tablets of stone but on tablets of human hearts." 2 Corinthians 3:2-3

Now they call it snail-mail. Regardless of the affection you may harbor for snails, this is a derogatory descriptor intended to cast aspersions on its lack of speed. It was coined as subversive technological hype to make us see paper mail as a second-rate, low-rent, outmoded commodity, and I don't like it one bit. The deep love I bear for the kind of mail that's made of paper and ink and is delivered to an actual, literal metal mailbox out by the street bristles at the insinuation that it is inferior in any way.

I know that e-mail has its place, and yes, I realize that you can actually print it off and hold it in your hand, kiss it, and stash it away as though it were REAL mail, but it lacks the authenticity of personality and intimacy that comes with handwriting scrawled imperfectly and irregularly across a page on which that very hand rested as it wrote. All this and more make this kind of mail more precious, more real than cold, predictable lettering that is popped to me with some impersonal clicks and no stamp applied by a beloved finger.

I love this verse perhaps because it explains why I love mail from loved ones the way I do. It describes living love letters written by the Supreme Maker and Lover of our souls. They come on personalized stationery, the color and texture varied according to the heart that bears it, but always inscribed with the same distinctive handwriting. They have been sent from afar to remind me that I am dearly loved and remembered and held dear in spite of the distance between us. They always bear a stamp with a clear image of the Author, proving that I am worth all He paid to send this blessing to me. They are sealed and sent with the holy intention of acting as a deposit of good will until their Author can see me and say these things to me face to face. If I should become lonely or discouraged, the letters are there for me to re-read and be reminded that Someone cared enough to fashion with His own hand an image of a piece of His heart for my keeping. I will treasure each one I am sent and handle it tenderly lest from misuse and careless treatment it be damaged or lost.

To be sure, we have different levels of commitment to different people in our lives, and rightly so. To some, we were sent to do more than just pop in once in a while and then disappear into cyberspace. Now that we are signed, stamped, and sealed, let us pray to be *delivered* to the right addresses.

~JUNE 1~
ULTIMATE DILEMMA

"I consider that our present sufferings are not worth comparing with the glory that will be revealed in us." Romans 8:18

I want to be pretty; I want to be plain.
I want to be a barefoot dancer in the rain...

But then again, on the other hand,
I'd rather be practical and wear brown wool,
Something that will make me invisible.

I'd like to be nameless with a face to forget,
Like a chameleon that blends in and graciously fits.
(But, oh, this desire to be a rebel in red
Blazing through pinks with a chicken on her head!)

I want to write poetry, be romantic and lacy;
I want to break bottles, break rules, and go crazy.
I want to be vivid; I want to be pale.
I wish to inspire; I'd like to regale.

I want to resist tossing love out
When its arrows pierce deeply and cause me to doubt.
I want to believe there's some other way
And deny the pain until some other day.

But something inside remembers too much
And warns the believer to shrink from soft touch
And warm eyes that give promises in cracked, leaky cups.
"It's a lie!" she shouts. "It doesn't add up."

So the mathematician shows the poet her proof,
And the bone-weary dreamer,
the enabling deceiver,
the naïve believer
gives up and turns loose.

If the mathematics has been winning out over the poetry in your world, and your heart is weary from loving and believing, remember Jesus on the cross on Friday and what happened on Sunday. Ask Him to give you strength to bear the wounds and keep loving just for today. Then tomorrow do it again.

~JUNE 2~
DO EVERYTHING IN LOVE

"Be on your guard; stand firm in the faith; be men of courage; be strong. Do everything in love." 1 Corinthians 16:13

That the Corinthian church was steeped in troubles isn't surprising considering the rampant immorality of that city. With a population of about 250,000 free persons, plus as many as 400,000 slaves, it contained at least twelve temples, the most infamous of which was one dedicated to Aphrodite, the Greek goddess of love, whose worshipers practiced religious prostitution. At one time, 1,000 "sacred" prostitutes served her temple. There was even a Greek verb named for this city: "to Corinthianize," which meant "to practice sexual immorality." Nevertheless, Paul was able to plant a church here. His first letter to the Corinthians revolves around his concern for their continued development of holiness in character.

At first it seemed to me a bit of an irony that so much of this book is about *love*. With such a background of loose living and sexual promiscuity, you'd think that "love" would be a word that Paul would just as soon not bring up. You'd think that he would be more singly focused on hitting them hard on upright living rather than spending a big chunk of it on love. He begins by instructing them on the dangers of division in the church, lawsuits among believers, sexual immorality inside and outside of marriage, allowing open sin to be congratulated rather than banished from their midst, improprieties in worship and the Lord's Supper. But then around what we call the twelfth chapter, he begins to focus on how we, the body of Christ, are to love one another. In fact, most Bible dabblers, when asked about this book, will tell you this is the book that has the famous love chapter. Besides chapter fifteen, which is a grand treatise on the resurrection and the second coming of Christ, Paul spends the rest of the book directing them as to what love really is. Considering that their whole culture was based on a counterfeit of love—the love goddess Aphrodite and all her religious prostitutes—it really isn't such an irony after all that Paul would see their need to have *real* love defined and contrasted with their false idea of love.

In this scripture, right here in a nest full of warnings about idolatry, weakness, and fear, he throws in "Do everything in love." At first glance, it again seems ironic, if not totally out of place. But I think the point is that the kind of love God created for us to share and live by is not something that comes at all naturally to the secular world. This is why he has gone into so much detail to explain it in the thirteenth chapter. What love really is is not selfishly feeding one's lust, gorging oneself with sensuality separated from caring; it is all about selflessness and sacrifice, thoughtfulness and patience. So after he tells them to stand for what is right and not be afraid to oppose those who are wrong, he tells them *how* to do that so they will reap new Christians, rather than just repelling the sinners.

It is a lesson for all of us: be strong to stand against evil, don't wimp out in the face of temptation, but in your response, let your life clearly define love as God does.

~JUNE 3~
A TIME TO LAUGH

*"There is a time for everything, and a season for every activity under heaven:...
a time to weep and a time to laugh; a time to mourn and a time to dance..."
Ecclesiastes 3:4*

He was just a baby in waiting so he had never read Ecclesiastes 3 to know that this was *not* the time for him to be born. In fact, it was about seven weeks early, and the medical staff in labor and delivery were not feeling too good about his surprise entry. They told us our three-pound son was in lots of trouble and likely wouldn't live. If he did, they were afraid he would be brain-damaged.

But bathed luxuriously in prayer, he did live— boy, did he live!— and aside from his crazy sense of adventure that knows no fear, his brain is not damaged. Everything about Ben grew and thrived spiritually, scholastically, and socially except his ears, which were chronically infected. At eleven he underwent radical surgery on his right ear that saved his hearing but left him with an ear canal as big around as a quarter. Having taught kids his age in school and knowing their capacity for cruelty, I was concerned that perhaps his self-esteem would suffer due to this obvious physical abnormality, especially since we were moving soon, and he would be in a new school. But I couldn't have been more wrong.

When we suggested that he grow his hair longer to help cover his ears, he gave it a try...for about two weeks. He liked his hair short, he said, so he went to school with everything laid out on the table. He was a sitting duck. When I asked him how school went, he laughed and told me, "Fine. The guys call me 'hole in one.'" Maybe they meant it as a cruel joke, but Ben, having always been a stand-up comedian, appreciated their sharp sense of humor, so he laughed. Not only had he saved himself some heartache; he had made some new friends. He was always creating new ways to enjoy his signature ear: seeing how many quarters he could fit in it and pulling them out to pay at concession stands, and stuffing long, plastic streamers down inside it and then waiting patiently until just the right time to begin nonchalantly pulling and pulling and pulling them out, inch by inch, foot by foot, to the bewilderment of the strangers sitting behind him at the football game.

A lot of us older folks learned a lot from Ben. What we feared might be a time for weeping, Ben obviously thought was a time for laughter. We thought there might be mourning, but Ben decided there would be dancing.

What a delightful gift creative humor is, and how enchanting is the quality of not taking ourselves too seriously! It rescues us from being held captive by stereotypes and preconceived notions. It takes what would be a persecutor and makes him a friend. It turns the vehicle the Enemy surely meant for heartache into a thrilling ride that lightens spirits and elicits smiles and laughter. And best of all, a joyful attitude is contagious.

The next time you are tempted to feel sorry for yourself because of someone's insensitivity, surprise him or her with some creative humor. You might make a friend for life.

"A cheerful heart is good medicine, but a crushed spirit dries up the bones."
Proverbs 17:22

~JUNE 4~
THE INFALLIBLE REFEREE

"Above all, love each other deeply, because love covers over a multitude of sins."
1 Peter 4:8

"I pray also that the eyes of your heart may be enlightened in order that you may know the hope to which he has called you, the riches of his glorious inheritance in the saints, and his incomparably great power for us who believe." Ephesians 1:18-19

Wanted: Referee

Oh, Lord, see this fight going on in here?
I really need you to be referee.
Blow your whistle when one is in trouble too deep,
And send both fighters to their corners—
The Vulnerable Second-Mile-Truster
And
The Hardened Independent Who's Learned the Hard Lessons;
The Mathematician who knows when things don't add up
And the Poet whose heart can't afford to notice;
The Wise Resolutionist, the Naïve Persister.

And please do all you can to make sure
That the best man wins
In the end.

We know we're supposed to love deeply. We know that all Jesus said on the Sermon on the Mount was about a higher law based not on an eye for an eye but on love at the very core of all our thinking. We know, in fact, that the whole Bible is just one story— and that in that one story the theme, rising action, conflict, climax, and resolution are all love.

But sometimes, loving hard, deep, and long just feels too expensive. We get hurt, disappointed, feel foolish, and thus grow disheartened and fearful of sticking our heart's neck out one more time. We want to escape the danger of disappointment and pain, so we pull in. We retract our antennae from all sensation because we know that some of those sensations will hurt. Like a turtle in trouble, we pull our heads in our shells and try to find comfort in the lonely darkness. However, as Christians, we cannot take ourselves out of this ballgame, no matter how many times we strike out or get bonked on the head by a foul ball. We are Ambassadors of the King.

What we need is not to duck out of sight or build around our hearts thick walls of determination not to love anymore. What we need is for the eyes of our hearts to be enlightened, just as Paul prayed for the Ephesians. When we see clearly the hope and the glorious inheritance we are called to, the pain of the moment can be put in proper perspective, and we can stick our necks out to love yet another day.

~JUNE 5~
WHAT IS THAT TO YOU?

"When Peter saw him, he asked, 'Lord, what about him?' Jesus answered, 'If I want him to remain alive until I return, what is that to you? You must follow me.'"
John 21:21-22

Reading these words on a page might tempt us to be stricter in our judgment of Peter than we really should be. Jesus having shown up to cook breakfast on the shore for his disciples, has just reinstated Peter. Three separate times— one for each of Peter's denials— Jesus has graciously awarded Peter the opportunity to reaffirm his love for him. And now, Jesus prophesies about the hard manner of death Peter will undergo someday.

Maybe it seems that after all this Peter is coming off as pretty childish and spiritually immature by asking Jesus to tell him if the same brutal future awaits John.

And maybe he is. But we are probably a pot calling a kettle black if are standing in this kind of judgment of Peter.

Do we look at others and wonder why they are faring better than we? Do we spend too much time feeling indignant about unfairness? What we signed up for when we became Christians was not like the traditional game of follow the leader, in which we all line up and do what the one in front of us does. Jesus did not soft-peddle anything in Luke 14 when he talked about the cost of discipleship. He even used the hyperbole of needing to "hate" our families and yea, our own lives in order to be his disciple. He challenged us to carry crosses; and let us not forget that when you saw someone carrying a cross back then, they were on their way to die. Look at His very words: *"And anyone who does not carry his cross and follow me cannot be my disciple."* Maybe it would help us in our argument against unfairness to understand the phrase to mean *"his **own** cross."* In other words, all of our crosses will not look alike. "Never mind," He says, "Just look at *me* and follow." Act, talk, respond as I would.

We are the Light of the World, the Salt of the Earth. Heaven knows there are a lot of different kinds of lost personalities in this world caught in all kinds of different sinful situations. If Christianity were a cookie-cutter thing where we all suffered the same problems and everything was what we might call equal, how would all those different personalities find their individual ways?

It's probably not a coincidence that Jesus addressed this very thing using this very metaphor at the end of this parable about counting the cost. *"Salt is good, but if it loses its saltiness, how can it be made salty again? It is fit neither for the soil nor for the manure pile; it is thrown out"* (Luke 14:34-35.) He, of course, was saying Christians that don't act like Christ are no better than salt that doesn't act like salt. This is why we are given the Holy Spirit. It lives in each individual Christian as a Counselor to guide us. He is "the Spirit of Truth" to guide us as we look into His Word for our individual answers.

He never said it would be easy, but He did say it wouldn't last forever. If it seems a little too unfair sometimes, think of how John the Baptist must have felt when his head was being carved off for Herod's platter. Then remember Jesus' words in response to John's questions about Him, and know that He sympathizes and hopes we will trust Him: *"Blessed is the man who does not fall away on account of me" (Luke 7:23).*

~JUNE 6~
THE GENTLE INTRUDER

"Here is a trustworthy saying that deserves full acceptance: Christ Jesus came into the world to save sinners—of whom I am the worst. But for that very reason I was shown mercy so that in me, the worst of sinners, Christ Jesus might display his unlimited patience as an example for those who would believe on him and receive eternal life." 1 Timothy 1:15-16

Something I'm so familiar with; a disturbance I've felt before;
An unmistakable throbbing; it's you again at my door.
You're tapping at another window, pursuing me again.
You're reaching out your hand and asking for me to ask you in.
It's happened so many times before— Your fragrance fills one space,
And then just as we're resting comfortably there, You move to another place.
To another door of another room You entreat my invitation.
Your whisper and your eyes burn through the walls of my consecration.
I feel my complacency crumbling and my anticipation swelling,
Then you ask for my permission to venture deeper into this dwelling.

When you approached my heart that day; when your bright shadow fell
on my soul,
You could have blasted your way right in, and taken this fortress whole.
You could have beaten down every door at once, but you knew the
weakness of my kind.
So thank you, dear Father, for your patience and mercy to keep
knocking one door at a time.

God knows we need Him to take the whole fortress, for we alone are poor caretakers of any part of it. His patience in handling me gently is borne of a greater trust than I deserve, for sure. I'm sure He is tempted to jump on His horse and ride off in all directions as He looks upon the disheveled state of more than one room of this dwelling.

I would be so disheartened if He were not such a kind waiter. His Word is ever before me, yes, and in it are spelled out His desires for my life. But, is it just me, or do you notice that sometimes *some* of its words are in bold print while other times *other* words are? He sharpens my ears and eyes to a manageable number of tasks at a time. If He were to shine His glare on the whole list of His desired repairs, I would surely swoon at the burden of the task. I might just throw up my hands and quit. Maybe I should remember this when I am dealing with newborn babies in the faith.

Let us thank God for His gentle ways with us and pray that as a result, we, like Paul, can become to a dying world a display of His desire for everyone to have eternal life in Him.

~JUNE 7~
LIVING LIKE A BELIEVER

"For in the gospel a righteousness from God is revealed, a righteousness that is by faith from first to last, just as it is written: 'The righteous will live by faith.'" Romans 1:17

When the lovesick poet first penned his words "Roses are red, violets are blue. Sugar is sweet, and so are you," they were probably a very visual, even poignant way of expressing his feelings. Over time, however, the imagery has grown trite and worn out its original newness so that if one uses these words now, the recipient feels gypped. Her admirer could surely have done better if his affection were true. So it is with many words that once packed a punch. Sometimes they go in one ear and out the other without ever making a visual connection or registering any real meaning.

It's sad to think it, but it's very likely that is what has happened with the words "faith" and even "Christian." The Word of God is fraught with both of them. We memorize them and we sing about them. So many claim to be "people of faith" and "Christians."

Living by faith is no small thing, though. It goes against the grain of our nature to do this thing at a very high and consistent level. As Christians, we are called daily to do something so much harder than just surrendering to what comes naturally; we are called to live purposely *super*natural lives. We are to be demonstrations to the rest of the world of how to live in this world without falling prey to its counterfeit system of values. This takes spiritual muscles and guts. We must swim against the tide.

We must not confuse the meantime with the end time. Our lives should be lived in expectant surrender. People should look at me and say, "Your life doesn't make any sense unless there's a God." My life should bear witness to the sovereignty of God and should make sense in no other light.

We have to live outside a place where we feel comfortable. We have to do things we could not do alone. The greatest joy we'll ever know is seeing God fulfill His promises, but we tie His hands when we will not step out in faith. Playing it safe and keeping our lives predictably neat are not options if the world is to see Christ in action.

When the word "Christian" was first coined, it was used to describe those who followed Christ. That means they walked around acting and talking the way He did because they *believed* Him. Does your identity as a "Christian" mean that you are living like a *believer*?

~JUNE 8~
A PERNICIOUS ROOT

"People who want to get rich fall into temptation and a trap and into many foolish and harmful desires that plunge men into ruin and destruction. For the love of money is a root of all kinds of evil. Some people, eager for money, have wandered from the faith and pierced themselves with many griefs." 1 Timothy 6:10

Living in a world sold out to materialism and hearing praises to wealth constantly sung out on all the airways present us with all kinds of temptations. Most of us know this scripture and are aware of the dangers of money but would welcome the opportunity to fight this dragon. True, poverty, too, can bring out the foolishness in us and reveal our true mettle, but most of us don't jump into poverty with a foolhardy desire to conquer that beast the way we do with wealth.

We know that it isn't the money that is the root of evil but the *love* of money. Probably most of us think that we could have the money without the love of it that is attributed to so much evil. After all, having money seems to indicate things about us that we rightly want people to believe: we are smart, hard-working, and responsible.

But that is not all that money indicates about us. It brings with it a set of transparent curtains over our hearts, and much about our spiritual maturity can be seen through the way we handle our money.

Here are a few questions that might serve as some specific indicators of danger. Do we use our money to bless others or to indulge ourselves in the "good life?" If we choose to do the latter, does the supply change the demand? Are our "needs" constantly changing? Could the "good life" be so good that we dread leaving what we have here for a "heaven" of unknowns where we cannot take any of our wealth with us? Are we fearful of what would happen to us—where we would derive our happiness and security—if we were to lose our money? In other words, and the whole crux of the matter, are we trusting in God or trusting in our money to save us?

The way Paul describes what happens to some is so sad. He says they have "wandered from the faith." They had the faith but then somehow just wandered away from it gradually without realizing what was happening. Though I love adventure, I have very little directional sense, and so I can identify with the terror of finding myself lost when only a few minutes ago, I knew exactly where I was. Somewhere obviously I took a step too many away from all known landmarks. It isn't necessarily that we buy one too many *things* but that we look away from our true anchor— our Landmark— one too many *times*. We wander from the land of faith into a land of sight where Paul says we will be "pierced…with many griefs." Not just evil such as exorbitant spending on booze and drugs and wild living—but "grief." Leaving faith-living and entering into sight-living brings *grief*. Just as I have done after leaving the trail and getting lost all for the sake of salving my burning curiosity, we see our harmful desires for what they were and grieve that we were so foolish.

Yes, we should live by faith and not sight, but stepping out *in* faith never means stepping out *of* the faith. Whether we are rich or poor, keeping our eyes on the landmarks of the faith— generosity, humility, and trust in God— is the only way to find our way Home.

~ JUNE 9~
THE ANSWER TO THE LION

"Be self-controlled and alert. Your enemy the devil prowls around like a roaring lion looking for someone to devour. Resist him, standing firm in the faith because you know that your brothers throughout the world are undergoing the same kind of sufferings." 1 Peter 5:8-9

"For the eyes of the Lord range throughout the earth to strengthen those whose hearts are fully committed to him." 2 Chronicles 16:9

This is a war-torn country, no doubt. We are journeying through enemy terri-tory, and the Enemy's minefields are every bit as real as those in foreign countries where we send our soldiers. The evil that surrounds us is no more an accident than the evil that surrounds those soldiers who put themselves in harm's way. Things blow up unexpectedly in this battle, too, just as the cars and buildings and arsenals over there. Just as we who believe in God know that there can be no creation without a Creator, we also know that whenever something happens, there is always a *happener*. In light of our Enemy, it is imperative that we stay vigilant. We must watch and pray: watch for signs that we are aiding the Enemy, and pray for single-mindedness; watch for those who are succumbing to temptation and "snatch them from the fire and save them" (Jude 23).

But we will grow weary if we try to live this faith-life being motivated only by negatives. We cannot be a people who are so ruled by fear that we grow passively safe rather than actively faithful. Yes, there is a hungry, roaring Enemy, but remember that there is also a Sovereign Lord with ranging eyes.

I like the verb "range." Since it is more commonly used as a noun to describe both a wide-open space or an array, the verb, too, connotes vastness, both in space and variety. I see God with His great hand shading His squinting eyes from the sun as He slowly moves His head, searching from horizon to horizon over all the landscapes of the world for fully-committed hearts. He waits there with His hand

167

on the floodgate (or His finger on "Send") ready to release power to the faithful. It doesn't say that He will swoop down and annihilate or eradicate the problem or that He will deliver us to Him in a fiery chariot as He did Elijah— but that He will *strengthen* us.

He says it another way in the story of the Prodigal Son Luke 15. After a series of falls on his face due to foolish living, the son, finally "fully committed," says, "Father, I have sinned against heaven and against you. I am no longer worthy to be called your son." The Father has obviously been watching with "ranging" eyes for his son to return because we are told that he sees him "while he was still a long way off." The Prodigal Son might not be what you first pictured when you read "those whose hearts are fully committed to him," but honestly, isn't this the way most of us come to that point? Maybe we didn't run off to Babylon and take up with prostitutes or go on a drinking binge, but didn't we try to take our Father's riches and use them apart from a relationship with Him?

Aren't you glad that God arranged for us to know that the Father "filled with compassion for him, ran to his son, threw his arms around him and kissed him" and that we need not face the would-be lion without His ranging eyes and His waiting kisses?

~JUNE 10~
NEW WINESKINS

"No one sews a patch of unshrunk cloth on an old garment, for the patch will pull away from the garment, making the tear worse. Neither do men pour new wine into old wineskins. If they do, the skins will burst, the wine will run out and the wineskins will be ruined. No, they pour new wine into new wineskins, and both are preserved." Matthew 9:16-17

The way we act about rules is funny. The same person who will toe some intolerable line with unswerving consistency will bow her back and refuse to cooperate or even negotiate about some other rule that is infinitely less stringent. The difference lies in the rule-maker. If the one making the rules has already established a solid love relationship with us, we tend to trust and therefore bend to his or her desires, even if we don't fully understand. If, on the other hand, the rule is made by someone anonymous or faceless and voiceless, we are more apt to react with skepticism and even resentment or rebellion. Fear may cause the resentment or rebellion to remain masked, but it still is there to muck up the mechanism just the same. We don't normally like rules without relationship.

Jesus didn't just come to make a few little minor changes to Judaism; He came to fill the law with meaning, to impart, through faith in Him, a new kind of life that would be motivated not by following the laws, but by knowing the Law-Giver. He came down from Heaven, as part of the Trinity, to allow us to know God and to respond to His love for us. Jesus spent a lot of time on His Sermon on the Mount saying "You have heard it said, but I say…" in order to get past the externals of simply following a rule because God said so and into the meaningful depths of the *reasons* behind all these rules. The subject of love kept coming up every time He spoke anywhere. In fact, He kept telling everyone that if you could only follow two rules, you should choose to love God and your fellowman. If you did these things, everything else would take care of itself.

John's disciples came asking Him about fasting. If Jesus was trying so hard to get people to believe He was indeed the Messiah, then why weren't Jesus' disciples practicing fasting, a common trademark for all good believers? Since there were Pharisees around, maybe this is a two-layered answer- one for the sincere questioner and one for the hypocritical Pharisee who wanted to trap Jesus. His answer to John's group? Don't mindlessly follow a tradition that pays no attention to the relationship. Why fast, a sign of mourning, when Jesus was there with the disciples? Why not instead *feast* now, and then fast later when they were mourning His absence? If you cling to meaningless rules that defy belief in a love relationship, why should the world believe your Messiah is real? His answer to the Pharisees? This new Messianic order will not be so easy. It cannot be learned by rote—by just sewing on a patch or using the same old wineskin. It issues from the core of the heart. The heart must be cleansed before what comes from it can be holy. Otherwise, it is a sham.

Reformation without regeneration will not work for very long. Learning a set of rules will serve to fool a few, but without abiding in Him and being thus transformed, we cannot follow the Great Commission. We must do all it takes to get to know Jesus.

~JUNE 11~
HE RESTORES MY SOUL

"The Lord is my shepherd, I shall not want. He makes me lie down in green pastures, He leads me beside quiet waters, He restores my soul." Psalm 23:1-3

In the black velvet panoply of June,
Clouds rush past the face of the moon.
My feet tethered fast to the silent sod,
My heart throws wistful songs out to God.

Come and revive me and shine up my heart;
Wash off the dust and cleanse every part.
I stand still on your easel in the shadow of your face.
Reach down and refashion, repair, and erase.

When the sun brings tomorrow's duties and rush,
I'll draw on the peace from this reverie's hush
And see with my faith eyes your hand in bright noon
Touch my face like these clouds on the face of the moon.

We are His sheep and as such don't know all we should about how to take care of ourselves without His help. David's well known Twenty-Third Psalm starts off with the obvious needs all creatures have: food, rest, and water. Most of us can readily tell when we need food and water. Though we are a little slow sometimes to realize we need rest, our bodies, if not our minds, will usually cast the winning vote, and we will eventually lie down and rest. However, he doesn't stop there. He goes on to speak of the importance of the restoration of his *soul*. And this is where most of us really need some prodding.

We need to be mindful of our need for the revival and renewal of our faith. Without enthusiasm, our lights will grow dim and our salt will grow bland. Most of our budgets can't afford a soul-stirring odyssey to be dazzled by new vistas of God's creation, but we can go camping or lie down in the driveway on a starry night. We can go on a hike down a brand new trail or listen to some beautiful music with some good headphones. We can put out some bird seed and watch quietly as they feast. We can write a friend a long letter and share some favorite scriptures. We can sing hymns on our back porch or have a picnic on a fishing pier.

Ask God to help you get out of your rut and shine up your spirit. It always worked for David.

~JUNE 12~
PROVIDENTIAL INSOMNIA

"That night the king could not sleep; so he ordered the book of the chronicles, the record of his reign, to be brought in and read to him." Esther 6:1

"On my bed I remember you. I think of you through the watches of the night." Psalm 63:6

There is an interesting story in the book of Esther about King Xerxes. Two would-be assassins had been discovered by Mordecai the Jew, Queen Esther's former guardian, but the king had been so distracted by the antagonist Haman's requests to annihilate the Jews that Mordecai was never properly rewarded or even acknowledged by the King. Chapter two tells us that this information had merely been recorded in the book of the annals of the king. As this swiftly moving drama advances to its climax, we learn that on the night after the evil, anti-Semitic Haman had convinced the king to allow him to execute a certain offending Jew, King Xerxes was not able to sleep, and therefore, ordered that the book of the annals be brought in and read to him. He realized, after reading about the uncovering of the assassination attempt, that Mordecai had never been rewarded, and thus ended up ceremoniously honoring the very Mordecai that Haman had planned to have hanged. Ironically, Haman died on the very gallows he had constructed for Mordecai, who later was raised to high honor in the king's service. What started out as a frustrating night of sleeplessness wound up bringing about nothing less than the salvation of the Jewish nation.

Most of us suffer from sleeplessness on occasion. It could be that we have consumed too much caffeine or are too keyed up from the activities of the evening. Maybe health issues or too much sleep can explain our inability to sleep. Or perhaps, as in the case of the King of Persia, we are victims of providential insomnia. Perhaps we have fallen into the hands of God, the Lover of our Souls.

Are there those who come to mind that you need to pray for? Is there someone to whom you have outstanding debts of forgiveness that need to be brought to your otherwise too-busy mind? Does He find this the perfect time to awaken my slumbering conscience into festering about a matter that is bordering on becoming ingrown and invisible? Is this the time, with quietness and sleeping bodies all around, to set our minds to memorizing that scripture that once— a long time back— the Holy Spirit prompted us to learn? Or maybe just taking time to linger purposely in the presence of the Lord has been put on the back burner too long. Maybe this is your time to "Be still and know that [He is] God."

Whether the reason for sleep's escaping us is providential or natural doesn't need to concern us, for we know that we are welcome at God's throne anytime. The next time you find yourself staring at the ceiling or doing bed spins at 2:00 a.m., consider it His invitation into His chambers. He might have some justice issues to settle in the wee hours, as He did with Xerxes, or maybe He would just enjoy the pleasure of your company.

~JUNE 13~
WEDDING CLOTHES AND TOWERS

"Then they said, 'Come let us build ourselves a city, with a tower that reaches to the heavens, so that we make a name for ourselves and not be scattered over the face of the whole earth.'" Genesis 11:4

It wasn't enough to belong to Almighty God and to bear His name and be His people; these people wanted to "make a name for *themselves*." Thus, they began building and kept building higher and higher, believing foolishly that their earthly magnificence and might would be enough to foil even the plans of God. They were in denial of the truth of who they were and whose they were. Perhaps it was insecurity and fear, or perhaps it was conceit and vainglory, but whatever the motivation, the result was a separation from God's will for them that resulted in our loss of a common language and a common purpose.

Jesus tells us a parable in Matthew 22 about the same mistake. This time a man who has been invited to a king's wedding banquet for his son is chastised and expelled for not wearing his wedding clothes, though they likely have been provided for him by his host, since the man is invited in off the streets. Again we see someone who wants to obtain something by his own means, to take advantage of the king's munificence on his own, not the king's, conditions. We will make ourselves uncomfortable to gain admission into certain restaurants requiring formal attire— and that is so that *we* can pay for our meal! It seems pretty nervy that a guy fortunate enough to be brought in off the streets to enjoy, free of charge, a total stranger's lavish wedding feast would refuse to comply with such a simple request as to put on the proper clothing.

But before we make these stories too far removed from our own, let us take a look at the way we live. Are there certain givens that we just can't stomach? Does God require a little too much of us sometimes? I mean, does He really care if we fudge here and there about what He asks of us? Maybe some of those particulars were appropriate for there and then, but what about here and now? Does honesty mean the same as it did when all this was written? Hasn't He changed His standards by now about divorce and lying? I know He talks about cross-bearing, but isn't what He really wants just my happiness? Can homosexuality really be so wrong when so many today are embracing that lifestyle? Can the whole world be wrong?

Paul says in Acts 4:12, "Salvation is found in no one else, for there is no other name under heaven given to men by which we must be saved." It is by Jesus' name, and not one we make for ourselves, that we gain passage into the Feast. James asks "...don't you know that friendship with the world is hatred toward God? Anyone who chooses to be a friend of the world becomes an enemy of God" (James 4:4).

Do we dare take the chance that these have been updated somewhere and we have not received the memo?

~JUNE 14~
THESE TERRORS AND WONDERS

"Therefore, we do not lose heart. Though outwardly we are wasting away, yet inwardly we are being renewed day by day. For our light and momentary troubles are achieving for us an eternal glory that far outweighs them all. So we fix our eyes not on what is seen, but on what is unseen. For what is seen is temporary, but what is unseen is eternal." 2 Corinthians 4:16-18

You think this light is here to stay; your confidence is flowing.
But it will not last the day; the darkness is coming—You might as well know it.
Heavenly moments make earthly visits; we gather them to us to cherish.
But they, like we, are just pilgrims: earthly bliss was designed to perish.

All you can see is quickly dissolving; this ground is sinking fast.
Earth's sunshine is only a bright-colored shadow;
These terrors and wonders will pass,
And only investments in Heaven will last.
So grasp only loosely all you can see;
Tiptoe lightly on treacherous sod;
Hold with a death-grip to the Truth that endures.
Lean all your weight upon God.

You think your grief is here to stay; your tears in torrents are flowing,
But pain will be gone in a heartbeat; the Light is coming—
Take courage and know it!
Man's freedom brought hell to God's garden; it can mangle
and kill all we cherish.
But our days of anguish are numbered: earth's grief
was designed to perish.

All we can see is quickly dissolving; this ground is sinking fast.
Earth's sunshine is nothing but bright-colored shadow.
These terrors and wonders will pass,
And only our treasures in Heaven will last.
So grasp only loosely all you can see.
Tiptoe lightly on treacherous sod;
Hang on with a death-grip to the Truth that endures.
Lean all your weight upon God...
On the one indestructible God.

~JUNE 15~
HOLY FIRE

"And I will ask the Father, and He will give you another Counselor to be with you forever- the Spirit of Truth. The world cannot accept Him because it neither sees Him nor knows Him. But you know Him, for He lives with you and will be in you." John 14:16-17

Bush ablaze on Sinai's summit
Thunders the voice of Majesty,
Searing the life from idolatry's flesh,
And its only ashes, a covenant.

Divine Pentecostal inferno
Descends from Heaven's refinery,
Incinerating the aimless histories
Of three-thousand awestricken souls.

When Heavenly heat consumes a heart,
What's left is God's radiant candle—
A torch through night's birth canal into day—
Hot, holy hallelujahs!

Notice that everywhere Jesus speaks of His Spirit, He refers to it as a "He," not an "It." Understand this Spirit within you.

173

He leads (Matthew 4:1); He gives life (John 6:63, 2 Corinthians 3:6); He counsels (John 14:26) He fills us (Acts 4:31; 6:3; 9:17; Ephesians 5:8); He speaks to us (Acts 13:2, Revelation 2:7); He puts desires within us (Romans 8:5); He controls our minds (Romans 8:6); He testifies to our sonship in Christ (Romans 8:16); He helps us in our weakness (Romans 8:26); He reveals Gods wisdom (1 Corinthians 2:10); He is a deposit within us, guaranteeing what is to come (2 Corinthians 5:5); He produces lovely fruit (Galatians 5:22-23); He walks with us (Galatians 5:25); He can be pleased by us (Galatians 6:8); He nurtures the God-life within us (Ephesians 2:22); He grieves (Ephesians 4:30); He seals us for the day of redemption (Ephesians 4:30); He fights for us (Ephesians 6:17); He sanctifies us (2 Thessalonians 2:13); He vindicates us (1 Timothy 3:16); He inspired men to write the Scriptures (2 Peter 1:21).

And lastly, we are told in 1 Thessalonians 5:19 that He burns within us as a flame that we can either fan or smother. Paul pleads with the recipients of this letter, and thus with us, not to "put out the Spirit's fire," lest we lose that warm glow that should characterize all who follow Christ. Paul also reminds Timothy to "fan into flame the gift of God." He is asking him not to let timidity smother all God has given him to do.

Is there some way you are smothering the Spirit? Maybe it is by actively working against Him in some secret way that needs to be renounced before the spark goes out, or maybe it is by simply allowing your timidity to rule in some area where your faith should be ruling.

~JUNE 16~
GOD, THE MOTHER

"For the Lord's portion is his people, Jacob His allotted inheritance. In a desert land He found him, in a barren and howling waste. He shielded him and cared for him; He guarded him as the apple of His eye, like an eagle that stirs up its nest and hovers over its young, that spreads its wings to catch them and carries them on its pinions. He made him ride on the heights of the land and fed him with the fruit of the fields. He nourished him with honey from the rock, and with oil from the flinty crag, with curds and milk from herd and flock and with fattened lambs and goats, with choice rams of Bashan and with the finest kernels of wheat. You drank the foaming blood of the grape." Deuteronomy 32:9-14

"They made me jealous by what is no god and angered me with their worthless idols. I will make them envious by those who are not a people; I will make them angry by a nation that has no understanding...I said I would scatter them and blot out their memory from mankind, but I dreaded the taunt of the enemy, lest the adversary misunderstand and say, 'Our hand has triumphed, and the Lord has not done all this.'" Deuteronomy 32:21, 26-27

There comes a day when the Lord tells Moses that his life will soon end and commands him to teach the Israelites a song before they enter the Promised Land. They are to sing this so that it will become a lasting testimony to the generosity of their God and the unfaithfulness of their fathers and perhaps result in more faithful future generations (that's us.) Perhaps it is because God directly dictates this song to Moses that so much is revealed about the emotional side of God that is rarely seen in such concentration.

The imagery is, of course, matchless, since it flows from the very tongue of God. He begins by telling how He took to be His very children "Jacob," whose name is later changed to "Israel," and thus the name of the nation that God plants from His people. With the language of a mother with a baby He is said to have "shielded him and cared for him." He guarded Israel "as the apple of His eye." That phrase literally means "the little man of his eye," and refers to the pupil, which above all must be protected since it is the mechanism that allows for vision. God shielded his children just as we shield our eyes with protective goggles when welding. His tenderness cries out not only in His protectiveness but also in His provisions: riding "on the heights of the land"; eating "the fruit of the fields," "honey from a rock," reaping olives from rocky soil, plenty of milk and meat from the fattest herds and flocks, and a bountiful supply of bread and wine. The tender care in every aspect of their lives was unmistakable.

Therefore, when they turned away from such tenderness to cling instead to idols, God, the Father, vowed to punish them, as any good father would. But what we might fail to notice is what God, the Mother, went through. His tender heart was broken.

In this required song, God chose to reveal both sides of Himself to us. Perhaps we will more likely be moved by God if we can remember that He is moved by us.

~JUNE 17~
WAITING TO BE NAMED

"To him who overcomes …. I will also give him a white stone with a new name written on it known only to him who receives it." Revelation 2:17

Abram became Abraham, Sarai became Sarah, Jacob became Israel, and Saul became Paul. Each received a new name to indicate entrance into a new relationship with the Lord. Isaiah 62 speaks of Jerusalem receiving a new name "that the mouth of the Lord will bestow" in order to show her new status as the "crown of splendor in the Lord's hand." She would no longer be Jerusalem the captive, but Jerusalem the victor; Jerusalem the way God had always wanted her to be.

Since my first encounter with this scripture in Revelation, I have been more than just a little intrigued by it. Having been raised in a culture where most people name their children according to something as trivial as the tickling of the ear, I have always been fascinated by the Bible names which were almost always moti-

175

vated either by some character trait or some identification of ancestry or geography. It is particularly interesting when God comes along into someone's life and chooses to change his name to fit what He wants or has already seen.

I learned from my teaching years how very important names are. Every school year things were a little shaky until about Thanksgiving, when suddenly everyone began to relax and we felt at home together. Finally I figured out that the reason for the change had to do with my having at last learned well the names of all 120 of those kids who came into my classroom daily. Once I could call them by name, they apparently began to feel that we had a personal relationship. It is as though once we know someone's name, an invisible equal sign goes up behind it followed by a blank waiting to be filled in. Eventually the blank is filled with a word or a phrase that paints a picture of something deeper than the skin of what it means to be Jan, Judy, Cynthia, Dennis, or Larry.

If all this happens to us humans who can know another only as much as she allows, imagine how it must happen with God who knows every wrinkle, every heartbeat, every brainwave. Due to shyness, fear, shame, or modesty, we might succeed in hiding our true character from even those closest to us, but we can hide *nothing* from our Creator and Father. Psalm 139 describes graphically just how well He knows us. *"You know when I sit and when I rise; you perceive my thoughts from afar. You discern my going out and my lying down. You are familiar with all my ways. Before a word is on my tongue, you know it completely."* David goes on to describe how we can never hide from Him and how He formed us inside our mothers and knows how many days we will be on this earth.

Is being known something you cherish or fear? How we feel about being really, really known reveals a lot about us. There is One who knows us through and through. He knows so much more than just the name everyone else calls us. He knows exactly what goes in the blank right now. But thanks be to God, He also knows we aren't finished becoming yet. He is waiting to give us our true name. Every minute He gives us is another opportunity to become the name we hope to read on that white stone.

~JUNE 18~
A MERCIFUL SNARE

"Your rod and your staff, they comfort me." Psalm 23:4

There is some irony in this verse, but you might not see it if, in your attempt to quote the whole thing without stopping, you get caught up in the rhythm and don't think about the words. There is nothing unusual about a sheep being comforted by the shepherd's staff, for that is the instrument he uses to rescue a sheep that should slip off down a steep hillside. But the rod is used over and over in the wisdom and poetry books of the Bible to mean an instrument of punishment. Why would David say that he is comforted by the Shepherd's rod of punishment?

David would grow up to be a king who would learn how prophetic those words were. Having been prodded by lust into an adulterous relationship with Bathsheba, David goes on to commit murder in an effort to hide his guilt. He is unsuccessful at this deception, however, because God uses His rod on David, reminding him, through his prophet Nathan, that nothing escapes His eyes. As a consequence of his sin, the baby he and Bathsheba have conceived dies. David goes on to serve God so well that God names him "a man after my own heart." Psalm 51 is a beautiful and poignant testimony of David's godly remorse and true repentance after his visit with Nathan.

When I was six, I crossed a busy street alone, although my parents had warned me against doing this time and time again. When they asked me about this, I lied, not knowing about the eyewitnesses. I was caught, and the "rod" of my daddy's belt was applied straightway. I didn't think of this as a comforting thing at the time, but now I know that it was. Had I not been caught the first time, I would certainly have done it again and could have been killed as a result of slippery deceptive techniques. I also learned that lying isn't as easy to get away with as I thought, and so I was not as eager to try it again as I would have been had I not been caught. Comforting.

The same is true for David. Had God not confronted David, he would have gotten good at deception, believing that he had fooled everyone, even God. Deception is not a part of God's heart, so it is doubtful that had he practiced deception over and over he would ever have been known as "a man after God's own heart."

There is no sin as deadly as successful sin. We reap what we sow, and the more we sow seeds of sin, the "better" the harvest will be. We know that the more we practice a thing, the better we get at it. If what we are practicing is ungodliness, the sooner we are foiled, the more merciful it will be for us. In some cases, we can even begin to think that God approves, and our consciences can become seared to a very dangerous degree.

Romans 1 contains a detailed description of some who persisted in their evil ways until God finally "gave them over" to sexual impurity (v. 24), shameful lusts (v. 26), and "since they did not think it worthwhile to retain the knowledge of God, he gave them over to a depraved mind" (v.28).

It is a wise practice to ask God to reveal our sins to us, to be merciful and to comfort us with His rod, if need be, and confound us in our sins before we become lost sheep.

~JUNE 19~
HEAVEN LURES US

"So the man gave names to all the livestock, the birds of the air and all the beasts of the field. But for Adam no suitable helper was found...Then the Lord God made a woman from the rib He had taken out of the man, and He brought her to

the man. The man said, 'This is now bone of my bones and flesh of my flesh..."
Genesis 2: 20, 23

For those who have lived awhile, we know we'll never find it, but still we keep searching for it everywhere. It comes in different forms. Sometimes the vision is so defined it's almost palpable: the dream of a fairytale romance, the quest for the perfect friend, wanderlust that takes us over oceans and back, hunger and thirst for the nectar and ambrosia of the gods and goddesses. Other times it is a nebulous thing that wafts its elusive scent before our nostrils and disappears into the ethereal as quickly as it came, but we keep remembering what it was like to catch a whiff of it. We think maybe next time we will be quick enough to snatch it to ourselves and at last be satisfied. But we never are, and what's more, we never will be— at least not the "we" we are right now. You may object and hold out as proof that time you went to Switzerland or that steak you had at that new restaurant or that Christmas Eve it snowed ten inches. Yes, there *are* times that our grasp does equal our reach and reality actually does exceed expectation, but do any of these times *last*?

It seems that in the Garden, God made a point of parading all those animals He had made before Adam. Since it was Adam's responsibility to name them, He knew Adam would have to study each one carefully, and maybe that's just why He gave him that job: so that Adam would recognize his need. He would look at them all and realize that his need was not for any of these, but for something, actually some*one* higher.

And so now, we have paraded into our lives people and experiences that each seem to be an opportunity for us to ask the same question: Could he be the One? Could this be the Time? Is this, at last, that Place? But we are always eventually disappointed, and our need is highlighted. We know we must be good sports about it and be thankful for what we have, but we know it isn't ideal. We had something Higher in mind, whether we talk about it or not.

This may sound bleak and fatalistic, but it isn't meant to. Actually, it is very good news. Because we can desire it, it is there ...somewhere. Malcolm Muggeridge said, "Because of our physical hunger, we know there's bread; because of our spiritual hunger, we know there is Christ." [1] The desiring and dreaming and hungering and thirsting are not accidents or a sign that we are just inherently hard to please (well, in a way we *are*, but we were *meant* to be). It is God telling us there *is a fulfillment*. He tells us that He is a jealous God, and rightly so, unlike us when we are jealous. God knows until we love Him most, we will be settling for something other than life.

Robert Browning said, "Ah, but a man's reach should exceed his grasp, or what's a heaven for?"[2] That heavenly aroma is there to lure us to Him, to remind us of what is real, to whisper, or sometimes to *shout*, to each of us to follow our noses and soldier on. What we are made for awaits us; we are in the process of readying ourselves for it. It will take no less than a lifetime, but It will be worth every minute of it.

~JUNE 20~
THE GRAND INFILTRATION

"...go and make disciples of all nations, baptizing them in the name of the Father and of the Son and of the Holy Spirit, and teaching them to obey everything I have commanded you." Matthew 28:19

They had been with Him for three years, watching Him like hawks, clinging to Him doggedly, sometimes even to the point of trying to talk Him out of the climax of His very purpose for being here. He was their Rabbi, and this ragtag group of unlikelies couldn't get enough of Him. Then He had been taken and killed—just like that. His capture and execution had been ridiculously easy— like taking candy from a baby. Some dark hours followed before they saw Him again, back from the grave, ready this time to prepare them for their true purpose at last: the Grand Infiltration. They would go out into the world—all of them and those they would infect— as new Christs.

This was His Great Commission. This was the one that told them and us how to carry on here in the absence of His physical presence. (Of course, He made it quite clear before He left the first time that we would not be left Fatherless, as orphans. He would impart to us to live in us His Spirit that would guide, counsel, and comfort.) But it wasn't just a casual parting statement telling them to be good and not get into trouble. What He said we must do is not just to live morally, but to live *interpretatively*.

First of all, we must *be* His devoted disciples, just as those who followed Him around hanging on His every word. Well, yes, it will necessarily look a little different without a flesh and blood Rabbi leaving actual footprints for us to follow on the path. Still, we must determine to walk as He would walk, and this will take a lot of *study* of how He walked. Are we studying Him closely enough to know how that looks? It will look different from the way the rest of the crowd walks for sure, just as it did when He was here. Those footsteps will enter into places most will not. They will veer off the beaten path to linger awhile with unsavory women at wells and short tax collectors who must be called down from trees. They will start early or come in late in order to leave the masses of other footprints and blaze a trail alone to some place of solitude to spend with the Father. They will fall to their knees for help as they enter the valley of death, and then they will not flee when the soldiers come. This is no less than what it means to be a disciple, and no less than what we are to be when we teach others. We must live interpretive lives for the sake of those we teach and baptize and teach (notice that there is teaching both before and after baptism in this scripture).

And then we must make *disciples*. Most of the time I fear I blend in a little too much to be doing this thing right. I know I must be out in the world and approach others in a way as not to scare them off when they see me coming. But then, somehow, they must see in me this radically different way of viewing and living life. They must find in me a capacity to love deeply with a heart that is hardy but never hard, with the tenderness to be hurt but not to shrink away from pain as though the wounds are mortal. They must notice that I am energized by a hope that hangs on through what others might call disasters. And my hope must be strong enough to be contagious. I somehow must really look like a "little Christ."

~JUNE 21~
EXTINGUISHING THE FLAMING ARROWS:
ME ACCORDING TO THE TRUTH

"Do not conform any longer to the pattern of this world, but be transformed by the renewing of your mind. Then you will be able to test and approve what God's will is—His good, pleasing and perfect will." Romans 12:2

"...take up the shield of faith, with which you can extinguish all the flaming arrows of the evil one." Ephesians 6:16

We are told in Romans to *be transformed.* This is a passive verb form, and thus means that the subject is being acted *upon* rather than *doing* the action himself. It could be a frustrating thing to need something as much as we need transformation and find that it can only happen if we are acted upon— if we are the *do-ee,* rather than the *do-er.* But then in the very next phrase we are told how— by the *"renewing of our minds."* So if we can find the right way to renew our minds, we can be transformed. According to the context, it has something to do with not conforming to the standards, the morality (or lack thereof), of the physical world all around us, the one we can see with our natural eyes. When we try really hard to do this— to buck the ways of the world—we find that the world is not an easy thing to throw off our backs. He is a tenacious rider who wraps his legs around our belly, hangs on with a vice grip to the saddle horn, and with the determination of fire ants and cockroaches, wills to break us. It is so hard that it feels like something almost *alive* is fighting back.

In fact, this stubborn rider, this something that is fighting back really *is* alive. It is our Enemy, Satan, who has not only set out to tame us when we try to throw him off, but shoots "flaming arrows" at us. We learn in Ephesians about the importance of our wearing God's armor to be able to stand against his "schemes." The arrows in his quiver are many and varied, but all are shot from the taut bowstring of a lie. We are being lied to. He comes peddling lies to us hoping to undermine our determination to fight back. Some lies are more treacherously camouflaged than others. One of his favorite surely must be the one about what we will lose if we turn to Christ, or for those who already have, if we draw near enough to let Him have our whole vessel.

It seems that most of us proudly believe that we have a "Self" worth saving. We talk of *our* dreams, *our* desires, *our* philosophies, *our* tastes as though we ingeniously made these choices, much like an artist would choose his brushes and colors, to come up with this masterpiece, Self. Maybe we fear that if we sell out to become Christian, or *more* Christian, we will lose our unique identity and take on a cookie-cutter personality. But really, this is far from the truth. When we are abiding in the world, rather than in Christ, we are simply a by-product, a shadow, an echo, a mimicry of what we have heard and seen. The more sold out to the world, the more people become *alike*, not different. Whereas, because we serve such a multi-faceted God, when we give over ourselves to become "little Christs," then we get a *real* personality. It is then, in fact, when we become more who we *really* are than ever before. It is only then that I become me according to the *truth*, rather than me according to the *lie*.

~JUNE 22~
THE CURRENCY OF LOVE

"… where your treasure is, there your heart will be also." Matthew 6:20-21

"Be still and know that I am God." Psalm 46:10

"…his delight is in the law of the Lord, and on it he meditates day and night." Psalm 1:2

What we sometimes spend in order to show our love is money; everyone enjoys gift-giving, and I'm for it as much as the next person. However, gifts bought with money can be suspect: is this because I bought her something? Is this something they already had and didn't want anymore? Am I receiving this because he thinks buying a gift is the right thing to do? And the saddest question of all: is he giving me this as a substitute for giving me something costlier? And sometimes it's true that what we can best "afford" to give is our money.

The "something else" the person asking this question usually wants is *time*. Just as the coin of perfection is practice; the coin of love is time. There is nothing that better reveals our love and dedication, nothing that is so telling of our devotion as the amount of time we give. Money well spent on a loved one can be seen as a wise and unselfish investment, but if the investment falls through, it is always possible that we can earn the money back that we "lost." Not so with our time. Except once a year in the fall when we go off Daylight Savings Time, there is no getting back the time we spend. We make the choice of how to spend this coin knowing that we will never get this chunk back. The clock is unforgiving. And that is why our time is the most unselfish and extravagant gift we can give.

Most Christian parents know the value of spending time with their children. We know that even though sometimes the kids might think they prefer a life of back-to-back excursions to Disneyworld and the like, those who get their wish sooner or later long for what they lost out on to get it: their parents' undivided attention. Wise parents understand the folly of making their kids experience-rich and relationship-poor. Roller-coasters and water slides are a sorry substitute for listening ears, adoring eyes, and soft shoulders. Our children are our treasures, and we want them to know that they have our hearts, not just our money. We wanted the same thing from our parents, didn't we?

What is perplexing is that this thing that the marriage of love and wisdom has taught us about our children escapes us when it comes to our relationship with our greatest Treasure. Jesus told us that the greatest commandment was to "love the Lord your God with all your heart and with all your soul and with all your mind and with all your strength" (Mark 12:30). How protective are we of the time we spend with our Lord? So many answer with an apology about busy schedules. Although many times the busy-ness is worthwhile and attempts to make a good case for time spent "with God," it isn't the kind we, as kids, wanted from our parents or the kind we are content to give to our own children. It lacks stillness; it lacks gazing; it lacks separation from the world which clamors for our attention. It is for this very clamoring world that we need to be reflections of Him, but, alas, turbulent waters cast a poor reflection.

~JUNE 23~
DISAPPEARING INTO CHRIST

"Do nothing out of selfish ambition or vain conceit, but in humility consider others better than yourselves." Philippians 2:3

Humility is the glue that holds the church together. Where it is absent and pride abounds, even with the fattest budget and the finest equipment, our plans founder and growth is stunted. Pride keeps us in the devil's back pocket. Where humility is present, much is accomplished even against all practical odds. Humble spirits work together for the glory of God without caring who gets the credit. The absence of the spirit of competition in places where competition is clearly inappropriate leaves room for God to move in ways He cannot move when crowded out by power struggles and one-upmanship.

Paul's short letter to the Philippians is usually remembered for its strong emphasis on joy. He says that one of the ways this church can make his joy complete is by "being one in spirit and purpose." He knows that a church that works together in humility and unselfishness will receive a great deal of joy, too. And what works for the church in this area works for all Christian relationships. The family who is led by a humble and unselfish man will likely reap great harvests in God's kingdom and find rare joy.

Wise parents begin early praying for a Christian mate for their children. We know that the spouse our child ends up with will be the single most influential person in his or her future. Should they fall in love with and decide to marry a secular-minded person, your children's struggle for godliness will be much harder than if they marry Christians. When we began praying for the man God was preparing for our little girl, we visualized one who would cherish and take care of her, one who would be a tender and wise father and would always have in sharp focus their souls' journey to an eternal home with God.

Our prayers were answered with even more than we knew how to ask for in our son-in-law, Jeremy. He is one of those quiet men whose life clearly explains to the world what God had in mind when He spoke so often in His word of the far-reaching benefits of humility and unselfish service. Being a coach, Jeremy knows well the meaning of competition, but he also knows where it is to stop in order that Christ be glorified. The service he renders to his family, friends, and church is inspirational without being sensational. Rather than drawing attention to himself and manipulating others' gratitude and appreciation, he comes closer to *disappearing* so that only his good works remain as a testimony that he was there. His is one of those beautiful lives that doesn't make sense by the world's standards. Some might wonder what's in it for him that he will work so hard for others. Much of his life doesn't make sense if there isn't a God.

Such is the spirit of true humility. It is a stepping away from instant gratification for something better. It is a choice that can develop into a good habit about which those who do not yet know Christ will scratch their heads. There will always be some who ridicule it as foolishness, but there will be others who recognize it as an unmistakable hallmark of Christ. *"Submit to one another out of reverence to Christ."* *Ephesians 5:21*

~JUNE 24~
DYING TO LIVE

"Or don't you know that all of us who were baptized into Christ Jesus were baptized into His death? We were therefore buried with Him through baptism into his death in order that, just as Christ was raised from the dead through the glory of the Father, we too may live a new life." *Romans 6:3-4*

Denominational lines are drawn at this point so many times. We *love* each other, we even *like* each other, we *feel* united, but then when we begin talking about how salvation occurs, we realize that, even though we claim to be in the same book, we are not on the same page.

Of course the obvious answer to this problem is that we need to be on *all* the pages. Just as a trial must look at all the testimony before the verdict is reached, so must we when we are seeking God's will as revealed through His Word. Taking bits and pieces from here and there won't do; all the bits and pieces must been seen together before we have a true picture. Doug Groothius makes a startlingly obvious point: "Everyone may be entitled to his own opinion, but everyone is not entitled to his own truth."[3] Unlike the world, Christians believe there is absolute truth, and that truth is found in Jesus.

Are there many ways to be saved? Can we choose our own philosophy about this according to the way we analyze God? Do we have the luxury of our own opinion when it comes to The Truth? One thing we know: the Word will lead us into all truth.

183

In John 18:37 Jesus says that He came into the world to testify to the truth. He adds, "Everyone on the side of truth listens to me."

Ephesians 2:8-9 reads *"For it is by grace you have been saved through faith—and this not from yourselves, it is the gift of God—not by works, so that no one can boast. For we are God's workmanship created in Christ Jesus to do good works which God prepared in advance for us to do."* First Peter 1:21 compares the water of the flood that washed away wickedness while holding afloat the saving ark to the waters of baptism that wash away sin: *"In it [the ark] only a few people, eight in all, were saved through water, and this water now symbolizes baptism that now saves you also— not the removal of dirt from the body but a pledge of a good conscience toward God. It saves you by the resurrection of Jesus Christ..."*

In studying the whole and not just a part, we see that God's grace saves us when we live by faith. We also see that the point at which the grace is applied and our sins forgiven is at the death and burial of the old man and the resurrection of the new man raised to "live a new life." We just can't divorce one part of the truth from the other part and call it the whole truth. Why would we want to settle for half-truths when we have access to all of it? Agreeing that there is life in Christ is only half the truth; the other half is that death must come first.

~JUNE 25~
THE CAUSE AND EFFECT OF REPENTANCE
PART ONE

"'Therefore, let all Israel be assured of this: God has made this Jesus, whom you crucified, both Lord and Christ.' When the people heard this, they were cut to the heart and said to Peter and the other apostles, 'Brothers, what shall we do?' Peter replied, 'Repent and be baptized, every one of you, in the name of Jesus Christ for the forgiveness of your sins. And you will receive the gift of the Holy Spirit'...Those who accepted his message were baptized and about three thousand were added to their number that day." Acts 2:36-38, 41

Somehow the role of baptism has grown into a controversial issue though its importance is hard to deny considering that some of the last words the Bible records Jesus speaking on earth were about it: *"Therefore, go and make disciples of all nations, baptizing them in the name of the Father and of the Son and of the Holy Spirit, and teaching them to obey everything I have commanded you"* (Matthew 28:19); *"Go into all the world and preach the good news to all creation. Whoever believes and is baptized will be saved, but whoever does not believe will be condemned"* (Mark 16:16). All of Christendom calls these words "The Great Commission." Most will admit that baptism is indeed "important," but unless we look at the whole testimony concerning it, we are likely to miss the truth about its real function. We will believe *more* or *less* about it than we should, and neither will be the whole truth.

Before hearing or reading the truth about who Jesus is and what He came here to do, we are people inhabited by hearts that live pretty much by sight alone. We operate in a practical, down-to-earth, self-protective mode that doesn't allow for the reality of something as ephemeral as spirituality. We think that what we see is real, and that what we can't see is, at very best, suspect, and at worst, imaginary. But when the Good Seed is dropped on willing and fallow soil, these hearts relinquish the dry, hard husk of self-survival, and the pulsating, vulnerable heart that God created in us is exposed. The seed of faith begins to grow, and now we can have a living hope in the strength and wisdom of Someone greater than ourselves. As when we fall in love, we are changed. *Faith is what changes the heart.*

This realization of what true Reality is and this new belief that God, His Son, and His ways are superior to us and ours is called repentance. We turn from that kind of thinking that elevates us above Him and instant gratification above an eternal viewpoint and begin to "demolish arguments and every pretension that sets itself up against the knowledge of God," and "we take captive every thought to make it obedient to Christ" (2 Corinthians 10:5). *Repentance is what changes the life.* It is much like becoming engaged to be married in that we realize that our kind of freedom will no longer satisfy and nourish us; we are ready to commit to One and Only One.

~JUNE 26~
THE CAUSE AND EFFECT OF REPENTANCE
PART TWO

"When the people heard this, they were cut to the heart and said to Peter and the other apostles, 'Brothers, what shall we do?' Peter replied, 'Repent and be baptized, every one of you, for the forgiveness of your sins. And you will receive the gift of the Holy Spirit.... With many other words he warned them; and he pleaded with them, 'Save yourselves from this corrupt generation.' Those who accepted his message were baptized, and about three thousand were added to their number that day." Acts 2:38, 40-41

Any girl with an engagement ring on her finger will tell you that this is not a satisfactory stopping point for her relationship with her beloved. She looks forward to the marriage that this engagement foreshadows. She is not yet really his, and as wonderful as the proposal was, the real celebration still lies ahead. *The wedding is when the relationship changes;* it is at that point that what she feels and desires realizes its fruition. Until that day— in fact, until a certain *moment* of that day that can be recorded on a clock— she is not married. For the rest of her life, when you ask her when she became his Mrs., she will be able to tell you the day and the hour.

This is the way it happened in the book of Acts over and over again. They were "cut to the heart" and asked "what shall we do?" Like them, we respond by obeying the command of the Great Commission: we surrender to baptism, the death and burial of the old self and the resurrection of the new. We are "dead to sin but alive to God in Christ Jesus" (Romans 6:11). We have put on Christ; we are "clothed" in Christ (Galatians 3:27). Now, with our sins washed away and His Spirit dwelling within us, we are added to His body, the church. *Baptism changes the relationship*. Now we are married. When asked later on when we became a Christian, we will not need to shrug and answer in some fuzzy historical terms. It is our new birthday.

And is it really so strange that upon our entering into the most important covenant relationship of our lives—ours with God— that He would arrange for a *sign* of that covenant? God has always been so very visual with us. The trees of Life and of the Knowledge of Good and Evil, the rainbow, altars of remembrance (Ebenezers), the Ark of the Covenant, circumcision of all Jews, and the Lord's Supper that recalls for us the Passover were all *His* ideas. They are solid and visual and often even tangible. He does not leave our memories to chance abstraction; He is concrete.

So there is faith, repentance, and baptism. The first means little without the second. But the second cannot be maintained for long without the third, an actual change in the relationship. The first says our hearts are changed. The second says our lives are changed. The third says we will, in fact, die to our old life. It brings about forgiveness of our sins and ushers us into the kingdom, a covenant relationship. Like the wedding, it seals the relationship change.

It is the beautiful consummation of supreme love.

~JUNE 27~
EXTRA EFFORT TOWARD THE BOND OF PEACE

"Make every effort to keep the unity of the Spirit through the bond of peace."
Ephesians 4:3

The importance of a spirit of peace between brothers and sisters cannot be overemphasized. (Of course there are exceptions when to be at peace with man is to be in rebellion against God, and then we must stand firm at all costs rather than to trash Truth just so everyone can "get along.") But the rule in scripture after scripture is to make every effort to maintain this blessed bond of peace that Christians so need in order to build up the Body.

One of the deadliest deterrents to the maintenance of this bond is miscommunication. James emphasized the importance of listening well, thinking before we speak, and bridling the tongue. But sometimes, miscommunication arises for other problems with our tongues. Sometimes we don't say *enough*. Sometimes we don't *ask* enough.

Years ago I shared with my friend my inability to understand why she seemed to change so often in her feelings for me. Some days she was warm and lingered, obviously desiring my company, while a few days later she seemed cooler and more hurried. I honestly was skeptical that she was just fickle, and I worried about trusting her. Her explanation was that her love for me was "plaid." I wished I had never asked; by my interpretation, her answer was more painful than my wondering. The picture I conjured of plaid was an area of *something* followed by an area of *nothing*. I wanted her to love me *all* the time, as I loved her, not just *sometimes!* Our friendship remained strong, and she seemed as intent upon maintaining it as I was. Still some sadness would surface when I would remember that her love was only "plaid," not solid. Rather than discussing it, though, I took this as a heavenly lesson in humility.

Then one day, *six years later,* I laughingly referred to her "plaid" kind of love for me, and she knitted her brow, squinted her eyes, and made it known that the context in which I spoke of that was nowhere *close* to what she had meant! She eagerly explained to me that to her "plaid" meant different *colors* placed side by side covering an *entire* area. "Hmmm," I thought. "I guess that *is* a pretty accurate description of plaid." She explained that it was all about the different *ways* she loved me and needed our friendship— sometimes face-to-face in a *dancing* way and other busier times, side-by-side in a *marching* way; sometimes brilliantly and sometimes softly, *like plaid.*

All those years, I had misjudged my friend's affection for me; and, all those years, I had needlessly battled heartache. If only I had asked her *six years earlier* to better explain her figure of speech! If only I hadn't jumped to conclusions!

Is there something that still haunts you? Perhaps a bond that should be strong and encouraging is suffering simply because of an underdeveloped explanation or an unasked question.: "What do you mean?" Don't let your silence rob you of another dance.

~JUNE 28~
THE PURPOSE OF TRUTH

"...make every effort to add to your faith goodness; and to goodness, knowledge; and to knowledge, self-control; and to self-control, perseverance; and to perseverance, godliness; and to godliness, brotherly kindness; and to brotherly kindness, love. For if you possess these qualities in increasing measure, they will keep you from being ineffective and unproductive in your knowledge of our Lord Jesus Christ." 2 Peter 1:5-8

"Who is wise and understanding among you? Let him show it by his good life, by deeds done in the humility that comes from wisdom." James 3:13

When we have finally progressed from seeking to become experts about only worldly things to pouring ourselves into God's Word in order to learn *real* Truth, there awaits yet another possible snare: misunderstanding what we are to *do* with this Truth.

We can easily become so excited about all the Bible is teaching us that if we are not very careful and prayerful, our new knowledge can go to our heads and *stay* there rather than finishing its trip to our heart and thus changing our lives. Having much knowledge stored up in our heads without a life of godliness to match is a subtle, yet sinister, type of spiritual pride.

Truth is for more than just argument. We need to listen to the way we respond to others who don't see eye-to-eye with us. Especially dangerous are the topics we have studied diligently, for we might be tempted to re-route the focus on a lovingly entreating Savior to our expertise. The would-be Bible study can turn into a prideful match of the wits that contradicts everything about truly following our Rabbi and making disciples as He told us to do in the Great Commission.

Truth is for changing lives. Once we get a thing in our heads— especially when that Thing is God's Word— it should not just wait there in storage for the right time to use it against someone else. (What a vicious armory such knowledge can be!) The Truth needs to saturate us so that it is *lived* out rather than just *spoken* out. Without our attempting to live the things we teach and preach, we have no real understanding of the difficult struggle against the flesh that we are asking others to undertake. This empathy is vital; it was for this that Jesus was sent to live among us.

The key to this challenge, as with everything else about Christianity, seems to be humility. Pride would have us boastfully proclaim our victory to the lost; humility would have us come alongside, take her hand, and guide her through the minefield. Pride would have us win the argument; humility asks us to save the soul. Pride makes us a strict and heartless taskmaster; humility restrains us by calling us to a remembrance of our lostness; it holds out hope and offers second chances.

Jesus once told some new followers that if they would "hold to" what He taught them, then they would know the truth that would free them. He was telling them and us that Truth doesn't set us free just by "knowing" it but by doing it. Empty-headed or brilliant, we are still behind bars until our knowledge is *visible*, not just audible.

~JUNE 29~
HOW TO BE TRANSFORMED

"Do not conform any longer to the pattern of this world, but be transformed by the renewing of your mind. Then you will be able to test and approve what God's will is—His good, pleasing and perfect will." Romans 12:2

All it takes to be transformed is a renewing of the mind. Now, if we can just figure out how to renew our minds, we'll have it made. We know that what Paul states so succinctly is anything but easy and natural. It is a defiance of gravity. We are helped some by what He tells us in 2 Corinthians 10:5: "We demolish arguments and every pretension that sets itself up against the knowledge of God, and *we take every thought captive to make it obedient to Christ.*" We must somehow learn how to look *way out there* at what we are *about* to start dwelling on and decide if it is worthy of a vessel for Christ before we let it enter. But many times, either because of a fast-paced life which lacks enough introspection or because of naïveté to all the wiles of the Enemy, we can't see that far ahead. We aren't in touch with where we are heading; we're just trying to get through the day. Sometimes we don't even stop to see if where we've been was good territory, so we aren't all that careful not to travel the same path again.

Another hard thing about transformation is that it never gets fully finished! This is not a destination we ever reach this side of Heaven. *"And we, who with unveiled faces all reflect the Lord's glory, are being transformed into His likeness with ever-increasing glory, which comes from the Lord, who is the Spirit"* 2 Corinthians 3:18. We are supposed to reflect God's glory for people on earth to witness better and better the longer we know Him. All of us who have turned to the Lord have had the "veil" removed that once covered our eyes and hearts; therefore, we *should* be able to see Christ with our spiritual eyes and have hearts to *live* out His message, rather than just *speaking* it out. Still, the world crowds in on us so thickly and so constantly that even if we have been *somewhat* transformed somewhere back there in our past, the process hasn't continued. Often Christians look back to take a measurement of spiritual growth and find that they are either treading water or sinking a little below the surface rather than moving closer to the shore. The transformation from one degree of glory to another has been stunted into a past-tense experience that happened one time and then ended, rather than a present-perfect situation that had a definite beginning but is still not finished.

If your sanctification has dissolved into dissipation, take heart; there is something you can do to help change your pattern. Remember that the more we are with God, the more we look like Him. Purposely arrange for regular times for renewal. This intense kind of gazing upon the Lord and speaking honestly with Him will require solitude. In these times of solitude, pray to have your sins revealed. Agree with God that these sins are working against your becoming all He wants you to be. Just let Him know that you agree that He is right and you are wrong. Apply His Word specifically to your needs.

You can assure the family you are "deserting" for a while that their sacrifice will be worth it because you will come back looking more like God.

~JUNE 30~
"A FULL UNDERSTANDING OF EVERY GOOD THING"

"I pray that you may be active in sharing your faith, so that you will have a full understanding of every good thing we have in Christ." Philemon 1:6

Read this scripture again. Does anything about the last part strike you as odd? I think most would have said it this way: "I pray that you may be active in sharing your faith *because* you have a full understanding of every good thing we have in Christ." Not Paul. He wants them to share their faith *so that* they will have this full understanding of "every good thing we have in Christ." In his view, the understanding is the *effect* of their sharing, not the cause. What might Paul be suggesting to Philemon here? What are some of these "good things" he's talking about?

Anyone who has shared his or her faith with very many others has a pretty good idea about at least part of this question. We see God at work when we share our faith. Although it is true that each person we speak to about Jesus may either accept or reject Him, if we keep at it with the heart of a learner as well as a teacher, we will certainly see how God moves in us and through us in some very surprising and unexpected ways. We will see Him show up to sit beside us as we teach the "hard" ones, the unlikely ones who have wasted their lives on selfish and foolish pursuits. Many times— most, in my experience— we will get to watch Him miraculously peel away their worldly vision and give them new, spiritual eyes that can see their emptiness and His fullness. We will get to hear the voice of the Holy Spirit whisper at just the right time a scripture— or four, or twelve— that, by persistent repetition, we "hid in [our] heart[s]" all those years ago but haven't thought about since. We will see Jesus make Himself crystal clear in His parables to these whom the "wiser," and more sophisticated have given up on although they, themselves, can't make any sense of a pearl of great price or a mustard seed, new wineskins, and lights on a hill. These inside views of God at work serve to bolster our faith in an "unseen" but very alive Power and weaken our dependence upon ourselves. This is a "good thing" because there are too many different kinds of people for any one human to know just what approach to take and which words to use for every single one. In fact, until we have some of these faith-sharing experiences under our belts, we are likely to vacillate between the extremes of terror and conceit. When we give up on our expertise and trust God to use us as a vessel He fills daily, then we begin to experience the *joys* of sharing the Lord. This joy is definitely one of those "good things."

Another "good thing" is the people we come to love that we would have never guessed we could have. We meet and learn about people from completely different worlds from ours. We get educated about problems and viewpoints that better equip us to help ourselves and others. My heart delights in some of the friendships that have come as a result of sharing my faith with "unlikely" candidates. I understand better now what Jesus meant by tenderly befriending some of those He befriended and soundly berating some others who seemed more "likely."

And this is just a *partial* understanding of *some* of the good things!

~JULY 1~
CHOOSING WHAT WE WEAR

"Therefore, as God's chosen people, holy and dearly loved, clothe yourselves with compassion, kindness, humility, gentleness and patience. Bear with each other and forgive whatever grievances you may have against one another. Forgive as

the Lord forgave you. And over all these virtues put on love, which binds them all together in perfect unity." Colossians 3:12-14

Paul is giving the Colossians some rules for living holy lives. His basic premise for these expectations is "Since, then, you have been raised with Christ, set your hearts on things above, where Christ is seated at the right hand of God. Set your minds on things above, not on earthly things" (Colossians 3:1-2). As a result of their now being "hidden with Christ" (v.3), they are to quit nourishing and nurturing the old earthly nature, to resist wrapping themselves in the old rags of degeneracy and rather to "put on the new self, which is being renewed in knowledge in the image of its Creator" (v. 10).

What he is asking them to do, in effect, is to reject one "reality" in favor of a new one. Where do we get our view of what is real and true? Don't we get these mainly from what we expose ourselves to most? If we don't energetically and purposely *choose* to follow the real Leader, life will take us by the tail and pull us day by day by a kind of gravity that after years becomes part of our substance. What *others* have decided, then, has become *our* lives. After years of letting life happen to us, like pinballs that are bounced off one wall onto another, we are still "infants tossed back and forth by the waves, and blown here and there by every wind of teaching and by the cunning and craftiness of men in their deceitful scheming" (Ephesians 4:14).

What might be "natural" every day is to stay in our pajamas or to climb back into the same clothes from yesterday that we left on the floor beside the bed last night. But most of us realize that is an instinct that we must fight, so dragging ourselves out of our sleep clothes and kicking our dirty ones aside, we go to the trouble to choose something clean, presentable, and appropriate to wrap up in for the day.

Paul pleads with us to take charge in choosing our clothing every day rather than letting slothfulness dress us. The discipline we muster up for our physical body's sake must be applied even more so to our spiritual being. *This* is the body that goes forth not just to appease or please the eyes and nostrils of those we will encounter today, but to call the dying lost out of the darkness into the Light of Hope. Look at the list again: compassion, kindness, humility, gentleness, patience, forbearance, forgiveness. He challenges us to defy gravity and do what might *not* come naturally until from habitual practice, something better comes more naturally. And then in a separate sentence, he admonishes us to put *over* these, somewhat like an overcoat of extra warmth and protection, *love*. This is sometimes the hardest for us to do by command because it seems too basic a thing for us to control. But it isn't if we give the control of it over to God, who is, Himself, love. When I am most at a loss as to how to deal with people's quirks, lifestyles, habits, and annoyances, I find that praying to *love* them does wonders.

~JULY 2~
TO KISS THE UGLY

"Above all, love each other deeply, because love covers over a multitude of sins."
1 Peter 4:8

"...whatever you did for one of the least of these, you did for me." Matthew
25:40

When our oldest granddaughter was only two, she interrupted the prayer at our Thanksgiving table to correct the adult praying. Normally a quiet and compliant child, she shocked all of us by announcing with the boldness and authority of an old-time prophet of God: "When we pray, we say 'Our Father.'" None of us knew where she got these instructions, but it served as a foreshadowing of the spiritual heart growing inside this little girl.

Another instance when Allison surprised us with her view into the Heavenlies was one that we at first saw as just plain funny. I had some of those ugly fake teeth that I liked to pop in stealthily at just the opportune time to catch everyone off guard, preferably in public. With a very straight face, my voice and general demeanor suddenly conformed to these very homely and unsightly teeth. My friends and family always responded with embarrassment, begging and threatening me to take those things out NOW, while strangers either stared in open-mouthed horror or broke out in snorting laughter behind their hands. But the first time I did this with Allison around, rather than responding in any of these ways, she did something totally unexpected: she looked at me with big, sad brown eyes of compassion and leaned right over and *kissed* me on my grotesquely uninviting mouth! We thought it was so cute that we went through this ritual with her over and over to see if she would do it again and again. And yes, she would.

But it didn't seem like a funny game to her at all, and I decided that she was not savvy to our manipulating this cute response from her. She was simply responding to someone who looked like she could use a little love. The more we watched her as she grew up, the more sure we were that this was the case, even at such an early age.

Some say that babies come straight from God and that is why they are so precious and loveable. I don't know. But if this is true, it's a shame how as we grow older, most of us lose our grasp of compassion. The very fact that we considered it *funny* that she would kiss something that looked like that tells you *something*. With most of us, the uglier it is, the less we want to do with it. If we can stand at a distance, we will. We might find some other way to help, but to snuggle up with repulsiveness is not high on our list of 'druthers. Why do we unlearn this much needed grace, and can we possibly reteach ourselves?

Jesus touched lepers and women with lifelong issues of blood; he fraternized with prostitutes and washed people's feet. He was not put off by superficial dirt but called those who looked clean and together on the outside "whitewashed tombs." Jesus showed us how to do it and called us to follow Him.

Yes, with a realization of our reluctance, a penitent heart, and prayer, we can once again become as little children.

~JULY 3~
A HEART FOR THE TASK

"Whatever you do, work at it with all your heart..." Colossians 3:23

"Delight yourself in the Lord, and He will give you the desires of your heart." Psalm 37:4

It is a brisk autumn day full of bright yellow sunshine adorning a deep blue West Texas sky. I write this having just finished an invigorating motor scooter ride down a country road near the ranch house where I have secluded myself to write. On my way back inside from feeding the cows, my curiosity pulled me to drag out the old scooter lying on its side and try my hand at reviving it. After messing ignorantly with this knob and that switch, kicking this lever, and turning this crank, much to my delight, it puttered to life, and away I cruised. It was exhilarating! As I came back to my writing table, I bowed my head and thanked God for helping me start that old scooter.

Giving thanks for something like this might seem inappropriate, for certainly taking a motor scooter ride is not a dire need or anything I couldn't have lived without. There are days in my life that are lived well and productively without any thrills or wildness to punctuate their predictability (...but I have to admit to you, there are not *many*!) Still, to me it is not only *appropriate* to give thanks for fun but nothing less than *vital* that I do so. I know the importance of a heart that knows what it means to be thrilled.

Having fun is for so much more than just having fun. We know that choosing deliberately to clothe ourselves in all those Christian characteristics that we read about in Colossians is crucial if we are to waylay the gravity of sloth and worldliness. And even though in time they will grow into more natural and unforced graces, there will always be some of these callings that are harder for us than others. There is no denying that we were not put here primarily for fun, or Jesus would not have used the picture of heading off to die when He told us to "take up our crosses and follow Him."

But there are many Christian duties that, even though our sighs might indicate differently, we know good and well they don't require anything *close* to death. They are the woof and warp, the everyday staples of productive Christian living. We *do* them all right, but often we do them as Shakespeare described the young boy: "creeping like snail unwillingly to school."[1] What if we could somehow learn to think of these tasks as *fun*? What if we could learn to throw our *hearts* behind them and not just our *wills*? It can happen. I have watched it happen in others, and

I'm beginning to experience it myself. Take Psalm 37:4 as God's literal promise to you.

What I am suggesting today is this: As you go down your prayer list, rather than just praying for their health and safety or wisdom in making decisions, pray that God will give those you love a *heart* for the work He would have them do. Pray that they will learn to *love* what God calls them to do rather than tolerate it with a sigh.

I'm going to pray for my loved ones to *enjoy* this day in God's vineyard as much as I enjoyed my motor scooter ride in the country.

~JULY 4~
LESSONS FROM PROVERBS

"Trust in the Lord with all your heart, and lean not on your own understanding; in all your ways, acknowledge Him, and He will make your paths straight." Proverbs 3:5-6

Proverbs has thirty-one chapters, just the perfect number for reading one every day of every month. By the end of the year, you will have read this whole book of wisdom twelve times. Here is a sampling of its lessons:

1. *Don't be a sluggard; take the initiative.*

2. *Distinguish between "fake" riches and true wealth.*

3. *Avoid sexual sin. Don't underestimate the strength of this temptation and its consequences.*

4. *Choose a mate carefully; marriage is for a lifetime. Once you are in one, work always to strengthen it.*

5. *Parent wisely. Bring up your children in the Lord. Discipline them, for the impact continues for generations.*

6. *Use wisdom in relationships. Choose your friends wisely.*

7. *Control your tongue. Don't underestimate the harm it can cause.*

8. *Control your emotions, especially anger.*

9. *What seems right isn't always. Get true understanding from God's Word.*

10. *Guard your heart, for from it springs the kind of life you will live.*

11. *Be generous. A selfish man will fall while a generous man will be lifted up.*

12. *Overlook insults. Only a fool shows his annoyance immediately.*

13. *Commit to the Lord whatever you do. If you can't in good conscience involve God in it, don't do it.*

14. *Give gentle answers if you desire to diffuse anger.*

~JULY 5~
IN YOUR MOUTH AND IN YOUR HEART

"Now what I am commanding you today is not too difficult for you or beyond your reach. It is not up in heaven, so that you will have to ask, 'Who will ascend into heaven to get it and proclaim it to us so that we may obey it?' No, the word is very near you; it is in your mouth and in your heart so you may obey it." Deuteronomy 30:11-14

"Whatever you do, work at it with all your heart, as working for the Lord, not for men, since you know that you will receive an inheritance from the Lord as a reward. It is the Lord Jesus you are serving." Colossians 3:23-24

Our American congregation in Germany, composed primarily of military families, had just lost several families who had finished their tour and returned to the States. There were now only two classes for kids: one for the babies and another for everyone from ages six through eighteen. The older kids— all five of them—decided they needed a little time away from the younger ones and asked if we would sponsor a youth retreat for them. What the adults pictured was taking these five on a little overnight trip and giving them some deeper instruction in the Word than was possible in their regular class with so many young kids. But that is *not* what our daughter had in mind at all. Twelve-year-old Emily went to school the very next day and invited pretty much everyone she saw and was able to bring fifteen of her unchurched friends to the retreat.

Her whole life has been a lesson in taking on more than one person should. Nothing is too difficult for Emily. It is as though the part of her brain that should tell her to look at things realistically was never formed. Once in junior high on a summer trip home from Germany she saw a friend with some unique shoe-laces she liked, so she asked us to buy what we considered a ridiculous number of pairs for her to bring back to Germany to sell. We did, and she did, making a reasonable profit and a bunch of happy junior high girls. In high school she discovered that she had a talent for sketching children, so what started out as a gift to mothers of children she babysat progressed into her being commissioned to sketch from old pictures beloved, deceased parents and children for aching relatives. As a mother of two she throws all her energies behind celebrating her children's birthdays with an amazingly imaginative creativity that makes most of us tired just to think about. As an elementary teacher, she takes willingly into her already swollen classes— even sometimes requesting them— the special needs children. One summer when their church was between children's ministers, she took that role upon herself without pay and arranged service activities and trips to hospitals and nursing homes. It is an understatement to say that her refusal to shrink from difficulty is inspiring. The King James Version calls this "working heartily as unto the Lord."

You probably know one or two like her, but these vessels of untiring industry are definitely in the minority, and the inspiration they contribute is sorely in demand. We are equipped more than we realize: it is *already* in our mouths and in our hearts.

~JULY 6~
STRUGGLING TOWARD GOD

"You will seek me and you will find me when you seek me with all your heart."
Jeremiah 29:13

This place we're living is not conducive to faith-seeing or faith-walking, and almost everyone falls prey at some time or another to doubting God. Is He real? (So few really believe in Him.) If He's real, is He good? (So many terrible things happen.) If He's really good, is He powerful? (So many times a chaos seems to rule over which No One seems to be in control.)

We usually say in these times that we are "struggling with doubt." But when we say that, are we always telling the truth? (Well, actually, maybe we are, considering those actual words. Maybe we are struggling *with* doubt, when we should be struggling *against* doubt.) Do we really put up a good fight against this doubt, or do we run scared and powerless, and maybe even hang out a white flag over our heart?

"For our struggle is not against flesh and blood but against the rulers, against the authorities, against the powers of this dark world and against the spiritual forces of evil in the heavenly realms" (Ephesians 6:12). Because of such all-out war against us and our belief in God, we are admonished to arm ourselves to the teeth. Our defense consists of a suit of armor, a shield and ready feet, but our offensive weapons are "the Sword of the Spirit, which is the Word of God" and prayer. When strong doubts assail, we should remember that this is what Paul is talking about here and take full advantage of his very specific advice. Diving deeply and seriously into the Word of God at these times is how we wield our sword against Satan. Pushing everything else aside in order to study the Bible and pray diligently is how we struggle *toward* God and *away from* doubt.

In studying we will be reminded of all God has done in the past for those who trust Him, and we will review His promises for us who will lean heavily in His direction and believe more in Him and what He says than in what we see, hear, or feel.

In addition to doing these things, we need to make some plain old common sense arguments for Him. After all, doesn't He deserve the benefit of the doubt? Think of all the stupid things we trust our lives to that in no logical way should inspire our trust: Most of us get into our cars everyday without ever climbing around underneath to see if there is a bomb that could kill us; then we trust every single stranger on the highway enough to get on there with them and mix it up. We visit restaurants we know nothing about and fearlessly eat food cooked by people we never see and about whom we know nothing. List all the good things in your life, and think hard about this: Did every single one of those things happen because *you* made it happen? A little honest introspection will work wonders in helping us to lean more in the direction of God and His goodness and omnipotence.

When doubts come, don't take them lightly assuming they will just go away. Honor God by believing and acting upon these words He spoke through Jeremiah.

~JULY 7~
BLESSINGS OF RESTRICTION

"Reuben, you are my firstborn, my might and my sign of strength, excelling in honor, excelling in power. Turbulent as the waters, you will no longer excel... "Simeon and Levi are brothers— their swords are weapons of violence. Let me not enter their council, let me not join their assembly, for they have killed men in their anger...Cursed be their anger so fierce, and their fury so cruel! I will scatter them in Jacob and disperse them in Israel... Genesis 49: 3-4, 5-7

Genesis 49 is dedicated to Jacob's blessings over his sons. However, though they are called "blessings," some of them were blessings we would choose to bypass, given our 'druthers. We might wonder, with blessings like these, who need curses? Beth Moore, in her study *The Patriarchs*, effectively uses these "antib-lessings," as she calls them, to point out some important lessons to all of us.

Reuben, Simeon, Levi, and Issachar, much like their forefathers, Ishmael and Esau (Genesis 16:12 and 27:39-40), received as their "blessings" prophecies of turbulence and servitude rather than praise and honor. Beth calls these "bless-ings of restriction" because of how in the very essence of their negativity, they do indeed bring about real blessings, not just to themselves but to the nation of Israel. By hindering a success based upon dangerous character traits, they and their nation are saved from the rampant and widespread extremity of evil that eventuates from unbridled sin.[2] We might liken this to a rich man addicted to money being given the "blessing" of bankruptcy in order to save his soul, or one addicted to drugs or alcohol losing her driver's license before she took her or someone else's life.

Up until I was thirteen, I received little parental discipline. Occasionally my daddy would spank me, but since he was gone a lot, most of the response to my rebelliousness fell to my mother, who couldn't find it in herself to dole out the stringent discipline that befit my crimes. Her trusting and lenient nature was deserved and honored by my older sister and would have been a coveted blessing to many of my fifth-grade- peers, but it was ill-spent on me; I ran wild and bare-foot all over town and through the woods until late at night and eventually fell into hooky-playing, cigarette-smoking, shop-lifting, and squirrel-shooting with my b-b gun on the town square.

But in the seventh grade, my parents divorced for the second time, and in the eighth grade, my daddy, who had custody of me, married Dorothy. In stark contrast with my mother, Dorothy was a no-nonsense kind of person. My daddy would no longer hang out at night and on weekends with his buddies, and I would never again roam the streets armed and dangerous. Both of us fell into line without much argument, but I missed the warmth, affection, and trust of my sweet mother. Even so, I became a respecter of authority and a model student. She was not perfect, and neither was I, but the kind of life I led throughout the rest of my high-school years in no way resembled my life before Dorothy. I can't say that I completely comprehended what was happening to me at the time; I am absolutely *sure* that I did not look upon her as an absolute *blessing*. However, she *was* a tremendous blessing, and now I know that. I know that she afforded me the *blessings of restriction* that I so desperately needed if I was ever going to be able to hear God's direction for me and follow. I wish I had thanked her more before she died for her hand of restraint. I am, however, thanking God for orchestrating it.

~JULY 8~
CHASING FOOLISH RABBITS

"All a man's ways seem innocent to him, but motives are weighed by the Lord."
Proverbs 16:2

There is something rather titillating about being pulled by our passions. When those passions are centered on God, we are in for the time of our lives. These are surely our greatest adventures. But when we find ourselves swept away by passions that are centered on ourselves, heartache looms on the horizon. We might start off by dabbling in some little thing which in moderation might be a harmless distraction from time to time. But unchecked, there is a danger of falling into the vortex of a whirlpool of trivial pursuits that destroy our focus on operating as an effective vessel for our Lord. Vanity can easily become our Achilles Heel— the screaming demands of an aging or otherwise changing body to be slim, attractive, and youthful. This might evidence itself in the amount of money and time we spend on the particular rabbit we are chasing at the moment. (There are so many rabbits of this particular breed!) Maybe it's the exercise rabbit that runs behind so many bushes that we haven't the time to do anything but chase it hither and thither. What started out as an honest desire for a healthy body soon turns into a ravenous hunger for one more way to improve the flesh. Or maybe it's the surgery rabbit that calls us to cut away or enhance or smooth or plump more and more. If we have enough money, this rabbit can run us ragged and leave us broke and disappointed over and over when gravity once more comes calling.

Maybe the rabbit we chase is more of the intellectual type than the model type. Perhaps we have learned a few things and found the experience so heady that we contract a kind of intellectual fever. It struts its pseudo power, flexes its rubber muscles, and whispers seductively about the glory it can buy for us. So now rather than enjoying studying and listening to what others might teach us, we become addicted to our own spewings, restless and impatient until it's once again our turn to enlighten these by our authority.

When we get caught up in the chase, we trade off valuable time that we could be spending with people who might love our company or need our comfort, or even more important, need to know our Lord. Neither do we have the time we need to learn more of Him.

Many times once we are spinning around in circles on our way down into the whirlpool, rather than ditching the ballast that is holding us under, we excuse it by calling it something nicer than it really is. We tell others, and even ourselves, that all of this striving is for a noble reason. This isn't about vanity; this is about having a healthy body; or this is about remaining attractive so that I might draw others to me so that I can teach them about Jesus. And maybe it is; maybe it really is.

But this scripture in Proverbs certainly caught my eye and helped me to realize that sometimes I don't examine myself as I should or listen to wise counsel of those who know me best. Let it work on you now. Pray for God to reveal any invisible rabbits.

~JULY 9~
DISCRETIONARY WISDOM

"Blessed is the man who does not walk in the counsel of the wicked, or stand in the way of sinners or sit in the seat of mockers. But his delight is in the law of the Lord, and on His law he meditates day and night." Psalm 1:1-2

How fitting that the book of Psalms begins with such a beautiful and concise blanket statement describing the righteous man. There are only six verses, so it isn't hard to memorize, and yet its imagery covers a vast territory of do's and don'ts. The contrast it draws between the way of the righteous and the way of sinners is clear and definite.

The Psalm begins by speaking of some of the activities a person of discretion will not take part in. Parallelism, the most unmistakable hallmark of Hebrew poetry, effectively helps us to picture someone in three different postures: walking, standing, and sitting; therefore, we are quickly and easily drawn into the picture.

First of all, the godly person of discretion will not "walk" with the wicked. Should the wicked invite him to go along with them, he will refuse. Since the word "counsel" is used, likely the psalmist is referring to a more figurative walking that a literal one, although it logically follows that anyone whose advice we would not trust is someone with whom we would also not want to travel or spend time in fellowship. Next, we are not to "stand" with them or to station ourselves with them. Maybe you have heard the expression "I will stand with you," or "beside you," or "behind you," all suggesting "in defense of" you. So, not only are we not to go with them, thereby encouraging what they do by our joining in, but we are also not to defend their actions. Thirdly, we are not to "sit" with them or settle in with them who are scornful about the things of God. This might hit more nerves than the first two, which are not so difficult for most of us to do. This third admonition suggests that we are not to blend in with those who sit around and laugh about spiritual matters, clearly testifying that those who believe the invisible are fools. It is hard to know how to stand for the truth sometimes when we are outnumbered by those with whom we are sitting around. We know better than to join in actively, and yet we fear that we will come across as spiritually pompous or Pharisaical should we blow the whistle on them. Even those who have been Christians for years have trouble with this.

The psalmist gives us some advice about how to start in the very next verse: "But his delight is in the law of the Lord and on it he meditates day and night." In other words, we choose to *walk*, *stand* and *sit* with God. He tells us to "speak the truth in love." So we study to know the truth, and then we pray to love those to whom we will impart it. We could probably do this more effectively one-on-one than any other way.

We trust in God to help us, and we take courage from the words that Mordecai spoke to Esther: "And who knows but that you are here for such a time as this?"

~JULY 10~
BEING THE TREES WE WERE MADE TO BE

"Blessed is the man who does not walk in the counsel of the wicked or stand in the way of sinners or sit in the seat of mockers. But his delight is in the law of the Lord, and on his law he meditates day and night. He is like a tree planted by streams of water, which yields its fruit in season and whose leaf does not wither. Whatever he does prospers. Not so the wicked! They are like chaff that the wind blows away. Therefore, the wicked will not stand in the judgment, nor sinners in the assembly of the righteous. For the Lord watches over the way of the righteous, but the way of the wicked will perish." Psalm 1

After the psalmist finishes his description of what a righteous person does *not* do, he goes into what he *does* do: He delights in God's Word and meditates on it "day and night"— all the time. Some versions use the word "dwells" rather than "meditates." The original word is *hagah*, meaning literally to chew, as a lion would. It brings to mind a sort of vicious and violent, wholeheartedly- focused *gnawing*, as to get all the goodness out of it that he can. He wants to waste nothing, to leave nothing behind. Such a focused study of the Bible is not something we do casually or incidentally; it is a purposeful wrestling-type thing that we do for dear life. The closest most come to that is cramming on the night before a test. Imagine what a difference we would see in our lives if we actively tried to suck dry the Word the way students prepare for tests in medical school. And they must! Doctors can't afford *not* to know, for lives are placed in their hands on a daily basis. But since our *eternal* souls and those that are placed in our paths are even more important than the *temporary* bodies that house them, shouldn't we be studying at least that hard?

Next comes the beautiful tree imagery that has made this Psalm so memorable. This tree is healthy. It is planted near the water so as to draw regular nourishment. We have already seen, in the previous verse, what this nourishing water symbolizes: a constant dwelling on the Word. The Word is our anchoring root, and our regular drinking from it provides our only proper nourishment. Interestingly, the tree is doing nothing fancy or extraordinary here; it is just doing what is was made to do— yielding its fruit in season and hanging onto its leaves against the wind so as to send out its blessings of food and shade.

Like this tree, Christians flourish and bless, standing strong against earthly winds that buffet and are secure in the judgment to come, only when we are properly nourished. Without the nourishing root, we become fruitless— "chaff that the wind blows away."

~JULY 11~
QUALITY THAT SURVIVES THE WIND AND THE FIRE

"Blessed is the man who does not walk in the counsel of the wicked or stand in the way of sinners, or sit in the seat of mockers. But his delight is in the law of the Lord, and on his law he meditates day and night. He is like a tree planted by streams of water, which yields its fruit in season and whose leaf does not wither. Whatever he does prospers. Not so the wicked! They are like chaff that the wind blows away. Therefore, the wicked will not stand in the judgment, nor sinners in the assembly of the righteous.
For the Lord watches over the righteous, but the way of the wicked will perish."
Psalm 1

"For no one can lay any foundation other than the one already laid, which is Jesus Christ. If any man builds on this foundation using gold, silver, costly stones, wood, hay, or straw, his work will be shown for what it is because the Day will bring it to the light. It will be revealed with fire, and the fire will test the quality of each man's work. If what he has built survives, he will receive his reward. If it is burned up, he will suffer loss; he himself will be saved, but only as one escaping through the flames." 1 Corinthians 3:12-15

201

Dear Father,

I willingly and willfully relinquish this desire for a glory that gives me sawdust instead of meat, tin instead of gold, vinegar instead of the nectar that you offer. I want to invest myself in learning more of You instead of pouring all my energies into trying to impress others. Help me desire more to invest myself also in other people's eternal souls rather than spinning my wheels trying to kid myself about this mortal body that is fading and weakening daily. Take me deeper into your heart that does not cling to such vanities so that I won't be like "chaff that the wind blows away" or a foolish builder who used cheap and flimsy materials that will be burned into cinders on the day it is all brought to light. I don't want to make it to You "as one escaping through the flames." I want to build wisely upon Christ. I want to meditate on your words "day and night" until they become me and I become them.

Be my everlasting, filling, rich, overflowing portion now and forevermore. So may it be possible, my precious Father, because of your perfect Son.

~JULY 12~
THE KEEPER OF OUR STORIES

"Peter said to Jesus, 'Rabbi, it is good for us to be here. Let us put up three shelters—one for you, one for Moses and one for Elijah.' (He did not know what to say, they were so frightened.) Then a cloud appeared and enveloped them, and a voice came from the cloud: 'This is my Son, whom I love. Listen to Him!'" Mark 9:7

Peter was not insinuating that He did not love Jesus, and I don't believe God was chastising Peter for not wanting to listen to Jesus. It seems to have been a teachable moment that God didn't want to waste to teach some things to Peter and all His other children who would eventually read these words.

One of the lessons was to Peter and us like him who feel that we always must *say* something. "He did not know what to say," says the scripture. Could God have been saying, "Then why did you say *anything*? In His reply, He might have emphasized the word "listen." "This is my Son, whom I love. *Listen* to Him." Just *listen*, Peter; no speaking necessary. Many of us don't know how to leave a silent moment alone. We have either never heard the expression, "Silence is golden," or we don't have a very high regard for gold. Here we learn the valuable lesson from God's own mouth that there is a time to speak and a time to listen, and when we don't know what to say, that is one of the times to listen.

Another lesson is that although Peter might not have been *meaning* to dishonor God's Son by honoring Moses and Elijah, God wants there to be no doubt about who our authority is. There were many great prophets, but now that Jesus has come, *"Salvation is found in no one else, for there is no other name under heaven given to men by which we must be saved" (Acts 4:12)*. There is a stirring story in Acts 17 about Paul's employing a holy shrewdness among the Athenians in order to teach them this very lesson. Left to our own devices and imaginations, we are apt, like them, to enshrine many gods— one to serve us in any situation in which we find ourselves. But there is only one God, and He embodied Himself in the flesh of Jesus to come to us to be seen and to be heard above all other voices. In this case, God might have emphasized the word "Him": 'This is my Son whom I love. Listen to *Him*!' Until we listen to Jesus above all other voices in all circumstances, we dishonor God.

Maybe because of the spiritual stature of Moses and Elijah, Peter was just overwhelmed by all the holiness surrounding him. But are we not sometimes tempted to listen to flesh and blood too? Do we not want to give more authority than we should to opinions from mouths other than Jesus'? God's answer to us today, as it was to Peter on Transfiguration Day, is that no person, even Moses and Elijah, can tell us what we need to know. Moses knew his stories, and Elijah knew his— both operating with the limited authority needed within the time and space God placed them; and maybe your friends and family possess a certain amount of wisdom, too, but only Jesus has been given "*all* authority in heaven and on earth" (Matthew 28:18). We must *listen to Him!*

He alone is the faithful keeper of *all* our stories.

~JULY 13~
BE WHAT YOU LOOK LIKE

"Seeing in the distance a fig tree in leaf, He went to find out if it had any fruit. When He reached it, he found nothing but leaves, because it was not the season for figs. Then He said to the tree, 'May no one ever eat fruit from you again.'" Mark 11:12-14

"On reaching Jerusalem, Jesus entered the temple area and began driving out those who were buying and selling there. He overturned the tables of the money changers and the benches of those selling doves, and would not allow anyone to carry the merchandise through the temple courts." Mark 11:15-16

"In the morning, as they went along, they saw the fig tree withered from the roots. Peter remembered and said to Jesus, "Rabbi, look! The fig tree you cursed has withered." Mark 11:20-21

Here is a very cryptic section of scripture. There are all kinds of questions one could ask: Why is Jesus so upset that this tree is not bearing fruit when it isn't even in season? Why is He so upset with the people selling sacrifices at the temple when it is true that everyone had to have one? Why does Mark go *back* to the fig tree, drawing our attention this time to the fact that it has indeed withered?

On at least five different occasions, Mark employs a literary technique of sandwiching an important faith lesson from Jesus between two similar events or between the beginning and the ending of one story. He liked to show how Jesus seized every opportunity to teach his disciples from the objects and situations at hand. So what do these two events have in common?

Both the fig tree and the merchants seemed to be something other than what they were. (Try to forget for the moment that it wasn't the season for figs; almost all analogies have limits of similarities.) The fig tree flourished with healthy foliage that belied its present fruitless condition. Anyone looking at it would *expect* some figs to be hiding in that lushness. Likewise, the temple merchants *seemed* to be helping others with their religious duties. Really, though, by setting up their animal pens and money tables in the Gentile Courts, they had desecrated the only place the Gentiles were allowed to worship and pray. Likely they were also selling their goods at exorbitant rates.

Mark demonstrates how Jesus took His disciples from a benign symbol—the fig tree—into a real-life situation where people's behavior spelled out their heart's rejection of His message and purpose, back to the end result of the symbol—a withered fig tree—in order to teach parabolically an important lesson: you should *be* what you look like you are. And so we should. Our lives should not be false advertising. We should not tease others into drawing near or bait them only to reel them into their soul's destruction. Heaven forbid that we allow ourselves to become withered fig trees by taking an unsuspecting soul who trusts us, like those poor who so needed the doves of sacrifice. We should look carefully and prayerfully at our lives to see if we really are what we seem to be.

~JULY 14~
EAGERNESS REDIRECTED

"But eagerly desire the greater gifts." 1 Corinthians 12:31

When I hear the word "eager," I always think of my daddy. He was the poster child for hyperactivity before the word was even coined. Some of my earliest memories are of his whistling and pacing the floor, impatient to leave. Wherever it was we were going, he was always the first one ready. Whether we had five minutes until we were to be there or forty-five (which was usually the case), he was anxious to go. As I grew up, I saw his eagerness manifest itself in every new thing he learned, and he was always learning something new. He had a "burning desire" (one of his favorite expressions, by the way) to teach somebody else the thing he had just learned. With him, the learning process didn't seem to be complete until he had taught it to someone else. Whether it was playing a guitar, learning a new memory technique, mastering all the states and capitals, or reading a fascinating book, Daddy always insisted that the rest of us try it too. He did not have to *make* himself tell us as though it were some kind of parental duty; his eagerness constrained him to share it.

This is the way Paul was. This scripture is his transition sentence into his beloved and well-known treatise on love found in 1 Corinthians 13. And he was one to listen to; Paul knew all about eagerly desiring. It was the story of his life. Everything we read about him reflects his feverish desire to throw himself into a cause, whether to persecute the Christians, to carry the gospel of Christ throughout the world, or to get to Rome so he could testify to Caesar, the most powerful man in the world at that time. In his testimony to King Agrippa (Acts 26), he says he was obsessed against Christians and would go to all lengths to persecute them. We read at the beginning of chapter eight of his part in Stephen's stoning and of his door-to-door ministry of dragging people from their houses off to prison. No wonder God waylaid him on the road to Damascus. Nothing was too hard for Saul, nothing too much trouble, nothing beyond his imagination. God took the passion he had created in this man which had been tragically misdirected and redirected it to be used *for* His cause rather than *against* it. You see, it was not Paul's obsessive tendency that was sinful; it was the way it was *directed* that was wrong. In the hands of the right Master, the trait that compelled him to do evil became Paul's most noble and useful characteristic for bringing about good.

I grew up thinking my daddy's kind of eagerness to share what you know was pretty normal; it settled in beneath my skin and is a part of me as surely as my straight hair and bunioned feet. Maybe you can identify. An eager nature can serve as a strong impetus for sharing the Truth, but it also can take us off on side roads where we might linger too long and be caught up in some mundane undertaking that tempts us to waste time and energy expounding on some trivial nonsense. If you know how it feels for a desire to well up inside to throw more of yourself than you should into teaching someone something stupid rather than about your Savior, before you leave your prayer closet, lay your eagerness in the hands of God.

"For I resolved to know nothing while I was with you except Jesus Christ and him crucified." 1 Corinthians 2:2

~JULY 15~
FEELING ALIVE VS. BEING ALIVE

"...If anyone would come after me, he must deny himself and take up his cross daily and follow me. For whoever wants to save his life will lose it, but whoever loses his life for me will save it. What good is it for a man to gain the whole world, and yet lose or forfeit his very self?" Luke 9:23-25

What really makes us *alive?* I mean aside from the literal, physiological life, isn't there something more that *life* means? Jesus surely spoke as though there is. He once said that He came that we might have life and have it more abundantly (John 10:10). All that He encountered already had breath in their bodies, so what did He mean by His being the One to *give life?* What is this "life" he calls us to lose in order to find?

These are pretty deep questions to ponder, so let's start with something easier: What makes you *feel* alive? Now we're getting somewhere. Almost everybody can find at least one answer to that question, even if we do not want to be honest about sharing those answers with anyone else. Sometimes we are ashamed because what gets our hearts to pumping strongly enough to finally *feel* is either a forbidden and unholy desire or harmful addiction, in which case the guilt is appropriate since idolatry might be eating away our very life; or, something that, though not unholy, seems somehow less than spiritual. In this case, we might find, upon further consideration, that when invited, God can use what we love to accomplish spiritual ends, as long as we keep our priorities right and not value the better above the Best. But is what makes us *feel* alive the thing that really makes us *be* alive, in the way Jesus meant? Well, I say no; feeling alive is not the same thing as *being* alive. The Enemy specializes in deception. What we may *feel* is bringing us more life might *in reality* be killing us.

But feeling alive *can* be what helps us to know our potential. It might very well be an itch put in us by our Creator. The scratching that we do when we pursue our loves gives us a certain amount of satisfaction, gets our blood pumping, and causes us to feel heavenly possibilities. We say these things make us feel *alive* because honestly, we spend a lot more time feeling kinda numb, sorta dead. It isn't that our life is so bad—it might even be overflowing with blessings— but still we live it in a somewhat regular cadence. Occasionally, though, we find a way to take a break from the cadence, the routine, the marching, and we plunge into a *rhapsody*, a *dance*, a *freefall*, or a *swan dive*. We call this "feeling alive" because it seems as though this is what we were made for.

Jesus is telling us here that we must trust Him enough to be willing to give up even the *very* thing that makes us feel most alive if it keeps us from following Him. It really might *be* the last breath of literal life He asks us to give in order to follow Him. But likelier, it will be something else: money, time, recognition, appreciation, a lavish lifestyle, a voracious desire for thrills. It is sort of a gauge. Which holds our highest allegiance? Which will we protect at all costs— the kind of adventure we already know or the more abundant kind that He desires to show us? Are we afraid to risk the one bird in our mortal hand for His two in His Eternal bush? Losing is the only way to win.

"So we fix our eyes not on what is seen, but on what is unseen. For what is seen is temporary, but what is unseen is eternal." 12 Corinthians 4:18

~JULY 16~
WHAT HAVE WE COME HERE FOR?

"All that the Father gives me will come to me, and whoever comes to me I will never drive away." John 6:37

"Many will say to me on that day, 'Lord, Lord, did we not prophesy in your name and in your name drive our demons and perform many miracles?' Then I will tell them plainly, 'I never knew you. Away from me, you evildoers!'" Matthew 7:22-23

Here is one of those situations about which we are tempted to just shake our heads and assign to the "Great Mysteries" column. Opponents of the Bible's veracity could use this to accuse the Bible of having contradictions or to accuse Jesus of speaking out of both sides of His mouth. It seems that the "evildoers" Jesus is speaking to here are the same ones He said He would never drive away, doesn't it? But Jeremiah warns us that there will be times like this when His truth seems to be beyond our finding out. He tells us at these times we are to seek Him with all our hearts (Jeremiah 29:13). It was the same way when Jesus spoke in parables; what He wanted was for those who really cared to understand to ask more questions.

Look at the ones He is calling "evildoers." These He claims never to have known have done great acts in His name: prophesying, driving out demons, and performing many miracles. It might seem strange to us that people can do such things without the benefit of God's power, but the scriptures, old and new testament alike, plainly tell us about pagan magicians who could compete up to a point. Remember when Moses' staff turned into a snake, Pharaoh's magicians' staff did the same. Then Moses' snake ate the magicians' snake (Exodus 7). Also, remember that Simon the Sorcerer, even before he became a Christian, "amazed all the people of Samaria" (Acts 8). Ephesians 6 reminds us of the strong evil forces that we battle. To say that they have no power is to refute God's Word and to leave ourselves vulnerable. That these people in Matthew 7 did these things is not what Jesus is arguing, nor should we. Jesus is saying that they used His name for selfish reasons. What they were after was not Jesus Himself, but the fame and power that dropping His name could buy them. This is why Simon the Sorcerer was chastised so severely by Peter when he attempted to buy a "new trick" from the apostles.

Those whom He will never drive away, however, have come to Him for Him alone. They have been drawn by the Father out of their poverty of Spirit that Jesus speaks of in His Beatitudes. He says "theirs is the Kingdom of Heaven."

Are we here just for what bearing His name can do for us? Might we gain something for ourselves that is less than Heavenly, less noble than what we will need in order to bring more glory to Him, less mission-minded than what will draw others to Him? Jesus wants a relationship with us. This is what prayer is all about. He wants us to be united with Him in a way that allows Him to shape and mold us "from one degree of glory to another."

Are we gazing upon His loveliness in order to be like Him or using Him as a lucky charm to benefit us without changing us? What, *really*, have we come here for?

~JULY 17~
EVANGELISTIC BALANCE

"For whoever keeps the whole law and yet stumbles at just one point is guilty of breaking all of it." James 2:10

"We proclaim Him, admonishing and teaching everyone with all wisdom so that we may present everyone perfect in Christ." Colossians 1:28

In Homer's *The Odyssey,* the hero is presented with the deadly dilemma of sailing his ship between Scylla, a six-headed sea monster, or Charybdis, a whirlpool which could swallow the entire ship. He finds himself "between the devil and the deep blue sea." Both edges of this narrow tongue of sea threaten death; clearly his only safe course is to navigate straight down the middle.

This is the way it is sometimes. Although many times the Christian life calls for leaning hard in one direction and giving no sway to any kind of middle ground, there are other situations that call upon us to steer directly down the middle.

James warns us not fall to the temptation of believing we've got it *all* down pat and thus use ourselves as excuses to condemn others. Jesus tells us to be careful to see where our own sinful inclinations lie lest we attempt to remove a speck from someone's eye using sight hindered by an embedded plank. Sailing here is deadly; some are sure to be eaten alive by the monsters of self-deception, spiritual arrogance, and harsh judgmentalism. These are the rough waters of tyranny.

However, the other side of the channel is just as dangerous. If we decide that we have no business speaking to anyone about sin just because we can't live perfectly, we rob others of help they need to remember what the Ideal looks like. We endanger others when we refuse, because of our imperfections, to remind them of the truth about an eternity that is certain to come. We misunderstand Jesus' saying, "Judge not lest you be judged" if we think that means we are not to continue admonishing others and pointing out sin. We have only to read a few verses later where He says, "Do not give dogs what is sacred; do not throw your pearls to the pigs" to realize that there is some discerning— a type of judgment— involved in order to determine who the dogs and the swine *are.* I have even known parents who refuse to lead their kids down the right paths because they did not choose those paths when they were kids. They feel this is hypocritical, but it isn't. Hypocrisy is having no intention of doing what you are preaching, not waywardness that is finally seen as such and repented of. These are the deadly waters of isolationism. Here lurks the danger of letting the whole ship go down for lack of involvement.

We can afford to be neither tyrants nor isolationists. We must realize that really the only way we can take planks from our eyes is by means of the atoning blood of Jesus. So what Jesus is asking us to do is realize *we* need Him as much as the other guy. But the other guy *does* still need Him, and we must be faithful to remind him of that.

"Instead, speaking the truth in love, we will in all things grow up into Him who is the Head, that is Christ." Ephesians 4:15

~JULY 18~
A MIND SET ON FULFILLMENT

"Jesus turned to Peter and said, 'Get behind me, Satan! You are a stumbling block to me; you do not have in mind the things of God, but the things of men.'"
Matthew 16:23

Jesus has just finished warning His disciples about the suffering and death that are soon to come upon Him in Jerusalem. Peter has rebuked Jesus for His words and avowed that no such thing will happen. This just does not fit the visions Peter has of Jesus' ministry. Here Jesus chastises Peter even though Peter's motives do not seem purely selfish: he is not trying to save his own life but the earthly life of Jesus. Nevertheless, Jesus seems every bit as opposed to Peter's desires and addresses him with every bit of the sternness that He would had his request been on behalf of himself rather than Jesus.

In fact, maybe Jesus knows that regardless of how Peter's motives *sound*, there is indeed some selfish motivation. The entire time Jesus has spent with these men has been about gaining their unflinching trust and devotion to their Rabbi and Master Jesus. He has continually warned them about choosing their life over their dedication, their safety over their devotion. Up to this point Jesus has spent most of His time teaching the crowds in parables and healing the sick, so his disciples have become accustomed to watching and learning at His feet where their trust in Him has come fairly easily. He amazed them on a daily basis; why shouldn't they believe in Him?

But now, they have reached a different place where Jesus' plans require more trust. Rather than making the proper connections and crossovers from what they have learned about who He really is, Peter, at least, finds it very tough to step away from what he has grown accustomed to in order to honor Jesus with his trust. He is screaming, "Encore, Lord! Please, just give us an encore of what we have already seen! Let's not leave the shores for the deep waters. Let's not fix something that isn't broken."

An important question we all must eventually ask ourselves is whether we trust God because of what He has done for us or because of who He is. The same disciples who watched Jesus feed multitudes on a few bites and heal every kind of disease trembled in a storm although He was in the boat. They failed to learn the big lesson. They couldn't see the forest for the trees. We so often do the same thing. We watch God answer some very hard prayers in ways that we desire and then grow confused and doubtful when He is silent or seems to be working in ways contrary to our visions. He is the same God all the time, though, and He is just as omnipotent and omniscient when He answers one way as when He answers the other. He is still worthy of the same trust.

God had a plan that required Jesus to go to Jerusalem to die, so Jesus went. He has plans that require certain things of us, so we, too, must trust Him and go there. Today's big question is this: Is my mind set on fulfilling *God's* plan for my life, or is my mind set of getting God to fulfill *my* plan?

~JULY 19~
BEFRIENDING HUMILITY

"All of you, clothe yourselves with humility toward one another, because 'God opposes the proud but gives grace to the humble.' Humble yourselves, therefore, under God's mighty hand, that He may lift you up in due time." James 5:5-6

I really believe that what our language needs is another word for what some people call pride. From an early age we hear about it in glorious contexts: "family pride," "team pride," "proud to be an American," "I am so proud of you." The Bible, however, is noticeably devoid of any positive mention of pride and starkly abounding with negative commentary concerning it. Likewise, humility, on the lips of the world, is a dreaded and shameful position to be avoided at all costs, whereas on the pages of God's Word, it is the only means by which we can be lifted up by God. Once we become serious students of the Word and lovers of its Author, we must undergo some serious retraining of our minds in regards to pride and humility. If we fail to reprogram our value system about these two words, we will suffer repeatedly in our relationships.

In fact, in our most cherished earthly relationships, pride is our greatest enemy. Marriages are dissolved, families are splintered, and friendships are wrecked because of the insidious evil of pride. It is the Enemy's trump card because it can be used so effectively and subtly against Christians of all levels of maturity. Since it is the root of all selfishness, the very immature Christian is vulnerable for obvious reasons. Once we recognize our selfish tendencies for what they are and can fight them with prayer and discipline, we might become vulnerable to spiritual pride, the tendency to become inwardly arrogant and thus overly judgmental due to our grip on discipline. We have merely slipped out of one messy, undisciplined situation into another. The devil rejoices when he can get us to play his game without our even realizing it.

One of the specific pitfalls at this level is thinking that being in opposition to wrong automatically makes us right. There is usually more to being right than just being opposed to wrong. Gary Thomas in his book *Sacred Influence* used what he learned from Elton Trueblood to help me see the point that there are many ways to miss the bull's eye, but there is only one way to hit it. In our ardor against a *wrong* way someone we love is behaving, we might fall into the deadly belief that we have cornered the market on the *right* way to behave. Our pride might blind us to the truth that opposing wrong doesn't automatically make us right. Pride wants to stop us right there at the first step; humility would have us go some steps further by asking if I might be aggravating any of the other person's bad behavior, if there is any way I might need to change to help him or her change, or if there is some kind of compromise we can make that is even more right than either of us was alone.[3]

Nothing less than befriending humility can help us defeat the ever-present enemy of pride. Today let us begin that most important friendship. Study, pray, practice.

~JULY 20~
HUMILITY FROM THE ROOT

"Do nothing out of selfish ambition or vain conceit, but in humility consider others better than yourselves." Philippians 2:3

"Therefore, whoever humbles himself like this child is the greatest in the kingdom of heaven." Matthew 18:4

If we are to befriend this attribute of humility, we need to see what it *really* is and not just what it *seems* to be. Humility is often counterfeited by something easier and cheaper but vastly less effective at its original purpose of bringing glory to and strengthening faith in God. It seems that humility is commonly thought of somewhat like an ornament we hang on our tree— an outward response that is called for at certain times. Some of these times that propriety might call for this ornament are when we receive a compliment and when we do something well and feel good about it. We feel we must be ready at these times to shuffle the glory away from ourselves and fuss at ourselves for any self-commendation. Such responses *might* be indications of true humility or at least our desire to be humble, which are both commendable, but they, in themselves, are *not* humility. James tells us to "clothe" ourselves in humility, and maybe this is what he is talking about: wear the right kind of clothes long enough, and you will begin to be the kind of person your clothes say you are. (This is one of the main justifications for school uniforms.)

But Jesus indicates strongly that humility is a fruit that issues forth from a root, not just an ornament that is hung mechanically on a branch which didn't give it life. The kind of humility Jesus desires is that kind we want to cultivate. He says we are to humble ourselves like children. What could that mean? Paul seems to understand this kind of humility; in his letter to the Philippians, he says we are to "*consider* others better than ourselves." He could have just as easily used some other word than "consider," one that would have indicated a less interior motive and more of an outward, or ornamental, discipline. *Considering* is something we do on the inside before we ever get to the action part. So, perhaps what Jesus means when he uses a child as a visual aid for humility is that we act exactly like we feel like acting. A little child's actions issue directly from his feelings rather than from some circuitous route that filters out his "wants" from his "oughts." Children have to be *taught* propriety, good manners, thoughtfulness, and consideration of the feelings of others; they are not born with those attributes. And parents who teach their children such are certainly justified; without such attributes as a foundation, a Christian character cannot be grown. But Jesus seems to be challenging us to desire the guilelessness of an untrained child when it comes to being humble. He knows the problems with what He is asking; He came down here and lived this life.

There is only one way we can *become* humble from the roots out and *grow* humility: we must desire it enough to *pray* continually for it.

~JULY 21~
TRUST: THE ROOT OF HUMILITY

"I tell you the truth, unless you change and become like little children, you will never enter the kingdom of heaven." Matthew 18:3

In order for *us* to become humble, we must come before the humble Jesus, gaze upon Him prayerfully, and pray to Him gazingly. We must do more praying about our roots that grow the fruits than about ornamental things or even ornamental responses. So *much* about becoming Christlike depends upon prayer. You can't read the New Testament ten seconds without coming upon a form of the word "pray." We are admonished about it by example and command over and over. The example Jesus gives us is as follows:

> "Our Father in heaven, hallowed be your name,
> your kingdom come, your will be done
> on earth as it is in heaven.
> Give us this day our daily bread.
> Forgive us our debts as we also have forgiven our debtors.
> And lead us not into temptation,
> But deliver us from the evil one."
> (Matthew 6:9-13)

Since this is how Jesus tells us to pray, what can we learn from this prayer that will help us better understand how to nurture the root of humility? Perhaps something else Jesus said about children might help. Before He mentioned the specific virtue of childlike humility, He says in a more general way, *"You must change and become like little children."* The requests of this model prayer are pretty simple and direct. This is not a complicated prayer; it sounds like one a child might pray. "Father, you are wonderful. I can't wait until we are together in the same place. I wish people down here would act like you and Jesus and the angels do up there. Please give us what we need today— food and forgiveness. Help us to forgive others, too. Please keep the devil away from us today. AMEN."

But the key is not just in saying the words as a child might; the childlike thing He wants from us most seems to be our trust in Him to answer these requests, our belief in His power to deliver, our trust in His care. If we could really live with that uncomplicated childlike trust and believe in Him more than ourselves, humility would issue forth from us a natural byproduct. No longer would we be confused about Who really deserves the credit for the good we do. No longer would our looking after ourselves hinder our serving others; we would know that *He* would look out after our interests. We would know whatever good happened was the result of one or more products of prayer: His directly answering our or someone else's prayers; or, our becoming more like Him as a result of our time spent with Him in prayer. This is what being in relationship with Him is all about—conforming us more into His image.

He wants us to become like Him because being like Jesus is the only thing that will change our world, and spending much time gazing at Jesus is the only thing that will make us like Him.

~JULY 22~
WRITING OUR OWN TICKET

"For if you forgive men when they sin against you, your heavenly Father will also forgive you. But if you do not forgive men their sins, your Father will not forgive your sins." Matthew 6:14-15

"And when you stand praying, if you hold anything against anyone, forgive him, so that your Father in heaven may forgive you your sins." Mark 11:25

What we are after is the real fruit that grows from a pure root—not just ornaments to be attached to our branches. We want all the fruit of the Spirit mentioned in Galatians 5—*love, joy, peace, patience, kindness, goodness, faithfulness, gentleness and self-control.* We want to be truly *humble* so that we can be lifted up by God since we know that anything or anyone else who lifts us up are only temporary props. We know that the only way we can learn to be like Jesus and thereby grow this fruit from the inside out is to be in relationship with Him, and as in all relationships, that requires spending lots of time with Him. It is true that no amount of prayer will ever really *entitle* us to all God does for us; we, in ourselves, are not deserving of the least bit of it. It is always by His grace from start to finish that we even have the chance of a relationship with Heaven. Yet, in a way, we are allowed to write our own ticket to receive or to be denied that grace.

Matthew records that immediately following Jesus' model prayer, He adds this condition about forgiveness. He has already alluded to the connection between *forgiving* and *being forgiven* in His prayer. He seems to want us to understand that these ideas are placed together not just for the sake of organization because they are both on the topic of forgiveness; there really is a cause and effect relationship between what we do with the virtue of forgiveness for others and what we expect Him to do with it for us.

This whole concept of anything conditional with God is foreign to some. The Bible is packed with examples and reminders that His *love* for us is unfailing, but unless we have the correct definition of love, the condition placed upon our forgiveness might seem contradictory. Even earthly parents understand the wisdom of reinforcing good behavior and discouraging bad behavior. God's absolute holiness will not allow Him to bless us when we are on the fast track to hell. John tells us about this in no uncertain terms: *"Anyone who claims to be in the light but hates his brother is still in the darkness (1 John 2:9).* You may say that your unwillingness to forgive someone doesn't mean that you *hate* him; let's not quibble over words here. Its use here means "to be angry" (see Matthew 5:22).

Prayer is powerful for sure, and it is our single best avenue for an image-changing relationship with God, but our relationship to God is *directly* related to our relationship to *others*. It is not farfetched to say, then, that according to how much we love each other, the words we offer to God will arrive at His throne in one of two ways: "golden bowls of incense" (Revelation 5:8) or "babbling, like the pagans" (Matthew 6:5).

~JULY 23~
SWEPT CLEAN IS NOT ENOUGH

"Remain in me, and I will remain in you. No branch can bear fruit by itself; it must remain in the vine. Neither can you bear fruit unless you remain in me. I am the vine; you are the branches. If a man remains in me and I in him, he will bear much fruit; apart from me, you can do nothing…This is to my Father's glory, that you bear much fruit, showing yourselves to be my disciples." John 15:4-5, 8

The same one who might argue for morals alone getting us to heaven would argue against the odds of a broken-off branch continuing to grow cherries. How pitiful to be so shallow and nearsighted when our very souls are at stake!

I have heard women in drug and alcohol rehab centers say that they are there to get their lives "cleaned up." They are concerned about getting the bad things out of their lives so that they can live lives of joy and fulfillment. However, Jesus tells us a parable in Luke 11:24-26 that helps us to see that a good housecleaning is at best a temporary measure and at worst an invitation for even more trouble to enter in. *"When an evil spirit comes out of a man, it goes through arid places seeking rest and does not find it. Then it says, 'I will return to the house I left.' When it arrives, it finds the house swept clean and put in order. Then it goes and takes even other spirits more wicked than itself, and they go in and live there. And the final condition of that man is worse than the first."* I remember that the first time I read this I was more than a little shocked at the ending. I thought that because the man had his house all cleaned up, the evil spirits would not want to go in. I thought the man would be proved prudent and be rewarded for cleaning up his act. But there is a hint in what He has said just before He gives the parable: *"He who is not with me is against me, and he who does not gather with me, scatters" (Luke 11:23).* This is all about being *with* Jesus. He seems to be saying that what is most important is that we are *attached* to Him. If we are not attached to

Him, whatever we are doing, whether it looks moral or not, actually "scatters," rather than bringing things together.

Morality alone is neither good nor bad. It can be used by both the Lord and the devil. Morality for its own sake is empty and powerless. God didn't create us for the purpose of being moral, as strange as that might seem. He created us to belong to Him and to be in a Father-Child relationship with Him. The entire Bible is one long love story of God's pursuit of us for the very purpose of being united with Him. Because of God's absolute holiness, He cannot be in a whole relationship with what is not holy. This was the whole purpose of the blood of the perfect Lamb, Jesus. We can be washed in and covered by His blood and be united with Holy God. Holy living is definitely conducive to our coming to find and to maintain that relationship with God through Christ, but it is so much more than just good morals.

Being swept clean is not enough. This just leaves us empty and vulnerable again. We were not made to be empty. We were made to be filled with the Spirit of God. We were made to be *attached* to Him, the True Vine, and to produce His fruit. Apart from Him, outside of a relationship *with* Him, morals or no morals, regardless of how clean we may look and how proud we may feel of that cleanliness, Jesus reminds us, we can do nothing.

~JULY 24~
WITH UNVEILED FACES

"We are not like Moses, who would put a veil over his face to keep the Israelites from gazing at it while the radiance was fading away... It has not been removed, because only in Christ is it taken away...But whenever anyone turns to the Lord, the veil is taken away...And we, who with unveiled faces, all reflect the Lord's glory, are being transformed into his likeness with ever-increasing glory, which comes from the Lord, who is the Spirit...The god of this age has blinded the minds of unbelievers, so that they cannot see the light of the gospel of the glory of Christ, who is the image of God." 2 Corinthians 3:13-18; 4:4

Paul uses a literal historical occurrence to symbolize the danger that lurks at the door of all mankind. This fading glory image points to the fading away of the old law. He says this veil, this refusal to see, will remain over the eyes of all who do not want to see Christ, for indeed, Christ *is* the glory of the Living God, the very *incarnation* of the God we could not see before. Trying to see God without looking at Him through Christ is like trying to see something clearly through a veil. Our refusal to focus on Christ as the true image of God might be something we do at first just out of skepticism or rebellion to our parents' religion, but here the Bible makes it clear that this kind of veiling is nothing to fool around with, for we are playing right into the hands of "the god of this age," who knows that against his evil lure, Christ is our only hope, the only glory that doesn't fade; rather in Him we are transformed "with ever-increasing glory."

Satan tries in many ways to veil us from the Truth. He knows there is only one ultimate Truth, and that is Christ Jesus, the Incarnation of God, the Propitiation for our sins, and the Victor over death. He may sell himself to us, as in the context of this letter to the Corinthians, as a way to God through Moses or some other prophet other than Jesus, or he may sell himself to us as the sufficiency of morality alone. Perhaps he will peddle himself to us through intellectualism, or a philosophy that embraces getting all the "gusto" we can right here, right now, since we only live once. Many times he buys us through hedonism, an insatiable desire for pleasure at any cost. He is all too successful in his claims that pride is the winners' way, while humility is for losers. He veils many by means of scrambling our sense of shame, telling us to be ashamed of a strong stance for Christ but to feel proud of learning how to blend with the world.

This last one causes many of us to hang our heads with the realization that we are allowing that dangerous veil to come over our eyes. The gospel message taught and preached by the early Christians never encourages such catering to this base instinct to fit in. On the contrary, read the exciting and challenging words of Paul as he comes to the climax of this part of this letter: *"We are hard pressed on every side, but not crushed; perplexed, but not in despair; persecuted, but not abandoned; struck down, but not destroyed. We always carry around in our body the death of Jesus, so that the life of Jesus may also be revealed in our body...Therefore, we do not lose heart. Though outwardly we are wasting away, yet inwardly we are being renewed day by day (2 Corinthians 4:8-10, 16).*

~JULY 25~
TO EVERYONE WHO ASKS

"Always be prepared to give an answer to everyone who asks you to give the reason for the hope that you have." 1 Peter 3:15

This scripture teaches us that we must study the Word so well that when others ask us why we believe as we do, we will not have to hem and haw around or fake a coughing spasm until we can sneak off and call the preacher to get the answer. These words show us that an inherited faith is not enough. We should be like the Bereans spoken of in Acts 17:11 who were nobler than most because they studied the scriptures to see if what had been preached was correct. Life comes at us fast sometimes, and if we're not careful, we will adopt a kind of second-hand Christianity based upon someone else's views simply because we will not bother to take the time to study on our own. In fact, it is tragically common to find someone we admire and trust and try to get to Heaven on his or her coattails. This ride will not last forever, though, for we are told in Romans 14:10-12 *"For we will all stand before God's judgment seat. It is written, 'As surely as I live,' says the Lord, 'every knee will bow before me; every tongue will confess to God.' So then, each of us will give an account of himself to God."* And the Hebrews writer reminds us *"Nothing in all creation is hidden from God's sight. Everything is uncovered and laid bare before the eyes of him to whom we must give account"* *(Hebrews 4:13)*. Our souls are eternal, and whom we entrust them to will make the difference between how we fare in that never-ending era. We must go straight to the source and know the why's of our life's choices, not just for those who might ask but for our eternal welfare, as well.

But this is getting the cart before the horse. What we should ask first when we read this scripture is "Is anyone asking?" The scripture assumes that we will be asked about our hope, but are we? If we are not, then we need to ask ourselves why. Is there anything peculiar about our lifestyle? Are we set apart in any way from the garden-variety human being? What is this hope Peter talks about? Leading up to this point, Peter has been talking about suffering for doing good. He has issued such instructions as *"Do not repay evil with evil or insult with insult, but with blessing, because to this you were called, so that you may inherit a blessing...Who is going to harm you if are eager to do good? But even if you should suffer for what is right, you are blessed. 'Do not fear what they fear; do not be frightened.' But in your hearts, set apart Christ as Lord"* *(1 Peter 3:9, 13-15)*. These are the kinds of actions that arouse the curiosity of the world. These responses to ill treatment and suffering are totally irrational to the world. They fly in the face of looking out for number one. Witnesses to these kinds of Christians who have "set *Christ* apart in [their] hearts as Lord" rather than fear realize that hope must be found somewhere other than in human strength, strategy, or wit.

Words are cheap. We need the boldness and faith to live out the words so that the world will wonder, ask, and learn from us about the hope found in Christ alone. Be ready!

~JULY 26~
THE MYSTERY OF GODLINESS

"Beyond all question the mystery of godliness is great:
He appeared in a body,
was vindicated by the Spirit,
was seen by angels,
was preached among the nations,
was believed on in the world,
was taken up in glory."
1 Timothy 3:16

Here Paul writes to Timothy to say that although he hopes to come to him soon, if he is delayed, here are some things he wants Timothy to know about how people ought to conduct themselves in *"God's household, the church of the living God, the pillar and foundation of the truth"* *(1 Timothy 3:15)*. Paul uses these words, likely a hymn, to help unveil some of the mystery of godliness. "He" refers to God, of course, but Paul reasons that if we are to become godly, a close look at God is our best means.

"He appeared in a body." First of all, you can *tell* that godly people have been with God. It is interesting that most of us understand that bad company really does corrupt good morals, but we hardly ever turn that around to look at the positive inverse: good company corrupts bad morals. (Understand that "corrupt" here is used in the verb form meaning "to alter.") The more time we spend with God, the more we look like Him. The more time we spend studying His Word, the more we begin to sound like Him. He shows up in us and thus appears *"in a body,"* specifically, the body of godly people.

"Vindicated by the Spirit" means that we entrust justice to God. Godly people are not vindictive. They show by their refusal to get vengeance that there is indeed some restraining Agent, some Comfort beyond revenge that can work upon the human heart—Something from out of this world. It is not *natural*, but *supernatural*, for us to accept injustice mildly. One of the first phrases our kids learn to put together is, "That's not fair!" Growing out of that happens only by being transformed, reborn, through Christ.

"Seen by angels" as applied to us indicates that our main audience is not earthly, but heavenly. Our actions should not be for the praise of men but for the eyes of and to bring glory to God alone. We are on a bigger stage than meets the eye.

"Was preached among the nations and believed on in the world." Godliness has wide-ranging influence; in fact, it changes the world!

"Was taken up in glory" reminds us of the ultimate reward for our godliness, for dying to ourselves and being hidden in Christ. *"Your life is now hidden with Christ in God. When Christ, who is your life, appears, then you will also appear with Him in glory"* (Colossians 3:3).

The mystery of godliness *is* great. It is *"Christ in you, the hope of glory" (Colossians 1:27).* Through Christ the mystery can be unveiled. That is why He came.

~JULY 27~
SLAVES OF DEPRAVITY

"These men are springs without water and mists driven by a storm. Blackest darkness is reserved for them. For they mouth empty, boastful words, and by appealing to the lustful desires of sinful human nature, they entice people who are just escaping from those who live in error. They promise them freedom, while they themselves are slaves of depravity— for a man is a slave to whatever has mastered him" 2 Peter 2:17-19

Earlier in this passage, Peter has identified these men as "having left the straight way and wandered off..." What could have so corrupted these, who were once walking aright, to this extremity? Notice that they are not content just to wallow in sin alone; they entice others to go with them, promising them freedom. Obviously, then, these men must have felt that the constraints of Christianity were too great and thus have thrown off the fetters for a reckless romp in the green fields of freedom. They sound so authoritative with all their boastful promises. You can almost hear their voices as you read this entire chapter Peter devotes to warning others about them. He describes their empty promises by calling these deceivers "springs without water," something that once brought refreshment but has now dried up to nothing. Their carousing nature shows that they do not see themselves in this light and probably cannot imagine that their good times will ever come to an end. They have become sick and tired of being told what to do and what not to do and are out for a big gulp of life, for a change.

I don't know what went wrong for them. I do know, though, that it still happens. People who start off strong grow weak in the spirit and stout in the flesh. Perhaps they tried harder to empty themselves of badness than to fill themselves with the goodness of Christ and thus found that "the demon returned and brought seven more with it." Or perhaps their hearts were the hard path that the good seed did not penetrate or the rocky soil where no root developed to protect it from persecution or the thorny soil tangled with the worries of this life or the deceitfulness of wealth. Maybe, like the prodigal son, they felt safe dabbling in a little of this sin and a little of that until one day they found themselves in quicksand and decided it was easier to enjoy the mud bath than fight to get out. One or more of these reasons caused these, and some you might know, to throw up their hands one day and say, "Enough!"

But verse 19 reveals the bottom line of all their sayings and doings in the name of freedom: *"They promise freedom, while they themselves are slaves of depravity—for a man is a slave to whatever masters him."* This is the way with Satan. After he captivates, he destroys his prey. Look at the demoniacs in the Bible; the demons entered into them, apparently needing a body to inhabit, but no sooner had they gotten inside than they began to destroy their host. *"The thief comes only to steal, kill, and destroy" (John 10:10),* never to *increase* life in *any* way. About Jesus, John adds in the same verse, *"I have come that they may have life and have it to the full."* He is the Good Shepherd.

We will never be free agents. We will serve somebody. We must be careful to make this choice with eternal eyes.

~JULY 28~
WELLS WE DID NOT DIG

"Each of you should look not only to your own interests, but also to the interests of others." Philippians 2:4

"...a land with large and flourishing cities which you did not build, houses filled with all kinds of good things you did not provide, wells you did not dig, and vineyards and olive groves you did not plant— then when you eat and are satisfied, be careful that you do not forget the Lord..." Deuteronomy 6:12

The Israelites have been mercifully delivered out of their Egyptian bondage, and now Moses prepares them for the time soon to come when they will finally be settled into the land God promised to their fathers. His whole purpose in this famous chapter in Deuteronomy is to ensure that neither they nor the generations to come ever forget the bountiful deliverance and constant care the Lord their God has afforded them. Soon they will overtake nations who will leave for their survival and enjoyment all of these ready-made luxuries. These words are sharp arrows aimed at hard human hearts prone to scorn their Provider by denying the truth about the origin of their blessings.

I, too, have drunk from wells I did not dig. I have eaten and been satisfied from vineyards that I had absolutely no part in planting, and my house has been filled with luxuries that I received ready made. You see, I have a big sister.

One of my first memories is of my big sister absolutely adoring me. I have heard the stories of how it was before I could know how to take note and remember: that little four-year-old girl thought I was *her* baby, and she was diligent to give me the kind of loving care and protection any good parent would. I suppose it isn't so hard for some to be smitten with or even to find irresistible an innocent, little baby, but I am here to tell you that as I grew, I became increasingly resistible and decreasingly innocent. By the time I was in junior high, I had metamorphosed into a definite thorn in her teenaged side. Still, Judy responded with remarkable grace and forgiveness, all the while managing to see me through the same rose-colored glasses she always had. No matter that I told on her for the one or two mischievous acts she ever dared to engage in so that she could finally suffer some of the wrath of our parents that I was more than a little familiar with; no matter that I treated the love of her life at that time with rattlesnake venom, she could never stay mad at me for more than a few minutes. And absolutely nothing I could do would deter her from snuggling up to me at night after reading the Bible to me, kissing me tenderly, and making a sisterly pact with me for us both to "try to be better tomorrow." I remember always wondering at those times how anyone *could* be any better than she was. Judy's unconditional love for me was my strongest proof of God.

I did nothing to deserve her— in fact, I did much to antagonize her— but there she always was welcoming me with love in her eyes every morning and teaching me about God the last thing every night. I believe an x-ray might show Philippians 2:4 tattooed on her heart.

"Give thanks to the Lord, for He is good; His love endures forever." Psalm 107:1

~JULY 29~
OUT ON GOD'S LIMB:
WHAT THE "THEREFORE" IS THERE FOR

"Then Jesus said to his disciples: 'Therefore, I tell you, do not worry about your life, what you will eat; or about your body, what you will wear...But seek His kingdom and these things will be given to you as well." Luke 12:22, 31

Luke 12 relates a parable Jesus told about a wealthy but foolish man. The parable ends with words of warning to anyone who is rich in money but is not rich toward God. Most modern Bibles include italicized headings between sections of scripture that seem to need dividing for some reason. I suppose whoever did that had good motives. Maybe they were trying to be sure we had an idea what was coming, so they inserted these themes, of sorts; or maybe they just wanted to be sure our attention didn't wane, so they added these words in script to wake us up if we started to nod off before we reached the end of what someone else earlier sectioned into "chapters," (again, likely for some similar unknown reason). Whatever the reason, there is one of those divisions right here after this parable and right before a "therefore," which everyone knows is a transition word meant to connect where we are to where we were. Everyone knows, but I wonder how many do what I did until a few days ago—just mentally erase it.

The italicized phrase in my NIV Bible reads, *"Do Not Worry."* Maybe I am just too impressionable, but because of that heading, I have always believed that the main purpose in this section of Jesus' talk was to explain how He is willing and able, as God, to take care of all of our needs, and He wants to announce, as the angels announced His birth to the shepherds, that we are now set free from the curse of worry. Certainly it does that, and I shall continue to use these words to chastise myself and discourage others in regards to worrying. However, recently I saw this chapter in a new light that excites me even more than the security of knowing I have a book, chapter, and verse that relieves me of the morbidly cherished responsibility of worrying.

I have no problem with the commonly-held idea that Luke 12 is a lesson about stewardship, but now I don't believe that Jesus' main point is about money in the parable or about worry in the "therefore" section that follows. I think He is asking us to look closely at where our treasures, and therefore, our hearts, are making their home. That "therefore" hooks back to His warning about not being rich toward God.

He wants us to see stewardship in a deeper sense than whose pile we put each part of our money. He is talking about single vision, an undivided heart that is placed unreservedly in God's column. This parable is about a man whose heart was so distracted by a practiced and perfected, cherished longing for goods that he lost his focus on what his real treasure was. His eyes were so filled with the stars of success and self-sufficiency that he could no longer see anything else clearly, not even the God who had given him the crops he was busy compounding in his storehouses. He lost sight of his source of ability, and he lost sight of what it meant to be humbly grateful.

May God grant us the wisdom of gratitude so that our hearts may make their home in their true Home.

~JULY 30~
REMEMBERING OUR FIRST LOVE

"But I have this against you, that you have abandoned the love you had at first. Remember, then, from what you have fallen, repent and do the works you did at first." Revelation 2:4-5 (RSV)

The crowds thronged around Him. There were so many places to go and people to see, but one day Jesus found the opportunity to sit down with His disciples on the Mount of Olives and have a bit of private conversation. Jesus had been saying things that didn't make a lot of sense to them. Sometimes He spoke of going away without them; sometimes He responded to them in puzzling ways. His wisdom and authority were undeniable, but there was something they couldn't quite nail down about the nature of this "King." One thing was certain: He was like no other king they had ever heard about; He was like no one else period.

And now He was saying that a time was coming when the very temple they had just left would be utterly destroyed. They had so many questions: When will this happen? What signs will mark your return? What will the end of the age look like?

As He answered them, they probably wished they had never asked, for the forecast went from bad to worse as He described the clashing of kingdoms, famines, earthquakes, and persecution. He explained that, as a result of the vast increase of wickedness, the love of most would grow cold.

And now years later, John, likely the only disciple still alive, takes dictation from God: a letter to the Ephesian church. He explains that they have done many things right: they are hard workers, do good deeds, do not tolerate wickedness, and have endured persecution for the name of Christ. But there is one thing lacking that He obviously needs to point out to these good folks: the fire of passion they once felt for Him and His cause has grown cold.

Why, we might wonder, if He is able to find all these other good things to commend them for, does He care about this? He has been speaking of their good deeds and hard work in present tense, so what's the problem?

Maybe the reason we tend to want to ask this question is that, sadly, we can identify. After all, doesn't the way we *walk* supersede we way we *feel*? Aren't we to be commended when, against all that we *feel*, we continue to *do* what is *right?* Well, yes, but then again, no. God did not create us primarily to *behave.* Good behavior, good deeds, hard work are noble, and when we buck the temptations to quit, God is pleased with us. But He is not pleased if we settle into and finally, settle *for* a consistently pale, limp, tepid, and numb *love* for Him. We are told to worship Him *in spirit and in truth*. Worship involves adoration, and adoration involves our emotions.

Yes, we are to be good soldiers who march into battle whether we are weary and reluctant or effervescent and eager. But the *feet* can't go on indefinitely without some recharging of the *heart*. We need to refresh our memories about how it was when we first met Him. Then, we need to take off our boots, fall into His arms, and *dance* with Him.

~JULY 31~
DANCING LESSONS

"The Lord your God is with you, He is mighty to save. He will take great delight in you, He will quiet you with His love, He will rejoice over you with singing." Zephaniah 3:17

"...At that time I will deal with all who oppressed you; I will rescue the lame and gather those who have been scattered, I will give them praise and honor in every land where they were put to shame. At that time, I will gather you; at that time, I will bring you home. I will give you honor and praise among all peoples of the earth when I restore your fortunes before your eyes." Zephaniah 3: 19-20

"For the eyes of the Lord range throughout the earth to strengthen those whose hearts are fully committed to Him." 2 Chronicles 16:9

"O, Jerusalem, Jerusalem, you who kill the prophets and stone those sent to you, how often I have longed to gather your children, as a hen gathers her chicks under her wings, but you were not willing." Matthew 23:37

Lest we think that these agonizing words in this final scripture were addressed only to the Jews, look at this reminder from Paul: *"If you belong to Christ, then you are Abraham's seed, and heirs according to the promise" (Galatians 3:29).* No, we are *all* heirs of the promise; we are *all* invited to be participants in the divine nature. Listen to the Mother-sigh of Jesus as He longs for what could have been. Listen to the God-sigh in fleshly form lamenting the ruin of what He wanted for us. This was not the heart of a power-hungry ruler whose rebellious constituents are about to be taught a lesson. This is the heart that prompts the words, "Father, forgive them, for they know not what they do" through parched and bleeding lips from lungs emitting their final few breaths. Ironically, the Father to whom He makes His request is the One who has sent Him for this very hour because of our helplessness. And ironically, the One who is being punished is the only One who doesn't deserve it. Here is an "outlaw" so offensive that he doesn't even get a trial, yet so obscure that his opponents have to pay one of his followers to identify him so they could arrest Him. Here is a King so poor that he owns only the clothes on His back and with no place of His own even to lay His head.

Surprise after surprise, irony after irony. There is so much here that is illogical, so much that is irrational.

But isn't that the way with love? Doesn't true love take us by storm? When it is new, doesn't it render us a little bit foolish and provoke responses that defy reason?

When we first discover the love of our life, don't we act in some extreme ways? Doesn't this "first" love muster in us energy we didn't know we had, and inspire in us poetry and music we never knew were there? This is the love the Ephesians in Revelation 2 had lost.

Go back and read these scriptures again. Aren't they enough to jazz up your marching? Now read John 3:16. Look at the love in this scripture anew, through the lens of what we know love to be at its strongest.

If that's not dancing music, nothing is.

~AUGUST 1~
SWAP-MEET MAGIC

"He has sent me ...to bestow upon them a crown of beauty instead of ashes, the oil of gladness instead of mourning, and a garment of praise instead of a spirit of despair. They will be called oaks of righteousness, a planting of the Lord for the display of His splendor." Isaiah 61:1, 3

You don't see them much anymore, but once the signs were a common weekend sight along the highways: "Swap Meet Today." (Once Larry and I even saw a sign that read "Dog Trade Every Third Saturday.") Just last week I drove past a car-swap. Hundreds had come pulling on trailers old cars they hoped to trade in for someone else's old car. Of course, at these meets everyone's eyes are fully open to the fact that the value of the things traded would be close to the same. There's nothing really magic about giving someone two nickels and getting a dime in return.

But when we were little girls, my sister and I used to lick trading stamps to fill little books for our mother to trade in at a "redemption center" for things worth ever so much more than the little green square inches of paper we gave for them— like a bike, a b-b gun, a chemistry set, or a transistor radio. To us, it was the ultimate redemption magic to go into a store with generic paper that wasn't even money and come out with a brand new bicycle.

The message Isaiah spoke to the Jews of Judah after their northern brothers had been taken captive by the Babylonians must have sounded like that same kind of magic. He spoke of a time when the Lord's favor would come to light upon them in unmistakable dimensions. First he spoke of good news for the poor, mending for the broken hearted, freedom for slaves, release for prisoners, comfort for the mourning. The good news then graduated from basic deliverance into Something More, blessings of elaborate proportions for the grief-stricken—not just deliverance, but a Divine potpourri of extravagant trade-in deals: for their ashes, a crown of beauty; for their mourning, the oil of gladness; for their spirit of despair, a garment of praise; for their reputation as vulnerable, shriveled, fruitless bushes in the desert unable even to produce a little much-needed shade from the blistering sun, the name of "oaks of righteousness, a planting of the Lord for the display of His splendor." It was a foreshadowing of what happened in Jerusalem on Pentecost shortly after Jesus went back into Heaven after His resurrection. Peter, using the keys to the Kingdom bestowed upon Him by His Rabbi and Savior, stood up and preached the crucified Jesus as the long-awaited Messiah to a crowd undeserving of His news but ripe for the hearing. *'When the people heard this, they were cut to the heart, and said to Peter and the other apostles, 'Brothers, what shall we do?' Peter replied, 'Repent and be baptized, every one of you, for the remission of your sins. And you will receive the gift of the Holy Spirit'" (Acts 2:36-38).* And there it was again— the same unbelievable trade-in magic. We bring to Him our sins, and in return He gives us His very Spirit to live inside us—to protect, guide, and comfort us *eternally*, if we so choose.

This isn't a dime for two nickels or even a '57 Chevy for a little red wagon. This is eternal life for certain death. Ponder it afresh today, and be exhilarated and swept away by the Magic of your redemption. Live out your gratitude in service to Him today.

~AUGUST 2~
A FEW ANSWERS FOR SKEPTICS

"The wrath of God is being revealed from heaven against the godlessness and wickedness of men who suppress the truth by their wickedness, since what may be known about God is plain to them, because God has made it plain to them. For since the creation of the world God's invisible qualities— His eternal power and divine nature—have been clearly seen, being understood from what has been made, so that men are without excuse." Romans 1:18-20

"If God is really in control..." begins many a question from skeptics of the existence and/or goodness of our God. Without bothering to go to the most logical of all places, His Word, to learn of God, they easily condemn our beliefs in an all-wise, all-loving Father-God. Usually they cannot understand how there could be evil if He is who we say He is.

One of the common foundational truths overlooked by skeptics is the fact that this is a love relationship we are in, and in any good love relationship, love must be *chosen*. Second Corinthians 4:4 reads, "The god of this age has blinded the minds of unbelievers, so that they cannot see the light of the gospel of the glory of Christ, who is the image of God." God can't take the direct approach and force us to love Him because that would defeat His purpose of having a mutually loving relationship with us. This is not one of the ways He chooses to use His power. Therefore, He is present enough so that those who want to know and experience Him are able to, but absent enough so that those who don't desire that aren't forced to. The first chapter of Romans shows us that God will give us the "privilege" of living in sin if we insist. The consequences, even on this earth, will likely bring us torment, but it will be a torment of our own choosing.

Many have trouble understanding why God allows certain people to die, but they have forgotten that God is the God of *all* of history, not just ours right here, right now. Perhaps He allowed that person to die because truly it was the lesser of two evils in some bigger way than we can imagine. Romans 8:28 explains that "*All* things work together for the good of those who love the Lord and are called according to His purpose." He doesn't say here that all things work *separately* for our good, but that all things work *together*. We usually see just one puzzle piece at a time in this limited world we live in, but there are times throughout our lives when we can look back and see how some of those seemingly random pieces fit together with exact nicety.

God surrendered some of His control over the workings of this world when He allowed for evil to be a part of this world. However, it was for our freedom that He chose to do so. Therefore, we can and do suffer as a result of people's evil choices. God is still ultimately in control, though, because He can't lose the final battle. He has already defeated death through Jesus. God continues to control the fact that we do not have to be defeated by evil if we choose to be in relationship with Him through Jesus.

"It is for freedom that Christ has set us free. Stand firm, then, and do not let yourselves be burdened again by a yoke of slavery." Galatians 5:1

~AUGUST 3~
THE LOCUST YEARS

"I will repay you for the years that the locusts have eaten—the great locust and the young locust, the other locusts and the locust swarm…You will have plenty to eat, until you are full, and you will praise the name of the Lord your God who has worked wonders for you." Joel 2:25-26

Every August 3 I relive in detail this day a few years ago. It was a day of tears and laughter, losing and gaining, a day of goodbye and hello. After ten years of having the luxury of my dear bosom friend living only six minutes away from me, she was moving to Hawaii, of all places. Not just to a new town, not even just across a few state lines, but all the way across an ocean— and a big ocean, at that. Although we both kept reminding each other that God knew best and would continue to hold us together in His big hand, it was a cup I was having a very hard time swallowing.

But as the minutes of the last night ticked sadly away before I would take her to the airport early the next morning, something else was happening five-and-a-half hours away—something wonderful and blessed: my grandson was making his way into this world. The Lord was taking away, but He was also giving. By the time she was in the air, he was snuggled safely in his mother's arms. They named him "Joel,"("The Lord is God")— yes, of sad goodbyes that, in Him, always blossom into joyous hello's.

Joel is a bright, active little guy who plays dangerously hard and gets more than his share of goose eggs on his head. One of his favorite words at age two is the question, "Ready?" When we hear this, we know we aren't. We also know we have no longer than three seconds to prepare for some kind of fierce action coming our way. We are pretty sure there will be roughness all through the day, but we know just as certainly that when bedtime comes, he will lay his tired little blond head on some lucky shoulder, listen to a story, recite a Bible verse, say his prayers, and give sweet kisses. And all of the cyclonic energy required of us through the day will be more than compensated for.

His parents named him aptly. The prophet Joel had some hard news for God's people in Judah. They would be victims of great swarms of literal locusts that would devastate their agricultural livelihood. (This is not to mention the swarms of figurative ones that would plague their and their ancestors' future, the Babylonians, Medo Persians, Greeks, and Romans.) He called on everyone of every age and profession to repent, for this onslaught was the Lord's army reminding them that "the Day of the Lord" was at hand. But what this prophet is best known for is the message he brings concerning the aftermath of the destruction: the Lord will send *"grain, new wine and oil, enough to satisfy you fully...I will drive the northern army far from you...Be not afraid, O land; be glad and rejoice...I will repay you for the years the locusts have eaten" (Joel 2:19-20, 25, 28-30, 32).* And sure enough, if we keep reading, we come to Acts 2, the beginning of the fulfillment.

We need never let the locust years before our life in Christ tempt us into hopelessness that saps our energy for the day. A lovely evening has rolled in, and comfort lies on our shoulder. Now we can rest. Praise Him who has worked wonders.

~AUGUST 4~
REAL LIFE

"Above all else, guard your heart, for it is the wellspring of life." Proverbs 4:23

Part of this no one had to tell us; we knew it a long time ago. Life—the *real* kind that gurgles, bubbles up, and swells ecstatically around us—cannot be separated from feelings. We describe life at its best through the media of feeling words. When someone describes her life as "just putting one foot in front of another," we know she is merely surviving, not really living. We all somehow *know* that life is not something just to be survived, but to be *lived* to its fullest with our hearts to their fullest. Those who throw in the towel due to sustained pain or disappointment somewhere down the line always regret that they did. Those who will themselves to numbness wish that they had stayed vulnerable, and maintained, at all costs, the ability to *feel*. They learn at a great price that when they closed off their heart to further possibility of pain, they also closed it off to further possibility of joy. They thought that a thick wall would protect them and help them to survive, but they learned that what they ended up with was no life at all. The heart they sought to protect shrivels into nothing *to* protect. It hardens into stone. True, stone cannot cry, but neither can it laugh. It is just a cold, dead lump of heaviness.

But can the heart be *trusted*? According to Jeremiah, who calls the heart "deceitful above all things," absolutely not! He knew it was the wellspring of life which evil must not be allowed to contaminate. The heart left to itself—left to our *selves*—cannot be trusted. Solomon tells us more than once that *"There is a way that seems right to a man, but in the end it leads to death" (Proverbs 14:12; 16:25).* Left to ourselves, we follow what *seems* right, but our unguarded, untrained heart from which the *seemings* issue is not a trustworthy guide. Strife, bitterness, lust, fickleness, vengefulness, selfishness, and greed seek us out; without invitation, they nip at our heels. But peace, patience, kindness, self-control, gentleness, and faithfulness come to abide in us only as a result of a well-nurtured, well-nourished Spirit- the Holy Spirit of God, given to us when we become Christians as a "deposit guaranteeing what is to come" (2 Corinthians 1:22). A malnourished Spirit *shrivels*, and the heart is left prey to the defaults of worldliness; a well-nourished Spirit *thrives* and overcomes the default. The water from the former is putrid, infested with disease, and its consumption is sure to poison; the water from the latter is clean and pure, and its consumption brings life and health. Many well-meaning but misguided Christians have given up the fight to live. They have decided that the heart is just too fragile, too prone to being wounded in battle, or that it is too demanding and hard to control, so they have in one way or another effectively killed it. They have cut themselves off from the wellspring of life.

Wisdom tells us not to kill the heart, but to *guard* it. Protect it from evil by filling it with goodness. Remember the man Jesus spoke about with the demon who, after being evicted, later returned to move back in with his seven buddies? The reason? Emptiness. Taste His goodness (Psalm 34:8). Become enthralled with His beauty as He is with yours (Psalm 45:11). Let Him fill you up. It is the best way— the only way— to guard your heart.

~AUGUST 5~
A PRAYER FOR A GUARDED HEART

"Blessed are the pure in heart, for they will see God." Matthew 5:8

We guard our hearts by filling them with God, not just emptying them of evil. In fact, without God's filling, we cannot keep them emptied of evil. Jesus calls the well-guarded heart a "pure" heart. If our hearts belong purely to God, unadulterated by anything else, Jesus promises that we will "see God."

Think of it! Seeing God doesn't mean just when we get to Heaven, but right here on earth, we can see God and know how to follow Him.

Take a close and honest inventory of your heart. Pray, as you do this, that God will reveal to you any weaknesses, any impurities there. When I did this recently, He was faithful to answer me with clarity and immediacy. I wrote down the things I needed to be vigilant about and began praying for them specifically and earnestly. Here is how my prayer went:

Dear Father,

Times like these help me realize how weak and frail my heart can be. I believe I am beginning to understand what you meant in the Beatitudes about being "poor in spirit." Maybe the way the poor in spirit receive their blessedness is by at last falling on their faces before your throne in abject hopelessness of anything less than Your thorough healing of the heart really answering their needs for very long. Here I am, then, Lord, seeing so clearly how desperately my heart (the heart of all my matters) needs Your touch. You have surely given me these words of request to bring to You. Please give me a heart that is generous, gracious, humble, and complete in Christ. I can see no reason why you wouldn't be pleased with all these aspects, so I ask boldly, Lord, believing Your words that whatever we ask in Your name you will give us, and that when we delight ourselves in You, You will give us the desires of our hearts. I truly can say that above all else in this world or my imagination I want these things— a heart that is generous, gracious, humble, and complete in Your Son.

I ask for generosity because I am selfish-hearted. I ask for graciousness that I might extend grace to others rather than being demanding and judgmental. Help me be a gracious rememberer and forgetter— remembering the times I have received grace from You and others, and forgetting when frail or busy flesh has let me down. Please give me some gracious blind spots. I ask for humility that I may have Your perspective of me, not some inflated delusion of grandeur. And, finally, I ask for a heart complete in Christ, so that I will not continue expecting and depending upon anything this side of Heaven for peace and nourishment. Amen.

Begin this very day to let Him show you what you need to pray for in order to guard your heart and keep it pure for His use. Be specific! It will prove an exercise in faith that will draw you nearer to the perfect Wellspring of Life.

~AUGUST 6~
ON THE ANVIL OF SILENCE

"I am still confident of this: I will see the goodness of the Lord in the land of the living. Wait for the Lord; be strong and take heart, and wait for the Lord." Psalm 27:13-14

"Search me, O God, and know my thoughts.
See if there is any offensive way in me
And lead me in the way everlasting."

229

...Silence upon silence
day after day—
the weaning of a heart needing Pure Blood and Water
but caught up in a thirst for pride's false nutrition.

Heartache upon heartache
night after night—
the Plan in full swing of a Savior who pleads
for His suffering child on the anvil.

Prayer upon prayer
after tear upon tear—
the slow, certain dirge to the burial site
of Satan's lost stronghold.

How long ago was this blueprint fashioned
to deliver me to the reckoning?
"Such knowledge is too wonderful,
too lofty for me to attain."

The anvil of sustained heartache and silence is a hard place to lie still. Sometimes *He* has placed us there to bring us to the end of ourselves and our shallow notions of what is necessary in our lives. Sometimes we are there in spite of and against all of His desires; our rebellion has convinced us of a better way than His. We pray and listen, waiting in the silence for Him to burst through the door and deliver us from this place. We don't understand. Are we are no longer spiritually discerning; have we tuned into a different frequency from His? Or is this waiting the very medicine, ripening, or fermenting we need to grow more into His likeness? Is this His way of beckoning us to come up higher?

These times give us the opportunity to exercise our *faith*. Once faith was just a word in the Bible or a song—so easy to read and sing; we could even get emotional about it in its abstraction. But here it is in the concrete of our very lives, no longer an abstract philosophy, lovely but untried, but an *absolute* that demands a decision. Is He worth waiting for, or will we decide, either quietly or aloud, that He, like our faith, was, after all, just some ink on some pages? Whatever we decide, we will never be the same.

~AUGUST 7~
"I CAN'T GET NO SATISFACTION"

"Satisfy us in the morning with your unfailing love that we may sing for joy and be glad all our days." Psalm 90:14

The dreams we dream of others can only come true in Him.
Our high-piled hopes crumble sadly into wishes;
Our bright expectations grow dim.
What looked like certainties and felt like promises
Turn out so often to be whims.
The dreams we dream of others can only come true in Him.

Mick Jagger and the Rolling Stones aren't the only ones who can't get any satisfaction. Confined to an earthly search, we are all in the same boat.

Time and time again, we are forced to abandon the noun and settle for the adjective. Sometimes we grasp onto the heaven*ly* relationships, but they never turn out to be *Heaven*. Something is always there to mar them out of the excellence we hoped for and into a settlement for something less. True, we have out moments, but the rub lies in their lack of permanence; they are not a place we can stop and put down roots or capture in a jar to have as often as we like. We remember them longingly and hope to have some more.

This is the way it is here on earth. And this is the way it is with earth*lings*. No one can fulfill our deepest hearts' desires. Most of us refuse to believe this until we have tried it for ourselves many, many times and failed just as often. But those who "are being transformed into his likeness with ever-increasing glory" are ecstatic to have finally figured this out. We no longer have to feel the heartaches of being disappointed time and again when the flesh we had hoped would be Divine was, after all, just flesh. We have given up the illusion.

But this is not to say we have given up *hope*! On the contrary, we *now* know how to focus on our one *true* Hope. He is the person of Jesus. He is not Someone we have to wait for; He is here with us now. When we finally allow God to be God in our lives, then, and only then, are we free to allow flesh to be merely flesh.

Give those you love the *most* extravagant gift: the freedom to step down from that pedestal once and for all. They're probably weary and bruised up from all the times they have had to fall off.

~AUGUST 8~
DANGEROUS MEANDERING

"Therefore, since we are surrounded by such a great cloud of witnesses, let us throw off everything that hinders and the sin that so easily entangles, and let us run with perseverance the race marked out for us." Hebrews 12:1

We are beset time and time again by undue fearfulness and swollen pride and all kinds of perversion of His perfect will. How foolishly we can meander through our days, oblivious to the way our fruit is rotting from the core! How we need to be aware that our core needs the continual care that can only come from reaching upward and not inward for sustenance! Such disturbances as a bristling when we must play second fiddle and devastation when we realize that we are not cherished in our selfishly prescribed ways indicate that our security is rooted in the wrong places, not in God, as it should be.

When we know that we should relinquish it all to Him but we know also that we cannot truly say that we have, let us at least say to Him, "Oh, Father, I *want* to!" When useless fretting and selfish anxieties cling to us like lint on black wool, let us not believe that we are beyond help. Though we know that He won't wrench it from our white-knuckled grip, can't we at least tell Him that we *desire* to loosen our grip? Can't we petition Him to reveal to us what we must *do*, how we must *change* to be able to give up all this foolishness?

Can we ask Him to reveal to us as we study His Word the crossroads where we have chosen badly? Can we ask Him to open our eyes and take us back there and lead us out of our earthly choosing? Can we ask as we read His Words that He will persuade us to look harder and in a different way this time?

Dear Father,

If the pain comes with the territory, and this is the territory where I belong right now, then I accept and even embrace it and ask for your courage to receive it well. But if I'm not in the territory you created me for at this time, or if this pain is a sign of my sin and waywardness, I beg you to take my outstretched hand— or show me how to stretch it our further to you—and lead me back to your perfect path for me.

I pray with hope and confidence because of Jesus. Amen

~AUGUST 9~
FINDING JOY THROUGH THE SUFFERING

"I then, as Paul— an old man and now also a prisoner of Christ Jesus— I appeal to you for my son Onesimus, who became my son while I was in chains... I am sending him—who is my very heart—back to you." Philemon 9-10, 12

The letter to Philemon is only one chapter long. It is a kind of postcard parable in that there is a transgressor, an interceder, and a master. The interceder asks the master to accept with grace and mercy the transgressor who has been made "new."

The good news is that Onesimus has become a Christian. The bad news is that he is a runaway slave. To complicate matters, Paul, who has just become a spiritual father to Onesimus, knows his master, Philemon. In fact, Philemon is a Christian in the church in Colosse that Paul helped establish. In this little post-card, Paul addresses not just Onesimus' master but the entire church as he pleads with Philemon to accept his returning slave as a brother, rather than a slave. It is a tender reminder that people can change; Paul hopes that Philemon will exercise mercy rather than the justice that he has the right and power to wield now that the one returning to him has enslaved himself to a higher Master. The fact that the slave does indeed return to throw himself at the mercy of his master is good evidence that Onesimus is a changed man ready to do what is right, even when it hurts.

By sending the letter to be read by the entire church, Paul set Philemon up for success in what might have been a hard temptation to overcome considering the power Philemon possessed over Onesimus. This is how we should help others: Christian peer pressure. Rather than to delight in always testing each other, we should try to find ways to *help* each other succeed in doing the right thing.

Another understanding we can glean from this little letter is that the kind of joy Christ means to bring to His followers must be a joy *through* suffering—not one that removes the suffering to get to the joy. (Otherwise, Jesus would not have died on a cross.) We try to make it look easier, but truly it cannot be. Paul said Onesimus was going back—possibly to continue being Philemon's slave. His true freedom, like ours, could only come by accepting the fact that he was a lawbreaker and thus deserved punishment. Only his master had the power to set him free.

"Jesus said, 'I tell you the truth, everyone who sins is a slave to sin. Now a slave has no permanent place in the family, but a son belongs to it forever. So if the Son sets you free, you will be free indeed'" (John 8:34-36).

~AUGUST 10~
INVESTING WISELY

"Remember Your Creator in the days of your youth before the days of trouble come and the years approach when you will say 'I find no pleasure in them'... Remember Him—before the silver cord is severed, or the golden bowl is broken; before the pitcher is shattered at the spring, or the wheel broken at the well, and the dust returns to the ground it came from, and the spirit returns to God who gave it." Ecclesiastes 12:1, 6-7

If we are honest, most of us deal with vanity in one form or another on one level or another. If we are not careful, we will become overly invested in trying to *look* a certain way. Sometimes vanity's roots are wrapped fairly tightly around our hearts before we ever notice their invasion. By the time we take notice, we can be deeply diseased by it.

It is a disease not limited by age. Growing out of the years of easy outward beauty does not make us immune to vanity. In fact, for some of us, the hardest battles against it come when we are old enough and experienced enough to *know* better. But as with so many besetting sins, what we know *intellectually* doesn't always transfer wisdom to how we *live*.

It can start rather harmlessly as a challenge to see how long we can hold off the gravity of aging and reign victorious over the ordinariness of appearance we were born with. It might work the way a gardener's challenge does: See if you can take a plain piece of sod and turn it into something beautiful to behold. An avid gardener might spend hundreds or thousands of dollars to accomplish this thing.

And like the gardener, we might have trouble backing out after we have already invested so much, so we just keep throwing more and more of our energies into it. When the seasons begin to change and like the gardener, we realize the folly of trying to build a visual paradise in the dead of winter, we have nothing of ourselves invested anywhere else. Our whole life has been invested in this plot of sod. Our beautification investments are no longer paying off, and we are poverty-stricken in all other areas.

The root meaning of the word "vanity" is "emptiness." The book of Ecclesiastes is all about it. When we vainly pursue something, we conclude with emptiness. When we pay too much attention to our shell, our cores get nothing. We are *empty*. Solomon warns us about many different kinds of empty pursuits. He says that when we invest our whole lives in the pursuit of physical beauty, financial success, and fame, we do so at the expense of the inward man, our Souls, which were created to strive toward and be richly invested in fearing God and keeping His commandments. He says this is "the whole duty of man." Compared to this, everything else is meaningless.

Take an honest inventory today. Where are you most seriously invested? When the outward glory ends— and it will— "When the keepers of the house tremble, and the strong men stoop, when the grinders cease because they are few, and those looking through the windows grow dim," will your investments still be working for you?

~AUGUST 11~
A LOOK AT BOTH SIDES OF THE COIN

"Since you call on a Father who judges each man's work impartially, live your lives as strangers here in reverent fear." 1 Peter 1:17

For all who have grown up in the shackles of legalism, may I offer a different viewpoint? May I share a view from some different shackles others have grown up in? While you have felt enslaved by "Be good!" "Follow all the rules," and have found a taste of freedom in the other side of that coin that reads, "Trust God for your goodness," "Break free from the law and fly in the breeze of His love and mercy"— some have come *from* and *to* other places and have found freedom in looking at the coin in another way.

Think about the word "anchorless." Imagine trying to fish from a small, anchorless vessel out on a windy sea. Imagine the frustration of trying to enjoy your picnic lunch in this boat with no anchor. With every bite you try to enjoy, your food sticks in your throat from the vague fear of drifting too far away from shore in directions you may not be familiar with. This is how it feels to grow up with only lip service to God's Word. When your spiritual education is derived from a strictly social gospel— how to get along with people, how to be a good citizen, how to be the kind of people others will like— your schooling doesn't go too far. When you find you can't "get along" with people because you don't see eye to eye, who's to say which viewpoint is right? When it's time to be a good citizen and vote on candidates or proposals, how do you judge which is best? What if the people you want to like you have a different moral code from yours or the character traits you always have held to are questioned? What is the *correct* standard for character and morality? Out of all the choices we are given, all the directions we can choose to travel, how do we find true north? Or is there even such a thing as true north? Go into a library, or turn on the t.v., and you will soon find that everyone seems to have a different idea about that.

It is undeniably true that there is such a thing as harmful legalism; Jesus met the Pharisees and teachers of the law head on about this time after time. This is the kind of law-keeping that ignores or tramples over and lays waste to the deeper root of all of God's lawmaking: love, peace, and reconciliation with Him. If this is what you flail against, flail away. You are certainly following your Rabbi when you reject this kind of focus on lawkeeping.

But look carefully, and be honest. Be sure you are not just trying to disfigure who God really is into something you had rather He was. He is love and mercy and longsuffering and sacrifice, but He is also a jealous God who will not allow evil to win out over good. He calls us to present ourselves as living sacrifices, which requires laying down our lives as *we* might want them to be and taking up some kind of cross that is hard to bear. Many of His followers have been and still are being martyred for standing against the evil that is out to devour those in its path who have not availed themselves of the blood of His Son. He sent Jesus to show us that true love is not just linking hands with the whole world no matter what it embraces but rather that it is *counter*-cultural and might require us to give our very lives to testify to its authenticity.

The Word of God is the true north that leads us to the right answer to every character issue. It is the solid rock— the only one on which we can stand with no worries that it will crumble under our feet. Taking God's Word seriously— all of it, not just the parts about loving, but also that parts about obeying and honoring right over wrong, *even if it offends someone*—is the anchor without which we will always be adrift.

~AUGUST 12~
TWO DIFFERENT SHOES

"The second is this: love your neighbor as yourself." Mark 12:31

I have noticed that God, as He listens to my pleadings, looks down upon my doings, and muses on my judgments of others, often responds by affording me with another perspective.

For instance, when I have felt a little emotionally shortchanged by someone, it isn't long before I am stopped in my tracks as I walk away or hang up the phone from someone to whom I have just done the same thing. I realize with chagrin that what felt like a glancing blow when it hit me felt like only a little bump when I was the perpetrator. What I did was not meant at all maliciously; it just happened with no thought at all. I withheld from the other, or cut her short, not because of anything I was feeling or because of any ill intention, but rather simply because I didn't think about it all. I was preoccupied with other thoughts or I was truly in a time bind and could not afford to stretch out the conversation. In these times when Something causes me to catch on and make the connection between being the victim and the victimizer, I realize that God is using His Spirit to point some things out to me and heighten my sensitivity to someone other than myself.

One of the things I can learn is that God is "the God of all comfort." He was with me when I felt the blow of rejection, and now He has appeared to change my perspective on it so that I can rethink my bruised feelings. He might be reminding me that I was a little more focused on myself than I should have been. Otherwise, I would have given the other person the benefit of the doubt and tried harder to play the role of her defense attorney, which is, of course, what I want others to do for me when I come across in a short or curt way.

Another lesson He might want to teach me is that what I do without thinking can hurt others. I might have been imagining myself to be above such unthought-fulness. This will help me to try harder to clear my mind of distractions and truly focus on the one before me.

Or I might have been critical of someone's overly sensitive nature. This is especially true when all this happens in the opposite order, and I do the deed first that later gets done to me. This is useful in growing more Christlike because I realize I, too, am indeed vulnerable. Thus, hopefully, I will be both a more patient and more understanding sympathizer.

Whatever the situation, we can be blessed with growth when we are given the opportunity to find ourselves standing in both shoes. Hopefully, we will better understand the left foot because of the perspective the right foot gives us. We should thank God and pray that we will notice and use these opportunities to move both feet forward as we try to walk more in the footsteps of Jesus.

~AUGUST 13~
CUT FROM HIS FABRIC

"Be self-controlled and alert. Your enemy the devil prowls around like a roaring lion looking for someone to devour." 1 Peter 5:8

"For the eyes of the Lord range throughout the earth to strengthen those whose hearts are fully committed to Him." 2 Chronicles 16:9

Satan comes hidden under lust-colored drapings,
Dancing and swirling, he tempts and he taunts,
Writhing voluptuously with seductive appeal
Perfuming his stench, he needles and taunts.

Silky and slick, darkly intense,
Eyes burning deeply and skin hot to touch.
Shrewd, lithe, and limber, darting and flitting—
Scratching our itches and promising so much.

Then snapping his ropes we are wafted away.
He loses his prey; we slip from his hands.
Our cries to our Father's listening ears
Have severed his ropes and shattered our bands.

Ripping madly at those trappings of darkness that failed,
He runs to his dressing room to don something bright,
Sashed with complacency, arrogantly seamed,
Or zippered with a consuming zeal to be right.

Or one with threads soaked in pride's deadly mire
Or colored with the dye of defensiveness and doubt;
Or one that clings warmly with resentment's appeal,
He simmers and wheedles, frets and pouts.

Desiring us to doubt those whose love we know best:
"To give them the benefit of the doubt, you're a fool!"
He recites and entices, "You must second guess!"
Throwing ashes and tarnish on God's golden rule.

His wardrobe is as varied as our weaknesses.
He comes out in one then another.
One knitted of jealousy or of self-indulgence;
And yet another of slandering our brother.

But God is waiting to strip him naked,
Expose his true colors and put him to shame,
If only we'll cut our lives from His fabric
And seam all our days with the strength of His name.

~AUGUST 14~
SURRENDERING OUR CROWNS

"...the twenty-four elders fall down before Him who sits on the throne, and worship Him who lives forever and ever. They lay their crowns before the throne and say, 'You are worthy, our Lord and God, to receive glory and honor and power, for you created all things, and by your will they were created and have their being.'" Revelation 4:10-11

Here we have described for us a scene in Heaven of some saints laying their crowns down before the throne of their Master. They seem to do this willingly, even eagerly, because, fully convinced of the incomparable Holiness and Majesty of God, they wish to present Him with anything that might indicate any competition. It reminds me of some songs I have sung that speak of our laying our crowns at His feet.

I had always sung those words with little effort or thought until a few years ago when I went through some heartache involving some unexpected losses. It was then that I realized that the reason I was having such trouble adjusting was that I was being asked to lay down before God some "crowns" that had played a large role in my self-esteem, and which had indeed been more of an anchor than they should have been to my very security. I had to make some hard confessions about the immaturity of my spirituality. I had *felt* as though I was trusting in my identity in the Lord. I would have sworn that my security and joy were Heaven-based and not earth-based. I sincerely believed that I had crowned Jesus as King of my universe with no reservations.

But when things started changing in my life, I had to come face to face with the truth that these estimations just weren't true. I was being held down by some invisible strongholds that needed to be brought to my attention. The root of the problem was that I had allowed some aspects of my life— some conditions and situations that I took for granted would always be mine— to become *crowns*. They were not worthy of being crowns; they were false props. Now I was being asked to surrender them at the feet of Jesus—just to turn loose and trust that His grace would be sufficient for me, that *He* would be enough.

It is not an easy or natural thing to surrender a crown. It is very difficult to think of going through life without something that has become such a part of you. It is very, very difficult to walk away from a lovely and cherished crown. Its loveliness to own and to wear is compelling; what it means is so thrilling. It casts over us a feeling of chosenness. It gives us a powerful thrust to feel that we have aspired to and ascended to a place of our dreams. But He knows we are dreaming for less than we should be.

The huge problem with all this is what wearing a crown so clearly indicates: *that we belong on a throne*. Proverbs 16:2 reminds us of a profound truth: "All a man's ways seem innocent to him, but motives are weighed by the Lord." When God weighs our motives and sees that something in our life has become a crown that deceives us into believing that we belong on a throne, we should thank Him profusely when He shows us that we must surrender it to Him. When things start going that must, we must ask Him to help us to let go graciously. Hanging on for dear life will only stunt our growth and possibly even take the life of our spirit. Offer Him any would-be crowns this very day.

~AUGUST 15~
FEASTS AND OFFERINGS

"Be holy because I, the Lord your God, am holy." Leviticus 19:2

The book of Leviticus deals with the duties of the Levites, the tribe in charge of worship. Here we learn about the various Jewish feasts and sacrificial offerings God desired. Though it contains detailed descriptions of the priestly duties concerning tabernacle worship, its main thrust is holiness. Leviticus called the Jewish nation to a close focus on living holy lives before their holy God. Every time I read through the book of Leviticus I am excited to get to the end of it. It is bone wearying to think of all they had to go through in order to make some kind of pleasing atonement—all the raising and gathering of all the right kinds of animals for each kind of sacrifice, all the blood-letting and all the cleaning up, all the laundering of all the bloody priestly garments after each sacrifice. I wonder how there was any time left for anything else except their religious responsibilities. (Hmmm. Maybe there wasn't. Maybe our problem is *too much* leftover time!)

I also come away very, very grateful that Jesus came and changed all that for me. I know that in spite of how hard it is to read, it is always a good thing for me to have done it, for it never fails to give a new shine to the meaning of deliverance. Jesus came and paid the blood price once and for all. The closest I have to come to the hardship of all that physical work is to read about it from time to time to remind me how blessed I am to be on this side.

However, Romans 12:1-2 reminds us that this change in dispensations means in no way that God no longer cares about holiness. *"Therefore, I urge you, brothers, in view of God's mercy, to offer your bodies as living sacrifices, holy and pleasing to God— this is your spiritual act of worship. Do not conform any longer to the pattern of this world, but be transformed by the renewing of your mind."* This means that we need to be about the business of interpretive living. Our lives— and the sacrifices involved in the choices and decisions we make on a daily basis— interpret to the world who God is. Indeed, Hebrews 12:14 tells us that "without holiness, no one will see the Lord."

For now *we* are His priests, and the sacrifices we bring to Him are our very lives. Ephesians 5 is a wonderfully specific chapter about what this means. It is to Christians what Leviticus was to the Jews. If every Christian would memorize Ephesians 5:1-21 and strive to live it in a literal way, we would put an end to a lot of the corruption we are subjected to. Here is just a sample of our challenge: *"Be imitators of God, therefore, as dearly loved children and live a life of love, just as Christ loved us and gave himself up for us as a fragrant offering and sacrifice to God. But among you there must not be even a hint of sexual immorality, or any kind of impurity or greed, because these are improper for God's holy people"* *(Ephesians 5:1-3).* Not even a *hint*, it says.

Ironically, this kind of sacrificial living proves to be not just an offering but truly a feast. That holy living might bring us into some kind of famine of fun is the Enemy's lie. Holiness is what we were made for; it is a lavish feast, both now and for eternity.

~AUGUST 16~
THE ROOT OF OUR FRUIT

"But the fruit of the spirit is love, joy, peace, patience, kindness, goodness, faithfulness, gentleness, and self control. Against such things there is no law." Galatians 5:22-23

"Taste and see that the Lord is good." Psalm 34:8

"Do not think that I have come to abolish the Law or the Prophets; I have not come to abolish them but to fulfill them." Matthew 5:17

"By your fruit you will recognize them. Do people pick grapes from thornbushes, or figs from thistles? Likewise every good tree bears good fruit, but a bad tree bears bad fruit." Matthew 6:16-17

Outside-in versus inside-out; easy versus hard; quick versus slow; sloppy versus thorough; shallow versus deep. "You have heard it said... but I say unto you..." Jesus shocked people of His time by saying things that caused Him to come across as not just a puzzling master of paradox but sometimes even an anarchist. I imagine more than once someone rolled his eyes and said, "Here's that rebel again trying to trash the sacred law."

Of course, that wasn't true. The law of love that He came to proclaim and exemplify perfectly fulfills all the other laws; it just does it from the inside-out. It accomplishes it through the heart rather than the skin. It begins in the root instead of the fruit.

Trying to turn a hardened criminal into a good citizen by working on the symptoms alone is usually akin to trying to control a forest fire with a water gun or preventing a cage full of rabbits from propagating with a wag of the finger. About the time you succeed in one area, flames or baby rabbits break out from somewhere else. Just as production of the fruits of the flesh won't be *stopped* by plucking them one at a time off the tree, production of the fruits of the flesh won't occur by merely hanging them on the tree like a crate full of Christmas ornaments.

They are nourished into health and beauty only by means of the root— the Spirit. It is not as though *we* create our charming attributes, but rather the Lord and His Spirit *afford* us these graces. Only by giving Him total control over the entire tree will our fruit become plump, ripe, and tasty to those whom it contacts.

~AUGUST 17~
JAR POURERS VS. JAR BREAKERS

"Therefore, my dear brothers, stand firm. Let nothing move you. Always give yourselves fully to the work of the Lord, because you know that your labor is not in vain." 1 Corinthians 15:58

"But we have this treasure in jars of clay to show that this all-surpassing power is from God and not from us." 2 Corinthians 4:7

"Remain in me, and I will remain in you. No branch can bear fruit by itself; it must remain in the vine. Neither can you bear fruit unless you remain in me." John 15:4

Free Love for Sale

If you would listen closely you would hear a whiny sighing,
And isn't that mouth shaped somewhat like a pout?
But if you'd ask, I'd answer right away that I'm a lover,
Giving love profusely beyond the shadow of a doubt.

If I can't do it for free, Lord, let me call it prostitution;
And when I wait for return to come, Oh Father, just don't let it.
Keep at me 'til I learn to give my love away and not sell it,
To hand it over, turn around, and graciously forget it.

We can't fool the fruit with synthetic fertilizers or enhance production by short-cut means or store-bought mulch. We rightly dedicate the tree to the Master only when we turn it over fully to His care. He instructs faithfully through His Word. When His Word would prune off ravishing yet barren branches but we scurry to hide the shears, then we are acting as jar pourers rather than jar breakers.

Have you ever been disappointed, discouraged, or even devastated when your gifts or services seemed to go unnoticed or unappreciated? This seems to be such a common denominator of even the most dedicated Christians that I believe it must be one of Jesus' hardest teachings for us to digest. Instead of feeling disdainful, perhaps we should be *thankful* for these sandpaper sensations. They alert us, as we lavish our fruits upon imperfect creation, to turn our hearts and minds more fully to dedicating our roots to the ever-faithful, never-blasé Creator.

Nothing done *for God* is ever wasted.

~AUGUST 18~
SATISFY ME IN THE MORNING

"Satisfy me in the morning with your unfailing love that I might sing for joy and be glad all my days." Psalm 90:14

"Satisfy me
Satiate me, fill me sopping-sponge full!
In the morning
Ah, the bright, cool, fluttering wings
Of a clean, new day
When night has finished its job of restoration
And gets itself a rest,
And the sun pours yellow all over the waiting green earth
To turn it all pink and orange and purple.
With your unfailing love"
Always dependable, never tired or fickle,
Requiring no guesswork or apprehension
When I approach You for another few minutes
Of intimate touch and quiet gazing,
Hitting the mark every time,
Assuring me over and over
That you will be delighted to be with me always,
Even to the end of the age,
And that You, indeed, have gone before me
To prepare a place where you will take me
To live in your presence always,
And I shall, indeed— Oh, Blissful Realization!
Dwell and dwell and dwell
In the House of my Lord
Forever!

~AUGUST 19~
THAT I MIGHT SING FOR JOY

"Satisfy me in the morning with your unfailing love that I might sing for joy all my days!" Psalm 90:14

"That I might sing for joy
Hot, holy Hallelujah's!
Energizing, heart-throbbing, celestial-reaching
Notes of praise
To my Maker and Redeemer
And be glad

Exceedingly glad, sigh-evokingly relieved,
Hand-clapping, foot-stomping,
Tear-bringing, heart-racing, tongue-loosing,
Can't-shut-up-about-it ecstatic!
All my days!"
Not just two or three a month
Or a week or on Saturdays and Sundays
Or only months with "r's"
And days without stress or disappointment,
Or days that allow freedom from hard work or tight schedules
But every one of them that I wake up to—
Even those when I'm old and trembly
And saggy-baggy wrinkled
And too bent to stand straight on my feet
(Much less on my head to make kids smile)
Or cook a good meal,
Or sit in my garden,
Or read and write
Or be loved by friends
Or appreciated by my family
Or remembered at all
By any living soul;
Days when I can no longer run
Or even walk;
Listen to music
Or hear anything at all.
All My Days—
(And yea, my nights also!)

~AUGUST 20~
HEART SURGERY

"For the Word of God is living and active. Sharper than any double-edged sword, it penetrates even to dividing soul and spirit, joints and marrow; it judges the thoughts and attitudes of the heart. Nothing in all creation is hidden from God's sight. Everything is uncovered and laid bare before the eyes of Him to whom we must give account." Hebrews 4:12-13

Heart surgery is a time-consuming and critical process. The sharp scalpel cuts deeply, and the bleeding is profuse. One could die in the midst of this procedure whose goal is to restore normal and safe living.

And yet, no shortcuts can be allowed; the entire tedious and painstaking distance must be accomplished to restore this life-sustaining organ to its original design and function. *No* shortcuts— even though the healing process will take much longer and be much more painful when the cuts are deepest, to repair the most serious damage. Some, hearing of the pain, the danger, and the long period of recovery and convalescence, choose not to go through it, though the doctor pleads, explaining in vain that a reasonably secure life cannot be had without it.

And although the doctor might even attempt sometimes to explain the malfunction and the procedures he will use to correct or alleviate the problems, the patient rarely fully understands, never having been a heart specialist or surgeon. She must decide whether to trust the doctor and submit, lie down on his table and be cut into, or decline, and limp through the remainder of her life in an unwhole and precarious condition.

It is all so easy to see when we put it this way. Most of us, after thinking seriously about the alternatives, choose to have the surgery. We choose to entrust our lives to basically a stranger who will cut into our organs and do whatever he chooses, rather than the alternative of having our lives cut short. But the Great Physician comes to us in His word pleading His case for our spiritual health. Page after page he admonishes us to get that death-threat we are harboring taken care of, to let His sharp scalpel cut out the malignant intrusion that is little by little, day by day, eating away the life of our spirits.

That's the way most people lose their spiritual health— not in one huge leap off God's bandwagon but by sliding a foot off, then a leg, a hip, and finally lowering himself another few inches onto the world's highway. Today come to the Doctor and ask to be diagnosed. Take the medicine, get the surgery, take the cure no matter how long and slow the healing process might be. The truth is that although our bodies will die, all souls live eternally. Hopefully, that is good news to you! If it isn't, the Doctor is in.

"...knock and the door will be opened to you. For everyone who asks receives, he who seeks finds; and to him who knocks, the door will be opened." Matthew 7:7-8

~AUGUST 21~
LEAVING EGYPT

"Have I not commanded you? Be strong and courageous. Do not be terrified; do not be discouraged, for the Lord your God will be with you wherever you go...go in and take possession of the land the Lord your God is giving you for your own." Joshua 1:9, 11

The first chapter of Joshua is full of encouraging words from God, not just to Joshua and the Israelites he was preparing to enter the Promised Land, but also to those of us who have been grafted in and invited to enter a new Promised Land. Joshua's original audience had left Egypt as slaves on their way to a land prepared for them by God. After years of wandering in order to lose their stubborn ways and independent thinking, now they were on the verge of entering in at last.

When we become Christians, we too, leave our slavery to sin and enter into a Promised Land. The land we enter is full of wonderful inheritances that we can either take advantage of or not. If we don't, then although we have freedom offered to us, we still remain in Egypt.

This is a land of release from sin's enslavement. Paul tells us in Romans 6:17: *"...though you used to be slaves to sin, you wholeheartedly obeyed the form of teaching to which you were entrusted. You have been set free from sin and have become slaves to righteousness."* If we continue to allow sin's corruption to speak to us unhindered by the transforming power of God's Word, we are not taking advantage of one of the benefits of this new land we were given.

This is a land of refreshment. Once we awoke each morning and put on the same old clothes, ate the same old food— staples of the life of a slave who is doomed to making the same old bricks for the same old master. Life before the Promised Land was one of monotony that was borne of the hopelessness that comes from meaningless living. Life in the Promised Land is one of meaning and purpose. We are on a great adventure that is filled with possibilities beyond our wildest imagination because we are fueled and driven by the imagination of the God of all creation.

This is a land of rest. Yes, we work— not *so that* we will have salvation, but *because* we have it— but this work is the kind that reaps for us a joy that carries us above anxiety and despair. We no longer have to worry about a cruel master who might take away the straw we need to make our quota of bricks. We can rest in the arms of a loving Father who will supply all our needs and knows the number of hairs on each of our heads.

Our preacher, Joe Keyes, recently pointed out that we can "own" something without really "possessing" it. He used as an example the books in his library that he rightfully "owns" but does not possess until he reads them and internalizes their information. Might we in a sense "own" salvation but be missing its benefits? Have we really *taken possession* of all it offers? So that this would not happen to Joshua and those he led, the Lord instructed Him: *"Do not let this Book of the Law depart from your mouth; meditate on it day and night so that you may be careful to do everything in it" (verse 8).* Proclaim the Word, ponder the Word, and practice the Word: good advice for leaving Egypt and fully entering into our Promised Land.

~AUGUST 22~
DECIDING TO DECIDE

"Trust in the Lord with all your heart, and lean not on your own understanding; in all your ways acknowledge Him, and He will make your paths straight. Do not be wise in your own eyes; fear the Lord and shun evil. This will bring health to your body and nourishment to your bones. Honor the Lord with your wealth, with the firstfruits of all your crops; then your barns will be filled to overflowing, and your vats will brim over with new wine." Proverbs 3:5-10

At the end of our lives, we will be where we are and what we are as a result of the decisions we have made, one by one, day by day. As Christians, we must be committed to taking our stand for Christ at every crossroads. Indecisiveness is not an option, for if we do not make our own decisions, someone else will surely make them for us. Ronald Reagan told a story of a time when he was young and a shoemaker needed to know whether he wanted round-toed or square-toed shoes. Since he couldn't decide, eventually the shoemaker brought him a pair of shoes with one round-toed one and one square-toed one. He didn't make the decision, so someone else did.

In just a few verses, Solomon reminds us about some crucial decisions we make as we live and grow. The decisions will be made; there is no question about that. The question is whether we will make the decisions or let someone else make them for us.

First of all, we decide whom we will trust. In trying to follow Christ, there is really no such thing as fence-sitting. We may balance there for awhile, but eventually we will end up on one side or the other. Jesus said, *"No one can serve two masters. Either he will hate the one and love the other, or he will be devoted to one and despise the other" (Matthew 6:24)*. Most Christians know better than to serve money or "mammon" (KJV), or anything so obviously of the world over the Lord, but there is another would-be master less obvious whom we might choose to trust: ourselves. Jeremiah 10:23 reminds us that *"a man's life is not his own; it is not for man to direct his steps,"* and Proverbs 14:12 and 16:2 say respectively *"There is a way that seems right to a man, but in the end it leads to death"* and *"All a man's ways seem innocent to him, but motives are weighed by the Lord."* If we don't take care to trust God, we will follow our own feelings.

Secondly, we decide whether to "acknowledge him" or not in choosing our paths. Will we choose the easy path, well-beaten due to its many takers, or will we choose a higher, harder one that God will have to accompany us on in order to remove the obstacles and deliver us to our goal? I Thessalonians 4:7 reminds that we are called to live a "holy life," and I Peter 1:3-4 reminds us of the rewards: *"an inheritance that can never perish, spoil, or fade-kept in heaven for you."*

Verses 9 and 10 address our decision about how we will handle our assets. We either choose to honor Him with our "firstfruits" or give Him the leftovers. The rich fool in Luke 12:16-21 did everything right economically. When it came to financial savvy, he was no fool. But he was ultimately a fool because He forgot to account for the living, active, and observing *God* who provided every single thing he owned.

The way of the world is the default. "I just haven't yet decided" *is* a decision.

~AUGUST 23~
BY CONSTANT USE

"Anyone who lives on milk, being still an infant, is not acquainted with the teaching about righteousness. But solid food is for the mature, who by constant use have trained themselves to distinguish good and evil." Hebrews 5:13-14

The Hebrews writer is encouraging these Christians to grow up. The time for subsisting upon milk alone has passed, and yet they still will not give up their bottles. This kind of nourishment requires so little work— a little relaxed sucking can even be done while reclining. No chewing is required; it just slides easily down the gullet. It is necessary for babies, whose digestion can handle nothing stronger, but alas, it lacks all that is needed for growing past infancy. There comes a time when milk, though it still might appeal to the taste, has no value in nourishing growth. Milk, like the "elementary truths of God's word," has its limits for one who desires to grow into full man—or womanhood—in Christ, and therein lies the rub.

Maybe it really isn't spiritual milk you crave. Maybe you can honestly say that you have advanced beyond your spiritual ABC's. The question to keep asking ourselves is whether we are *continuing* to grow a taste for and nourish ourselves on more and more solid and substantial fare. Are we stronger and better equipped to swim against the stream of the worldliness we are so surrounded by than we were this time last year? Are we learning what we need to move onward and upward, closer and closer to the footsteps of Jesus, or have we leveled off so that we are walking on a plateau? Do we anger as easily as we once did? Do we forgive any faster? Have we begun to form habits such as praying for our enemies, turning the other cheek, and walking the extra mile? Is it any less important for others to know about our good deeds and any less crucial that we hide our bad ones? These are among the questions we need to ask ourselves on a regular basis so that we don't get lulled to sleep by the easy ride.

A good way to look at the difference between milk and solid food might be to ask if we are still stuck where we were when we first learned to believe in God and in Jesus as His Son. That is the taking-in phase. We take in new information, let it sink into our hearts and find a home there. We study, learn, and become solidified in this knowledge. However, this is not where we should stay. If we did, we would not be very close followers of Jesus, who went about *doing* good, not just *knowing* good. When we add to the *taking-in* some *putting-out*, then we are growing up. Though we never quit taking in, we should, *"by constant use"* of what we learn, serve God by serving others with it.

In other words, we go from just believing *in* God to actually *believing* God— believing not just that He is the Almighty Creator of us and our universe and that Jesus is His Son—but that what they say to us in the Bible is *true* and to be believed above all else the world shouts, and believed so strongly that we will act in a kind of faith the world finds extraordinary enough to marvel at.

"For we are God's workmanship, created in Christ Jesus to do good works, which God prepared in advance for us to do" (Ephesians 2:10).

~AUGUST 24~
A BROKEN AND CONTRITE HEART

"Cleanse me with hyssop, and I will be clean; wash me, and I will be whiter than snow...Create in me a pure heart, O God, and renew a steadfast spirit within me...The sacrifices of God are a broken spirit; a broken and contrite heart, O God, you will not despise." Psalm 51:7, 10, 17

I ask to be washed, but what do I mean?
Do I really understand what it means to be cleaned?
Do I dare apprehend what should happen to me
To be transformed from *this* to the thing I should be?
Like the clothes I throw into my washing machine,
I must tumble and soak before I am cleaned.
My fabric's condition must weaken and change
To be pure again, to be free of the stain.
If the blemish were obstinate insisting to stay,
I'd give up my efforts and throw it away.

It is no trivial thing to ask to be clean...
Such simple words with such painful means.
It's bearing crosses I'd rather throw down;
It's wearing thorns instead of a crown.

One measurement of spiritual maturity is the condition of our consciences. Psalm 51 is David's heart's cry after Nathan confronted him with his sin with Bathsheba. Second Samuel 11:1-12:25 tell the story of this "man after God's own heart" sleeping with another man's wife and then having him killed to help cover up his own sin. Though David committed these atrocious sins, his heart was quickly turned back to God when the prophet painted a picture of just what this looked like to God.

The whole Bible is at our disposal to accomplish this very thing. It is there to point us to the truth that without Jesus, we could never be washed clean. It is there to show us the impossible chasm between ourselves and Holy God that we *should* have to bridge but cannot. Can our consciences still be pricked? Are our hearts still tender enough? Or have we rejected His voice so many times that we no longer can hear it over the call of the world we so love?

Just reading and meditating on His Word can help so much. It can change the soil of our heart from dry or thorny or rocky to receptive and fertile and productive. If this hits a little too close to home, take a day (or a week) away from the world's reach, pray and fast and study and meditate on God's Word.

"For the word of God is living and active. Sharper than any double-edged sword, it penetrates even to dividing soul and spirit, joints and marrow; it judges the thoughts and attitudes of the heart" (Hebrews 4:12).

~AUGUST 25~
PREVENTIVE MEDICINE:
TAKING OUR SPIRITUAL VITAMINS

"Therefore, holy brothers, who share in the heavenly calling, fix your thoughts on Jesus, the apostle and high priest whom we confess." Hebrews 3:1

In Hebrews, an anonymous author writes to remind Jewish converts not to revert to Judaism but to cling to Jesus, "the author and perfecter" of their faith. He gives them five warnings to help them in this challenge. The warning to us, now that we are "a new creation" (2 Corinthians 5:17) is not to fall back into our old ways, our old habits.

- *"We must pay more careful attention, therefore, to what we have heard, so that we don't drift away" (2:1).* Notice he uses the word "drift" rather than "run." Isn't that usually what happens? Little by little we lose our focus on God's way when we allow the world's way to have more input into our hearts and minds.
- *"But encourage each other daily...so that none of you may be hardened by sin's deceitfulness" (3:13).* Sin is indeed quite deceptive and can appeal to us unto destruction if we have no one around to remind us of its lie. He says it is important on a *daily* basis that we give and take encouragement from other Christians. Make a visit or phone call or write a note asking for or giving encouragement.
- *"Therefore let us leave the elementary teachings about Christ and go on to maturity..." (6:1).* Rather than just going over the same things we already know, let us move on to a closer imitation of Jesus. Let us challenge ourselves and each other to be bolder, to reach out to more people, to forgive faster, and to study harder. Think of fruit: if it's not growing, it's dying on the vine.
- *"Let us not give up meeting together, as some are in the habit of doing, but let us encourage one another..." (10:25).* This sounds much like the second warning since it concerns encouragement, but this one is specifically talking about drawing near to God congregationally. We are reminded here about the importance of the body, the church. It is so important that it is called "the bride of Christ" (Revelation 19, 21).
- *"Make every effort to live in peace with all men, and to be holy; without holiness no one will see the Lord" (12:14).* Chapter twelve is the "therefore" part of chapter eleven, which describes great heroes of the faith—the "great cloud of witnesses" that surrounds all of us now. We

are encouraged by their holiness to *"throw off everything that hinders and the sin that so easily entangles and run with perseverance the race marked out for us" (12:1).* This is rightfully the last of the five warnings— the climax— because it is what can result if the other four are employed. We are to desire holiness, not run from possible accusations of it, as some do because they'd rather blend in than stick out. But He says *"without [sticking out], no one will see God."*

I always learn so much from teaching others. Study the list above, and go out and teach it to someone else today.

~AUGUST 26~
"GODLESS LIKE ESAU"

"See that no one is sexually immoral, or is godless like Esau, who for a single meal sold his inheritance rights as the oldest son. Afterward, as you know, when he wanted to inherit this blessing, he was rejected. He could bring about no change of mind though he sought the blessing with tears." Hebrew 12:16-17

Genesis 25:29-34 tells a pitifully sad story about a boy who, under the power of his taste buds and belly, sold his birthright—no small possession back then— for "a mess of pottage" (KJV). There is much we can learn from this story. (Go back and read it now if you are not familiar with it.)

When I first read this story, I wondered why Isaac couldn't have just said, "Oh, since I see that your brother cheated, I revoke the blessing I gave him and bestow it upon you. There! Everything is fixed!" But there are at least two reasons that this could not happen. Both of them have value for us.

For one thing, the Bible is filled with examples of Old Testament events and situations whose meanings are not completed, or fulfilled, until the New Testament. (This *fulfillment* is what Jesus was all about.) There is a very short and perplexing parable about a man who goes into his storeroom and takes out both the old and the new. In other words, something new he has gained in knowledge or ability finally makes the old have meaning, like learning to read the books stored there or learning to play that old piano. We learn the rest of the Genesis 25 story when we get over into Hebrews. Now we see that this was not only historical but parabolic in that it teaches us the extreme gravity of our choices. *"He could bring about no change of mind though he sought the blessing with tears."* Think of the warning that is to us right now: there comes a time when choices reap their due consequences.

Secondly, because of the terrible deception plotted by Jacob and his mother, we might feel sorry for the victimized Esau. But Hebrews suggests that Esau's grief was something less than *godly* sorrow and connects the results concerning his blessing with his former folly about his birthright. It seems that had Esau not been so willing to trade something of great and lasting value (the birthright of the firstborn) for something of little and temporary value (a bowl of red stew), he would not have had to go through this terrible mess later when it came time for the coveted blessing to be transferred. There is nothing now, nor was there then, anything inherently sinful about red stew; Esau's foolishness (Hebrews calls it "godlessness") lay in the fact that he chose the lesser over the greater. The Hebrew writer is telling the Jewish converts to continue to choose the Law of Christ over the Law of Moses and not to be brought back into slavery when they have been set free.

We must keep close watch over our choices. What we choose to do with our time, our money, our concentration, and our dedication is crucial and has eternal consequences. Pray for wisdom to discern the greater from the lesser. Let us not be godless like Esau.

~AUGUST 27~
THE WAY THAT I FEEL

"For in my inner being I delight in God's law; but I see another law at work in the members of my body, waging war against the law of my mind and making me a prisoner of the law of sin at work within my members. What a wretched man I am! Who will rescue me from this body of death?" Romans 7:22-24

Oh, Father, I wish I truly could say
That all I desire in the world is your will,
But it is not true, for I'm begging you now
To make special arrangements for the way that I feel.

I want you to take this hurting away.
I want you to give me a heart free from cares.
But something keeps saying that if you did that,
You'd have to pull up the good wheat with the tares.

Like the ones you prayed for who crucified you
Were ignorant and blind to what they were doing,
I suspect that I have no clue what I'm asking
Or what my nearsighted heart is pursuing.

I long for the day when I truly can say
That all I desire in this world is your will,
But now I'm caught shamefully between Heaven and Hell,
Frozen in time by the way that I feel.

So many times when I thought for sure
That I'd chained up my will and left you with the key,
My ghost slithered out as alive as before:
I'm afraid that I'm doomed always to be me.

I arrive at dark places that I call conclusions
Time and time and time again,
But the sun comes up and the road stretches further
To new beginnings you make from my ends.

Oh, Lord, I'm selfish and stubborn and vile
To worship at the shrine of the way that I feel,
But I will keep hoping that the bright day will dawn
When all I desire in this world is your will.

"Thanks be to God— through Jesus Christ our Lord!" (Romans 7:25)

~AUGUST 28~
A LIGHT FOR MY PATH

"Your word is a lamp to my feet and a light for my path." Psalm 119:105

Temptation comes to us in a myriad of forms. First it comes overtly in garish and predictable ways. Later, after we grow in Christ and are more spiritually discerning, the wolf must dress more like a sheep in order for us to take even a second look. Satan is wily and fits the temptation to our Achilles heel.

More mature Christian are sometimes caught off-guard by certain feelings, certain desires—not necessarily the obvious ones like sexual temptation or greed—but subtler ones: weariness in well-doing that tempts us to give up on a good work, hurt feelings that tempt us to despair and very quietly, very secretly doubt the listening ear or the good judgment of God.

One of the best remedies at times like these is a good soaking in God's Word. Just to retreat oneself and get alone with some drawn out time to read and meditate on His words to us is good medicine. In so many ways we are reminded in our reading about the ways God has demonstrated His wisdom to His people through the ages. Over and over we are reminded of those who did not give up and were rewarded, of those who realized they could keep going because in their labor, they struggled "with all *His* energy" (Colossians 1:29). We read of others whose hearts were bruised who leaned themselves upon the Rock (Psalm 19), who rested in shadow of His wings and found a comfort beneath his feathers (Psalm 91). We gain refreshment from David's stirring praise of his God in Psalm 63 as he hid from deadly enemies in the Desert of Judah: *"Your love is better than life...My soul will be satisfied as with the richest of foods...I sing in the shadow of your wings."*

We know that bad company corrupts good morals, and it follows that good company does just the opposite. It builds us up and enriches, not just our morals, but our spiritual health in every way. There is no better company than God's Word, and we should have one handy for those unexpected times of dire need or those unexpected times of waiting.

Psalm 119 also says, "I have hidden your word in my heart that I might not sin against you." The more time we spend reading the Word, the more we are hiding it in our hearts. If we are wise, we don't throw away our pocket change at the end of each day but rather tuck it away somewhere knowing that eventually it will build into enough to be of some value on a rainy day, or maybe even take us on a vacation. The same is true (but moreso because of the value of its rewards) with the way we should look at picking up our Bibles when we have a little spare time. We are building up our hearts for a rainy day. We are tucking away wisdom and devotion for future refreshment and encouragement, not just for ourselves, but for others God will put in our path.

"If your law had not been my delight, I would have perished in my affliction. I will never forget your precepts, for by them you have preserved my life" (Psalm 119:92-93).

~AUGUST 29~
UNWHOLESOME TALK

"Do not let any unwholesome talk come out of your mouths, but only what is helpful in building others up, according to their needs, that it may benefit those who listen." Ephesians 4:29

There is a pitiful story in Numbers that exemplifies in a pointed way the problem Paul refers to here. When the twelve spies returned from their reconnaissance mission into the land God had promised to the Israelites, all but two of these guys were trembling in their boots. They couldn't see the forest of God's promise for the trees of their human limitations. They admitted to seeing "a land flowing with milk and honey" just as Joshua and Caleb saw, but they added the word "but" to the report. "But" the people are too powerful, the cities are too well-fortified. Number 13:32 says that because of their fear, "they spread among the Israelites a bad report." Chapter 14 recounts the tragic results: a whole community weeping and wailing and railing against their leaders— "If only we had died in Egypt! Or in this desert! Why is the Lord bringing us to this land only to let us fall by the sword? Our wives and children will be taken as plunder. Wouldn't it be better for us to go back to Egypt?" And finally, the Lord responds to their grumbling by striking down the men who spread the bad report and leaving them in the desert forty more years (one year for each of the forty days they explored the land), all because of someone's mouth. Joshua and Caleb, who used their mouths to build up and encourage faith in God and faithfulness to him, were rewarded by being allowed to live and enter into the Promised Land.

Isn't the word "unwholesome" interesting in the context of this story? The ten unfaithful spies left out the part in the story of God's promise concerning the land they went to see. They did not tell the "whole" story; this was "unwholesome" talk. That's the problem with much damaging testimony; it tells only *part* of the story— maybe the part that causes someone we were already a little prejudiced against to fall into doubtful shadows and thus justify our preconceived notions.

The book of James has much to say about the dangers of the tongue. It compares the power of this tiny organ to that of a bit in the mouth of a powerful horse, the small rudder on a mighty ship, and the little spark that destroys a great forest. He warns us that there is no sense in thinking we can "tame" it, for no man can. To tame something is to change its natural tendency so that it becomes a different kind of creature— one that can be trusted to lie still and benign at your feet. He says we must, therefore, be vigilant about keeping "a tight rein" on it (1:26); those who cannot have a religion he calls "worthless."

In Ephesians, Paul gives us some guidance on how we might accomplish this. Notice that he not only encourages the Christians to empty their lives of certain sins, but he seizes the opportunity to take them into the fullness of righteousness. Just previous to this exhortation, he has discouraged stealing by adding the encouragement of using their hands productively so they may have something to share with the needy. Here not only does he discourage unwholesome talk, but he encourages talk *that builds up the listener*. He doesn't seek to *take out* the sin and leave a *vacuum* but rather to *replace* the sin with an *act of righteousness*. Let this be our challenge for today.

~AUGUST 30~
WHEN JESUS STOOD

"And do not grieve the Holy Spirit of God, with whom you were sealed for the day of redemption." Ephesians 4:30

"'Look,' he said, 'I see heaven open and the Son of Man standing at the right hand of God.'" Acts 7:-56

Stephen was the first Christian martyr. His story is a stirring one, and it is hard to understand how anyone could read it and not be inspired to greater faithfulness. He is brought before the Sanhedrin, the powerful high court of the Jews, to defend himself against charges of blasphemy against Moses. Rather than shrinking in fear or succumbing to the drain of energy that often results from a situation that seems so hopeless as single-handedly converting the whole Supreme Court, Stephen takes a deep breath and starts at the very beginning, way back there with Abraham. He tirelessly recounts how God worked through Abraham, Joseph, Moses, Joshua, and David, building up to his climax: the Most High God wishes to dwell no longer in a place, but in us! At this point, having gained the strength and courage that can only come from thrusting oneself fully into a holy cause, he accuses them of resisting God's Holy Spirit which has resulted in their betrayal and murder of His Son. *"When they heard this, they were furious and gnashed their teeth at him. But Stephen, full of the Holy Spirit, looked up to heaven and saw the glory of God, and Jesus standing at the right hand of God" (Acts 7:54-*

55). He saw Jesus *standing* at the right hand of God— not *sitting*, but *standing!* This is different from the other descriptions about Jesus' position in proximity to God. Luke 22:69 tells us, in Jesus' own words, *"But from now on, the Son of Man will be seated at the right hand of the mighty God."* But here Jesus is *standing*, as if to honor Stephen, as if to give him a standing ovation.

Isaiah 30:18 sheds some light on the occasion. *"Yet the Lord longs to be gracious to you; He rises to show you compassion. For the Lord is a God of justice. Blessed are all who wait for Him!"* Stephen, being a good Jew, no doubt knew about this scripture and took great comfort in all it meant to him that fateful day: He is reminding me of His compassion; He is reassuring me that justice will be done by His own hand; therefore, I can be content to wait for Him to do that in His own good time. It is not such a wonder, then, that his last words were the words of Someone else who knew these same truths: *"Lord, do not hold this sin against them."*

Can't this be a thrilling encouragement to us, too? When we acknowledge, cherish, and nourish rather than downplaying by quenching, grieving, resisting the Holy Spirit that He has so bountifully given to us, He honors us too. Jesus, in fact, promised that it would be so. *"Blessed are you when people insult you, persecute you and falsely say all kinds of evil against you because of me. Rejoice and be glad, because great is your reward in heaven, for in the same way they persecuted the prophets who were before you"* (Matthew 5:11-12). May we remember, when we find ourselves against a wall for His sake, that Jesus gives standing ovations.

~AUGUST 31~
RIGHT NOW THROUGH ETERNITY'S EYES

"The nights of crying your eyes out give way to days of laughter." Psalm 30:5 *(The Message)*

Arrival in Zurich
(En Route to Tel Aviv)

Flying through hours easterly bound,
Time chomps down hungrily seven full hours,
While all we have done is adjust our watches
And try to adjust our sleep.

This short night we've passed had no time for a middle,
Only a beginning and end.
There was sunset, a lingering, orangey surrender,
A wee bit of blackness, and then came the dawn.

I believe when we finally reach Heaven's shores,
We'll bask in the yellow of Eternity's dawn,
Look over our shoulders at the black fear of Life's night,
Remember the promise of Psalm 30:5,
And say, "What a short night that was!"

God is always teaching us little parables with our lives. Every time we fly over an ocean or pass through several time zones in the air, we get another glimpse of what He means by so many of His words: "The struggles we're going through now are nothing to be compared to the glory that will be revealed in us," "Jacob served seven years to get Rachel, but they seemed like only a few days to him...," "For our light and momentary troubles are achieving for us an eternal glory that far outweighs them all." They are all reminders that when the joy comes in the morning, the long night will fade into oblivion. What once was the dream will be reality. We will have finally awakened to the Real World. All the lies Satan has tried to feed us will be revealed for what they were, and we will no longer see "a poor reflection as in a mirror; then we will see Him face to face." We will fully know God and be known by Him.

Psalm 126 prophesies beautifully *"Those who sow in tears will reap with songs of joy. He who goes out weeping carrying seed to sow will return with songs of joy carrying sheaves with him."* The "seed to sow" we carry is the hope of all God promises us. Sometimes when the weeping comes long and hard, this "seed" is all we have. Some tragically lay it down in the pool of their tears rather than holding on to it in spite of them. They allow Satan to discourage them out of sowing their hopes; they never come back singing songs of joy because of the sheaves they reap.

Don't be fooled by the darkness out the window. Soon we will see the lights on the runway and at last land safely At Home.

~SEPTEMBER 1~
THE POTTER'S FIELD OR THE KINGDOM'S KEYS

"Because of the Lord's great love, we are not consumed, for His compassions never fail. They are new every morning; great is your faithfulness" (Lamentations 3:22-23).

Of the Bible's most tragic characters, surely one of the saddest is Judas Iscariot, the disciple who betrayed Jesus for thirty pieces of silver. We remember that he sat close enough to Jesus to use the same dipping bowl only hours before he led the authorities to Him in the garden and that he later suffered such regret that he threw the money away and took his own life.

Of the Bible's most heroic characters, close to the top is the apostle Peter, the one who was so gung-ho for Jesus that he was always jumping out of perfectly good boats to try to get to Him. Once he even attempted to walk to Him upon the water. He's the one who so loved Jesus that when Malchus showed up to arrest Him, Peter slashed his ear off. He is the apostle who preached the sermon on Pentecost that ushered in the Lord's Church, the very Body of Christ that would represent and do the work of Jesus after He had ascended into Heaven after His resurrection. This is the sermon that "cut to the heart" those who a month earlier had rallied for Jesus' crucifixion, the sermon that stirred three thousand to be baptized that very day. He is the one history tells whose only objection to being crucified for honoring his Lord was that he was not worthy to die in the same manner, so he had the executioners crucify him upside down. Definitely a heroic character.

But this is not all we remember about Peter, is it? He was the apostle who, only a few hours after vowing that he would die for Jesus, blatantly denied *knowing* Him, not once, not twice, but *three* times. Peter the Rock, under just a little pressure from people he didn't even know, miserably crumbled into Peter the Coward. Not so heroic. In fact, not a lot different from his fellow apostle, Judas. So what's the difference between Judas and Peter? Both of them betrayed Jesus, and both of them felt rotten for having done so, but their lives ended up so radically different. Why?

The difference is that Peter decided to accept forgiveness, and Judas did not. Could Jesus have forgiven Judas for such a heinous crime? Undoubtedly. After all, He asked God to forgive those who wielded the hammers that drove the nails into His hands and feet. Just as Peter was welcomed to the seaside breakfast Jesus cooked for His apostles after the Resurrection, Judas, had he stayed around, would have been also. This parallel is one we sorely need to grasp. Satan is out broadcasting the lie that enough will finally be enough; that there is a line over which we can step that regardless of our earnest desire to return, Jesus will tell us no. We can run away and never give Him the chance, of course, but if our heart is fully repentant, as Peter's was, we will receive His healing forgiveness that will restore our usefulness to Him. Peter thought there was a chance he could be reinstated, so, unlike Judas, he stayed around to see. As a result, his life was lived out— and even snuffed out— to the glory of God rather than ending tragically in a potters' field.

You might not have a lot of faith in yourself, but never underestimate Him.

~SEPTEMBER 2~
AND WHEN HE IS OLD

"Train a child in the way he should go, and when he is old he will not turn from it." Proverbs 22:6

My brother-in-law Jerry is a wonderful example of this scripture's fulfillment. Jerry was raised much like Timothy, by a mother completely sold out to God and fully dedicated to Christ and His ways. He grew up to be a successful lawyer but fell victim to alcoholism in midlife. It was a terrible thing that wreaked financial destruction and emotional hardship on his family for years. Though we prayed, it was very hard to visualize any relief for the situation, and though he was extraordinarily sensitive to the individual desires of all he loved and was always taking our kids to professional baseball games, preparing our favorite meals, buying us exactly the right gifts, and composing humorous poems on all kinds of occasions, he was enslaved by the power of alcohol. He could play the guitar and piano, sing every word of ten thousand songs, and cook like a chef, but he could scarcely go a day without drinking.

Then one day, much to our surprise, he checked himself into a recovery center, and after having stayed there for sixty hard days, he came home clean and sober, never to take a drink of alcohol again. He became a faithful member of AA and was instrumental in helping many others, especially other lawyers, to learn the truth about their disease and to turn their lives around as he had. He came back to the basic truth that is the keystone of all humanity: we are powerless to control our lives and must submit to God if we are to live truly productive lives.

I believe that Jerry was able to come back to this truth when he was old because of what his mother instilled in him when he was young. Stories like this are a great encouragement to those of us who have raised or will raise children of our own. I have heard some say that we have had that scripture all wrong and that the training "in the way he should go" refers to helping our kids find their particular gifts and talents. But the original language does not bear this out. "Train" here means "to dedicate for or to the cause of righteousness" as in 1 Kings 8:63 (the temple) and Genesis 18:19 (Abraham's household). I suppose there is some amount of subjectivity as to quantity and quality, but the message is that wise and consistent nourishment of the young and tender shoot can reach so deeply into its core that even the full-grown tree is greatly affected. I know that the inverse is also true, for to this day I still do battle with natural tendencies to be self-centered and manipulative, traits that were not trained out of me when I was young.

Just as with Jerry, although in the mid years a restless desire to try a different way from our parents can corrupt the direct path and bring about a deadly and circuitous route, there still remains a great hope that what was ingrained in our formative years will eventually be mined from the rubble. As any kind of mentors to the young, our job is to implant firmly our charges the way of righteousness that, even if abandoned for a season, will be there for them to return to. After all, most who have known that one way works won't have to try very many other ways that fail before they circle back around to what first worked.

~SEPTEMBER 3~
ELIMINATING THE CHAFF

"Not so the wicked. They are like chaff the wind blows away. Therefore, the wicked will not stand in the judgment, nor sinners in the assembly of the righteous." Psalm 1:4-5

My first association with the word "chaff" was in my first study of the book of Ruth. There we learn about Providence leading Ruth to the barley field of the merciful kinsman-redeemer Boaz, who insures that Ruth's gleaning is productive. There the workers threshed the barley, or shook and beat it, so that the chaff, or the utterly useless part of the grain, would fall away to be disposed of and all that would remain would be the edible produce.

In Psalm 1 we are reminded of another kind of chaff, the chaff of wickedness. After the psalmist has described in detail the righteous man as one who "yields its fruit in season and whose leaf does not wither," he contrasts with that the wicked. He says that "they are like chaff that the wind blows away." The next word is "therefore," so we know that what causes the wicked to be unable to withstand God's wrath in the judgment has something to do with the characteristics of chaff—it is utterly useless to God.

We read a New Testament version of Job in Luke 22:31-32. Here Jesus' reveals that Satan has asked to "sift...as wheat" the disciples, obviously hoping to bring His purposes to ruin. Jesus suggests that Peter will be first, for He tells him to strengthen his brothers after he has turned back. This sifting of Peter comes to pass before the day is over; Peter denies Jesus three times. Afterward, however, Peter does turn back and indeed strengthens many brothers for the rest of his life. Just as in Job, Satan "asked," and God allowed it. Had not there been something that needed sifting in Peter and the others, Jesus would not have allowed it.

I suppose as long as any of us lives upon this planet, there will be parts of us that could be described as chaff— flesh that needs to be shed so that we can be fully useful to God. That's what Christian growth is—growing from one degree of glory to the next (2 Corinthians 3:18). It's a terrifying thought that we might become *totally* chaff, as Psalm 1 speaks of. The psalmist is warning us that unless we are faithful to let God have His way in pruning us, lopping off offending elements, we could little piece by little piece dry up into lifelessness until that is the sum product of what we are. For a good illustration of the value of polishing off the rough edges, just look what sandpaper does to finish fine furniture.

It takes courage to be sure, but we all need to be brave and trusting enough to ask God to sift us. We can never fully trust ourselves in our own hands, but we can always trust ourselves in His. The sifting process might hurt, but that kind of pain is ever so much better than the deadly numbness and uselessness that will come of us later if we do not submit now.

~SEPTEMBER 4~
DRESSING UP IN JESUS

"You are all sons of God through faith in Christ Jesus, for all of you who were baptized into Christ have clothed yourselves in Christ." Galatians 3:26-27

C.S. Lewis describes in *Mere Christianity* what this means by analyzing pretending. There are two kinds of pretending— good pretending and bad pretending. The bad kind of pretending, such as saying, "I will show up to help you set up for the fellowship dinner tomorrow" when you know you will not is just an out-and-out lie. But there is another kind of pretending which can serve as a means to achieve a very good end—an end you may be able to envision but haven't quite laid hold of yet.[1]

Take baseball, for instance. When I was a little kid, my daddy told me anything I could really envision myself doing, I could do. When I was having trouble hitting a baseball, he made me stand there at the plate with my eyes closed and tell him when I had mentally hit the ball, when I was running, and which base I had reached. In the middle of all that, he asked me what color my shirt was. I thought how peculiar a question that was until he explained that if I was truly *envisioning* myself hitting and running, I should be able to answer that question. Once I had gotten the hang of becoming a successful homerun hitter in my mind, then I was ready to have some balls actually pitched to me. He told me to stand there with my eyes open and look like the hitter that I was when I did it mentally. Although I still had not hit a real ball, he told to me to *pretend* that I had hit a thousand.

This is the kind of pretense that leads up to the real thing. Most of us already know that when we are not feeling particularly friendly or patient, the best medicine is to just go ahead and pretend that we are. Most of the time this pretense leads to the real thing, and soon we are no longer pretending. This is called walking in faith.

Many days we go to some trouble to make ourselves look a certain presentable way on the outside as we venture out to meet the world. Inside we might be a dead-tired bundle of frazzled nerves on the verge of tears, but we hope that the way we make ourselves look on the outside will convince others, as well as ourselves, that we are not. And here we are knowing our tendencies to fail at all we hope to do and be, our fears of letting God down by allowing the old man to rise up and bully the New Creation that we are, but we bow down and pray "Our Father" anyway. We may not *feel* like a Son of God Almighty, Omniscient and Omnipotent, but we accept the role anyway. God not only lets us get away with pretending to be something we're literally not; He commands it. He knows that if we are "clothed in Christ," that is, *dressed up as Christ,* this will lead us to the end He desires. When we remember that we are dressed up as Christ, there are things that we can no longer do, no longer say, ways we can no longer act. For now we are representing Christ. Just as an actor who goes onstage must stay in character with his role, so must we when we wear the identity of Jesus.

Jesus told His disciples in John 14 that dressed up as Him, we would do even greater things than He did: He would no longer be limited by the flesh which confined Him to only one place at a time. Now His Spirit in all of us would infiltrate the world. And we, dressed up in Christ, are those blessed vessels.

~SEPTEMBER 5~
SURRENDERING TO THE PLOW

"By their fruit you will recognize them. Do people pick grapes from thornbushes, or figs from thistles?" Matthew 7:16

Some of the most frustrating days of my life have been those wasted on shortcuts. I remember the vacation that my whole family missed out on skiing in Colorado because of my foolish navigational advice to my husband, the driver. The "shortcut" was much longer and curvier than the map indicated, so we got to the ski area just as they were closing down the lifts. Other times, in an effort to do *less* work, I have brought about many *additional* hours of it. How many of us have skipped reading the long instructions of assembling a swing set only to find at the end of the day that our trial and error method took ever so much longer than the reading we wanted so much to avoid?

Jesus seems to be suggesting here that laziness and all attempts to short-cut His methods will not pay off. He tells us that *He* is the Way, which is to say that in the very least He is meaning that *His way* is the Way. He means for us to give ourselves up to Him and His way. He tells us that in order for us to work right we must die to our very selves; we must lay down our lives and take up His cross. How many more ways could He have said it? He seems to really mean this; there is no other way to the Way than to be completely born again, to have completely new wineskins, to become completely new creatures.

He wants us to turn ourselves over to Him, but what we want to do instead many times is to keep "ourselves" and just change a few habits, to keep the old house and just move the furniture around. "Ourselves" means our wishes, our dreams, our philosophies, and our feelings about the way things are or the way they should be. He wants us finally to see that we are *not* the authority, regardless of just how strongly we may feel about matters. He would have us, if need be, be rigged up with blinders like horses who are being taken somewhere they would needlessly fear to go if they could see. If we don't submit, we can never be what we really *desire* to be, although this is a hard concept to realize. We must, if we are ever to bear figs, give up the notion that we can do so if our soil is not planted in figs. Perhaps we are planted in clover, and perhaps we can keep that clover pleasantly green and neatly trimmed, but it will never produce figs, no matter how pretty it looks. In order for us to produce fruit "in keeping with repentance" (Matthew 3:8), we must give Him the whole field and let Him plow it up and start over. Trying to hold onto our say about our lives while trying at the same time to live as a Christian is a vain attempt at a shortcut that will never get us to our destination.

"Our say" means holding out in certain places— knowing how Jesus felt about something, how He treated it, but finding a reason it will not quite work for us. He told us to "be perfect," and that seems really hard, but it is harder yet to find satisfaction in living with a foot in two different worlds. He must have us on His terms.

Take a close look at the red letters in your Bible. Study those over and over until those pages are thinner than the rest. Let the Pattern soak into your conscience until it becomes your subconscious, until when you close your eyes, you can see Him there sowing in you what He wants you to become.

~SEPTEMBER 6~
A NEW CREATION

"So from now on we regard no one from a worldly point of view. Though we once regarded Christ in this way, we do so no longer. Therefore, if anyone is in Christ, he is a new creation; the old has gone, the new has come." 2 Corinthians 5:16-17

In the margin of my Bible beside this scripture I have written "Cheryl." Although all of us are new creations, hers is the face I see first when I read this scripture.

Cheryl was one of those unlikely responders to the gospel message. I saw her as an extremely worldly, sensual, materialistic person whose physical beauty was almost certainly the only god she would ever know. When a friend asked me to study the Bible with her, I had strong reservations about the fruitfulness of such an effort. I had a lot to learn, and in time I learned it well. As is true more often than not with teachers and students, "teaching" Cheryl was one of the most valuable lessons I have ever learned.

Mark 4:26-29 is called the parable of the growing seed. It describes the power that is in the Word of God like this. "A man scatters seed on the ground. Night or day, whether he sleeps or gets up, the seed sprouts and grows, though he does not know how." Little did I know that this parable had been proving itself mightily in beautiful Cheryl.

No sooner had she walked through my doorway, before she could even sit down, she began to weep. With head down and hands over her mouth, she declared to me, pretty much a stranger to her at this point, "I have never loved God! I have never loved God!" She went on to explain to me tearfully that she had learned this from reading John 14:23-24, *"Jesus replied, 'If anyone loves me, he will obey my teaching...He who does not love me will not obey my teaching."* After I recovered from my shamefaced shock at just how wrong I could be about a person, we proceeded to study about all the ways Jesus woos the lost to return to Him and how He longs to lift up the humble and give them a new start. Cheryl wasted no time responding to His call and has blessed her children, her grandchildren, and countless others with the grateful, gracious, and humble life she lives every single day.

Like most of ours, just in more vivid colors than some, the old Cheryl's life had wreaked havoc upon most of the people she loved. She set out to make amends to those she had hurt, and in a way only a heart "snatched from the fire" can (Jude 23), to warn others against the life of emptiness and destruction she had fallen into. She suffered bravely and humbly through some terrible consequences of her old life, including going to jail for a time. Then she resolutely set out to be trained to take on a profession that would put her in contact with many, many women whom she could encourage and speak to about the goodness of God.

About the time my amazement at her seems to be at its fullest, she surprises me with yet another milestone of growth and productivity in God's vineyard. Indeed, the old *is* gone. The new *has* come... and just keeps on coming! She is truly a new creation, a walking miracle, who never ceases to grow "from glory to glory."

Never, never underestimate the power of God's Word!

~SEPTEMBER 7~
OUR REAL IDENTITY

"Therefore, there is now no condemnation for those who are in Christ Jesus, because through Christ Jesus the law of the Spirit of life set me free from the law of sin and death." Romans 8:1-2

My passions and moderations loom perverted and sing off-key.
I'm on fire for concerns of my mortal being and lukewarm for the crucial needs.
I am wandering around in the wilderness, fallen away from grace.
I'm a foreigner to righteousness behind a familiar face.

But thank God the mercy that's snatched from me is by my hands alone.
Praise God! Father has made provision and tells me to keep marching on.
The wretchedness that slays my grace is sin disguised in me;
Father has sent His Spirit to set my real spirit free.

Free from this selfish nature I hate, free from the shackles of sin;
Free to take up this threadbare tent and head toward Home again.
His Spirit testifies with mine of all I have received.
I'm His child, not ruled any longer by fear, if only I will believe!

The hopelessness that floods my heart when sin looks like the winner
I now reject, for I am bought too dearly to die a sinner.
My precious Jesus who surrendered Heaven understands my plight.
He conquered death to intercede; He has taken up my fight.

My body, which seems like all of me, is already as good as dead,
But because of Christ, my spirit lives on by righteousness instead.
How difficult to understand the way sin does its deed—
It tells us we're defeated, that we'll never starve this greed.

It swears that we are bankrupt, destitute and doomed,
Shipwrecked alone with no vision of Home, hopelessly marooned.
But no, we're more than conquerors, so I must accept the grace
That's offered to me full-strength and brand-new every time I gaze on His face.

When sin struts before me and shouts in my ear of its power
to consume me with fire,
I must be convinced that my real identity is Christ and that sin is the liar.
Oh, Abba Father, keep opening my eyes to the things I need to see.
To believe in your power to outlast my sins, and finally, indeed, set me free.

~SEPTEMBER 8~
THE BEAUTIFUL DEATH OF DESIRE

"I do not understand what I do. For what I want to do I do not do, but what I hate, I do...For I have this desire to do what is good, but I cannot carry it out." Romans 7:15

"And if the Spirit who raised Him from the dead is living in you, He who raised Christ from the dead will also give life to your mortal bodies through His Spirit, who lives in you." Romans 8:11

Romans 7 and 8 strike chords of familiarity in every Christian I have ever talked to. We all can identify with the dilemma Paul chronicles here. It is the struggle between the old man or woman and the new creature. It is the conflict between flesh and spirit. It is the internal evidence of the spiritual warfare spoken of in Ephesians 6. In chapter seven he describes the dire straits we find ourselves in with our inner being delighting in God's law and "another law at work in the members" of our bodies that "wages war" against that desire. Finally he cries out, "What a wretched man I am! Who will rescue me from this body of death? Thanks be to God— through Jesus Christ our Lord!"

Chapter eight is all about how through the Spirit of life which raised Jesus from the dead, we are also given just such a resurrected life as Jesus was. Just as He came forth alive from the tomb which He entered dead, our bodies of death can also be restored to life. He reminds us that we are no longer controlled by our sinful nature that once gave us no options. We have only to cherish, and thus nourish, this spirit—to lean in God's direction and give Him our vote of confidence— for it to keep us alive and free from sin's bondage. Before we had this spirit, sin was our master, and whenever we became a little uncomfortable in its midst, the Enemy would just move the furniture around a little to appease us. But alas, we were still in the same prison, the same "body of death." Now that we have received the Spirit of life, we have a choice.

The problem is that if we do not remember that the choice is now ours, sin will bully us into giving in again. He will lure us back into our chains. Now when we sin, it is not because we are helplessly alone and unarmed; no, we are armed to the teeth with the Holy Spirit willing to raise us from this death with the same power He raised Jesus. Forgetting that, though, and failing to call upon God through this wonderful power within us, failing to nurture, nourish, and trust this Spirit, would render us as powerless as before. This is why we are warned against putting out the Spirit's fire (1 Thessalonians 5:19). Without its fire, we may be overcome by despair. We might allow ourselves to believe that we will *always* desire the thing we cannot have, that we must *always* fight as hard as we are now to overcome our weak tendencies. Sometimes the fight is harrying and exhausting. To think that we have to fight this hard *forever* without letting up a minute in order to stay true to God might be enough to cause us to throw up our hands and quit on day two. But Romans 8 is here to remind us that God desires to crucify that body of death *along with its strong desires* that war against Him. I once read a poster in a library that said "Those who do not read are no better off that those who cannot read." Don't ignore or neglect the Spirit. Nourish it by feeding it on God's Word. The desires will subside, and you *will* arise from the dead.

~SEPTEMBER 9~
DO NOT LOSE HEART

"Consider Him who endured such opposition from sinful men, so that you will not grow weary and lose heart." Hebrews 12:3

"Therefore, since through God's mercy we have this ministry, we do not lose heart." 2 Corinthians 4:1

"...because we know that the One who raised the Lord Jesus from the dead will also raise us with Jesus and present us with you in his presence...Therefore, we do not lose heart." 2 Corinthians 4:13-14, 16

What does it mean to "lose heart," and why are we warned about it so often? There could be multiple meanings, one of which is surely to lose hope. It is interesting, though, that though the word "hope" would certainly be easy enough to use in these instances, the word "heart" is chosen instead. I have thought a lot about this, especially in times when my own heart was aching to the point I thought it might "break." Which brings me to my next question: What does it mean to have our hearts "broken"?

One of the ways we "lose" heart is bound up in what we mean by a "broken" heart. Maybe losing heart means having it broken off one piece at a time. Pieces can break off when we are so hurt that for one reason or another, part of us never heals. Part of our heart is rendered useless by atrophy and seems just to fall off from the living part. Other pieces break off when as a result of the fear of hurt, we wall it off from all attention or nourishment and it dies from malnutrition. Yet other pieces may break off when as a result of hurt or resentment, we feed our heart poisonous fuel whose continual burning eventually dries the life out. Losing heart happens when pieces of our heart ache to the cracking point and then because they are mistreated, they finally just break off.

If this seems too metaphorical to wrap your mind around, think of it like this: I am loving another Christian the best way I know how, but I keep getting hurt (neglected, ignored, and indirectly or even directly rejected). I know as a Christian that *not* forgiving is not an option, so I pray for a soft heart to do so, but still I am confused as how to proceed. How do I love more wisely? Should I continue on the same path and ask that God give me strong feet for the journey, stand a little more at a distance, or move away entirely? It is vital that we pray and search the scriptures seriously. *However* I proceed must *not* be motivated by self-protection and pain-avoidance alone, for that would leave me vulnerable to something even more tragic than the original hurt: a dry and brittle heart in danger of losing some of its parts. Since we are told *not* to lose heart, there must be some way that God can take the aching and cracked pieces and mend them so that they are not lost.

For healing, we must keep our hearts open, tender, and in His presence. The mission Christ has set us on requires a *whole* heart. We must continue to pray in these times that God will mend ours so that we can love Him with all of it and throw all of it into following close upon His heels. A dying world depends upon our thriving hearts.

Take any endangered pieces to His feet for healing before it is too late and they are lost.

~SEPTEMBER 10~
TRIVIAL PURSUIT

"Remember this: Whoever sows sparingly will reap sparingly, and whoever sows generously will also reap generously...You will be made rich in every way so that you can be generous on every occasion..." 2 Corinthians 9:6, 11

Oh, Father, I'm on such a trivial pursuit;
How I am panting for Mammon!
How did it sneak in?
How thick is its root?
How long have I missed your
Transmissions of warning?
How long is delay time
From Heaven to Earth?

The perfect image can almost be bought;
The heavenly visions lie close to my grasp!
But now I see that as expensive as it is
To buy all the trappings,
The enhancement of the façade is even still
Less costly than that of the heart and the soul.

Oh, Father, indeed your Word is so sharp!
It has cut me to shreds,
And I bleed on my velvet.
I foul my perfume and encrust all my baubles.
And all I can ask at this point of such need —
When you see the deep folly
Of my shallow pursuits,
And smell only death in my costliest nard —
Again, once more, for the ten millionth time,
To smear on my doorpost
The blood of dear Jesus
And invoke your dire mercy
As you point me to those
I once felt so sure you called me to save.

I think that I hear your message to me
In their plenty of poverty and goods and appeal;
In your ways that are so much higher than mine:
You call me to focus with a gaze that burns deeply
And to be stricken by the poverty
That hides in my wealth.

~SEPTEMBER 11~
THE ATTACK ON AMERICA
PART 1

"Because you have rejected this message, relied on oppression, and depended on deceit, this sin will become for you like a high wall, cracked and bulging, that collapses suddenly in an instant." Isaiah 30:12-13

Anyone alive in 2001 will not come upon this day without haunting memories of that shocking American Tuesday. On the days and weeks that immediately followed many words of inspiration and encouragement were spoken in grocery stores, on the air, in schools, and in churches. Stores sold out of American flags. People talked about the wonderful unity that came out of the tragedy, and our hearts were warmed by the support of volunteers in such a grave time of need. But there were also many questions. People called in on radio and TV talk shows asking questions of just about every nature: What kind of people would do such a horrible thing? How can anyone be so filled with hate? Some were asking questions about God: Where was He on that Tuesday? How could He have allowed such as this to happen? Isn't He a good and loving God? Isn't He stronger than evil? Strongly authoritative statements of certainty thickened the air about the extremity of evil personified by the planes that crashed into our strongholds and killed thousands of innocent people.

All of these are honest and legitimate questions, I suppose, but I am afraid that they missed the whole point. Really afraid. And after these several years have passed, I wonder if we've missed a prime opportunity to grasp the depths of a message that we pray will not have to be repeated. Certainly evil was involved, but probably not so much in the way most people seemed to view it. Everybody knows that it was evil for those people to have taken it upon themselves to destroy thousands of people who were going about their peaceful lives minding their own business. Expressing this obvious sentiment over and over is just a waste of breath. Some people seemed to be *trying* to see God in it, as evidenced by some of the questions, but it seems those questions were only treated and maybe even *intended* as rhetorical ones— just words put forth poetically and emotionally to indicate that the speakers had some measure of depth in their thinking but never really meant to be answered. If any replies were made at all, they were usually by well-meaning people—even Christians—who answered, "There are some things that we cannot understand on this earth. We just have to trust Him."

But I don't think they should have been or should be now treated rhetorically at all. I think "Where is God in all this?" is exactly the right question, and I believe that if we don't spend lots of time in serious thought and prayer over the answer, we have absolutely no hope in saving the life of this country we seem to be so in love with.

My answer to the question, "Where is God in all this?" is right in the middle of it. Ask yourself another question: Where was He when His perfect and sinless Son Jesus was tortured and killed at the hands of the Jews and Romans? Talk about an innocent victim! I mean no offense to anyone when I ask this question, but I must ask it: were the people who died on 9/11 any more innocent than Jesus?

~SEPTEMBER 12~
THE ATTACK ON AMERICA
PART 2

"In those days Israel had no king; everyone did as he saw fit." Judges 17:6, 21:25

Except for those who compare this attack with the one on Pearl Harbor in 1941, we act like this is a brand new story. Why aren't we comparing it to Nineveh, Assyria, back in the days of Jonah and Nahum? Remember the story? Jonah was sent by God to preach to the ungodly Ninevites about their detestable lifestyle and total disregard for Him and His laws. Jonah knew so well that his God was the One of mercy in the face of repentance that, unable to stomach the thought of God's sparing and even adopting these wicked enemies of God's people, he ran away only to be swallowed and later spat out again by some kind of big fish. He went, and just as he thought, this depraved metropolis humbled themselves before Him, repented, and God did not destroy them after all. By a hundred and fifty years later, though, they had fallen back into their ungodly ways, so God sent Nahum. This message was not one of mercy, as Jonah's had been; this was a message of doom. To this city of 120,000 (and, yes, many of them were "innocent women and children" and even "innocent" men!) Nahum delivered the exceedingly bad news that the "river gates [would] be opened" for a destroying army. The destruction of Nineveh by the Babylonians was so complete that its site was forgotten. When Alexander the Great fought a battle near its site of this great city in 331 B.C., he could not even tell there had ever been a city there. No trace of it was seen until 1845 when Englishmen uncovered some ruins of the magnificent palaces of the Assyrian kings. Together the stories of Jonah and Nahum illustrate God's ways of dealing with nations —

with messages of pleading, followed by longsuffering grace in response to confession and sorrowful repentance, but finally with just and terrible punishment in the face of repeated apostasy.

Some might argue that this is different because Assyria was not a nation founded directly upon God's principles, as our nation most assuredly was. But what about all the other stories in the Bible?

Way back before all this, in the time of the judges, the Hebrew nation, God's own beloved people delivered out of Egypt, fell into a life of neglect of the God who had delivered them miraculously through the parted waters of the Red Sea. It just seems to slip their mind that He had fed them daily by His own hand and destroyed their enemies so that they could inhabit a "Promised Land" to live as His special example to a hell-bound world. During the first three hundred years in this "Land of Milk and Honey" they misinterpreted God's slowness to anger over and over again, and went through seven cycles of 1) sin, 2) servitude, 3) supplication, 4) salvation, and 5) silence (toward God) and therefore, back to the beginning of the cycle again.[2] His own beloved people, says Judges in two different places did what was right in their own eyes (sound familiar?), they "did evil in the sight of the Lord," and so He chastened them.

~SEPTEMBER 13~
WHY SILENCE IS GOLDEN

"My dear brothers, take note of this: Everyone should be quick to listen, slow to speak..." James 1:19

"There is a time for everything, and a season for every activity under heaven: ...a time to be silent and a time to speak..." Ecclesiastes 3:1, 7

Though I'm not finished talking about 9/11, I must interrupt to honor Betty's on her birthday.

I'm still not normal, but I'm closer than I used to be. Practically from the womb, I have had more than my share of energy, causing me to find sitting still and being quiet more of a challenge than most. For years one of my New Year's resolutions was not to interrupt. Maybe it's because I am an abnormally fast talker that I have struggled with waiting for others to finish their sentences before I jump in and begin mine. It's a terrible character flaw, and I am ashamed of it. But thanks to Betty's influence in my life, I'm a little better in this area than I once was.

Betty became my sister-in-law when she was seventeen years old and after I already had twenty-one years of transgression under my belt. Even at such an early age, Betty was a good teacher. Her methods, though, were neither purposeful nor direct; she simply practiced her magic on me until I realized that the beauty of a serene spirit can bring out the gold in silence. I learned from her that there is, indeed, a time for silence. There is a time for quietly gazing into another's soul, not with nervousness about what to say next, but with a lovely and expressive poise that speaks more eloquently than many spoken words. Her way of fixing her gaze upon me and listening so intently was quite a rare experience for me, and at first the pauses made me nervous. Later I found them delightfully comforting. I knew she had really heard me and was not mentally distracted, as I often was, calculating my response or looking around for what I might need to do next after the conversation ended. She taught me the value of undivided attention and purposefully delayed responses. I began to see the dangers of being quick to speak and the wisdom of a thoughtful answer.

I have loved Betty as a friend and a sister for many years since those first lessons, and still when we rush together in reunion, I can hardly wait to finish our hug so that I can stand back and take a swan dive into those beautiful listening brown eyes that have comforted and encouraged me through almost forty years' worth of life's up's and down's.

I pray for every hyper person reading this the treasure of a Betty in your life. I pray for every quick tongue a meditative set of eyeballs and eardrums across the table.

And for all the Betty's out there, know that you have a valuable ministry! *"Your beauty should not come from outward adornment, such as braided hair and the wearing of gold jewelry and fine clothes. Instead, it should be that of your inner self, the unfading beauty of a gentle and quiet spirit, which is of great worth in God's sight." 1 Peter 3:3-4*

~SEPTEMBER 14~
THE ATTACK ON AMERICA
PART 3

"Love the Lord your God with all your heart and with all your soul and with all your strength. These commandments that I give you today are to be upon your hearts. Impress them on your children. Talk about them when you sit at home and when you walk along the road, when you lie down and when you get up. Tie them as symbols on your hands and bind them upon your foreheads. Write them on the doorframes of your houses and on your gates." Deuteronomy 6:5-8

God punished His children for persisting in doing things as they each saw fit without regarding Him. He "handed them over to" and "sold them" into the hands of many oppressors— the Mesopotamians, Moabites, Ammonites, Amalekites, Philistines, Canaanites, Midianites, Amalekites (again), Ammonites (again), Philistines (again), Sidonians, and Maonites. He kept raising up judges (godly and courageous heroes and heroines) to deliver His people once they reached the supplication stage of their cycle. You've heard of these people: Gideon, Samson, and Deborah are probably the most famous. These weren't perfect people by any means, but they humbled themselves before God, inclined their ears to Him, and reached out for His forgiveness and help, refusing to stay and wallow and finally drown in the quicksand of sin. They tried hard to do what was right in the sight of God, unlike the others who "did what was right in their own eyes" (KJV).

Later, after the reigns of Saul, David, and Solomon as Israel's kings, the nation divided, and once again another generation of God's people "fell into" sin (get the picture here of just mindlessly living a life of less and less regard for God's desires), Assyria and later Babylon routed the Jews, destroyed even God's temple, and carried them off into captivity—back into slavery, into another Egypt, to start all over again. This happened because they failed to remember what their ancestors had to learn back then. They failed to study God's Word that had been passed down to them to be honored and obeyed. When the people humbled themselves after falling away and being defeated or carried off as captives, and God took them back, for a while they would do extreme things like tearing down altars to foreign gods and making bold and glaring speeches to each other about having the words of God read publicly and not allowing sin in the camp. God's message was not wasted on them; they GOT IT, at least for a while.

I can't help but wonder, with this preponderance of evidence, why we seem to be missing the point and why more of us are not confessing sin and stopping in our tracks to turn back to God and His desires for us. Why aren't more people asking the *relevant* question: what does *God* desire? In what ways have we offended and dishonored Him? What does "righteous" mean, and what does a godly life look like?

Why don't we get the message? I am afraid the answer is tragically simple: we don't know the stories. Aside from the stories we learned in Sunday school as children, most Americans are not very serious students of the Word, especially the Old Testament. Compare the amount of time that the modern American reads the Bible with the instructions given in Deuteronomy 6. "Impress them...Write them...Talk about them."

~SEPTEMBER 15~
THE ATTACK ON AMERICA
PART 4

"Not everyone who says to me, 'Lord, Lord' will enter the kingdom of heaven, but only he who does the will of my Father who is in heaven." Matthew 7:21

271

Coming and going, rising and settling down, don't let them out of your sight, and don't even let there be a chance that your children might grow up without a thorough knowledge of the importance of my will. These were God's instructions to His people in the beginning.

Life in the twenty-first century holds such allure. We have so many varied options of how to spend our time that even though many of the choices are delightfully harmless and many of the winsome temptations have an appearance of relevance and fulfillment, most are not *eternal*.

The New Testament has much to say about the fruit we are to produce. "Produce fruit in keeping with repentance" (Matthew 3:8), "...every tree that does not produce fruit will be cut down and thrown into the fire" (Matthew 3:10 *and* 7:19); and, "By their fruit you will recognize them" (Matthew 7:16, 20). And then Jesus shocks His listeners with this statement: "Not everyone who says to me, 'Lord, Lord' will enter the kingdom of heaven, but only he who does the will of my Father in heaven. Many will say to me on that day, 'Lord, Lord, did we not prophesy in your name and in your name drive out demons and perform many miracles? Then I will tell them plainly, 'I never knew you.'"

Perhaps you disagree with my whole premise. Perhaps you see the 9/11 attack as just a result of freedom of choice run amuck in the hands of evil people. Or maybe you see these acts as the work of the devil. I realize that this interpretation is disputable.

But there are some other things that are not, at least not if you claim to believe in the basic biblical ideas of eternity. The Bible teaches clearly that this fruit God requires in order for us to keep standing in His vineyard and drawing nourishment from the source is *righteousness*. He wants us to care about righteousness and to stand up for it and speak against evil and spend our time producing good fruit. This is the recurring message throughout God's Word— both the Old and New Testaments.

It is also indisputable that all who died that Tuesday were bound for one of only two eternal homes, Heaven or Hell. And whether or not Jesus returns in our lifetimes, the same narrow choice of conclusions awaits us all. How can we not realize this and deal with proper and prudent preparation in light of so many deaths in one day's time? Many have unrealistic and self-fabricated notions of God as being completely tender and gentle like a sweet, old grandfather. The stories recounted earlier completely destroy that notion. If we studied Him more, we would know His nature. The Bible offers every genre anyone could prefer to give us a correct picture of the True and Living God. If we don't agree on the underlying cause or the source of this tragedy, at least we probably do agree that Jesus calls us to a narrow way. *"Enter through the narrow gate. For wide is the gate and broad is the road that leads to destruction, and many enter through it. But small is the gate and narrow is the road that leads to life, and only a few find it." Matthew 7:13-14*

~SEPTEMBER 16~
THE ATTACK ON AMERICA
PART 5

"Those who cling to worthless idols forfeit the grace that could be theirs." Jonah 2:8

If we are not living a *deliberately* God-fearing life, if we are not hotly pursuing holiness, we are not on that very narrow road that Jesus speaks about. The life God desires is lived deliberately. Hell is real, and God is serious about His call for us to live upright lives and not to depend upon what *seems* right "in [our] own eyes."

I agree that the deeds of September 11, 2001, really are all about a whole lot of sin and evil, but I believe that the main issue we must recognize is that the evil that came rushing into our lives via jumbo jet came as a result of our own evil in this land that God has birthed and fed, dressed, led, and blessed over and over again in practically countless ways. God wants America to claim His Fathership of us and to bear His name in the way we live, raise our children, spend our time and money, vote, and make laws.

But America is a big place, and how can we stem its great and heavy tide if it is hell bent?

In truth, America is just a bunch of individual people, each of us is one of them; we are each a living cell in this great big organism. What each of us does, the choices we make, the way we react to God's individual 767's that crash into our own little worlds and cause us pain—all of these things matter! We should be asking all the time, "What is all this pain about? Could God be trying to mold me into a different shape than I am trying to mold myself?"

Instead of just praying that we will survive all this and that He will defeat our enemies and keep us strong as a nation, if we pray also to know and follow His will and to change so that we reject evil uncompromisingly in our personal lives, and then study His Word to know what good and evil really are, then He will bless our efforts and our upright hearts, and we will learn to grow more and more into His likeness. If each of us is blessed, then once again, our whole nation will be blessed. The whole is simply the sum of its parts. *"...if my people, who are called by my name, will humble themselves and pray and seek my face and turn from their wicked ways, then will I hear from heaven and will forgive their sins and heal their land." 2 Chronicles 7:14*

~SEPTEMBER 17~
EVEN WHEN IT HURTS

"Lord, who may dwell in your sanctuary? Who may live on your holy hill? He whose walk is blameless and who does what is righteous, who speaks the truth from his heart and has no slander on his tongue, who does his neighbor no wrong

and casts no slur on his fellow man, who despises a vile man but honors those who fear the Lord, who keeps his oath even when it hurts, who lends his money without usury and does not accept a bribe against the innocent. He who does these things will never be shaken." Psalm 15

Psalm 15 describes the unshakable man. A one-word summation of this man is "upright." The man who stands most upright before the Great Judge is the one who will least likely lose his balance in the gales of sin. Lose his balance how? The answer might not be as obvious as it seems.

What exactly does it mean to "never be shaken"? The original meaning of "shaken" here is to have one's well being disturbed and his security unsettled. Rather than referring to a fall into an obviously sinful lifestyle that throws off all restraint and gives into every fleshly whim, "shaken" here means something more personal and harder for the eye of man to decipher. The wounds of so many who are "shaken" in this way are deep and sinister, hiding so far beneath the flesh that those who would and could run to encourage or rescue never see them. Wounds that are never brought to the light and air can fester into bitterness and hardness of heart.

David sends out God's challenge to live with such uprightness before the Lord that what others from below do and say can never quite go far enough or reach high enough to block this man's view of God and His expectations. This man so fixes his gaze upon the God of Holiness and desires so much more to live in God's sanctuary than in the sanctuary of anything or anyone lesser that when he is treated with disrespect or unkindness, when he is passed over and his gifts ignored, when his merciful ways are taken advantage of and his humble nature exploited, he continues to be faithful, to "keep his oath" to God. Since his heart is not hard, it hurts, but he does the right thing anyway.

I am honored to be friends with one of these unshakable men. Most would not want to walk in Allen's shoes, for the Enemy has tried diligently to shake him. But he has shown that it can be done, and because of his demonstration, some will be inspired to try. He stands securely in his faith when God is silent, hangs onto Truth in the deafening din of lies, maintains a peaceful heart and a wise perspective when others around him are making short-sighted or faithless decisions. When concerning their treatment of him, he gives them the benefit of the doubt and "casts no slur." He might be seen as naïve by some, but his answer will always be, "Jesus Christ has my back."

Rudyard Kipling in his beloved poem "If" put it this way: "If you can keep your head when all about are losing theirs and blaming it on you...You'll be a man, my Son." It is a high call requiring a brave heart and tough feet, but I am convinced it gets easier with practice. If beginning seems too idealistic to consider, I pray you will have the blessing of seeing it lived out and thereby catch an unquenchable desire to dwell in His sanctuary and live on His holy hill.

~SEPTEMBER 18~
LOSING OUR LIVES JOYFULLY

"The man who loves his life will lose it, while the man who hates his life in this world will keep it for eternal life." John 12:25

"Whoever finds his life will lose it, and whoever loses his life for my sake will find it." Matthew 10:39

If *knowing* you should be holy is not your problem, maybe finding joy in the *trying* is. Many of us look up one day to realize that we are living in trivial ways that we never stopped long enough to notice. It's not that we have abandoned the faith (or even the assembly!), but between the compartments of spirituality, we maintain compartments of worldliness, or at least a flirtation with worldliness. It might show up in ways we spend our time, ways we mindlessly spend our money, or fantasies that consume our thoughts and maybe even our hearts. On some subconscious level we probably know that leading the life of Christ requires sacrifices, and in moments of temptation, we just aren't so sure that what will happen will be worth all the struggle. Many times the root of this problem is that we are living a life without meaning and purpose. We aren't so sure what we are here for, so we bounce from one triviality to another much like a ball bearing off the rubber bumpers of a pinball machine.

But with a "why" we can bear up under any "how." If we ask God to show us and then dedicate ourselves to looking in the right places for His answers, He will make known to us why we are here and His purposes for us.

The Word makes clear to us some of the places our purpose, and thus *meaning*, will *not* be found. We learn from Ecclesiastes 1:14 that it will not be found in the pursuit of pleasure. To chase after pleasurable activities (as the world sells pleasure) in hopes of finding true meaning that brings lasting joy is "vanity," Solomon said from experience. We learn from Jesus' encounter with the rich young man in Mark 10 that making money and collecting material possessions will not bring purpose and joy to our lives. In fact, we see that because this young man was so attached to his, he walked away from Jesus *sorrowfully*. We must somehow give up the possessions that possess our hearts. Neither will the pursuit of power lead us to our life's meaning. Jesus, rather, calls us to meekness, that quality that turns away from the power it possesses in order to bring strength to those who are weaker.

Our purpose *is* to be found in denying ourselves in order to serve Christ and others. Meaning is found when we hide ourselves in Jesus and His purposes (Colossians 3:3). When we dare to become involved in things outside ourselves, we begin to live a life that moves from a trivial randomness with no meaningful pattern to a purposefulness that nourishes not only our own spirits but the spirits of many others. And sometimes it must be done just that way: on a dare. We must dare to take Jesus at His word if we are to claim to truly believe Him and not just believe *in* Him. If we find that the stockpile of our "life" gets in the way of serving Him, we need to take action to eliminate the hindrances. Some things need to be lost before we can win.

~SEPTEMBER 19~
GOOD PAIN VS. BAD PAIN

"Be joyful always; pray continually; give thanks in all circumstances, for this is God's will for you in Christ Jesus." 1Thessalonians 5:16-18

There are times when giving thanks feels like it is almost impossible. When we suddenly lose a loved one to a death that seems so random and purposeless, when storms sweep in and confound our understanding of God's will, it is very hard to feel grateful. In fact, what we sometimes want to do is just shut down emotionally and not deal with feeling at all. We sometimes wish that we had just never become involved. Things would be so much easier to bear if we had just better maintained our distance. We wouldn't be feeling this loneliness, nor would we be going through all these disturbing feelings about what God was thinking when He let this happen.

Recently I attended a funeral in which I was reminded that to live is to lose, and to lose is pain. (Jesus makes it clear that losing our lives for His sake is the only way we will ever truly find real life, so I believe this minister was referring mainly to our loss of loved ones to death.) Our choice is not between pain and no pain but between *good* pain and *bad* pain. We make a choice in the way we love others as to what kind of pain we will face should we lose them to death. The greater we love, the greater the pain of the loss.

But great pain doesn't mean bad pain; the worst kind of pain at all is numbness, the kind of pain that affects us somewhere inside, but we can't feel it, so we ignore it. Not to throw ourselves into loving will keep us safe from feeling, but it will make us more vulnerable to something worse. We lose touch with the plight of our fellow strugglers as we journey through this campland toward heaven. We become the walking dead; we will not have the worries of weeping and mourning, but the price we pay is that we will also not have the thrills of rejoicing and celebrating. For a while this might feel like the best path to take, but eventually, maybe on our deathbed all alone with no one to comfort us, this kind of life takes its toll, and we realize why arranging to feel no pain led ironically to the *worst* kind of pain of all, a kind that we have no time to go back and amend or take another path at a crossroads we cannot revisit.

God gave us each other to love. He came here to show us how to do that. He did not come here to teach us how to play it safe and remove ourselves from grief and pain.

A detail worth noticing about this command in 1 Thessalonians 5:17 is that it does not say that we are to give thanks *for* all circumstances but that we are to give thanks *in* all circumstances. What we are being admonished to do here is to remember that God is still almighty and victorious, and we are still His. For these things, we *can* give thanks. And we can be glad we loved enough to suffer great pain, for we have a great Comforter.

Another way to look at it is that when we lose something, we can still give thanks for all that is still left. What is always still left— whatever we lose— is our heavenly inheritance, our eternity with God and His Son, that inheritance that can never fade, and hopefully some beautiful memories we were not too afraid to make.

"And when the Chief Shepherd appears, you will receive the crown of glory that will never fade away." 1 Peter 5:4

~SEPTEMBER 20~
SEEING AND BEING SEEN

"So from now on we regard no one from a worldly point of view...if anyone is in Christ, he is a new creation; the old has gone, the new has come." 2 Corinthians 5:16, 17

There are so many good reasons to risk loving strongly and well. One of them is the benefit of learning what lies beneath the surface of one another. I am greatly motivated and inspired by knowing there will be a time when Jesus and I will meet face to face, and I will "know fully even as I am fully known" (1 Corinthians 13:12). Being truly known is to me the very best part of love.

We are called by Christ to look deeply at our Christian brothers and sisters, deeply enough to realize that they are sacred vessels inhabited by the Living God of the Universe. This verse reminds us that we must be sure that we do not fall into the temptation of viewing other Christians from a "worldly" viewpoint but rather to see them as the new creation that they are. We must struggle against thinking that we are somehow better than others who are inhabited by the same God as we carry around inside us. This means we squint our eyes to see things from their point of view, understanding that it takes many different shapes and functions to build the Body of Christ. This is not to say that we are never to correct or admonish one another when there is danger of taking the wrong path, but when one of us sees a *disputable* issue differently from another, we are to risk being overly generous rather than giving in to being overly suspicious. How do we know whether God might be reaching through our sister's viewpoint an entirely different set of souls than we will reach with ours? By accepting and encouraging in these times rather than condemning and abandoning, we fulfill the law of Christ. We look at another with an eye and an ear to learn and thus, to grow.

The other day I was again exposed to, for probably the twenty thousandth time in my life, the expression, "Thank you for seeing me through all this." It was written in a letter to me to me by the hand of a dear friend who was going through some extremely trying times that had rocked her world down to its foundations. In this case, I can honestly say that she, through all of this, had swerved none at all from her very faithful Christian walk. Nevertheless, for some reason the expression caught my eye in a new way. It is a figure of speech that we usually do not take apart and consider at face value— just one of those sentiments we spit out without questioning its origin or wondering how it managed to become such a successful idiom. In light of this scripture, it suddenly holds a new and precious meaning to me. I think of all the times I have said the same thing to others: "Thank you for seeing me through this hard time." What I was saying without really thinking was, "When things are so hard that they press me into an unfamiliar shape, thank you for looking deeply enough to find the real *me* in there beyond all the tangle. Thank you for remembering—when I must become inconsistent with my phone calls or visits, when I must grow quiet and serious, when I cannot think of anything deep or inspiring to say in response to your questions or problems because I am weary or used up already— that I am *still* who you know me to be, one who loves you and listens to God and will come back as soon as I can. Thank you for seeing *me* through all of *this*."

~SEPTEMBER 21~
SEEDS

"But we have this treasure in jars of clay to show that this all-surpassing power is from God and not from us." 2 Corinthians 4:7

Dull and unbecoming with no grace or brilliant hue,
A seed is dropped into the soil and waited on to do
A task impossible for one with no apparent power—
But caressed by sun and kissed by dew,
It blossoms into a flower.
With fiery garnet plume and all bedecked in an emerald gown,
Its glory hardly resembles the husk once rough, unsightly, and brown.
Left alone to light the world, our lanterns have no spark.
Our fuse is dry and cold and powerless to light the dark.
But touched just once by the Finger of the Keeper of the Flame,
The reluctant wick sparks into a blaze
That will never be the same.
And the hide we walk around in is no better than a tomb;
Like the unplanted seed, impoverished, we lie powerless and doomed.
But planted by the Master of the Vineyard, life breaks through,
And our carcasses take on sweet fragrance and a bright and brilliant hue.
Christ fans our flicker into hot flame and floods our trickle with power—
And the grace that warms the soil of His spirit embraces her newly-born flower.

The next time you're having trouble believing in the power of Jesus to transform human lives, rip open a package of zinnia seeds and put some in your hand.

Learn from the dull, dry, lifeless husks that contain all the power, under the right circumstances, to become glorious orange, yellow, red, and purple velvety flowers. It is not in us to figure out how it happens, but we all know that it can. God doesn't ask or expect us to understand how he can transform a hell-bent sinner into a creature bound for glory; He simply asks us to provide the right circumstances for Him to do His mighty work.

~SEPTEMBER 22~
CULTIVATING THE PATH

"A farmer went out to sow his seed. As he was scattering the seed, some fell along the path, and the birds came and ate it up." Matthew 13:3-4

Jesus' Parable of the Sower demonstrates our Rabbi's master teaching skills in that it "lays to the side of" (the original meaning of the word "parable") a difficult and abstract lesson a simpler and more concrete object lesson to aid His listeners' understanding. Most of us who have been Bible students for any length of time can easily enumerate and assign meaning to each type of soil, or heart, touched by the seed, or the Word of God.

But if we see the story as a mere diagnosis of three "poor soil" hearts and one "good soil" one, isn't this, rather than a lesson about making disciples, more just a discouraging commentary on three-fourths of the worlds' hearts? Surely Jesus didn't tell this long and detailed story as only a means of discouraging us; surely He meant it to be another lesson on discipleship. Neither is it a lesson designed to tell us where and where *not* to sow the good seed. Rather than taking this lesson as one that teaches us how to test the soil, Jesus makes it very clear that the farmer sowed his soil not sparingly and discriminately, but generously and without regard to where it might land. Therefore, when we read this parable, shouldn't we read it with an eye not just for soil analysis but also, in context with Jesus' other teachings and His very lifestyle, an eye for how we, the trusted "farmers" who hold the Treasured Seed can have a positive effect upon cultivating the "soil" God has put at our disposal, both our own and others? We must learn how to prevent soil from going bad and how possibly to improve it once it does.

In fact, I have a friend who used to do it every year. Somewhere around April gardening fever would set in and we would both make dozens of trips hither and thither to nurseries to buy our spring bounties. Being the impatient type given to short-term projects, I would usually rush home and begin digging, anxious to witness the full bloom of my tiny, closed up seedlings. But Candy would spend a little more time before doing the actual planting so that she could improve her soil. She would make a few more trips to buy bags of stuff ever so much less exciting and colorful than flowers and work it into her soil. It took me a while, but I finally realized that the extra time nurturing the resting place for her new blooms is what made the difference in the richness and health of our gardens.

The path or the "wayside" (KJV), Jesus says, is the heart that has become like the hard, beaten-down path of worldly traffic. Their self-indulgence has caused them to be "hardened by sin's deceitfulness"(Hebrews 3:13), and they have been rendered spiritually deaf and blind, totally oblivious to the danger they are courting. Certainly in this case, the prevention would have been so much more of a possibility than the cure, for such a worn path took a long time in wearing down.

What can you do to nurture a young heart? Even if you are not a parent, you can influence the "soil" of a child. My friend Angela invites all her neighbors' kids into her home once a week for a Bible study. Invite kids to church with you, or get involved in a bus program that brings in kids from unchurched homes. A heart on its way to becoming a hard pathway awaits your gentle plow.

~SEPTEMBER 23~
SOFTENING THE ROCKY PLACES

"Some fell on rocky places where it did not have much soil. It sprang up quickly because the soil was shallow. But when the sun came up, the plants were scorched, and they withered because they had no root." Matthew 13:5-6

In His explanation to His disciples, Jesus explained that the rocky-soil heart receives the word with joy, but because he lacks roots, he quickly falls away under the strain of trouble and persecution. By planting a literal seed in a very sparse, shallow, rocky soil, we can quickly observe just the result Jesus describes here when He speaks of this kind of a heart. The plant springs up almost immediately; little waiting is required to see some results. However, alas, without roots there can be no steady and continued growth, regardless of the immediacy with which the plant springs up.

What does this shallow soil and rootlessness really mean when we are speaking of the human heart receiving God's Word? Jesus seems to be putting forth the practical fact that shallowness is not conducive to good root growth. Though it might make the teacher feel good to see "immediate results," we are naïve to disregard the hard, rocky places that remain in that small amount of good soil that responded so quickly when the seed was dropped in. This is why counting the cost is always important when we are teaching others the gospel in hopes that they will become Christians. If *we* are in denial of their history and allow or encourage *them* to be, we are not properly preparing them for the road they must travel. The hard layer of rock cannot be ignored. The rocky foundation must be taken into account and purposefully and intentionally covered with good soil that can cultivate a root. This is not to say that one's heart must be perfect in order to embrace Christ; none of us could. But to say we come to Him while we still allow for hindrances to living His life is doubletalk. True conversion requires us to bring our habits of life face to face with His holiness and yield them fully into His control. The stony-ground hearer is likely to depend upon itself rather than upon God for growth. It might trust more in its own feelings and impulses than in what is to be learned from God Himself. A rock is an apt symbol because it is not easily broken— habits, thought processes, motives. A certain brooding over the Word and what it will mean to submit to Another's will is the cost-counting that assures that repentance is real, not only presently, but as a permanent way of life. It is essential to give the soil the depth it requires to grow strong roots.

And what, exactly, are these "roots"? They are what connect us to Christ and His life. Roots go from one place to another. To be shallowly rooted in the spirit is to be deeply rooted into self or into the world. If a non-Christian is not deeply enmeshed in worldliness, then he or she is likely deeply enmeshed in self-determination. Either way, there is no taproot to Christ, our only means of safe delivery into Eternity.

Rocky hearts can receive the Word and thus become Followers, but they require steady and consistent nurturing of the Holy Spirit to remove and crush hardness into soft, arable hearts that will grow hardy roots. We must look honestly at our own hearts, too, for any stoniness that still needs softening. A time might await us in the future which will require even stronger roots than we can imagine.

~SEPTEMBER 24~
THE THORNS OF LIMITED BELIEF

"Other seed fell among the thorns, which grew up and choked the plants."
Matthew 13:7

"The one who received the seed that fell among the thorns is the man who hears the word, but the worries of this life and the deceitfulness of wealth choke it, making it unfruitful," Jesus explained to his disciples. The thorns and weeds are those dangerous germs living within any soil which threaten to take over the good soil until there is no place left for the seed to grow. Unlike the rock that lies hard but dead beneath the shallow soil, these weeds have life and thus will continue growing if not pulled out by their roots. Just a simple shearing at ground level will not suffice; they must be dealt with for the noxious threat that they are. Anyone who has ever tried to grow anything knows that weeds need no cultivation in order to thrive. They come unbidden, just as sin that lies easily at hand whether we seek it or not. Grace, however, must be carefully cultivated. If our hearts are not kept fully under the searchlight of God's Word, if the Holy Spirit is not cultivated so that He can refine and enliven our character, old ways of thinking— old "truths"— will talk their way back into our newly-found life. If we just profess to believe the gospel, but we do not allow the gospel to sanctify us, to dispel the world's lies that were once truth to us, we will cultivate a whole new crop of lies. We will have simply moved our old furniture around so that the place looks different but indeed will still be the same old shack that is bound to fall down around us eventually.

What we *really believe in most* does not surface in every situation. Sometimes for a season we can talk the talk and even walk the walk. We can take on a new truth and begin to live it without even dispelling the old one, which was never true at all. Two of the lies that might never be dispelled when we take on our new belief in Christ is that He could not really care personally for us nor truly be depended upon to answer our prayers. This means that when worries of this life come, the limited belief system we have newly adopted (that Jesus Christ is God's Son) does not affect the way we respond. If we have not taken that belief as literally as we should— to realize that by our union with His Son, we are now united with the *Living and Almighty God*— we still will find ourselves confounded and panic-stricken by those worries. We will still look to the deceitfulness of wealth's security as our answer and to wealth's scarcity as our doom. The truth we accepted was not allowed to uproot the lies that challenged it. Those thorns, therefore, kept growing unchecked beneath the surface until finally they choked out the truth that we failed to cultivate.

Can it happen that just a few thorns are still growing beneath our surface, even after all these years? If we cultivate the Good Seed through continued prayer and study, God will give us the eyes to see and the will to grow uncomfortable with them until He helps us get at their roots. This is how we must see the thorns in both our own lives and the lives of those we teach. We must allow the Life of Christ to grow into all it can be, to be *all* the Truth, not just a compartmentalized section of our lives. We must not let any root remain that is in contradiction with this Truth, but we must see if for the lie that seeks to choke out the good fruit God desires us to bear.

~SEPTEMBER 25~
MAINTAINING THE GOOD SOIL

"Still other seed fell on good soil where it produced a crop—a hundred, sixty or thirty times what was sown." Matthew 13:8

Jesus further explained that this is the man who hears the word and "understands" it. This understanding depends not so much upon intellect as upon desire and purposefulness. We have all known Christians who soar spiritually but who barely hover above the ground scholastically, just as we known the spiritually bankrupt academicians.

God is no respecter of persons, and He seeks to bless those who seek Him. To the good-soil heart merely to read the Word is not enough. Just as the blessed man described in Psalm 1, he or she *meditates* upon the meaning of the words night and day seeking to allow them to affect his or her life. By earnest attention and prayerfulness, the heart of this hearer grows roots to its true Master and gains its nourishment only from Him. The life, therefore, takes upon it the semblance of that it dwells upon. This heart takes nothing for granted but measures all philosophies and experiences by the one true Plumbline, answering to no one less than its true Master. It never stops seeking for ways to grow more closely into conformity with its true Nourishment. It knows that its purpose is to bring forth eternal fruit.

This fruit bearing, however, must oftentimes be done with much patience. No one is exempt from pain and hardship on this side of Heaven, regardless of the soil of our hearts. If we had no hardship, if our reach did not exceed our grasp, then our faith would have no way to grow and become perfected. If we could go merrily on our way after becoming New Creatures, we would certainly forget any need for spiritual strength and become stunted and earthbound creatures. The fruit of the Spirit would never be fertilized, and thus power could never grow into meekness, self-sufficiency into humility.

James 5:7 reminds us to "See how the farmer waits for the land to yield its valuable crop and how patient he is for the autumn and spring rains." It is a call for us to be patient in suffering and an assurance that the rain will finally come that will produce our harvest. It also reminds us that Christ, too, will finally come and with Him our treasures we have placed in Him. So we obey, pray, and wait. And in the meantime, others, hungry for a life of meaning, will be watching the way we do this waiting and marveling at something too big to be contained in mere flesh. Even as we wait patiently for some slow fruits to grow and develop, other fruits will be blossoming because of that same "delay."

And thus, by making our only business to receive God's word and hold fast to it, we will be taken out of the bonds of self, become captivated by Christ, and produce, probably without ever knowing about much of it, "a crop, yielding a hundred, sixty, or thirty times what was sown."

~SEPTEMBER 26~
PAIN WITH A PURPOSE

"...though now for a little while you may have had to suffer grief in all kinds of trials. These have come so that your faith— of greater worth than gold, which perishes even though refined by fire— may be proved genuine and may result in praise, glory, and honor when Jesus Christ is revealed." 1 Peter 1:5-7

Where are you hurting right now? Are you hemmed in by circumstances over which you have no control? Has it been a glancing blow you didn't see coming, or is it a thing which has dripped and dripped day after day until the concave place worn by the first eon of this is fast growing into a hole? Do you pace in your cage and stare wistfully through the bars to a freedom that you can scarcely remember? Is hope dwindling into a word for naïve idealists?

Peter's first letter is addressed to "God's elect, strangers in the world, scattered through Pontus, Galatia, Cappodocia, Asia, and Bithynia, who have been chosen according to the foreknowledge of God the Father, through the sanctifying work of the Spirit, for obedience to Jesus Christ and sprinkling by His blood..." It is addressed to us. We have been chosen through the Spirit for obedience. That is why we are alive— to bring glory to our God by obedience to Him.

But obedience is such a big word. It is hard to keep our minds wrapped around everything that He requires of us at any given moment. Some times are easier than others to see what we are being called upon to obey Him in. And when we suffer, we wonder if it is because we slipped up somewhere and let something get past us whose consequences now must visit us as a result of our sloppiness or our negligence, our laziness, or maybe even some rebellion about which we have been in denial. When this happens to me, it doesn't take long to find something to convict in myself— usually several somethings. Of course, many times my suffering isn't so much related to anything I've done wrong. Maybe it's because of something someone else did or failed to do.

But the point of this scripture is that the place we should always look first is to God—and not just for answers to "why?" Maybe that's really none of our business right now. What is always our business is "what?" What can I do with this that will make me more genuine? How can I use this thing so that it will result in praise and glory to God? Ask Him these things, and then expect Him to answer you.

When you read this whole section of scripture, it really does sound like Peter has a tone of celebration even though he is talking about persecution. We must try to remember, in times of trial and suffering, that everything is not really centered on *us*. There is *much* going on within the kingdom of God, and *I* am not always the main character. I am *a* character, though, and therefore, I must be content to be used to resolve the conflicts and affect the outcome in the master plot. The Author is much wiser than I, and if I am to help His story along, then rather than wishing to tear out all the pages I don't like or mark through, like an angry child with a red crayon, all the lines I cannot understand, I must keep turning each page in joyful anticipation of what He will do next. That we can learn to celebrate in the midst of persecution is a great mystery, to be sure, but it is the way that Jesus Christ is revealed to the world.

~SEPTEMBER 27~
TRUE RELIGION

"Religion that God our Father accepts as pure and faultless is this: to look after orphans and widows in their distress and to keep oneself from being polluted by the world." James 1:27

I suppose one of the greatest values of suffering is for our testing, which whether we like it or not, is imperative if we are to become "perfect" as He is perfect. How can we know what stuff we are being made of if we never are called upon to use some of those attributes that can only shine in darkness? (I said "being made of" rather than "made of" because our perfection is an ongoing process, and as we go on, we take on and throw out characteristics that help or hinder us in our journey into the likeness of Christ.) It is good that God planned for us to be old enough to repent before we can, in the truest sense, become Christians; having already learned what it is like to "grow up" at least from infancy to childhood, we have some realm of experience to compare as we grow up from Christian infancy into maturity.

A hard, but good, question to keep asking ourselves is "How well am I maturing in Christ?" Before we answer, though, we must be sure we are using the correct standard of measurement. James gives us a no-nonsense way of measuring our progress.

I find that there are many detractors to meaningful growth in Christ— many impostors that tempt me to subscribe to something easier than but inferior to living out the kind of religion that "God the Father accepts as pure and faultless." Let me say before going any further that any of these can and might be *true* indicators if they are used to spur me on to doing good, but the problem so many times is that they stay on the cerebral or intellectual level and end up serving as a kind of pseudo-spiritual fluff.

I read a lot, and most of the time when I am finished with a book it is exceedingly marked up and dog-eared. Every underlined word, each dog-eared page testifies that right here the eyes of my mind flew open, the pupils dilated, my heart thumped a little louder and faster, and I was *impressed!* I am thinking, no doubt, as I underline and fold down corners that I will come back and revisit this place to make it my own somehow, to turn this ink into flesh and blood. In this way, I shall redeem the time I spent reading rather than acting out. It shall then have been not just leisure but truly an *investment*.

Also, in the past two years since I retired, I spend a lot of time alone. In those hours, I think many a noble thought and fashion many visions of deeds I might do to lift another's burdens. Having these thoughts and ideas makes me feel a bit deeper and *better* somehow just for having had them. But my rich new finery means nothing unless it actually makes me *behave* better. It is like Paul's comparison of speaking with angels' tongues to having *real love*. C. S. Lewis compares this kind of confusion to the sick person whose "feeling better" means nothing if the thermometer shows that his temperature is still going up.[3]

Sometimes to rescue our real souls from our romantic notions that would take them hostage, we must resort to practical means. If all this strikes a note of familiarity with you, sit down today and make a list. List ways that your ideas can be put into action and people who could benefit from your recent inspirations. Then take your notions on the road before you let yourself abuse one more book.

~SEPTEMBER 28~
RESTORING OUR SENSE OF AWE

"By the word of the Lord were the heavens made, their starry host by the breath of his mouth. He gathers the waters of the sea into jars; He puts the deep into storehouses. Let all the earth fear the Lord; let all the people of the world revere Him." Psalm 33:6-8

There is another side of the coin, however. Just because inspiration alone is a dead-end street, a life lived without any isn't any better. Inspiration and awe can spur us on to goodness and mercy and praise and all kinds of glorifying God. Life devoid of awe is as dry as sawdust.

Most of us have pet peeves, and one of my biggest is the blatant misuse of the word "awesome." I physically cringe almost every time I hear that word these days; usually the thing being described is about as close to true awe as playing a video game is to skydiving. I want people to leave that word alone. There just aren't any other words that are going to say what that one really means, and it makes me nervous to have it thrown around promiscuously until it is limp and pale beyond all recognition.

The word "awe" is a word in its own category. Nothing else even comes close. Just to say it is to realize how we got it: "Awe"— a guttural accompaniment to a dance of the mouth as it falls open and just stays that way as if paralyzed by what it just witnessed.

"He wraps himself in light as with as garment; He stretches out the heavens like a tent... He makes the clouds His chariot, and rides on the wings of the wind." "The heavens declare the glory of God; the skies proclaim the work of His hands...In the heavens he has pitched a tent for the sun, which is like the bridegroom coming forth from his pavilion, like a champion rejoicing to run his course." To read Psalm19, 33, and 104 is to understand that true meaning of "awe." It is an overwhelming sense of wonder. It is to marvel and be overpowered by the moment so that to say anything would be a sacrilege. Many of us rarely experience awe; we are too intellectual, and to be so emotional feels like a cliché. We feel we need to be original; expressing wonder at God's creation like these psalmists did might feel too much like jumping on a bandwagon.

But if it is a bandwagon, it is one we all need to jump on. Awe is important! It gives us perspective; we get to see ourselves as part of a grand story, not as the main character. It transports us into the timeless; we remember that our God is not limited to anything we can imagine. And since we are, through Christ, bound up in this God, *we* are not limited to anything we can imagine. Awe lays a deep foundation for spirituality. By beholding magnificence beyond our doings, we are reminded of a world beyond our literal vision, the real world that undergirds and supersedes the one our eyes and ears and sometimes even our hearts and minds try to bind us to.

Talk and noise, speed and busyness, entertainment and technology can choke out the awe from our lives. There is a remedy: Find a quiet, natural setting and be purposefully still. Read the story of Jesus healing the paralytic in Luke 5:17-26. Insert yourself into this amazing event. Let your marvel lead you to awe that can be expressed only in praise as it was with those people that day. Then read Psalm 33 and let your mouth fall open as you remember that this very same God is yours, and you are His.

~SEPTEMBER 29~
HOLY, HOLY, HOLY

"In the year that King Uzziah died, I saw also the Lord sitting upon a throne, high and lifted up, and his train filled the temple. Above it stood the seraphim: each had six wings; with twain he covered his face, and with twain he covered his feet, and with twain he did fly. And one cried unto another, and said, 'Holy, holy, holy, is the Lord of hosts: the whole earth is full of His glory. And the posts of the door moved at the voice of him that cried, and the house was filled with smoke. Then I said, 'Woe is me! For I am a man of unclean lips, and I dwell in the midst of a people of unclean lips: for mine eyes have seen the King, the Lord of hosts." Isaiah 6:1-5(KJV)

Holy, holy, holy! Lord God Almighty!
Early in the morning our song shall rise to Thee;
Holy, holy, holy. Merciful and mighty!
God over all and blest eternally.

Holy, holy, holy! All the saints adore Thee.
Casting down their golden crowns around the crystal sea.
Cherubim and seraphim falling down before Thee,
Who wast and art and evermore shalt be.

Holy, holy, holy! Tho' the darkness hide Thee,
Though the eye of sinful man thy glory may not see;
Only Thou art holy. There is none beside Thee.
Perfect in pow'r, in love and purity.

Holy, holy, holy! Lord God Almighty!
All thy works shall praise Thy name in earth and sky and sea.
Holy, holy, holy! Merciful and mighty!
God in three persons, blessed Trinity.[4]

What a worshipful song! I can see us casting down our crowns at His feet someday and the angels just throwing themselves at His feet to declare His majesty. I see us there with our new glorious bodies mingling with the angels— and we're all in a relieved and silent state of awe. We have finally finished this hard race and entered the rest that has been so elusive for so long. Disappointment is no longer even a remote possibility. No longer will it be true that time flies when you're having fun and creeps along when you're miserable. There is no more misery. There are no more goodbyes to those we dread leaving or any more wondering when and if we'll ever meet again. The shadows will be forever lifted, and we will see only the Truth, only the Light—always. No more faith-walking, ever.

287

~SEPTEMBER 30~
THERE IS NONE BESIDE THEE

"And they sing the song of Moses the servant of God, and the song of the Lamb, saying, Great and marvelous are thy works, Lord God Almighty; just and true are thy ways, thou King of saints. Who shall not fear thee, O Lord, and glorify thy name? For thou only art holy: for all nations shall come and worship before thee; for thy judgments are made manifest." Revelation 15:3-4

Holy, holy, holy! Tho' the darkness hide Thee,
Though the eye of sinful man thy glory may not see;
Only Thou art holy. There is none beside Thee.
Perfect in pow'r, in love and purity.[4]

The words of this verse always have an overwhelming effect on me. Though this is a beautiful song, and I don't want to miss any chance I get to sing every word of it with a body of worshippers, when I get to these words, I am always a little tempted to stop and have a conversation with Mr. Heber. I want to ask him what he was thinking when he penned this understatement of such magnitude. Was he trying to be a little humorous? "Though the eye of sinful man thy glory may not see." *May* not? Of course it doesn't! It hardly even *can*. So much debris gathers and settles between our eyes and God's glory. Even when we manage to clear it away for a blissful moment, it always returns in one form or another. The fallout of sin and the bluster of busy-ness are hard to keep at bay. I must fight the desire to be thought of as one who thinks logically and operates in practical ways; I know that to take God at His word and believe recklessly requires me to risk breaking free from the earth's pull. For me to glorify a God this Holy and powerful, I must be one who will be known for lifting my feet off the ground and gazing longingly upward in wild anticipation of things beyond my imagination. I must be willing to look a little naïve to the rest of the world. I must be willing to be caught with my mouth wide open.

"There is none beside Thee." I'm so glad he chose the word "beside" instead of "before" or "above." We know, of course, that there is none *"before"* God, but sometimes we act like there just might be something "beside"— *almost* equal. But there is nothing even *close* to His perfection of power, love, and purity. It's a big wonder to me that He wants to bring any of us into that pure realm with His absolute light. Oh, the unfathomable love He must have for us to bother cleansing our sin-dusted lives so that He can hold us close!

~OCTOBER 1~
NEW SEASON, OLD LEAVES

"They are autumn trees, without fruit and uprooted—twice dead." Jude 12

> I like the hush of autumn; its quietness is so huge.
> It falls like cotton around me, swallowing me whole with its cushiony throat.
> First my ears go down its gullet, and then my tongue is stilled.
> The rest of me falls motionless in a comforting paralysis.
> I think it is a most holy season when the din of fans can die,
> And finally we can listen unhindered to the whisperings of God.

Autumn is so lovely. Even its name—autumn—falls eloquently from the tongue and is beautiful to look at with its silent "n" just hanging out there so unobtrusively beside sister "m" who gets all the press. It seems to be just an in-between season hanging on to the leftovers of summer, when everyone came out to play hard, while serving as a harbinger of winter, when we all will go back in to recover so we can do it all again next summer. But it isn't just a memory of one time or a preview of another. Autumn is a glorious season by its own merits. It is a quiet glory, though, bidding us be still and listen to gentle rustlings. It can be a time when we slow down after summer's rush to listen to how God might want to be preparing us for the seasons ahead. It can be a time when we let old foliage fall away to make room for the fruit he is forming inside.

Some of the most beautiful imagery in the entire Bible is in the little book of Jude, just one chapter long, tucked between John's three epistles and Revelation. Jude's imagery here is a little confusing at first: autumn is not the time for fruit, so why should the tree be uprooted? And what does "twice dead" mean?

Jude, probably the half brother of our Lord, wrote this letter to warn his readers to be on guard against false teachers who were perverting the meaning of grace so as to give license to sin so that grace "could abound," to use the words of Paul. It occurs to me that many times I am my own worst false teacher of this doctrine. Sometimes I want to allow myself great liberties; I want to hold on to the thrills of a bygone season of my life when God wants me to shed those and enter into His deeper thrills. Because He has been gentle with me— bestowed such grace upon me— I fear the heartaches of letting go of what I *know* to reach out to what I *don't know* more than I fear *God* and the consequences He might allow if I *do not* obey Him. And so in this season when He desires to strengthen my roots in preparation for fruit to come in a future season, I refuse to shed the rapturously-colored leaves I glory in. Thus, I am "twice dead"—first, dead to the faith work I need to consent to right now, and secondly, dead to the possibility of the future fruit God envisions for me. Without his grace, I would already be uprooted.

On the brink of this new season, purpose to allow old foliage to fall away. Dare to embrace the naked starkness of the outside to enable every bit of the nourishment to go to the roots. Let us get silent before God and ask Him what must go in order for His way-down-deep growth to best be accomplished in us. Autumn to the branches can be springtime to the core.

"Therefore we do not lose heart. Though outwardly we are wasting away, yet inwardly we are being renewed day by day." 2 Corinthians 4:16

~OCTOBER 2~
CHOOSING OUR RENDEZOUS

"Do not be deceived: God cannot be mocked. A man reaps what he sows. The one who sows to please his sinful nature, from that nature will reap destruction; the one who sows to please the Spirit will reap eternal life." Galatians 6:8

From my car radio Whitney Houston crooned these words: *"A few stolen moments are all that we share/ You've got your family, and they need you there./ Though I try to resist being last on your list/ No other man's gonna do/ So I'm saving all my love for you./It's not very easy living alone/My friends try and tell me find a man of your own/ But each time I try, I just break down and cry/ 'Cause I'd rather be home feelin' blue/ so I'm saving all my love for you./ You used to tell me we'd run away together/ Love gives you the right to be free/ You said 'Be patient; just wait a little longer/ But that's just an old fantasy./ I've got to get ready, just a few minutes more./ Gonna get that old feeling when you walk through that door/ 'Cause tonight is the night for feeling all right/ We'll be making love the whole night through/ 'Cause I'm saving all my love for you."* [1]

Then I pushed in a Twila Paris tape, and this is what I heard: *"Quietly you lead me to an open place/ Hold me in the stillness 'till I see your face/ Waiting in the silence as you speak my name/ Rising like an eagle I will fly!/ Sweet victory over the enemy/ Gentle Power, all I ever needed/ Sweet victory, I take it finally/ Strength for running; it's been a long time coming/ Sweet victory./ In this place I rest in more than I can see/ High above the turbulence you carry me/ From deep in a full heart I will speak your name/ Rising like an eagle I will fly/ Sweet victory over the enemy/ Gentle Power, all I ever needed/ Sweet victory; I take it finally/ Strength for running; it's been a long time coming/ Sweet victory./ I held so tightly to my fear/ There were so many sins repeated/ But your love has brought me here/ And the victory is sweet—victory is sweet./ Sweet victory, the blood of Calvary/ Gentle Power, all I ever needed/ Sweet victory, I take it finally/ Strength for running; it's been a long time coming/ Sweet victory."* [2]

Two songs about rendezvous. One robs moments from the Lord to give to the devil, and the other robs moments from the devil to give to God. One speaks of trying to resist feeling unimportant since she's "last on your list," while the other fights to resist feeling *too* important. In fact, this second one has to be "held" in the stillness and made to "wait" in the silence. It's as though this one believes she could win on her own and struggles to defeat the clamoring self that would foolheartedly rush out to fight alone. The first has a lover who leaves her at home alone "breaking down," "crying," and "feeling blue." The second has a Lover who speaks her name and causes her to "rise like an eagle" and "fly." The first is saving her love for one who breaks promises after she has waited patiently and believed; the second has waited too: "It's been a long time coming"— but the One on whom she has waited delivers. He lifts her "high above the turbulence" and gives her "strength for running." One has just a few minutes more; the other has an eternity in the arms of the One who loves her.

The rest of our lives will be filled with many rendezvous; what will happen to our hearts as a result of these times depends upon the lover we choose.

"This is the kind of love we are talking about— not that we once upon a time loved God, but that He loved us and sent His Son as a sacrifice to clear away our sins and the damage they've done to our relationship with God." 1 John 4:10 (The Message)

~OCTOBER 3~
WHAT DO YOU HEAR FROM YOUR FATHER THESE DAYS?

"But the counselor, the Holy Spirit, whom the Father will send in my name, will teach you all things and will remind you of everything I have said to you." John 14:26

"Praise be to the God and Father of our Lord Jesus Christ, the father of compassion and the God of all comfort, who comforts us in all our troubles..." 2 Corinthians 1:3-4

"Be still and know that I am God." Psalm 46:10

"What do you hear these days?" We ask each other this question often about our friends and relatives who do not live closeby. The person asking expects that there has been *some kind* of communication due to the closeness of the relationship. The answer usually involves the recitation of a recent letter, phone call, or visit. If none of these things has happened and the answer is "Nothing," it is naturally assumed that something is amiss, either with the one who hasn't been heard from or the relationship between the two.

How often do we ask fellow Christians this question concerning their Heavenly Father?

Recently at a Bible study, a woman confessed that due to her upbringing, she really didn't expect to "hear from" God except through the reading of His Word. Then several of us reminded her of scriptures such as the ones from John and 2 Corinthians quoted above and gave her testimonies of times when we had indeed "heard from God." She was not the least bit argumentative, as some are when they have embraced a tradition rather than the Truth as found in scripture. In fact, she became very quiet and thoughtful. She was eager to hear stories of others who had received just what Jesus spoke of in John— teaching, reminders, comfort. When she didn't seem downcast or act as though she were cheated by not having had similar experiences, I suspected that I knew why: she knew that she could not blame God for not giving her something she had never asked for. When I expressed my hope that she would directly ask God to speak to her through His Spirit she had received at her baptism, she smiled and nodded with a lovely and joyful hopefulness.

But usually the situation is not this extreme. There are many who *believe* that God can and will give His guidance and reminders who, if asked "What do you hear from your Father these days?" would have to admit, "Nothing." It is not that God has stopped wanting to communicate and be heard; it is just that we have not given Him our ear. We might still be hurriedly giving Him our *voice* in prayer in the form of petitions or even thanksgiving, but all too often we do not purposefully arrange for times of silence so that we can hear His guidance or comfort. We don't turn off the TV or the music or purposely isolate ourselves from others.

It is true that He does speak mightily and even specifically to our needs in His Word. Nor will His voice ever contradict His written Word; if we think it does, then we are dealing with a false spirit and are not to be taken in. But He is *alive* and His Spirit within us will guide and counsel and comfort if we would but listen expectantly.

~OCTOBER 4~
DECREASING THE ODDS

"One of you routs a thousand because the Lord your God fights for you, just as He promised. So be careful to love the Lord your God." Joshua 23:10-11

This kind of talk from our God is not uncommon. So many of His words and actions reflect His passionate desire for us to be His, to let Him fight our battles for us, to give Him a chance to remind us, His children, and to teach the rest of the world that He is a God who can be trusted to take care of His own. In this farewell speech to his leaders, Joshua reiterates what he first learned from Moses who had received this promise from the very mouth of God: *"You will pursue your enemies, and they will fall by the sword before you. Five of you will chase a hundred, and a hundred of you will chase ten thousand, and your enemies will fall by the sword before you" (Leviticus 26:6-8).* This bountiful covenant was not one that God was approached about like we might approach a rich uncle to cosign a loan; this was all God's idea. So much did He desire to take care of His people that He went on to throw in more benefits: making them fruitful and giving them such an abundant harvest that they would still be consuming it when it was time to plow it up and plant another year's worth, dwelling with them, and walking among them. He reminded them of His deliverance of them from Egyptian slavery: *"I broke the bars of your yoke and enabled you to walk with heads held high" (Leviticus 26:13).*

Sometimes, maybe because most of us are not engaged in literal combat with the enemy of this context, we forget to apply these verses to ourselves. We find ourselves enmeshed in consuming worry or embroiled in bitter pursuits to avenge injustice done to ourselves or those we love, just as though we had never read these verses or those others about falling sparrows or the numbering of each hair of our heads. We wring our hands in despair in the face of the same One before whom we might have prostrated ourselves a few hours ago and called "God." Is it to such a weak and oblivious God that we pray? This very God promised to those who love Him that He would narrow all the odds. He is the One who helped the judge Shamgar strike down six hundred Philistines with a wooden stick used to prod oxen. He is the One who desired so much that His power be seen that he cut down Gideon's troops against the massive and fearsome Midianites from twenty-two thousand to three hundred men with nothing more than trumpets, torches, and empty jars. Gideon knew the truth of that victory, though, when the Israelites attempted to make him their hero. *"But Gideon told them, 'I will not rule over you, nor will my son rule over you. The Lord will rule over you'" (Judges 8:23).* He knew it wasn't his tactics.

And now will He really rule over us? Will we let Him rule over our enemies, or will we take them on alone? If we let something else rule us, like agitation or revenge, we will be no more effective than the horns, torches, and empty jars in the hands of men unaccompanied by God. The second part of God's message to Moses warns us of the other option. *"If you will not listen to me...you will flee even when no one is pursuing you" (Leviticus 26:17).* It is true, isn't it? When we are not faithful to trust Him completely, don't we find ourselves overtaken by all kinds of imaginary fears? God did not deliver us from the bonds of our slavery so that we could become paranoid, but so that we could be free. *"One of you routs a thousand because the Lord your God fights for you... So be careful to love the Lord your God."*

~OCTOBER 5~
THE LOVE OF OUR DREAMS

"The Lord your God is with you, He is mighty to save. He will take great delight in you, He will quiet you with His love, He will rejoice over you with singing." Zephaniah 3:17

Recently while working on a craft project, I watched the old, original version of *The Parent Trap.* When it got to the part where Maureen O'Hara stood face-to-face with Hayley Mills, the daughter she had not seen in years, I had to drop everything else I was doing and allow my longing eyes to latch fully onto the scene before me. For that one minute of playacting alone, Mrs. O'Hara deserved an Oscar. Her eyes widened a bit to focus in on and drink in every drop of the face of her child as one dying of thirst might swallow up the last drop of water in a canteen. The camera focused on the mother's green eyes to show them filling with a kind of light that turned them even greener and radiated out to brighten her entire face. Then ever so tenderly, her hands cradled her daughter's face as though she were touching something very rare and fragile that few others might ever get to touch. You knew that this mother was entirely in *this* place. She was completely undivided in her thoughts, so caught up in the moment that her heart knew no other love but this one that she gazed upon with no words and touched as fine china. She was swept away from any reality but *this one beauty* before her by which she was totally enraptured. As I watched, I knew why I must put everything else aside but this; I knew why I was so captured by this scene: it was my deepest longing. It was the epitome of *delight*.

One of the frustrations I have with the English language is its lack of words to describe all the different flavors of love. Whereas Greek has several words to describe various kinds of love, English seems to be stuck with a one-size-fits-all word, and the longer I live and love, the more certain I am that the word "love" is way too general to evoke all the appropriate messages it is called upon to do. Thus, we use it to describe everything from how we feel about the taste of enchiladas or the thrill of a riding a roller coaster to our deepest and most sacred familial feelings. Every time I am brought back to this scripture I realize that there *is* another word that says what I want it to about some of those very rare and special feelings: *delight!*

This scripture is one of my favorites and thus keeps popping up with regularity at the tops of these pages. It's not that God's Word isn't replete with inspirational messages so that I would *need* to repeat any of them; it's just that this one speaks vociferously to what I cherish most in my memories and dream of most as encores in the future: feeling delight, both *in* another and *from* another. Delighting is a very specialized kind of loving that means I am not just one-size-fits-all "loved," but that someone finds me captivating. There are so many shortcomings that scream that I am unworthy and unlovely that to learn that God could feel this way about me is the best news I could possibly hear.

I suppose to want to feel such adoration could be interpreted as vain and idolatrous, but God himself uses the same word to call us to Him. *"Delight yourself in the Lord, and He will give you the desires of your heart" (Psalm 37:4).* He knows what can come from pure delight. Fall into His arms today, feel His hands around your face, gaze upon the beauty of Christ, and delight in Him as He delights in you.

~OCTOBER 6~
THE MUSIC OF OUR LIVES

"Speak to one another with psalms, hymns and spiritual songs. Sing and make music in your heart to the Lord, always giving thanks to God the Father for everything, in the name of our Lord Jesus Christ." Ephesians 5:19-20

Romans 12:1 reminds us that it is not just when we sit in a church building that we worship God but in our living out each day we are given on this earth. Offering our bodies to be used in holiness for Him pleases Him. It is our "spiritual act of worship." Some translations even call it our "*reasonable* act of worship." Today's scripture speaks of musical worship, and I can certainly see why God would love the thrilling melody and harmony we bring to him when we raise our voices in song. But I am daring to stretch the illustration some and contend that there is something else "musical" about our lives that cannot be translated onto a treble or bass clef or be defined in a certain key—something *else* that might be music to the ears of God.

Something I read by Oliver Wendell Holmes, Jr. brought this to my attention a few years ago: "*Most people die with their music still in them.*" Another similar quote by an anonymous author is a little easier to translate: "*Every time a person dies, a library closes down.*" Obviously the "library" is all that I know, all the lessons learned from my experiences—things that I must share about doing or not doing. My library is also my repertoire of memories that I alone have and which, unless I share with you while I am still breathing, you will never get to "read."

But this *music*— what exactly is *that*? Without thinking analytically about this quote, we feel the sadness of it. We get some of what he was trying to tell us right off the bat: most people die before they are ever really known. The fact that Holmes used the word "music" indicates to me that there is something *delightful* inside that was put there to be a blessing, the way music is a blessing.

Mine is definitely connected with words. How I love them! They are little magic pieces of connective tissue between the nerves and muscles and heartbeat and brainwaves of one person to the same in another person. They can suffice if they are vanilla or plywood, peanuts or white bread, but I think those would be just a chant or a rap— something with a beat but no melody. In order for them to be *true* music, they need melody. They need to be jamoca almond fudge, solid oak, macadamia nuts, and pumpernickel— poetry—true strains of flowing, pulsing prose, lilting alliteration, scintillating simile. Then, for the whipped cream on top and the cherry on top of that, I offer up these words that are all music to bless my Lord, and the figurative becomes literal, the whimsy becomes tangible, my music becomes the music I must play and sing before I die. I must take this treasure entrusted to me by my Master and use it to His glory. I must open my mouth and let the music He has placed within me come out.

And so must you. Whatever it is, don't die with it still in you. Don't enshrine your treasures in a corpse. Ask Him to help you identify your music and "giving thanks to God the Father," go into the world and sing and play it with glad confidence. It will fall upon needy ears, and some sad and discouraged soul will get up from his dark corner and begin to dance. "*And whatever you do, whether in word or deed, do it all in the name of the Lord Jesus, giving thanks to God the Father through Him.*" *Colossians 3:17*

~OCTOBER 7~
DOING BATTLE WITH LEISURE'S LULL

"Let us not become weary in doing good, for at the proper time we will reap a harvest if we do not give up." Galatians 6:9

Choose carefully your discomfort, but above all, choose one!

For the last few years of my teaching career, toward the end of July I fell victim to the detestable habit of deeply sighing. I wasn't happy with myself for being this way; I knew better. I would hope that each sigh would be the last one— the final sigh of resignation which would signal my will to begin rolling along in its well-worn trenches. But toward the end, it seemed to take a while. I could remember that I loved the kids and even *liked* most of them, hardly ever had behavior problems, had my share of eager ones and witty ones who sent me home most days glad to do what I did; I could remember all the past smiles, hugs, and kind words that the upcoming year would likely bring again.

Still I struggled with inertia. I found myself leaning toward dreams of more leisure, less pressure, no set schedule to enslave me. The gravity of laziness weighed heavily on me, and I fought strong urges to stare across the fence to greener pastures. I kept wishing I could just stay home and read and write and garden. I thought that would be true comfort, true satisfaction, deep meaningfulness, solid stuffed-to-the-brim fulfillment.

Reaching the horizon of having one's own schedule is the desire of many, but the gravity of abusing it once we get there can be a temptation we are wise to fight. There are some questions worth considering as we think along these lines. Here were my specific ones: Would being my own master all the time really bring total fulfillment? Would those of us who are writers have much worth saying anymore? Is a Christian writer just an inscriber of words or a liver of the Word who runs up against truth that is worth the effort to mutter or scribble so someone else will benefit who is running the same course? Is a poet only a writer of poetry or a liver of it— one who, as she ventures through her minutes and days, discovers a lovely pattern— a rhythm and a rhyme—a parallel, a parable, simile and metaphor, the breath of God, personification, texture, sound, taste, and fragrance, imagery in every part of that life made up of these minutes she is given?

In other words, does doing our own thing foster growing in the Lord Jesus, or does it hinder it? Are we made to be our own masters? Are we really that smart? Did we create ourselves or write the instruction manual for how we best function? Rest and vacation time are valuable, of course, but should that go on forever, the sweet respite of it would soon turn bitter; we might lose our spiritual muscles and forget that our being here is not just so we can feast forever on the Lotus plant and forget all duty, but so that we can bring God glory with lives of service for Him.

God didn't put us here so that we could star in our own show; God put us here so that He could be here too.

~OCTOBER 8~
UNMECHANIZED DYING

"I tell you the truth, unless a kernel of wheat falls to the ground and dies, it remains only a single seed. But if it dies, it produces many seeds. The man who loves his life will lose it, while the man who hates his life in this world will keep it for eternal life. Whoever loves me must follow me; and where I am, my servant also will be. My Father will honor the one who serves me." John 12:24-26

"Therefore, I urge you, brothers, in view of God's mercy, to offer your bodies as living sacrifices, holy and pleasing to God—this is your spiritual act of worship." Romans 12:1

Oh, Father, I long to be thy machine—
An efficient thing
That flies on wings
Like lightning when you call my name.

Push my button,
And cause me to sing
Melodious praises that will honor my King—
But you say, "No. There'll be no such thing.

'Twill not be easy to choose my will,
To give up the thrill
Of all you long for
That delights your eyes,
The dazzling lies
That whisper and woo and tantalize.
I want a heart unmechanized
That chooses each time the truth or the lies.
I'll neither pressure nor terrorize

Until you invite me
To fuel and ignite
My Spirit inside you,
To soothe or to chide you—
Not a machine
But a soul that will lean
Unreservedly
Relentlessly
Upon its God."

~OCTOBER 9~
FROM PARADISE TO THE DESERT

"To this you were called, because Christ suffered for you, leaving you an example, that you should follow in His steps. 'He committed no sin, and no deceit was found in His mouth.' When they hurled insults at Him, He did not retaliate; when He suffered, He made no threats. Instead, He entrusted Himself to Him who judges justly. He Himself bore our sins in His body on the tree, so that we might die to sins and live for righteousness..." Peter 2:21-24

Many times we say— I have said it too— that Christ died so that we might live, and of course this is true. However, it is a huge oversimplification to leave it at this, insinuating that since He died, we can thus expect to have lives filled with nothing but frolic and festivity. This is, in fact, far from the true picture that scripture paints. It rightly indicates the final chapter, but it omits many of the chapters leading us to that point.

God offered Adam and Eve paradise in Eden, but it quickly became evident that they wanted something else— something "more" than what God considered "Paradise." They fell victim, as we do, to the Enemy's alluring lies about greener pastures. And just as happens with us, I am sure they deeply regretted their folly when they realized that what they had in Eden at the beginning— a life of unhindered fellowship with God— was indeed the greenest of all greens ever created. Since that time, life without troubles and sacrifice is not an option. Just as God had to remove them from Paradise to the desert, He must take us there, also, for He knows that it is not in us to appreciate the Promised Land He is leading us to without first suffering through some hot, dry miles in the desert. This is the dying that Peter speaks of that comes before the living.

When trouble comes, it feels as though something "strange" is happening. It feels as though something has gone seriously haywire. We can respond in one of two ways at these times: we can continue to obey Him and follow relentlessly in the footsteps of Jesus—forgiving and praying for our enemies, turning the other cheek, going the extra mile, giving our last "widow's mite," in other words, trusting Him as a good God who knows how to take care of the universe; or, we can take Option #2 and decide because of this strangeness, things must be off somewhere in the Heavenly realms so we must take care of ourselves, for surely in this strange time, if we don't Nobody Else will.

But Peter tells us about these strange-feeling times: *"Dear friends, do not be surprised at the painful trial you are suffering, as though something **strange** were happening to you. But rejoice that you participate in the sufferings of Christ, so that you may be overjoyed when His glory is revealed" (1 Peter 4: 12-13).* When troubles come, therefore, we can know that God has not allowed them so that we will die in the desert but so that an eternal character can be developed in us that will allow u to truly rejoice in a place beneath His wings. It is His desire to care for us, but until we die to our sins, our desire to take care of ourselves in a way we think is better keeps luring us away. We must go through the dying process in order to live. The cross we are to pick up and carry in order to be His disciple (Luke 14:20) is this willingness to go through with the suffering and self-denial rather than to wiggle out of it and take care of ourselves. It will be painful, but it is the only way to the Promised Land.

~OCTOBER 10~
FROM THE DESERT TO PARADISE

"Do not grieve, for the joy of the Lord is your strength." Nehemiah 8:12

"We were therefore buried with Him through baptism into death in order that just as Christ was raised from the dead through the glory of the Father, we too may live a new life." Romans 6:4

Baptism explicitly depicts what it means for one to be united with Christ. At this place where our sins are washed away (Acts 22:16), we are allowed to witness a microcosm of our lives' journey. We die so that we can rise up and live. Some versions say "that we may walk in newness of life." We need much help with this *walk*; we do not naturally jump out of the grave and do it perfectly. We stumble and proceed awkwardly as we learn how to follow in His steps as closely as we should. We *are* new creations (2 Corinthians 5:17), but as such, we must be willing to stay focused on the One by whom we have been given this new life. We are babes who are not readily apt to take to a growth process that requires us to take up our cross *daily*. And, of course, let us not forget that the one we have rejected will be hard on our heels to woo us back to him.

But Jesus, who *"made Himself nothing, taking the very nature of a servant... humbled Himself and became obedient unto death, even death on a cross"* wanted us to follow Him *through* the desert to the Promised Land. Philippians 2 goes on to say this: *"Therefore, God exalted Him to the highest place."* Romans 8 ties us to His victorious end: *"And if the Spirit of Him who raised Jesus from the dead is living in you, He who raised Christ from the dead will also give life to your mortal bodies through His Spirit, who lives in you...If by the Spirit you put to death the misdeeds of the body, you will live... Now if we are children, then we are heirs—heirs of God and co-heirs with Christ, if indeed we share in His sufferings in order that we may also share in his glory" (Romans 8:11, 13, 17).* The suffering is not for nothing; we *will* share in His *glory*, both here and into eternity, for indeed, eternity begins for us when we take on His immortal nature in this life. But we must remember in the desert times that we are being afforded opportunities to *grow* into His likeness. No one reading these words has suffered as much as Christ did. Hebrews 12:4 says, "In your struggle against sin, you have not yet resisted to the point of shedding your blood." In other words, the struggles we have been through have not killed us; in fact, wouldn't you say that with each struggle you have gone through *without taking yourself out of His hands*, you have become not *less* alive, but *more* alive? Someday some of us may indeed give our very lives in the struggle, but even then, we are promised "treasures in Heaven" (Matthew 6:20). We are also promised that these struggles are *"not worth comparing with the glory that will be revealed in us" (Romans 8:18).*

At the end of their wanderings, the faithful Israelites were delivered to the Promised Land. On the other side of the cross, faithful Jesus was delivered back into Heaven. On the other side of all our deserts, we will regain Paradise, too, if we see the desert for what it is and, in the dire heat, we do not take our lives into our own hands.

"As the time approached for Him to be taken up to heaven, Jesus resolutely set out for Jerusalem." Luke 9:51

~OCTOBER 11~
TRANSFORMATION, NOT IMPROVEMENT

"Do not conform any longer to the pattern of this world, but be transformed by the renewing of your mind." Romans 12:2

Here we were down here, ever since the flood, living out our lives and dying, most never at all *getting* what God meant about the adoption as sons. Although He repeatedly told the Israelites that He wanted to take them as a people of His very own, the vast majority didn't really understand what that meant. We were too steeped in doing things our way, bent on thinking with the mind of man, fearful of taking our feet off the ground as we knew it— as accursed as it was— to be lifted up by faith into a new way of seeing things, a new way of living. In Hebrews 11 we can read about some who did break the bonds of this fear and were rewarded not only *for* their faith, but *by* their faith; their reward was that they became this new kind of creation, they became His sons. But by and large, the world just didn't choose to go far enough off the deep end to really *get* it. By and large, we thought that the best we could aspire to was just to get better at what we were already being and doing. We didn't know what He was asking was not just that we *improve* but that we be *changed* into something quite *different* altogether.

So God sent Himself down as Jesus to us to show us how to become His sons, not just creatures who by trial and error were conditioned into doing some things and not doing others, depending upon whether they resulted in good feelings or bad feelings, a meal at the end of the maze or an electrical shock for having taken the wrong path. Jesus didn't think, speak, or do things the way the old creatures did. He went against all kinds of "normal" grains, rubbed a lot of the "best" people the wrong way, and spoke in paradoxes that were, to put it mildly, countercultural. He knew that His invitation to us wouldn't be easy, that it would require struggling against old norms, suffering, and even dying, but He also knew that all this was worth the sons we would become as a result.

Perhaps this is why His first words to a large crowd were ones that would right off the bat encourage us to go ahead and dive off into this deep and unfamiliar pool where He swam: "Blessed are the poor in spirit, for theirs is the kingdom of heaven" (Matthew 5:3). This was His way of encouraging us not just to try to *improve* this creature life, even if that meant making us into nicer people, but wipe our slates completely clean of this ambition, as high as it might be, and let Him draw for us the picture of a son of God. This one wouldn't aspire to getting better and better at what makes him or her "nicer," but would become a new wineskin that could hold a whole new set of truths. His Beatitudes continue to specify what this poverty of spirit would look like. It would mourn—from penitence, from compassion for ignorant, lost, or rebellious sheep that others would see as so victorious, strong, and shrewd that they had no need of a shepherd; it would be meek—that is, it would take the power it certainly possessed and willingly give it up so it could be led and broken into something more useful and meaningful than this power could ever bring about; it would hunger not for more power, fame, and fortune, but for *righteousness*, something most saw as a foolish trade-off that only a simpleton would make. This was not the same old can of worms glorified; this was a can of something else completely.

~OCTOBER 12~
OUT OF OUR MINDS, FOR GOD'S SAKE

"If we are out of our mind, it is for the sake of God...So from now on, we regard no one from a worldly point of view. Though we once regarded Christ in this way, we do so no longer. Therefore, if anyone is in Christ, he is a new creation; the old has gone, the new has come!" 2 Corinthians 5:13, 16-17

Redemption came not just to make us "be nice"; in fact, we need redemption in spite of and even sometimes *because* of our "niceness" When Jesus said, *"How hard it is for the rich to enter the kingdom of Heaven,"* let us not suppose he was talking only of those who were monetarily rich. He said so much in His Beatitudes. If our natural gifts include a calm reserve, a mild, easily managed temper, a good upbringing (which, by the way, is in no way to our own credit) which brought about in us a well-developed sense of responsibility, then we might be tempted to feel little need for "any better kind of goodness," as C.S Lewis puts it.[3] We roll along smoothly through our well-worn ruts for so long that when something foreign falls into our path and mere human habit lets us down, the complacence we had depended upon for so long is reduced to mere memory. Since we have done well "on our own" for so long, we have not bothered to cultivate a relationship with God through His Son. Our earthly account is depleted, and we have made no deposits in our Kingdom account. What we can see with our sight-eyes looks bleakly dim, and since we have thus far had no need for faith-eyes, we have no vision for our future at all.

But others who are more impoverished— the unbalanced ones who fall easily into foolishness and sin of all flavors— eventually learn that they have *nothing* and are *powerless* if they do take up the offer of Christ. They must *cling* to all His ways if they are to motor on down the road of life. They have no delusions of grandeur about what they can do—or at least what they *will* do—if left to their own devices. Jesus hung around with these types, and it drove the Pharisees crazy. He went to tax collectors' houses, visited with an adulteress at the town watering hole, and allowed a former prostitute to cry on his feet and wipe them with her hair, for Heaven's sake! He told the Pharisees that this type would enter the Kingdom of Heaven before they would. It wasn't that the Pharisees weren't a decent sort; they had just become so rich by their own devices and in their own brand of righteousness that they saw no sense in upsetting their well-organized and smoothly rolling apple carts. They had it made; why should they change?

Now obviously Jesus wasn't saying that we all need to become prostitutes or thieves in order to have a relationship with Him. He was warning us about our refusal, whether blatant or denied, to leave the well-worn path of our creatureliness in order to enter onto His path of sonship. To be a son of God means to be ruled by God rather than by our logical way of thinking, to honor God over our preconceived notions and above our limited scope of reality. It means to become meek and to humble ourselves before Him to the point that we risk looking foolish to the world. It means learning at His feet the limitations of our humanity when it comes to judging others; we can never really know anyone else's motives or temptations. Nor can we ever depend upon others' limited strengths, though we are tempted sometimes to do so to the point of idolatry. Thus, we are really all alone with God. But if we are His sons, we need not worry for our welfare, though the world may think us out of our minds.

~OCTOBER 13~
HOPE DEFERRED

"Hope deferred makes the heart sick, but a longing fulfilled is a tree of life."
Proverbs 13:12

An inferno, a flame, a spark,
Dying embers, cold ashes, the dark,
A sacrifice, a weaning, a purge,
Minor keys, sad refrain, a dirge.

Without death, life's a useless pursuit.
He said lest a seed die, no fruit,

Heaven's for later, not now,
So I'll keep my hand to the plow.

Dear Father,

Sometimes the deaths I must live through make me want to surrender the fight to smile and breathe. Sadness seems to hunger for me relentlessly and pursue me single-mindedly, to stalk my heart unceasingly as though I am his most fervent desire. In my weak moments I wonder what it would feel like just to give in finally, just to lie back and let Sadness have my soul, just to throw up my hands, throw in the towel, and let him swallow me whole.

And then I remember that you wouldn't allow me to be sifted if there weren't something that needed to be sifted. All the deaths I must undergo are so that life can come to me more abundantly. Oh, Father, I do want to dream your dreams for me. Please teach me what I need to know, show me what I need to see in order to more willingly allow every necessary kernel of wheat to fall to the ground and die. Help me believe in the life that will come from each death.

The difference between walking on the water and sinking in despair is in my own mind, in my own view of Jesus—whether I keep my eyes on Him or take them off. I want to keep my eyes fastened on your Son so that I, too, can truly live as your child, a transformed creation, not just an improved version of the old creature. Almost everyone learns *something* from their failures and mistakes; help me, Lord, to learn the *holy* something, the *life-giving* something, and not settle for lesser lessons. Help me learn to wait for the life that You alone can and will give, rather than rushing ahead after a death to take care of myself. I rest in Jesus' righteousness as I lift this prayer to you. Amen.

~OCTOBER 14~
DEAD FRUIT AND SUCKER SHOOTS

"The staff belonging to the man I choose will sprout, and I will rid myself of this constant grumbling against you by the Israelites...The next day Moses entered the Tent of the Testimony and saw that Aaron's staff which represented the house of Levi, had not only sprouted but had budded, blossomed, and produced almonds." Numbers 17:5, 8

Long years ago God did a strange thing to reveal to His people His choice of high priest. It was a type of contest. God told Moses to write the name of the leader of each ancestral tribe on twelve staffs in front of the Ark of the Covenant in the Tent of Meeting. The sign of God's choice would be that one of these dead sticks would sprout life. This staff which not only sprouted but actually bore fruit foreshadowed Christ as the vine from which we, the branches, gain the holy nutrition to bear fruit also. Matthew 12:33 and 35 say *"Make a tree good and its fruit will be good, or make a tree bad and its fruit will be bad, for a tree is recognized by its fruit...The good man brings good things out of the good stored up in him, and the evil man brings evil things out of the evil stored up in him."* We must produce fruit before we can be recognized as His; bearing fruit is a crucial part of preserving His witness on the earth, both by living as salt and light (preservers and rescuers) and by leading others to Jesus, the source of this light. Most of John 15 is about this fruit that is to grow from the true Vine. It begins with Jesus calling Himself the true vine, us the branches, and God the gardener who appropriately tends the plant according to how each branch is producing. Those which show no production He cuts off, and those which bear fruit, He prunes so as to make them even more fruitful. Anybody who has fruit or flower-bearing trees or bushes understands this concept. We clip away the dead blossoms and sucker shoots in order to prevent sapping energy from the rest of the plant.

God has a perfect image for us. Romans 8:29 tells us what it is: *"to be conformed to the likeness of His Son."* This pruning process is part of what it takes to get us to this point. Like the two things our plants need to be rid of— dead fruit and sucker shoots— we, too, need to be rid of dead works and sucker shoots. 1 Corinthians 3:12-13 helps us better understand these: *"If any man builds on this foundation using gold, silver, costly stones, wood, hay or straw, his work will be shown for what it is because the Day will bring it to light. It will be revealed with fire, and the fire will test the quality of each man's work. If what he has built survives, he will receive his reward. If it is burned up, he will suffer loss; he himself will be saved, but only as one escaping through the flames"* Services for wrong motives might be the wood, stubble or hay—the dead fruit devoid of life—that will not stand up under God's cleansing fire and will therefore result in loss of reward. These are just taking up space where new life could spring forth. They are a spinning of our wheels that is taking us nowhere. The sucker shoots might be our inordinate passions and affections which sap our energy by capturing our minds' full attention. These are not dead, like the old flowers, but they grow wildly and fruitlessly out of control, contributing nothing to God's desired image for us. These obsessions steal our focus from giving the plant the true nourishment it needs. We see these leggy shoots growing more and more out of control, and rather than facing the truth about their fruitlessness and cutting them back, we let our fear of the pain of their removal mar the health and productivity of the entire plant.

~OCTOBER 15~
GOD'S PRUNING SHEARS

"...while every branch that does bear fruit He prunes so that it will be even more fruitful. You are already clean because of the word I have spoken to you." John 15:2-3

"Consider it pure joy, my brothers, whenever you face trials of many kinds, because you know that the testing of your faith develops perseverance. Perseverance must finish its work so that you may be mature and complete, not lacking anything." James 1:2-4

To understand fully what Jesus means in these verses in John, it helps to know that the Greek word for "prunes" also means "cleans." Thus, when Jesus tells his disciples that they are already clean he is saying that He has been pruning them with every word He has spoken to them. God's foremost instrument for pruning us is also the Word He has spoken to us, the Holy Scriptures. This fact is the focus of the longest Psalm and the longest chapter in the Bible. Psalm 119:11 says *"I have hidden your word in my heart that I might not sin against you"*; verses ninety-two and three read *"If your law had not been my delight, I would have perished in my affliction. I will never forget your precepts, for by them you have preserved my life"*; and verse 105 proclaims *"Your word is a lamp to my feet and a light unto my path."*

But God uses another instrument to conform us to His image. James speaks of the circumstances that visit us in the form of trials whose testing can develop our perseverance and bring us to maturity.

I don't know about you, but the former is definitely more appealing to me than the latter.

Look how effective the shears of His Word can be when applied to us: *"For the word of God is living and active. Sharper than any double-edged sword, it penetrates even to dividing soul and spirit, joints and marrow; it judges the thoughts and attitudes of the heart" (Hebrews 4:12).* Do you believe that God really wants us to have to live in painful circumstances constantly? I believe that He had rather use His Word to help us grow into Christ's likeness and out of our own selfish earthly one. We could make our pruning process less painful if we heeded James 1:22-25: *"Do not merely listen to the word, and so deceive yourselves. Do what it says. Anyone who listens to the word but does not do what it says is like a man who looks at his face in a mirror and after looking at himself, goes away and immediately forgets what he looks like. But the man who looks intently into the perfect law that gives freedom and continues to do this, not forgetting what he has heard, but doing it—He will be blessed in what he does."*

Look at the result of all this pruning/cleaning. Look at what we will reap if He is able to cause our crop to flourish: *"I have told you this so that my joy may be in you and that your joy may be complete" (John 15:11).* We have already seen in James that our response to this pruning process does not have to be despair and grief; He says we should consider it "pure joy."

If we take this literally, we should be praying that God will identify for us our dead fruit and sucker shoots and change our focus from ourselves to knowing Him— what His Son should look like in our world— and then being just that.

~OCTOBER 16~
THE VALUE OF A STILLED AND QUIETED SOUL

"My heart is not proud, O Lord, my eyes are not haughty; I do not concern myself with great matters or things too wonderful for me. But I have stilled and quieted

my soul; like a weaned child with its mother, like a weaned child is my soul within me." Psalm 131:1-2

"You show that you are a letter from Christ...written not with ink but with the spirit of the living God, not on tablets of stone but on tablets of human hearts." 2 Corinthians 3:3

For most of my life I wrestled with the temptation to fret, to let anxiety take me by the tail and swing me around at will. I would awaken in the wee hours and imagine that things were much worse and much bigger than they really were. Being a working person with a clock ticking away beside my bed while I was losing valuable sleep increased my anxiety. I imagined 120 freshmen breaking out into frenetic partying the next day as I sprawled passed out and slobbery-mouthed on my desk so that the principal would come due to the noisy chaos, and I would be packed up and ushered out just shy of my retirement. Other times, in the broad daylight, I would fret over a botched schedule or whether someone had misunderstood me and thus misjudged me. I was a Christian who should have been resting confidently in the Lord and His providence, yet often I was a seething cauldron and a tempestuous sea.

Finding Psalm 131 was like discovering gold. I set out to memorize it that very day. Words cannot express the difference it made just to be able to close my eyes and speak Truth to my soul in the onslaught of clamoring lies. Learning these scriptures and seeing their effect brought once again into clear focus the truth of another Psalm: "I have hidden your word in my heart that I might not sin against you" (Psalm 119:11).

Even more inspiring than reading or reciting scripture, however, is watching someone live it consistently. It is as though that person is a parchment upon which God has almost literally etched his Truths for others to read.

I always wondered what kind of magic happened that I could relax and be refreshed when we visited my in-laws a few times each year in Oklahoma. I finally realized that, among other things, it is the restful nature of my father-in-law. No matter what kind of ill news we might all be living with, his smile and laughter never fail. His face radiates a peace that gently shades the glare of any mysteries we know not how to answer. It speaks with its perennial grins and chuckles of total surrender to a Kind Master whom he knows to be at the helm at all times. His ship is never really in trouble. Just looking at his face that says, "All is well" helps me remember that mine isn't either.

He is one of those dear love letters from our Father. The letter reminds us that we no longer need to cry out in feverish fear as an unweaned infant when its mother leaves his sight. We will never be forsaken or left hungry. He will always be our living water and our bread of life. There is no reason to fret. All is well.

~OCTOBER 17~
THE BLESSING OF A MENTOR

"...snatch others from the fire and save them..." Jude 3

There I was in a school brand new to me—and in a foreign country, no less. We were no longer in Texas, Toto, where even if all of our accents were not *exactly* the same, they had overtones of the same familiar flavor, and our idioms and colloquialisms made sense to each other. But here in this American high school in Germany, the teachers came from all over the USA, and they brought their own particular brand of the English language with them. About a week into school, some in the teachers' lounge hearing my East Texas accent shoot from my mouth at warp speed laughed and made a joke about my being an English teacher. I was not really bothered, for even in West Texas, where I attended college, some thought I spoke an unknown tongue. But someone else in the room took *great* offense at this jesting, and she hesitated not a second before jumping into the ring on my behalf. This fellow English teacher gave her peers a tongue-lashing in no uncertain terms and blatantly took them to task for numerous grammatical errors that had obviously been bees in her bonnet for years. This was my first encounter with Ronda, who grew into a wise and caring mentor who affected my life in ways I will probably never be able to count this side of Heaven. I never learned what exactly caused her to rush to take me under her wing so protectively, but there I rested and thrived for the next four years in Germany.

Ronda, an artistic and imaginative divorcee thirty years my senior, became a close family friend who dashed over to help our kids with school projects and supported us in any way she could. When my mother died suddenly, she grieved with me and took meticulous care of my business in Germany while I returned to Texas for two weeks.

She was not perfect. Eccentric in many ways, she expressed her opinions bluntly and without apology. Sometimes when she got on a disagreeable rant, staying around her took patience. At first I wondered if our age difference would be a hindrance to a good friendship, but I learned that the very obstacle I feared was the greatest blessing of our relationship. For Ronda had made many mistakes in her sixty years, and since she had no children to whom she could pass on the wisdom she had gleaned, I fell heir to much of it. This was no mild-mannered lady, and when she wanted you to listen and learn a thing, that was exactly what was going to happen. I can't count the times she took my face in her hands and with her face easily within spitting distance of mine, she "advised" me in her no-nonsense way about the specific dangers of taking this or that path. Her passionate advice on marriage, an area she admitted openly to having botched miserably, was invaluable. She predicted temptations that would assail me at fairly definite ages and exhorted me to respond wisely. She sang my husband's praises and listed definitively all the stupid ways I might go about losing him. Our friendship lasted even after we both left Germany and returned to different states. I am so thankful

I didn't avoid this crazy, unpredictable older woman whom God sent into my life at just the time I needed her.

Whether you are the older or the younger character in this story, may you glean from my experience. Someone younger and more prone to foolishness might be waiting for you; someone old and strange might be about to rescue you.

~OCTOBER 18~
PRAYING FOR PRUNING

"I pray that the eyes of my heart my be enlightened in order that I may know the hope to which you have called me, the riches of His glorious inheritance in the saints, and his incomparably great power for us who believe. This power is like the working of your mighty strength which you exerted when you raised Him from the dead..." Ephesians 1:18-23

"For I was hungry and you gave me something to eat, I was thirsty and you gave me something to drink, I was a stranger and you invited me in, I needed clothes and you clothed me, I was sick and you looked after me, I was in prison and you came to visit me...whatever you did for one of the least of these brothers of mine, you did it for me." Matthew 25:35-36, 40

Dear Father,

I invite you to go with me today down every path you have prepared for me. Fill me, please, with your full measure of Spirit so that I am a clear reflection and arm of you.

I desire to be like Jesus.

So much of me needs cleansing, Father. I am lacking in self-control when it comes to stewardship. Sometimes I want lots of stuff, God! I am so sorry when I fall under the enchantment of things and my shallow heart feels that they will bring comfort to the places that feel empty or neglected. I pray you will open the eyes of my heart at times of temptation and help me control my thinking so I can walk away rather than indulging myself.

I also pray for control over my tongue. I say many things that really weren't so bad until spoken. They seem to harden when they hit the air. I also speak whimsically thoughts that would soon pass, but after they are said, they haunt me because now someone believes they are serious thoughts. It seems I just spoke to break the silence, as if I am the designated speaker when no one else is speaking. Please help me be comfortable with silence.

...Which brings me to another sin: impure motives. I need help, God, controlling my desire to impress certain others. Just because it is the truth doesn't mean it needs to be said. Help me to keep holy secrets and trust you to bring about the love and recognition I need rather than trying to buy junk by counterfeit means.

And Lord, I need you to take these wrong feelings away that bring about anxiety. Please give me a heart of wisdom, not just a mind that can plan what to do but cannot do it with a heart of joy. The eyes of my mind I seem to be able to keep awake and alert, but I need you to open the eyes of my *heart*, Lord, to see what's really important— the Matthew 25 things— and use my energy to do these, rather than spinning my wheels feeling anxious about things over which I have no control.

I guess I am asking you to mature me, Lord— mature my heart— but oh, kind Father, do it gently. Above all, though, Father, gently or not, please continue pursuing me and those I love until we are fully yours.

I love you,
Jan

~OCTOBER 19~
A SHARP FOCUS ON LOVING WELL

"Love is patient, love is kind. It does not envy, it does not boast, it is not proud. It is not rude, it is not self-seeking, it is not easily angered, it keeps no records of wrongs. It does not delight in evil but rejoices with the truth. It always protects, always trusts, always hopes, always perseveres." 1 Corinthians 13:4-7

Many have said that a dog is man's best friend. When you examine this closely, you might find that the traits that motivate this belief are the same ones Paul writes about in his love treatise. The best kind of dog does all these things well in regards to his master. A dog, of course, doesn't struggle with nearly the temptations a complex human struggles with. (It's pretty safe to say that the "battle against spiritual forces in heavenly places" was targeted for humans rather than animals.) But humans who *do* manage a Christlike grip on these elements are definitely the ones we want for our best friends.

When bathed in the blessedness of being loved for years by one who loves so well, as I have been by my friend Sharon Marie, we know a lot more about Jesus than we otherwise would have. We become infected with a good "disease" that travels with us wherever we go; we become *carriers* of this thing, it seems, even though not necessarily stricken with its symptoms. We learn something of heavenly love through years of having it bestowed upon us that inspires us to try to live out its reality for others to bask in and feel Christ's love as we have been blessed to do. Even though we might never be as good at it as the ones who demonstrate it to us, we are better for having witnessed the ideal walking around as the same flesh and blood that we are. It always helps to *see* how it is done rather than just to read or hear about it.

Loving this way is certainly not an easy or natural thing, even to a Christian. In order for it to become the grace it was meant to be, its detractors and distracters must be attended to purposely with a tight rein and unwavering vigilance. The sum of the human problem seems to be that we can't focus on two things at once, as Jesus pointed out, and most of us choose to focus on something else to try to perfect. These other struggles against our would-be worldly natures might we worthwhile, but our great vigilance concerning them might be why we don't have such a sharp focus on the graces of loving well. Loving seems so basic that we might not even think that it requires a close eye or a ready ear; we might believe that if we are doing other things correctly, we will also love correctly.

One of the best things about being the recipient of true Christian love is what it does through the years to our way of viewing ourselves, others, and God. At first I thought I must be pretty special for someone to love me this way. But after years of messing up and being forgiven and not always returning love in the same volume or consistency as it was given, I realized humbly that this flood of love that had washed over me was not to my credit at all. I was simply and inexplicably a blessed recipient of a very close brush with God Almighty. There He was in the form of one who had faith to love His way woven auspiciously into my life. It caused me to give more thanks to Him and also to know I could possibly love others as undeserving as I am in the same way.

~OCTOBER 20~
THE SHEEP AND THE WOLF

"God, my shepherd! I don't need a thing. You have bedded me down in lush meadows, you find me quiet pools to drink from. True to your word, you let me catch my breath and send me in the right direction. Even when the way goes through Death Valley, I'm not afraid when you walk at my side. Your trusty shepherd's crook makes me feel secure. You serve me a six-course dinner right in front of my enemies. You revive my drooping head; my cup brims with blessing. Your beauty and love chase after me every day of my life. I'm back home in the house of my God for the rest of my life." Psalm 23 (The Message)

"Know that the Lord is God. It is He who made us, and we are his; we are the sheep of his pasture." Psalm 100:3

Awhile back when I had borne my heart inside out to God and spoken openly to Him of what sins I feared lurked in it, there came a new sort of freedom. And on the heels of that feeling, I thought, "If I am aware of why God may be letting or making certain painful things happen in my life, then why, rather than trying to "survive" them with grace and God's promised strength, do I not instead actually *help* Him? When looking at my life, don't I often say, "If I were God, I would do the same thing"?

Perhaps the reason I don't is that sometimes I forget what freedom in Christ feels like. Sometimes I get so used to going through these cycles that sin brings about in my life, that I think it is easier to wander around in the same old maze of heartache than it would be to learn a new map and go somewhere different this time. I have no delusions about being anything other than a sheep, but sometimes I act as if I have no shepherd. I plug my ears and put on blinders, it seems, just so that I can have the perverted privilege of falling off another cliff again. There is always the wolf, Satan, chasing me, too, and rather than learning after all this time that he alone is reason enough for me to stay close to the Shepherd, I foolishly believe I can outrun him and still be "on my own" away from the gaze of any caretaker. I think I can have a little harmless adventure outside the fold and then at bedtime I can sneak in and sleep under the Shepherd's watchful eye. What I fail to realize in my weaker moments is that I could possibly run so far from home that I could not find my way back. I know that in the parable, the Shepherd leaves the ninety-nine to go after one lost one, but I know that "losing" my way and "running away" are two different things. Romans 1 makes it clear that when we quit glorifying and being grateful to the God that we know, our thinking can become futile and our hearts darkened so that God finally gives us over to our waywardness. Second Thessalonians 2 says we can run so far away that God even sends us a delusion and allows us to *believe* the lie.

I know this kind of open rebellion is different from just leaning away from God's will, but I also know that the wolf is real and eagerly desires to have me. My stubborn will and my little wanderings make me an easy dance partner for his avid seeking whom he may devour.

Why don't I get on His side in this matter? Why do I not lean my actions in the same direction He is pulling the circumstances of my life? Why must He do all the work if I know why it must happen and that it is indeed necessary to break the growth pattern of my sin?

~OCTOBER 21~
RUNNING BACK HOME

"I am the Lord your God, who brought you out of Egypt, out of the land of slavery. You shall have no other Gods before me. You shall not make for yourself an idol in the form of anything in heaven above or on the earth beneath or in the waters below. You shall not bow down to them or worship them, for I, the Lord your God, am a jealous God..." Exodus 20:2-5

I.

Her world reduced to a marble,
Clutched in death-grip fashion;
Eyes awash with the blues and purples
Of unfamiliar silence;
Heart crammed full to overflowing
With no ocean to welcome the exuberant tide
Except the hearts that have forgotten the thirst
Or those that never knew to begin with...
Her options gone and no one at home
At the front door or the back,

She falls to her knees, surrenders her orb,
And thrusts her trust
Toward Heaven.

II.

Oh, take my world, Father,
And look at it hard.
Remodel it if that is your choosing
To fit a tender heart like mine
And cushion it from constant bruising;
Or maybe the heart needs changing—
Perhaps you should toughen it up.
Whatever it takes, Dear Father of Plenty,
Only You can fill this cup.

~OCTOBER 22~
THE LANGUAGE OF OUR ADVERSARY

"Then Eliakim, Shebna, and Joah said to the field commander, 'Please speak to your servants in Aramaic, since we understand it. Don't speak to us in Hebrew in the hearing of the people on the wall.'" Isaiah 36:11

In the fourteenth year of good King Hezekiah's reign as King of Judah, Sennacherib, the king of Assyria, attacked and captured the fortified cities of Judah. Now their goal was to overtake the great city of Jerusalem. But on their way into Jerusalem, they were met by three Israelites, bent upon defending the city, with whom they tried to humiliate into backing down, knowing that the defenders of the great city would not be so easily taken. What happened next serves as a graphic object lesson for all generations. In the middle of the Assyrian field commander's loud, threatening boasts, the three Jewish officials asked that he not speak in the language of the people, for they feared such talk might damage the morale of the people. The commander, desiring just such a result, continued in Hebrew to undermine King Hezekiah's leadership and frighten the general populace: *"Do not let King Hezekiah deceive you. He cannot deliver you! Do not let Hezekiah persuade you to trust in the Lord when he says, 'The Lord will surely deliver us; this city will not be given into the hand of the king of Assyria.' Do not listen to Hezekiah. This is what the king of Assyria says: Make peace with me and come out to me. Then every one of you will eat from his own vine and fig tree, and drink water from his own cistern, until I come and take you to a land like your own—a land of grain and new wine, a land of bread and vineyards. Do not let Hezekiah mislead you when he says, 'The Lord will deliver us.' Has the god of any nation ever delivered his land from the hand of the king of Assyria?"* (Isaiah 36:13-18). The people knew all too well of Assyria's military might, for their brothers in the northern kingdom of Israel had already fallen to them twenty years earlier. The people responded with silence because King Hezekiah had told them not to answer him.

This is the way it is with Satan when he approaches each of us. He knows very well our language, and he speaks it eloquently. He tells us not to listen to our king, Jesus, but to listen to him. He promises us all the comforts of home if we will give up our fight and go peacefully home with him. He tries to convince us that our King lies when he says He is powerful enough or good enough or wise enough to take care of us and that we would be foolish to allow ourselves to be misled by Him.

Hezekiah prayed. In his prayer he proclaimed God as the only God over all kingdoms, creator of heaven and earth, and he asked for deliverance by His mighty hand. And because of Hezekiah's prayer, God showed up: *"Then the angel of the Lord went out and put to death a hundred and eighty-five thousand men in the Assyrian camp. When the people got up the next morning— there were all the dead bodies! So Sennacherib, king of Assyria broke camp and withdrew. He returned to Nineveh and stayed there. One day, while he was worshipping in the temple of his god Nisroch, his sons Adrammelech and Sharezer cut him down with the sword ..."* (Isaiah 37:36-38). And bam! That's all there was to him, in spite of all his boasting and taunting. And so it will be with our adversary.

"When the thousand years are over, Satan will be released from his prison and will go out to deceive the nations in the four corners of the earth— Gog and Magog— to gather them for battle. In number they are like the sand on the seashore. They marched across the breadth of the earth and surrounded the camp of God's people, the city he loves. But fire came down from heaven and devoured them. And the devil, who deceived them, was thrown into the lake of burning sulfur, where the beast and the false prophet had been thrown. They will be tormented day and night for ever and ever." Revelation 20:7-10

~OCTOBER 23~
IN LOVE WITH WHAT WE LIKE

"Do not love the world or anything in the world. If anyone loves the world, the love of the Father is not in him. For everything in the world—the cravings of sinful man, the lust of his eyes, and the boasting of what he has and does— comes not from the Father but from the world. The world and its desires pass away, but the man who does the will of God lives forever." 1 John 2:15

What gets my pulse racing, gives my stomach butterflies, causes my pupils to dilate? What floats my boat? Which activities fall at the top of my dream list for having fun?

Next set of questions: Are these activities necessarily holy or unholy? When I finish them, how am I any better? Does this "betterment" have any definite spiritual benefits? How often? Is a little bit of this activity enough, or must I have more and more of it? If these activities grew into an addiction, would I or someone else be better off or worse as a result?

Before you jump to any conclusions, let me assure you that I am all for recreation. I believe in stretching and building up physical, mental, emotional, as well as spiritual muscles. I find great revitalization and reawakening in long, rambling hikes into the unknown. I like hikes in the mountains better than trips to the city. I can curl up almost anywhere with a good book or a crossword puzzle and be happy for hours on end. I prefer quiet reading to loud partying, writing poetry to doing math. Several times a week, I get a hankering and set out to the grocery store in search of ingredients to cook some exotic meal. Cooking, to me, is more fun than going to a banquet. I enjoy eating good popcorn at engaging movies, sitting around a table with family and friends playing games until the wee hours of the morning, fishing until it's so dark I can't see my bobber out there. These would be high on my list of favorite things to do. I also like some people better than other people.

The thing to remember is that we were not really put here for the *sole* purpose of recreating ourselves (which, I suppose, is what we mean by the word "recreation"). We were put here to be spent by him. If we allow ourselves to fall so deeply in love with what *we like*, we never get around to the main point of our lives. When we are too busy chasing our individual passions, we might never get to the part where we glorify God. It is thrilling to be swept away, and our archenemy is all too ready to indulge our appetites for what we like until we are used up and nothing is left for our First Love. This scripture is a good reminder of this danger.

"The world and its desires pass away, but the man who does the will of God lives forever." Since we know that all souls are immortal in one way or another, we must take the word "lives" to have special meaning—to *thrive* forever, perhaps. The converse of this would be that those who choose not to do the will of God will die forever. And this is really what scripture teaches. *"And if your eye causes you to sin, pluck it out. It is better for you to enter the kingdom of God with one eye than to have two eyes and be thrown into hell, where 'their worm does not die, and the fire is not quenched'"(Mark 9:47)*. The worm can never achieve death; it is always *dying*. What a dreadful picture. Unless we bridle our desires and give proper honor to our highest calling, this is what our future could hold. We must choose whether we are to have our treasures here or in Heaven.

~OCTOBER 24~
GOING WITHOUT A MAP

"The Lord had said to Abram, 'Leave your country, your people and your father's household and go to the land I will show you." Genesis 12:1

"And Thomas said to Him, 'Lord, we don't know where you are going, so how can we know the way?' Jesus answered, 'I am the way and the truth and the life...'"
John 14:5-6

Where are we going, my Jesus?
I'm trying to follow your steps.
I'm trying to look back and remember those times
You sat with your friends and wept.
If I can remember that picture
And know that you really knew how,
Then I can more easily feel you beside me
Weeping and listening now.

I need to stay close on your heels, Sweet Lord;
I must have been hanging back some,
For I'm still so surprised when I find myself fighting
Old battles I thought I had won.
I must have been looking beyond you
Or somewhere just short of your face.
I really am trying, but the air gets so hazy
In this less-than-heavenly place.

I'll take your hand, Father, and follow
For your love overshadows your wrath.
But where are you leading me, Jesus?
The light is so dim on this path.
I've asked for a peace that's abiding,
But it dwindles as quickly as it came.
I've even questioned your fairness
In the loneliness of my pain.

But you've always been faithful, Father,
So no doubt, you're still fathering now.
And you won't give me less than your vision for me;
I'm just missing your lesson somehow.
So keep leading wherever we're bound, Lord,
With this bond that can never be severed.
I'm foolish and blind with no sense of direction,
But I'm hanging on tighter than ever.

"By faith, Abraham, when called to go to a place he would later receive as his inheritance, obeyed and went, even though he did not know where he was going."
Hebrews 11:8

~OCTOBER 25~
A PICTURE OF COMPASSION

"Then, because so many people were coming and going that they did not even have a chance to eat, He said to them, ' Come with me by yourselves to a quiet place and get some rest.' So they went away by themselves in a boat to a solitary place. But many who saw them leaving recognized them and ran on foot from all the towns and got there ahead of them. When Jesus landed and saw a large crowd, He had compassion on them because they were like sheep without a shepherd. So He began teaching them many things." Mark 6:30-34

Teaching a multitude that day was not Jesus' original plan; what He had planned was a retreat with his apostles. Therefore, the first lesson I learn from this little story is that sometimes my well-laid plans are going to be waylaid in favor of something better God has in mind. And the plans that get changed could even be *good* plans, even plans with a holy motive, as Jesus' were that day. If I allow myself to persist in being such a goal-oriented person that I will not heed His Spirit when He wants to detour me, I might miss an opportunity God is giving me to be used in His behalf. If I love and serve my plans over His, who, *really*, is my God?

The second lesson might not be so obvious, but it is important. We can dig it from these verses by asking ourselves what picture comes to mind when we think of the word "compassion." I'll admit that for me these pictures included healing the sick, crying with the bereaved, visiting the imprisoned, clothing and feeding the needy— all those Matthew 25 things that in the end will be great consider-ations when separating the sheep from the goats. But this passage teaches us that these pictures are not the only ones that represent compassion. When Jesus was moved by compassion for these people who took out across the countryside to find Him, he began *teaching* them.

Probably the commonplace measurement of compassion is how desirous we are to help solve, or at least share, others' crises immediately. But Jesus shows us here that a different kind of crisis is at hand all around us that many who would consider themselves to be the compassionate sort overlook. Jesus perceived these people to be "like sheep without a shepherd," and lost sheep such as these are going to need more than just a little teaching. They are going to need the Bread of Life broken unto them specifically, pointedly, thoroughly, and consistently until the old man in them gives itself over to the new creation. They are going to need to hear the stories so they can know what a mighty God they are coming to follow— why He can be trusted and all that might come of their lives should they choose to surrender to His Lordship.

Jesus performed many acts that fit the traditional picture of compassion. He healed the sick and befriended the friendless; He even raised the dead. But there were times when He grew weary with those who wanted a sign or wanted a bread Messiah because He knew there was another kind of Messiah He was sent to be with another kind of compassion He was sent to show. Jesus came not just to fix our problems but to fix our Problem.

Sometimes those of us who teach berate ourselves for being people more of the "head" than the "heart." We might see our gift as something stiffer, more rigid, less tender than that of others "more compassionate," but now we know we are wrong to see ourselves this way. Jesus sees teaching as *compassionate,* and He had Mark to write about it so we would know this in no uncertain terms.

~OCTOBER 26~
INVITING JESUS INSIDE

"So the Pharisees and teachers of the law asked Jesus, 'Why don't you and your disciples live according to the tradition of the elders instead of eating their food with 'unclean' hands?' He replied, 'Isaiah was right when he prophesied about you hypocrites; as it is written: 'These people honor me with their lips, but their hearts are far from me. They worship me in vain; their teachings are but rules taught by men.' You have let go of the commands of God and are holding on to the traditions of men.'" Mark 7:6-8

Here we see another of those times when Jesus is approached by some fervently desiring to catch Him in some duplicity— some sort of illegality— so that they can expose Him as the fraudulent Messiah they wanted Him to be. This time it is about hand washing before eating a meal. Their accusation of Jesus and His disciples is their way of equating what they see as being outwardly filthy to being inwardly filthy.

The first thing Jesus does to refute them might be vague to us, but to them— had they had ears to hear and hearts open to understanding—it should have been a crystal-clear testimony of His uprightness: He quotes scripture *"as it is written."* Since the Pharisees and the teachers of the law were experts at the scripture, such a rehearsal of Isaiah should have been somewhat daunting to their agenda. But because they have dedicated their lives' focus to looking clean and together on the outside and negating what no one can see on the inside, they seem to miss that Jesus, among other things, is trying to point them back to the origin of their fame: a thorough knowledge of the Word of God. According to Jesus, "they have let go of the commands of God," as a result of their cleaving to the traditions of man. This is the way it happens. We might be brought to the dance with one person, but after we get in the door, we find other dance partners more to our liking, so we don't leave with the one "who brung us." These guys likely once had a pure desire to know God and therefore studied the scriptures diligently, but the fame they got for their knowledge swept them off their feet. They became so enamored of the peripherals, that they cast aside the Core to major in the minors. Jesus is calling them back to their Core, their First Love, but what they hear is the voice of a counterfeit religious fanatic who has the rude and socially unacceptable nerve to mess with their *insides.*

Do we feel this way sometimes? Do we concede to Jesus that no, we *don't* have all the answers, and yes, we *do* need to be spiritual, but to ask us to set aside our plans, to sacrifice our own agenda, *to lay down our lives* is going a little too far. After all, Jesus, don't you want me to be *happy?*

In the midst of this conversation, Jesus calls the whole crowd over and says, *"Listen to me, everyone, and understand this. Nothing outside a man can make him 'unclean' by going into him. Rather, it is what comes out of a man that makes him 'unclean'" (Mark 7:14-15).* A better English rendering might be "what comes out of a man *indicates* that he is unclean." Jesus gets more specific in verses 21-23 by enumerating some of the underlying roots of our external unclean acts. *"For from within, out of men's hearts, come evil thoughts, sexual immorality, theft, murder, adultery, greed, malice, deceit, lewdness, envy, slander, arrogance and folly. All these evils come from inside and make a man 'unclean.'"*

Jesus is saying to them and to us: "Don't just wear me on your lapel. Let me *inside,* where the sin is, so I can deal with it." I know of no clearer call in the Bible than this one for us to invite Jesus into our hearts. We need to reissue the invitation daily.

~OCTOBER 27~
HER MAGNUM OPUS

"And He said to them, 'You have a fine way of setting aside the commands of God in order to observe your own traditions. For Moses said, 'Honor your father and your mother,' and 'Anyone who curses his father or mother must be put to death.' But you say that if a man says to his father or mother: 'Whatever help you might otherwise have received from me is Corban' (that is, a gift devoted to God), then you no longer let him do anything for his father or mother. Thus, you nullify the word of God by your own tradition that you have handed down." Mark 7:9-13

In the middle of Jesus' answer to the Pharisees concerning hand washing versus heart washing, Jesus gives them another example of how they have traded off God's commands in order to enshrine their own. This one should have pricked the nerves of many, for it concerned the violation of one of the most basic of all foundational truths of Judaism, the fifth commandment.

Last week reading the prayer requests in our church library, I was reminded of this conversation between Jesus and these guys. An artist living in another state recently put her life's work on hold to return to Texas to care for her aging parents. This woman is sacrificing some of her prime years of productivity in order to take on an entirely different type of work. She has laid aside her brushes and easel and pulled a drape over her creative visions in order to take up the towel and the basin and use her skilled hands for bathing and feeding her mother and father. No one will parade by to offer big dollars or accolades for her work. Instead of gazing at some springtime blossom or autumnal scene of glory and transferring the vision onto a canvas to earn her fame and prestige, she sits at a bedside and gazes into the eyes of loved ones soon to be leaving this life. She carefully recreates for them scenes from the past—the album of her life's memories. In bold, vivid strokes she paints the laughter-filled days and adds pastel hues recalling intimate moments of grace and gratitude. She frames these renderings in silver tears and smiles gilded with tenderness and appreciation.

Her parents hold them to their hearts and feel an unexpected gladness at this crossroads met by many with trembling and dread. The memories these master-pieces conjure will remind them that their lives were wisely invested and will not be forgotten.

And standing closely behind her looking on is Jesus. He smiles upon the scene, nods His head in parental pride, places a hand on the artist's shoulder, leans down and whispers in her ear, "This, my Precious Daughter, is your greatest work."

"…whoever wants to become great among you must be your servant, and whoever wants to be first must be your slave— just as the Son of Man did not come to be served, but to serve, and to give his life as a ransom for many." Matthew 20:26-28

"Greater love has no one than this, that he lay down his life for his friends." John 15:13

~OCTOBER 28~
ENABLING OUR DELUSIONS

"Be perfect, therefore, as your heavenly Father is perfect." Matthew 5:47-48

"We proclaim Him, admonishing and teaching everyone with all wisdom, so that we may present everyone perfect in Christ. To this end, I labor, struggling with all His energy which so powerfully works within me." Colossians 1:28-29

Lately I've been coming on like gangbusters with crossword puzzles. These books are stationed all over my house and in my car so that whenever I have a few idle minutes that can't be used to do much else of productivity, I can snatch one up and exercise my brain. I've always heard this is a good way to keep the brain active and to stave off memory loss. Besides that, I have always loved words, long before I even knew what dementia was nor imagined a time when I might (Heaven forbid!) grow old. There's something very satisfying about sitting with a pencil and filling in a crossword puzzle successfully so that all the "across" words intersect sensibly with all the "down" words. I get a kick out of knowing another language— Crosswordese— that is spoken by only an elite few. There is something pleasantly secure about not having to wonder what they want when they ask for "Yeat's before"— it's always going to be "ere." I get a little buzz from being savvy about "hoopla" being "ado," "rushing about wildly" being "amok,"

319

and "furniture covering" being "antimacassar." But then yesterday a funny thing happened that put all my ill-placed security into proper perspective.

Digging around in my bookshelves, I discovered *another* puzzle book I had apparently bought a few years ago (so much for improved memory), so I eagerly set out to conquer one of these before I sat down to write. Hmmm... don't know that one. *That's* one I've never heard before. Hey, this thing expects me to know *French!* This is the way it went for the next fifteen miserable minutes. Humiliation. Self-doubt. Insecurity. I penciled in only a minute percentage of this puzzle, but I did come out of this debacle with a parable about Christian living.

Merely continuing to do what we have learned to do and being what we have learned to be might bring us a sense of accomplishment, but it will not serve us well if what we are after is growth. This kind of peace is just a pacifier that inhibits our maturity. We know this in many respects, and by this belief we raise our children without even thinking about it. We are thrilled when they get potty trained, and learn to tie their shoes, but if they expect us to continue for years to praise and reward them for these accomplishments alone, we quickly let them know how ridiculous this notion is.

Are we stretching spiritually so that we remain challenged and our muscles ache under the added stress, or are we resting on past laurels and calling it a day? Are we using an easy standard—comparing ourselves with ourselves? We must disable our delusions. The words of Jesus prod us upward to *perfection*. Maybe we won't accomplish it in this lifetime, but we cannot honor His counsel without continuing moving upward to more difficult puzzles.

"And we, who with unveiled faces all reflect the Lord's glory, are being transformed into his likeness with ever-increasing glory, which comes from the Lord, who is the Spirit." 2 Corinthians 3:18

~OCTOBER 29~
ASKING THE RIGHT QUESTIONS

"No one sews a patch of unshrunk cloth on an old garment, for the patch will pull away from the garment, making the tear worse. Neither do men pour new wine into old wineskins. If they do, the skins will burst, the wine will run out and the wineskins will be ruined. No, they pour new wine into new wineskins, and both are preserved." Matthew 9:16-17

I did only what I thought she had asked me to do. She said, "Will you help me proofread these sentences for errors?" I set out with finely-tuned eye toward the task. This comma needs to be deleted; this word needs capitalizing; a semicolon would work better here. When she turned to the answer section and began calling out the correct answers, the chagrin that befell me coursed through me like shrapnel. Much to my surprise, several of my carefully scrutinized answers were wrong, not because I didn't cross all my t's and dot all my i's, but because I had put the right punctuation on the wrong sentences. It was only when we looked at the answers that we realized that this exercise was concerned with something more basic than mechanics and the finishing touches. Rather than looking just at how the sentences were *punctuated*, I needed to be looking at whether what they actually *said* made any sense!

Jesus dealt a lot with people like this when He walked this sod. He was surrounded by obsessive T-crossers and I-dotters who plagued His ministry with their finely-tuned eye for mechanics. In this particular context, it was the disciples of John the Baptist, rather than the Pharisees, who came sincerely seeking an answer to a seeming duplicity between Jesus and His trailblazing Elijah who came before Him. Is fasting right or is it wrong? Other less sincere questions of less pure motives concerned picking grain on the Sabbath, washing hands before eating, and which of the commandments was the most important to keep. Jesus' answer about the old patch and the old wineskins went to the heart of their blindness: Since I have come to fulfill (fill full) the Law, now we can focus on the root rather than the foliage, the heart rather than the limbs. "You have heard it said...but I say unto to you..." Let us from now on examine our hearts and allow Truth to diagnose their condition.

Crossing all our t's and dotting all our i's is not necessarily evil, just as being a Pharisee was not in itself evil. We just need to remember in our mad frenzy to perfect the peripheral not to overlook the most important questions. May we look neither to the left nor the right but straight ahead into the perfect law of liberty to find what ails our souls and what brings them their truest delight.

~OCTOBER 30~
WHAT WE MUST ADD TO KNOWLEDGE

"His divine power has given us everything we need for life and godliness through our knowledge of Him who called us by His own glory and goodness. Through these He has given us His very great and precious promises, so that through them you may participate in the divine nature and escape the corruption in the world caused by evil desires. For this very reason, make every effort to add to your faith goodness; and to goodness, knowledge; and to knowledge, self-control; and to self-control, perseverance; and to perseverance, godliness; and to godliness, brotherly kindness; and to brotherly kindness, love. For if you possess these qualities in increasing measure, they will keep you from being ineffective and unproductive in your knowledge of our Lord Jesus Christ." 2 Peter 1:3-9

Do you ever think as you are poring over God's Word and taking it all in like a sponge that it could all add up to no more than brain-stuffing? Peter warns us that even though knowledge is one of the things we are to add to our faith— in fact, it is the first thing he mentions we are to add— that if we do not add some other crucial elements that allow us to participate in the divine nature, our knowledge of Jesus will be "ineffective and unproductive."

321

Jesus came down harder on the Pharisees than on any other group, and the Pharisees were the keepers, yea the guardians of the law that Jesus came to fulfill. Oh, they had knowledge all right; they knew every jot and tittle of the law. And Jesus did say that neither one jot nor tittle would pass away until all of it was accomplished, so obviously their knowledge of and desire to keep the law was not the thing Jesus criticized in them. The tragedy of the Pharisees was that they insisted upon keeping their old, tough, saturated wineskins instead of shedding them for the new wineskins that could properly contain the blessed new wine of Christ—the root, the purpose, the motivation, the *fulfillment* of this law. They lacked brotherly kindness and love.

The word "fulfillment" defines itself: it means "to fill full." Jesus came to give meaning to the law, to water us with His new wine so that we could bloom from the inside out, to give us some motivation besides strict obedience. This is why Peter's list ends with brotherly kindness and love. If he had stopped at godliness, we might be tempted to counterfeit it by intellectual law-keeping. He knew that the most powerful of all motivations is love. Love does whatever it takes. It keeps on when duty tuckers out. Love never fails.

Let us pray that all the knowledge of Christ that we take into our heads seeps down into our hearts so that we will be productive and effective for our Lord this day.

~OCTOBER 31~
SO SILLY IT'S SCARY

"So teach us to number our days that we may gain a heart of wisdom." Psalm 90:12

Dear Father,

Sometimes I think I get a glimpse of just how silly I really am. If I get a glimpse of my silliness in my worldly and foolish state, can I even imagine how extremely silly I am to You in Your true holiness and purity and wisdom?

So much clamors for my attention. How can I become so enamored of *things*? How can a new house— made of bricks and mortar— or a sleek and gleaming new car— a conglomeration of metal attached with screws— send me into a daydream? I look through a catalogue and imagine (for a moment) that it is in some way *important* for me to be dressed in this style or that color. I close my eyes to rest, and the pictures still parade through my mind. Clamor, clamor, clamor. "Look at me!" "Touch me!" "Try me on!" But Father, I know that these tangible trinkets are no worse than the intangible ones which charm me and tug at my heart.

I think of Ecclesiastes. King Solomon says over and over about everything under the sun: "All is vanity. Vanity, vanity, vanity." Vanity means "emptiness." It's ironic that the things that define vanity are the things and attitudes that tempt us to believe they will fill us up. The devil wants us to strive for them and feel the need for them so he can use up our mental and physical energy, waste our money and time getting them, and then stick his fingers in his ears and curl his lip and laugh at us: "Nanny nanny boo boo! HA! You're still unsatisfied! You've wasted all you could have been and all you could have used for God, and you're no further down the road than you were! People are still miserable that you could have helped. Hearts are still lonely that you could have cheered. Souls are still plummeting toward destruction that you could have noticed and rescued—and as a bonus for my added viewing pleasure, you are not any happier or more fulfilled than you were before you began this wild pleasure pursuit."

We have so much and yet need so little. When I think of what is really important, the list is so short. "To act justly, love mercy, and walk humbly with your God" (Micah 6:8). To please You requires so few material resources, and yet I have realized more and more how very much mental focus and energy it takes to get my eyes off the passions of this world and onto the higher, eternal one. How much do I allow myself to be robbed from Your use? How much am I allowing myself to be used up for trivial, vain, temporary pursuits?

I am so silly.

Father, I want to grow up and see with new eyes and gain a heart of wisdom. I want to bend my ear more closely to hear your Spirit's voice alerting me to the opportunities to make a few differences to a few people. I want to be more wary of this material warrior who parades all around me luring my heart away from its True North.

Please show me how to be true to You— how to be responsible and disciplined. I have written this so that I won't forget. I will need to remember this strong vision and conviction of my silliness. I want to hold on to truth with a strong grip and never let my eyes wander away when the pretties prance and clamor all around at the behest of the Enemy who desires to hypnotize me.

My hope in this prayer is through Jesus. Amen.

~NOVEMBER 1~
THE LAMP OF THE BODY

"The eye is the lamp of the body. If your eyes are good, your whole body will be full of light. But if your eyes are bad, your whole body will be full of darkness. If then the light within you is darkness, how great is that darkness." Matthew 6:22-23

What Jesus seems to be saying here is that an awful lot depends upon how we look at things. He says that our view of something will make great and far-reaching determinations, whether it be for good or for ill.

My niece, Tammy, is a good example. This child (aged 42, but still a child to me, since she's my niece) has had plenty of reason to see things more tragically than she has seen them. She has had what people disinclined to believe in God's sovereignty might call "more than her share" of struggles. Her parents divorced when she was eight, and as young as ten, weight problems forced her to begin dieting. After she overcame the weight problem and learned to live with the divorce, a lupus-induced life-threatening shutdown of her kidneys at eighteen forced her to drop out of college. She persevered bravely, fell in love, married, and had a beautiful set of twins granted to her only by the grace of God, according to the doctor who had feared her lupus would greatly jeopardize her and/or her babies' health. Then, when the children were still very young, her husband divorced her, left the family, and had very little contact with them as they navigated the dangerous waters of their teen years and entered into adulthood. Through all these obstacles, she went through the natural emotions of anger, fear, and sadness, but she never succumbed to the pernicious demon of self-pity. As a result, she could keep her focus off herself and on what her kids would need in order to stay out of trouble and grow into responsible and respectable adults. Rather than sinking into despair over what might have felt unfair, Tammy reached down to find all the gifts God had given her and used each one of them with amazing energy and confidence. She used her brilliant mind to secure excellent employment; she used her sharp sense of humor to bring laughter, rather than bitterness and despondency, to her family. Rather than using her disease as an excuse for isolation, she used her energy to reach out and make new and maintain old friendships. She absolutely refused to see herself as a pitiful person, and that kind of vision brought light into every corner of her and her children's lives. As a result, she won the love of a kind man who married her, and her children both made it to adulthood honorably, respectably, and responsibly. How easily she could have gambled all she had on the chance that self-pity might have bought her the sympathy of others who might have paved an easy road for her to travel. I'm so glad she resisted. So are her children, who learned first-hand the way to make it when the going gets rough.

Jesus didn't address these words specifically to self-pity; He wanted us to choose to have a spiritual—an eternal—perspective on everything that happens in our lives. He was saying that we have a *choice* about the way we process things. We can shed light on dark corners or throw a pall of darkness over the rays of light. Blessed are those who have someone wearing flesh closeby to demonstrate how it is done. Jesus showed us with His life how to be that blessing.

~NOVEMBER 2~
ON MOUNT MORIAH

"Then God said, 'Take your son, your only son, Isaac, whom you love, and go to the region of Moriah. Sacrifice him there as a burnt offering on one of the mountains I will tell you about." Genesis 22:2

Can't you just hear Abraham? "Oh, surely not, Father! Surely not Isaac, the child of promise, given to us miraculously in our old age by your very hand. Surely not, Lord! How can this be Your desire?" And yet, since this was the same man who obeyed when God told him a lifetime ago to pull up stakes and set out for a vague, distant land, we know he knew that even such an extremely bleak occasion was still not the time to start doubting the God he knew to be the only true, living God. His other son, Ishmael, had already been sent away at Sarah's request and God's approval, so truly, when the scripture calls Isaac his "only" son, this is more than just a modifier foretelling the scenario years hence when God would hold a knife above His own only begotten Son who also would be laid on another kind of altar of wood.

But unlike that moment in history when God let the knife be plunged into His perfect Lamb, he came to the rescue of Isaac and Abraham by providing a ram in a nearby thicket. Nothing less than the lifeblood of Jesus would suffice to take away the sins of the world, but in Abraham's case, willing obedience was enough. The fact that Abraham resolutely climbed Mount Moriah with the knife and the sacrifice in hand allowed our already omniscient God to "know" (yes, the scripture uses that word about God) that nothing could come *before* Him in Abraham's heart and therefore, nothing could come *between* them. For, whether Abraham knew it or not, God knew that if Abraham had not been willing to do this thing, Isaac would have been his idol. For a patriarch in the Family of God, idolatry had no place, and not only God, but also the Father of the Hebrew nation needed to know that for certain.

And for us, the children of such a glorious inheritance, the priesthood of saints called to participation in the divine nature, idolatry certainly has no place, and we, too, need to be assured that we are purged from all such godless obsessions. I hope this doesn't sound overly presumptuous, but I believe that because of the nature of mankind, there is a point in everyone's life where Something must die. We will have to stick a knife into it. Abraham did not literally have to stab Isaac's body and shed literal blood, but in a very real sense, he did stab in the heart any ungodly claim his love for Isaac might hold over his love and loyalty to God. He needed to express by his obedience that "his" son was not truly his. I need to express likewise, by obedience and not just words, that "my" family is not truly mine; "my" money is not really mine; "my" time is not really mine. Nothing of "mine" is more mine than it is God's. If I am unable to relinquish something or someone out of my keeping into God's, I am an idolator. I might as well throw my children into the fires of Molech or erect an Asherah pole in my front yard. Anything or anyone that we allow to countermand our loyalty to God is an idol. We must kill it, or it will kill us. Some of us are dying and don't even know it because we will not look inside to see the evidence of our life ebbing away. If we are still breathing, however, it is not too late.

~NOVEMBER 3~
THE PRICE OF DECEPTION

"Jacob said to his father, 'I am Esau your firstborn. I have done as you told me. Please sit up and eat some of my game so that you may give me your blessing.'"
Genesis 27:19

"In great fear and distress, Jacob divided the people who were with him into two groups, and the flocks and herds and camels as well. He thought, 'If Esau comes and attacks one group, the group that is left may escape.'" Genesis 32:7

"Then they got Joseph's robe, slaughtered a goat and dipped the robe in blood. They took the ornamented robe back to their father and said, 'We found this. Examine it to see whether it is your son's robe.'" Genesis 37:31

"Joseph said, 'I am Joseph! Is my father still living?' But his brothers were not able to answer him, because they were terrified at his presence." Genesis 45:3

What goes around comes around.

For any of us who have scratched our heads that a man as deceptive as Jacob could find such favor with the Lord, let us consider the rest of the story. True, Jacob, led by his mother, participated in some grossly manipulative shenanigans to deceive his poor old, blind dad into giving him his brother's blessing. We wonder how God could just overlook such and continue to take Jacob faithfully down his patriarchal path complete with angels on a ladder and supernatural success in livestock breeding. But we should not overlook the fact that just because God doesn't always choose to speak in words or to speak immediately does not mean that He is not speaking at all. Years later, when we least expect it, we see that Jacob indeed suffers when he becomes the brunt of his same brand of deception from his sons who snatch from his life the most precious of all his children, Joseph, the long-awaited son of his beloved Rachel.

But actually, Jacob's suffering starts long before this. He is about to meet up with the brother whom he has cheated in his dark dealings at his father's bedside. What's happening inside Jacob is no small gust; it's a tornado of cataclysmic proportions. Genesis 32:7 records it as "great fear and distress." He is paranoid about his come-uppances. He has danced, but now he is terrified about the price he must pay the piper.

Deception seems to have been a tragic heirloom passed from one generation to the next in Jacob's family. As Jacob's older sons, prompted by bitter jealousy, so mechanistically deceive their father, they sow the same wind which, just as their father has, they will later reap in the form of a whirlwind. Genesis 45 shows these great oaks of clever manipulation bowed low under the pressure of justice when they appear beneath the powerful and authoritative gaze of their wronged little brother in Egypt. So paranoid are they at his surprise identity that they cannot even talk; they are "terrified."

As a child I was warned not to "practice" deception. I learned in some hard ways that this wording was perfect: what we *practice* we become good at. For a while, deception seems to pay off: we get a lot for very little or nothing; we can artificially inflate others' opinions of us; we become naturals at navigating smoothly through life's obstacles. But on the other side of the coin lies the price for all this luxury: a deadly enslavement to fear and the possibility of raising children who do it just as well as we do.

~NOVEMBER 4~
ALL THE TREASURES OF WISDOM AND KNOWLEDGE

"My purpose is that they may be encouraged in heart and united in love, so that they may have the full riches of complete understanding in order that they may know the mystery of God, namely Christ, in whom are hidden all the treasures of wisdom and knowledge." Colossians 2:2-3

Paul, like John, fought the error of Gnosticism, a deadly teaching refuting all worth of anything physical since it offered competition to what was of true worth, the spirit. The danger lay in the harsh treatment of the body as a result of this asceticism: since anything material was considered evil, and the body is matter, whatever was done with it and to it was of no moral consequence. Therefore, licentiousness abounded. Salvation, to the Gnostic, lay in special "knowledge." They also denied Christ's humanity. Paul argues here that Christ's very purpose was to walk the same sod as we in the same kind of body as ours, so that by knowing Him we could better understand the heart of God.

All of us have questions we would like to ask God; maybe you have listed them for future reference—mysteries that we just cannot for the life of us fathom about this God of ours. I decided a long time ago that this was a *good* thing: if God is Someone a lightweight mind like mine can figure out, He would not be big enough to take care of everything *I* need Him to take care of, much less the whole universe! But here Paul makes a good point concerning the mystery of God. Though He is unfathomable, He sent us Christ, who walked and talked and ate and fished, laughed and preached and cried and prayed. He says that in Christ are hidden "all the treasures of wisdom and knowledge." He stresses knowledge here to refute this dangerous Gnostic idea that knowledge was spiritual enough in itself to save us. Paul says that these treasures are *hidden in Christ*. In other words, taking Christ at face value—believing He was God and yet man—is the way to all knowledge. We find there wisdom and knowledge in varying degrees, totally dependent upon how much energy we spend *mining* Him for them. He is the spiritual Goldmine, but like all treasures hiding in mines, we must go inside and dig for it. Jesus explained this when asked by His disciples why He spoke in parables. His answer reflected what Isaiah had said years earlier: even though all had ears and eyes, some would still not choose to hear and see. Many walked past Christ on the roads in Galilee and Judea and never took a second look; others strained just to touch the hem of His garment.

Which do we more resemble? Do we hear His name spoken and leaf through the scriptures about Him casually hoping to "catch" Him like a case of the measles, or do we excavate His treasures because we know that there is nothing anywhere to compare?

And look at what Paul says will help most in finding these mysteries that are hidden in Christ: encouraged hearts and a unity of love (verse 2). When we commit ourselves to loving and encouraging other Christians rather than isolating ourselves for the sake of safety or simplicity, we will more likely gain these riches of complete understanding found in Christ. For dwelling within the flesh and blood of His believers lie *"the glorious riches of this mystery, which is Christ in you, the hope of glory" (Colossians 1:27).*

~NOVEMBER 5~
JOSEPH'S FRUIT OF MANY COLORS

"His brothers then came and threw themselves down before him. 'We are your slaves,' they said. But Joseph said to them, 'Don't be afraid. Am I in the place of God? You intended to harm me, but God intended it for good to accomplish what is now being done, the saving of many lives. So then, don't be afraid. I will provide for you and your children. And he reassured them and spoke kindly to them."
Genesis 50:18-19

For a boy who started out with so little judgment about getting along with and endearing himself to others, Joseph grew into an amazingly Christlike figure.

In fact, some commentators believe that he is the most Christlike character in all of the Old Testament. He more than paid for the foolishness of his youth the first few hours in that cistern his brothers threw him into, but added to that he was then sold into Egyptian slavery, falsely accused of rape by his master's vanity-slathered wife, thrown into jail, and forgotten by a friend whom he helped set free.

Years later, after his life was on the upswing, Joseph had the perfect opportunity to make life miserable for these brothers who initiated him into all this misery when they came begging for food during a famine. In fact, he had the perfect opportunity to take their lives. They were fish in a barrel. But instead, he chose to forgive them because he understood that taking vengeance was a job too big for the likes of him, even though he was by this time an Egyptian ruler.

Joseph was the fourth generation from Abraham, the father of the Hebrew nation. A rudimentary study of the patriarchs Abraham, Isaac, and Jacob quickly reveals that they were far from perfect followers of Jehovah God. Cowardice, dishonesty, favoritism, and deception littered the lives of these men God used to bless every nation. Joseph's life, however, seems to have veered away from the generational stream of sinful tendencies. He contained all the strengths of his forefathers without their weaknesses. He was fruitful, faithful, and forgiving, having conquered immorality, materialism, and bitterness.

Of all the lessons we can learn from Joseph's life, surely his last words before the close of the Book of Beginnings contain one of the most crucial, if not the most crucial one. "Am I in the place of God?" It's no stretch to figure that the power he had attained in Egypt could have easily corrupted him into believing that yes, maybe he was in that very place. After all, he had almost absolute power due to his amazing prophetic feats and agricultural farsightedness. Obviously, though, Joseph never forgot where all those abilities came from, and to whom belonged the glory; he knew the answer to that question was "Never!" He knew he was but a vessel good for nothing but to be ground into dust, without the filling of God.

When it comes to forgiving, what a perfect question Joseph gave us to ask: "Am I in the place of God?" Can I see what motivates another to do what he does or to leave undone what she does? Do I have certain knowledge of anyone else's heart, motives, abilities, or weaknesses? Do I even have absolute recall that I myself have never done the same thing to someone else? Am I sure that something else I have done or might do is not just as bad or even worse from God's perspective? Do I really have all the information needed to withhold forgiveness from someone? "Am I in the place of God?"

~NOVEMBER 6~
REAL THRILLS

"You will be made rich in every way so that you can be generous on every occasion, and through us your generosity will result in thanksgiving to God." 2 Corinthians 9:11

Jesus explains in his Sermon of the Mount that our hearts' true location is revealed by the location of our treasures. Our physical investments indicate our heart's bounties.

Most would agree that one of our treasures is our money. Since most of us have to work hard to earn it, we discriminate about how we spend it. If we are wise we consider how to make the best investments of it so that it will give a good return.

Here Paul explains to the Corinthians the best motivation for prosperity: not to be able to live a lavish lifestyle but to be able to be generous in order to glorify God.

Having been raised with a practical rather than a faith-based philosophy of economics, I suffered quite a culture shock when I got married to this man of mine.

Larry's purposefulness in giving to God from the top, not the leftovers, was a leap I found somewhat daunting. With him, there was never a question about whether we would give regularly to God regardless of the up's and down's of our financial situation. Most would agree that *I* was the more adventuresome, fearless, even reckless one in this union, but when it came to this giving thing, I had to have some serious hand-holding and coaxing by my husband, who, though unwilling to skydive from an airplane with me, easily leapt into this freefall with an unbelievable peaceful demeanor. Learning this grace at his feet through the years of our marriage has been a great adventure because just when I think I catch up with him, he takes off on some new unmarked trail.

Larry learned from an early age the thrill of giving God the chance to show us His bountiful provision. While my kind of adventure was living on the edge of physical danger, his was finding people to rescue. Normally a quiet and serene man, Larry grows noticeably animated— dilated pupils and all— when he finds a way to surprise folks so that they get to have what they didn't think they could, or to go when they thought they'd have to stay home, or to eat a steak instead of cereal. Dizzying fun to him is finding a couple of strangers in a restaurant for whom he can secretly buy a meal. I can't count the times I have learned months or even years later about someone to whom he "lent" money with the only provision being that they give it to someone else when they were in a better financial position. It is his way of making a wise investment.

Sometimes when money grows scarce, he has to restrain himself a bit. But money is not his only treasure. Even after I had finally learned how to be a faith-giver of money, I was still tempted to horde another treasure: my time. But not my Larry. Somehow he has more hours than most of us, for he never seems to be tempted to think he will run out if he gives some unexpected visitor or caller a chunk of his time.

It is an inspiring thing to watch a person of faith investing his treasures. It causes us to wonder if maybe we've been settling for the merry-go-round when we could have been riding the roller coaster.

~NOVEMBER 7~
VICARIOUS JOY

"Each of you should look not only to your own interests, but also to the interests of others." Philippians 2:3

Since I grew up with only one sibling, there was enough attention to go around, and I was given my fair share of what I needed from my parents. Therefore, getting to do many things I wanted to do got somewhat embedded in me, and, thereby, I inherited a little bit of spoilage. But I have noticed that those who grow up in large families tend to know more about having to wait in the wings and sit on the back burner.

My mother, one of nine children, always disliked the water, having never learned to swim. Yet because her two daughters loved swimming better than eating and breathing, she faithfully took us each summer day for years when we were young, and when I grew up and had kids, she loaded us up and took us crabbing. She'd sit by the pool or on the shore and watch us with every bit as much delight as we were experiencing being smack-dab in the middle of the action. Then she would prepare the crabs, sit us down at a newspaper-covered table, and crack crabs, taking turns handing each of us the good meat inside. With a big smile on her face, she would crack crabs until her fingers were shriveled, and never eat one bite. One of her greatest thrills was cooking huge, tantalizingly delicious meals, though she rarely ate more than eight or ten bites. She'd push her plate aside and fix her gaze upon the rest of us as though just watching us enjoy ourselves was all the nourishment she needed. Somewhere along the way, she had learned to have fun vicariously. It never dawned upon me then, but I'll bet it had a lot to do with her growing up in a family where everyone had to wait his or her turn and where fun had to be seen in something more (or less?) than a self-centered way.

I confess that I am a connoisseur of fun. I am a thrill seeker from way back. I have learned well what titillates my senses and makes my eyes dilate, and I gravitate toward people who will join in with me in those activities. I even raised my children (and am presently hard at work on my grandkids!) to enjoy the same kind of fun that I did. But today on my deceased mother's birthday, I feel some scales falling from my eyes as I remember her and how she was different from me in this way. He who searches our hearts brought this scripture from Philippians to mind.

It occurs to me that I, and all Christians from small families, have the same opportunities to learn this lovely kind of unselfishness as those with many siblings. For, indeed, I am one among many siblings in this family of Christ. The church is another chance for me to learn the graces of second-fiddleism and back-burnerism. God knows this does not come naturally to most of us, so He reminds us in His word on more than one occasion that until we learn to decrease so that our brother can increase, until we learn to live for the good of the Body rather than for the desires of self, our growth will be stunted, and we will hinder rather than help the cause of Christ.

Today is the best day to start learning all this scripture has to teach. Maybe a good first step would be to commit it to memory.

~NOVEMBER 8~
KEEPING THE WORD NEAR

"Now what I am commanding you today is not too difficult for you or beyond your reach. It is not up in heaven, so that you have to ask, 'Who will ascend to heaven to get it and proclaim it to us so we may obey it?' Nor is it beyond the sea, so that you have to ask, 'Who will cross the sea to get it and proclaim it to us so we may obey it?' No, the word is very near you; it is written in your mouth and in your heart so you may obey it." Deuteronomy 30:11-14

There is more than one kind of gravity. Having things done for us time and time again tends to spoil us for any kind of survival skills that require diligence of muscle or will. Moses had led this bunch to the sea, across it, and through the desert. He had gone up on the mountain with God to receive His commandments for them, pled with God against destroying the whole lot of them when they transgressed time and time again, and now in the book of Deuteronomy he has restated for them what God requires of them before they enter into the land they have been promised. So when he encourages them to do their part here, in one respect he is saying, "I have already gone to the heavens for you to get this law! I have already trusted God for you so that He has opened the sea for us to go across!" The Law has been delivered to you. Now, just obey it!

Then he gets more specific about where the law is now that it is no longer up in the heavens or across the sea: it is "very near you; it is in your mouth and in your heart."

The rest of this chapter goes on to delineate their choices: life and prosperity or death and destruction; walking in God's ways and increasing and being blessed or bowing down to other gods and being destroyed. He concludes with this dramatically winsome invitation: *"Now choose life, so that you and your children may live and that you may love the Lord your God, listen to His voice, and hold fast to Him. For the Lord is your life, and He will give you many years in the land he swore to give to your fathers, Abraham, Isaac, and Jacob" (verses 19-20).* God had come to Abraham way back in Genesis 15:1 with similar words: *"I am your shield and your very great reward."*

If following God was not beyond the reach of the legal-bound Israelites, how much more accessible is that same choice for us who are recipients of God's ultimate promise to Abraham: "Through your seed, all nations will be blessed." Jesus is that blessing, and His Holy Spirit is our deposit guaranteeing our heavenly inheritance. If the word was in their hearts and mouths, how much fuller and richer should it be in ours?

True, things can fall out of the heart and do all the time. This is yet another kind of unfortunate gravity. How many times are we overwhelmed with emotion at the sight, sound, or touch of something lovely that we believe we will never forget or allow to fade or slip away only to squint our eyes later on as we try with no success to relive it? But if we had looked at a picture of it or listened to a recording of it *everyday*, the freshness could have lasted. This is the very way we keep the Word fresh and alive in our hearts.

And if it in our heart, it will be in our mouth. Jesus said, "For out of the overflow of the heart the mouth speaks" (Luke 6:45).

Have we chosen life? Christ went into the jaws of death to bring it to us. It is very near.

~NOVEMBER 9~
BECOMING SALT

"You are the salt of the earth. But if the salt loses its saltiness, how can it be made salty again? It is no longer good for anything, except to be thrown out and trampled over by men." Matthew 5:13

I take issue with the old saying "Familiarity breeds contempt." I'll bet whoever wrote that was forced to become "familiar" with someone who was *already* contemptible perhaps by virtue (or lack thereof) of a bitter heart or sharp tongue. In my experience, familiarity has usually bred love, affection, devotion, mercy, and all things good. *Usually.* The times that it has not bred these good things, it has bred something not as emotionally violent as contempt, but something that I will go so far as to agree does almost as much harm. Sometimes familiarity breeds *numbness*. When we mouth certain words over and over without stopping to consider what they really mean, familiarity breeds an insidious kind of robotic numbness. This is what I fear has happened with many scriptures, this one about salt being one of them. Let's look at it with fresh new eyes today, as though we are reading it for the first time. What did Jesus mean when he called us "salt"?

I am a salt freak. I crave salt the way many crave sugar and chocolate. I have been warned, threatened, and spied on in regards to my salt intake, and it thrills me to hear Jesus using salt here as a *good* thing. What was the goodness of it?

Obviously, one good thing is that salt enhances the flavor of things. When we walk around acting like Jesus, the world really does *taste* better. Without people who forgive instead of getting even, who smile in the face of death instead of fearing it like a plague, and who choose to share with others instead of lavishing all they have on their already glutted selves, life would taste terrible, like a bitter, unsalted lemon or entirely tasteless, like unsalted popcorn. Our saltiness gives this world a better flavor.

Salt also preserves. We are the ones who are meant to preserve what Jesus came here to bring. We are to remind others of what Jesus said in His beatitudes about meekness and humility when the world screams that truth lies in self-advancement and vaulting pride. We are here to preserve the truth that the things we can see are passing away but that there is a spiritual world we cannot see that will last forever.

Finally, salt makes people thirsty. Our lives should cause others to be thirsty. Spending some time with us should motivate a desire in those bound up in worldliness to throw away their junk food that fails to satisfy and seek out the refreshment of Living Water. When they ask, we should know how to take them to the well.

Mark 9:49 also speaks of salt, but it is not quoted so often: *"Everyone will be salted with fire."* Since Jesus has just finished quoting Isaiah to paint a graphic and terrifying picture of hell, some believe that this means that everyone who enters hell will suffer its fire. I don't think so; Jesus has already made this obvious. I think it is rather an introduction to his next topic, the importance of salt staying salty. It seems to me that Jesus is telling us *how* we become this salt that is so crucial to the world: through the purification of the fires of suffering. It should encourage us to view suffering as a necessary means to becoming the salt this world so desperately needs. Without salt, the world will perish. Without suffering, there can be no salt.

~NOVEMBER 10~
POINTS OF ELLIPSIS

"Do not be afraid, Abram. I am your shield, your very great reward." Genesis 15:1

"That night the Lord appeared to him and said, 'I am the God of your father Abraham. Do not be afraid, for I am with you." Genesis 26:24

"He had a dream in which he saw a stairway resting on the earth, with its top reaching to heaven, and the angels of God were ascending and descending on it. There above it stood the Lord, and He said, 'I am the Lord, the God of your father Abraham and the God of Isaac'." Genesis 28:12-13

"'Take off your sandals, for the place where you are standing is holy ground.' Then He said, 'I am the God of your father, the God of Abraham, the God of Isaac and the God of Jacob.'" Exodus 3:5-6

Wherever you start, you can't read very far in the Bible without coming upon God's reference to Himself as "the God of Abraham, Isaac, and Jacob." In the Old Testament, He is approaching someone and asking that they not be afraid based upon His relationship with his family. Later, in the New Testament, Jesus' spokesmen use this phrase to remind the audience that it is this God of their fathers, the One from the beginning, not mere man, who holds any and all power they might see demonstrated before them. A chronological study of this phrase reveals that God wanted each one in turn to trust Him because of what He had done for his father before him. He told Isaac to trust Him because of His record with his dad, Abraham; He told Jacob to trust Him because of how He was active in the lives of both his father Isaac and his grandfather Abraham. He didn't continue to add the names as He went down through the ages because it would have been absurd to deal with such a burgeoning list, but I think He still wants us to get the point that He is *our* individual God also and holds the same credentials, only more so, of course, because of all the history that has preceded us.

As I recently read this phrase, a picture came to me of three small dots and then the word "Jan." Points of ellipsis. These three spaced periods in a sentence indicate an omission of one or more words within a quoted passage. God actively pursued all these people He spoke these words to, and He wanted them to know that there was nothing random about their meeting with Him. They didn't just happen upon Him or beat the bushes to find a God that did not know them and was in hiding. He introduced Himself in a way that showed He knew them and was connected with their family from ages past. God keeps saying "I am the God of your Father Abraham, Isaac, and Jacob" so that we will supply the missing parts of the ellipses all the way down to our own name. He is pursuing us too, and there is no randomness at all about our meeting up with Him.

*"But about the resurrection of the dead— have you not read what God said to you,
' I am the God of Abraham, the God of Isaac, and the God of Jacob'? He is not
the God of the dead but of the living." Matthew 22:31-32*

~NOVEMBER 11~
MOUNTAINS FROM MOLEHILLS

*"Then the disciples came to Jesus in private and asked, 'Why couldn't we drive it
out?' He replied, 'Because you have so little faith. I tell you the truth, if you have
faith as small as a mustard seed, you can say to this mountain, ' Move from here to
there' and it will move. Nothing will be impossible for you.'" Matthew 17:19-21*

So slow of heart to understand: nothing I do is me—
The me I know could never do these things.
A tentative stroke of piano keys—
Reservedly, ill-at-ease;
The melody queries,
"Who grants stumbling fingers such wings?"

A teacher stands as a ramshackle house—
A cohabitation of light and dark.
Then the mud that should ooze from such a vessel of sod
Is refined into something useful to God.
Praise Him from whom all blessings flow
That holy fire rages from the Spirit's sure spark!

Yes, dear loving Father, it is decidedly so:
Nothing of my making will ever stand.
You have knocked on my door and asked me to give
This shroud that I cherish for the breath to live.
O, thwart all my strivings.
Slay my ambitions.
Glory to God in the highest!
Amen.

It's a twofold problem. We lack faith that God can make much of our humble
offerings, so we keep them pocketed, thinking they are only petty cash that
couldn't amount to much anyway. But eventually our hunger pangs prompt us
to seek *some* kind of recognition, some form of importance, "even if it can't be
spiritual," so we decide to invest, after all— our time, our money, our devotion,
our very heart— in things and pursuits that pay only worldly, therefore temporary,
dividends. We might feel full for a while, but soon our dividends end, and we are
both hungry and penniless.

God wants us to offer what we have to Him, even if it doesn't seem like much. He already sees our pennies as millions and our mustard seeds as bountiful branches of blessing.

The God of Abraham, Isaac, and Jacob comes reminding us that He knows us not only from way back but also way forward.

~NOVEMBER 12~
WAITING FOR JESUS

"It will be just like this on the day the Son of Man is revealed. On that day no one who is on the roof of his house, with his goods inside, should go down to get them. Likewise, no one in the field should go back for anything. Remember Lot's wife! Whoever tries to keep his life will preserve it. I tell you, on that night two people will be in one bed; one will be taken and the other left.'" Luke 17:30-35

Prior to these remarks, Jesus has been warning his disciples about the day when the Son of Man will return. He has compared it with the days of Noah and the days of Lot when "people were eating, drinking, marrying and being given in marriage…buying, selling, planting, and building" right up to the time of crisis when destruction came upon them. Here He predicts that the material things they have cherished will call to them, just as they did to Lot's wife causing her to take that last wistful backward glance. The things in their houses and fields that have occupied their time, cajoled them out of their money, and captured their hearts will no doubt continue clamoring right up to the moment He splits the clouds.

This is a graphic plea to all of us who are contained in this fading world for a while before we enter into the final phase of eternity ("final" because eternity is not something that will begin later but surely something that has already begun.) We struggle in differing degrees with the syndrome of Lot's wife and the people who failed to board the ark. The visible things of this world can worm their way into our hearts so that "the eyes of our heart" (Ephesians 1:18) fail to focus or focus only dimly upon the invisible but eternal things. Remember, He is saying all this to his disciples, not to some infidels or Pharisees who are decidedly opposed to Jesus and all He stands for. That means He is addressing us. Indeed, even the spiritually dedicated might go through days at a time without stopping to think about the truth that one of these days Jesus will indeed return and all of this will end. Life as we know it will come to a screeching halt, all of our stuff will be burned up, and all that will remain will be the treasures we have laid up in Heaven. When Jesus says "Whoever tries to keep his life will lose it, and whoever loses his life will preserve it," He is obviously using the word "life" in a worldly sense to mean all that we mistakenly hold most dear, all that we allow to substitute for the *real* life Jesus calls us to latch hold of with a white-knuckled death grip. He has already told us what that is: it is Jesus himself, the very Bread and Water of Life. It is this counterfeit life that He warns us not to try to keep. Obviously we must make a choice between the counterfeit and the authentic.

What He means by "one will be taken and the other left" is the subject of much controversy, but one thing is absolutely clear: regardless of how close we are to another person, salvation on that Day will be altogether individual. No one will ride into Heaven on anyone else's coattail. He will call our very names— yours and mine— and assign us to our individual places. This is the day we are all waiting for, whether we realize it or not. All this eating and drinking, buying and selling, even marrying and birthing must not be allowed to steal our focus from the glorious Day of the Lord. May not a day go by that your heart does not race with anticipation of the glory!

~NOVEMBER 13~
A GATHERING OF VULTURES

"I tell you, on that night two people will be in one bed; one will be taken and the other left. Two women will be grinding grain together; one will be taken and the other left...Where there is a dead body, there the vultures will gather." Luke 17:34-37

Last summer my three-year-old granddaughter and I came upon some vultures ("buzzards" to us) devouring a dead animal on the road. I explained to Callie that this might seem like a nasty thing but that God created these birds to clean up dead things as a way of keeping us safe from a lot of dangerous germs. A few weeks later, when she saw some again with her parents, she exclaimed brightly, "Nana *really* likes those birds!" I am pretty sure I would not think to name the buzzard as my favorite bird, but it seems to me that the quality of life would be more greatly affected by their absence than by the absence of hummingbirds, ladderback woodpeckers, or indigo buntings.

Luke 17 ends with this intriguing statement from Jesus about vultures gathering. Matthew also records these words from Jesus' Olivet discourse in chapter 24. The intrigue of these words lies in their graphic and mysterious nature: the picture of vultures gathering to pick apart corpses is not a fetching one; why would Jesus use such an ominous and unsavory image in regards to His second coming?

Perhaps it was not meant to be a picture of disgust at all but rather a picture of relief, like the one I was hoping to instill in Callie's mind.

One of the inevitabilities of this life is unfairness. You just can't live very many days in a row without coming upon injustice. This, of course, is a result of God's decision to give us freedom of choice in whom we serve and worship. As much as we wish everything could just be even and equitable and predictably just, it just isn't. We want all things pertaining to light and true Life to reign as sovereign over all things pertaining to shadows and death upon this sod we tread. We are tired not only of injustice at the hands of others, but we are weary to the bone of the temptations cast our way by the Evil One. We know that God desires that we not get even with those who persecute us because He will do that in His own good time, but sometimes His timing seems so sluggish to our way of seeing things. And we know also that He has promised to give us the strength to resist the evil. But it is hard to wait for fairness and light and life to rule over injustice and darkness and death. Sometimes aren't we tempted to wonder if things will *ever* really be made *right?* Will the stench and rottenness of evil ever go away?

These words of Jesus speak to our weariness with all this waiting and wondering. He has just finished describing how some will be "taken" and others will be "left," so it isn't too much of a stretch to deduce that these gathering vultures might be His image of the once-and-for-all final cleansing of every trace of menacing death from the presence of all the living. There *will* be a day— a glorious Day— when injustice, victimization, and temptation will be eliminated. The very bones of *death* itself will be picked clean, and only Life will remain.

"When the perishable has been clothed with the imperishable and the mortal with immortality, then the saying that is written will come true: 'Death has been swallowed up in victory'" (1 Corinthians 15:54).

~NOVEMBER 14~
THE MEMORIAL IMPERATIVE

"... Love the Lord your God with all your heart, and with all your soul and with all your strength. These commandments that I give you today are to be upon your hearts. Impress them upon your children. Talk about them when you sit at home and when you walk along the road, when you lie down and when you get up. Tie them as symbols on your hands and bind them on your foreheads. Write them on the doorframes of your houses and on your gates." Deuteronomy 6:4-9

By the time he died, he had been in the nursing home for so long. The last time I had seen him, over a year ago, he was in and out of reality, only sporadically recognizing those closest to him. The ravages of aging had overshadowed his sharp wit, his sparkly, mischievous eyes, and his perennial smile. I made my way to the memorial service with a heart fairly numbed after all these years barren of so much of the man I once loved and in whose presence I once took such vibrant delight. It would be a couple of hours of fellowship with the family and some words of comfort passed around in honor of a life we all had loved. But we all knew how hard these last few years had been on those closest to him. We knew about the hardships of uncertain diagnoses, frequent trips to the hospital, and long trips back and forth for the caregivers whose homes were not right there in the same town as the nursing home. Our knowledge that these heartaches were coming to a close served to squelch the heartache of losing him. At least it did for me. I assumed that everyone involved was pretty much on the same page.

But I was wrong. His children were not having a get together for the living, and calling it a "memorial service" just because that's just what you call these things. No, indeed. They were having a *Memorial* Service for their daddy. They had invited others to join them in remembering and celebrating their dad's life— *all* of it, not just the last few years of it. There were pictures from every phase of his life. A contagion spread rapidly to tell stories testifying to his fun-loving nature, his unselfishness, his enthusiasm as a loving daddy, granddaddy, and friend. I was hit full force by a violent gust of shame at having let him fade away. But now, gone were the few pale years. He was back in vivid color, making me laugh as only he could, making me cry for all I had lost, making my heart wake up to the whole story, testifying that he was so much more than a few years of fuzzy mind and failing body. The shadow of pain and numbness had been swallowed up by the reality of loving service and joyful life (2 Corinthians 5:4).

And then it hit me that this is what Deuteronomy 6 is all about. God knew that his children's Enemy was intent upon spoiling their relationship with Him. Because they would experience seasons of their Father's punishment as a result of their unfaithfulness and His silence as a result of their denial, He knew they would need to have regular memorial services to refresh their memories of the whole story, of the *real* story, that highlighted all those years before they embraced the Shadow, when their Father cared for them beyond their wildest imagination, when He guarded them as "the apple of His eye" (Deuteronomy 32:10).

We need them no less than they. He has done no less for us. Indeed, He has done immeasurably more; He has given us His Son! Turn your pinks red this very day.

~NOVEMBER 15~
ENCORE'S STUBBORN ALLURE

"Oh, the depth of the riches of the wisdom and knowledge of God! How unsearchable His judgments, and His paths beyond tracing out! 'Who has known the mind of the Lord? Or who has been His counselor?'" Romans 11:33-34

Not one of us can figure Him out or sum Him up. We cannot explain Him or predict Him; He is mysterious beyond all else. We know enough, though. We know that He is love and justice and mercy and truth. We know that He is pure goodness with no badness mixed in or warts on the other side of the coin. He cannot be tempted to be some other way, nor does He operate upon whim or with any randomness whatever. All that is good, whether from us or to us, is *really* from Him.

But even knowing all this, at times I have limited Him in a most unfortunate way. Sometimes I have acted, thought, felt, and lived as though *He* were limited— limited in His creativity, limited in His understanding, limited in His vision. If you asked me at these times if I believed God had limits to all these aspects, I would have answered emphatically, "No!" Still, my innermost fears and my actions resulting from them would tell the truth that I *did* believe that. And my beliefs about God do, in effect, "limit" God, at least insofar as they concern what

I allow Him to do in my life. How the people felt about Jesus in His hometown limited Him in that place, too.

A specific way I have allowed my small belief in Him to limit His work in my life is through my strong desire for *encores*. There have been experiences that have thrilled me so ecstatically that I have not only directly asked God to repeat them, but I have ground in my heels and gritted my teeth in an effort to *help* God reproduce them. It is as though I was saying, "Okay, God, you finally did it exactly right! Now, whatever you do, don't do *anything* to change this. Just keep doing *this* over and over." I must have been thinking that anything God did that was different from *this* would have to be worse, because it surely couldn't have been any *better*. I seemed to be advising Him, "If it ain't broke, don't fix it!"

There are all kinds of reasons my thinking was flawed about this. One of them has to do with the same reason it's wrong to wish for a person, even a wonderful, Christlike person, never to change. That's unbiblical. We are to be transformed into His likeness with ever-increasing glory" (2 Corinthians 3:18). Our experiences can produce and reveal glory in the same way. Another reason, connected closely with this one, is that our crucial need for an encore belies our belief in a God of boundless creativity. When we ask Him not to change something, we are revealing a doubt that He could make anything better or even as good as this one experience. How silly we shall feel someday in Heaven when we see that we so cherished this dandelion that we blindly rejected the rose He was holding in His other hand!

In recent years, experience has taught me not to be disheartened when the encore I wish for looks unlikely. Learning to rest in His providence has opened my nostrils to roses so fragrant that I am less likely to fear God "breaking" something that I view as "fixed." Let us keep our eyes and nostrils wide open in eager expectation of every new wonder He wants to show us. May our clamorings for an encore subside into peaceful rest in the arms of the unsearchable ways of the God of all creation.

~NOVEMBER 16~
FEELINGS MADE NEW

"Do not conform any longer to the pattern of this world, but be transformed by the renewing of your mind. Then you will be able to test and approve what God's will is—His good, pleasing, and perfect will." Romans 12:2

Our feelings can get us into big trouble.

Don't get me wrong; I'm all for feelings, and will go nose to nose against anyone who denies that our ability to feel is one of God's best blessings to us. The Bible is wallpapered with scriptures about the heart, the seat of our emotions. Jesus gave great dignity to its importance when He taught lessons such as "Where your treasure is, there will your heart be also," "Out of the overflow of the heart, the mouth speaks," and "Love the Lord your God with all your heart…"

Still, when untethered to the truth and allowed to run amok, our feelings can lead us into dark corners and down dead-end roads. Our enemy loves to take great advantage of this sway we give to our feelings to deceive us into turning away from all that is right.

We all have examples of people, maybe ourselves, who have admitted that they *knew* what they were doing was wrong, but they couldn't overcome their powerful *feelings*. This is an avowal that they have separated their feelings from their mind, as though one were vying with the other. "I can't change my feelings" becomes a justification for just going ahead and doing a swan dive into hell. The Bible is full of people who, because of these repeated swan dives into deeper and deeper pools, have ended up with hardened hearts that eventually became totally numbed to God. What tragic irony that overpowering *feelings* were the very root of such devastating *numbness!*

But Romans 12 tells us that there is a way that we can be totally transformed and by such transformation we will be able to *discern* the perfect will of God. The answer is the renewing of our *minds*. We start by studying (taking into our minds) God's will and then by taking "every thought captive to make it obedient to Christ." This goes hand in hand with demolishing "arguments and every pretension that sets itself up against the knowledge of God" (2 Corinthians 10:5). The "arguments" and "pretensions" are other names for *feelings*. The key to renewing our *feelings* is to renew our *minds!* We then gain the power to overcome rather than to be plummeted into a bottomless pit.

God wants us to be so filled with *knowledge* of Him that we can tell right away when our *feelings* are leading us astray. He knows that we will all struggle, but He expects us to lean against the wayward feelings in His direction. The way to do this is to continually renew our minds to deal righteously with each new temptation. If we feel too small for the huge struggle, remember Paul's words: *"We proclaim Him, admonishing and teaching everyone with all wisdom, so that we may present everyone perfect in Christ. To this end I labor, struggling with all His energy, which so powerfully works within me" (Colossians 1:29).* "Teaching," "wisdom"— these are *mind* words, the kind of mind words that hold *renewal* power. Renewed mind, renewed feelings.

"May God Himself, the God of peace, sanctify you through and through. May your whole spirit, soul, and body be kept blameless at the coming of our Lord Jesus Christ. The one who calls you is faithful, and He will do it." 1 Thessalonians 5:23-24

~NOVEMBER 17~
APPLES OF GOLD:
THE LUXURY OF A FRIEND

"A word aptly spoken is like apples of gold in settings of silver." Proverbs 25:11

A passionate nature is a delight when it ignites pleasure and pushes us down roads with happy destinations. It affords us who possess it thrilling roller-coaster experiences and fills our lives with unspeakable imagery and energy.

However, this very same passion feels like a curse when heartache cuts sharply and disappointment strikes bitterly. When my passionate nature escorts me into shadows and high-walled caverns, I want to trade it in on something with less flash and more function, something with fewer possibilities of extremes. Sometimes I have wished that I could amputate my sensitive antennae; that I could awaken tomorrow morning as one of those people who lives her life on an even keel, dependably traveling somewhere yawningly predictable. All the benefits, the sublime chill-bumpy emotional highs have dissolved from my memory, and my ardor goes on the auction block to the highest bidder.

I have a friend of many years who has my history etched on her heart. In these dreary times Candy dives deeply into my eyeballs, nods her head sweetly, smiles patiently and motherly, and reminds me with confidence about all the thousands of joyful mornings that have followed my nights of weeping. She recounts for me the details of my favorite true stories, bearing witness to her faithful listening ears and devoted heart. She is my safety deposit box filled with testimonials of hope. After all these years of listening to her recite my life, now it only takes one look into her eyes to remember the Truth: *"Weeping may remain for a night, but rejoicing comes in the morning" (Psalm 30:5)*. Best of all, after a little while in her care, I remember again why I am glad to be me, why it is *good* to feel things deeply. She even thanks God when she prays for me for the painful parts of my history because she knows they are part of what has made me the person I have come to be— the person she loves so much. No diamond or ruby was ever as valuable as words like these. Her prayers make me proud to be brave and eager to give passion another go.

I'm so thankful that God arranged for Christians to *belong* to one another, to be able to nurture the kind of fellowship that runs to our side and sings us our melody when our eyes are too clouded to read the notes and our memories too hazy to remember the loveliness, to step in as reinforcements when we are too weary to pray. Their words—just the right ones at just the right time— grace our lives and shimmer like "apples of gold in settings of silver."

One of the sweetest foretastes of Heaven is having a faithful friend who *knows* you well and loves you anyway. Never let her go unappreciated or take her for granted. Leave a love note on her windshield this very day.

"Two are better than one, because they have a good return for their work: If one falls down, his friend can help him up." Ecclesiastes 4:10

~NOVEMBER 18~
DANGEROUS SAFETY

"Now, Joseph and all his brothers and all that generation died, but the Israelites were fruitful and multiplied greatly and became exceedingly numerous, so that the land was filled with them. Then a new king, who did not know about Joseph, came to power in Egypt." Exodus 1:6-8

And thus began their journey out of the still eye of the hurricane into the tempest. For four hundred years they had reposed in Goshen, the best land in Egypt, as a result of a grateful pharaoh who had benefited from the godly wisdom of Joseph. But now their salvation from a famine's certain destruction is forgotten, and all this new king sees when he looks around at the growing population of Israelites is impending doom. Thus, the Israelites' lives are made bitter with hard labor. When this doesn't hinder their procreation, a directive is sent out to the midwives to kill all the Israelite baby boys.

But as a result, God raises up Moses to deliver the Israelites out of this pagan country and into His own where He can raise *them* up to get about the business of blessing all nations. It's a long, hard road ahead for the Israelites with many twists and turns and dead-end roads, but eventually time ripens into the day when the Messiah, the Promised One, will be delivered to earth to walk and talk among us, to bless us with His kindness and humility, to die, and to arise proclaiming death as the deposed king of our lives. God knew, as those four hundred years took generation after generation of His children, that Egypt was not to be Home but only a stopping off place, a campground. To live as slaves to pagans, whether in relative comfort or bitter hardship, was not His ultimate plan for us. He had better things in mind. And so, a pharaoh who did not know Joseph *had* to come along. What they saw as a disastrous memory lapse on the part of the kingdom of Egypt God used as the golden key for exit out of their "safe" doldrums into His dangerous but blessed hurricane.

Can you relate? Might He not do the same kind of thing with the dependable laurels we have rested upon for much of our lives? Isn't it possible, even probable, given how we love the comfort of predictability, that God will send something into our lives to disturb the predictability and uproot our security so that we might, even against our will, finally abandon our campgrounds and head more resolutely for Home? I remember how teaching my English classes for fifteen years had begun to feel like a security I could rest in. Oh, I still had some apprehension about what might be different each year or if these kids would finally be the ones that I couldn't reach, but by Thanksgiving of every year, I was settled into a fairly weather-worthy nest. Then it happened. My friend Janis suggested that I add an elective class in *Bible* at my public high school. Taking that on was, in many ways, like purposely leaving the calmness of the eye of the storm to enter its ferocity. Though, as with Moses, God paved the way for me and proved faithful to fill this weak vessel, I was unnested from the security of the predictability I had leaned upon for all those years. But what came for the next ten years was thrilling beyond words. To have stayed in the nest would have been to have missed the ride of my life and would have robbed hundreds of kids from a knowledge of God's Word.

To venture from our nests into the unknown will certainly feel like danger, but to stay could doom us to a most tragic safety.

~NOVEMBER 19~
JOYFUL SACRIFICE

"Out of the most severe trial, their overflowing joy and their extreme poverty welled up in rich generosity. For I testify that they gave as much as they were able, and even beyond their ability. Entirely on their own, they urgently pleaded with us for the privilege of sharing in this service to the saints." 2 Corinthians 8:2-4

According to what he says a few verses later, Paul is appealing to the Corinthians to compare their earnestness to the earnestness of others, in this case, the Macedonian churches. He goes on to say, "For you know the grace of our Lord Jesus Christ, that though he was rich, yet for your sakes He became poor, so that you through his poverty might become rich" (verse 9). Verse one seems to point to the reason these churches could be so generous: they were aware of God's grace to them. Apparently, they understood their need, their poverty when it came to saving themselves, and their wealth that came solely from Christ's atoning blood at God's expense.

In Matthew 13, Jesus uses a parable to point out the wisdom of what these churches were doing. He tells about a man who, after finding a treasure buried in a field, sells all he has to buy the field that contains the treasure. It is a very short parable—only two sentences long— and yet Jesus makes room for three words of modification that sometimes haunt us: "in his joy." *"In his joy* he went and sold all he had and bought that field." You might remember times when you did something without delay in your joy. In my joy, I have run right out to the grocery store and bought the ingredients for a meal my stomach influenced my imagination to excite my anticipatory brain into planning. In my joy I have jumped right out of my car— locking my keys inside— to hug a long-awaited loved one. I have, in my joy, left the house without my driver's license, run out into the pouring rain to get a long-awaited letter, spent more money than I should have when finally finding the right shoes, purse, blouse, or book, and raced into the airport leaving my plane ticket in the car.

Paul had a great pedigree and was on his way to greatness. He had sat at the feet of the best teacher, and he had excelled in practicing what he was taught— a "Hebrew of Hebrews" and faultless in righteousness. *"But whatever was to my profit I now consider loss for the sake of Christ. What is more, I consider every-*

thing a loss compared to the surpassing greatness of knowing Christ Jesus as my Lord, for whose sake I have lost all things. I consider them rubbish that I might gain Christ and be found in Him, not having a righteousness that comes from the law, but that which is through faith in Christ..." (Philippians 3:7-9). Attaining resurrection from death became the treasure for which Paul eagerly and joyfully sacrificed all he had, was, and could become. Paul, the man in the parable, and the Macedonian church members all knew that the treasure they had found was worth more than anything— in fact more than *everything*— they had, so they could joyfully sacrifice whatever it cost to own it.

Spend some honest time before Christ today. Ask Him to help you identify your greatest treasures. Let us make certain that rather than sacrificing *to gain* the real Treasure, we are not instead sacrificing the Treasure itself.

~NOVEMBER 20~
GLORIFYING GOD BY BELONGING

"A new command I give you: Love one another. As I have loved you, so you must love one another. By this all men will know that you are my disciples, if you love one another." John 13:34-35

The sacrifice we are asked to make might be, rather than money or fame, something else many of us cling to tenaciously: our time. Sometimes we want, more than anything, just to be left alone. For many whose week is filled with people, coveting isolation as a real treasure can threaten our possibilities of fulfilling our purpose for God. All of us know believers— maybe you are one of them— who because they have been hurt or disillusioned by the church, ask "Why do I need it?" But this scripture and others teach us that we glorify God best by living in fellowship with His family.

When we are born into Christ, we become members of His church. Joe Keyes, our church pulpit minister, puts it like this: "We can no more be Christians without being members of the church than we can become people without being members of a family."

No Christian is an only child; we work in community. A quick glance back at Genesis 1:26 reminds us that even God did not create alone; He did it as a part of the Trinity.

Consider just a few of the many "together" scriptures:

- *"In Him the whole building is joined together and rises to become a holy temple in the Lord. And in Him you too are being built together to become a dwelling in which God lives with His spirit" (Ephesians 2:21-22).*
- *"This mystery is that through the gospel the Gentiles are heirs together with Israel, members together of one body, and sharers together in the promise in Christ Jesus" (Ephesians 3:6).*

- *"After that, we who are still alive and are left will be caught up together with them in the clouds to meet the Lord in the air. And so we will be with the Lord forever. Therefore, encourage each other with these words" (1 Thessalonians 4:17-18).*

The Bible does not teach Lone Rangerism but *togetherness*. First Corinthians 12 goes into great detail about our dependence upon one another. We must be plugged into the body to avoid dangerous isolationism. First John 3:16 points out that not only should we be willing to give up our isolation for the body, but indeed "we ought to lay down our [very] lives for our brothers." Hebrews 3:13 tells us to "encourage one another daily ...so that none of you may be hardened by sin's deceitfulness," and Ephesians 4:3-4 tells us to "Make every effort to keep the unity of the Spirit through the bond of peace. There is one body and one Spirit— just as you were called to one hope when you were called—one Lord, one faith, one baptism; one God and Father of all, who is over all and through all and in all." And look at Ephesians 3:10: *"His intent was that now, through the church, the manifold wisdom of God should be made known to the rulers and authorities in the heavenly realms."* What reveals the wisdom of God "in the heavenly realms" is the unity of the church!

Being a kingdom citizen is more than just believing; it's *belonging*.

~NOVEMBER 21~
THE TREASURE OF QUIETLY PONDERING

"But Mary treasured up all these things and pondered them in her heart." Luke 2:19

"Your beauty should not come from outward adornment, such as braided hair and the wearing of gold jewelry and fine clothes. Instead, it should be that of your inner self, the unfading beauty of a gentle and quiet spirit, which is of great worth in God's sight." 1 Peter 3:3-4

God is so multi-faceted that in order to demonstrate His many distinctive characteristics, He created us to be *different* from one another. While I might hear His message and retell it in poetry or some sort of animated wordiness that might excite, you might relate the same message through dance, music, or even a certain kind of stillness that inspires through its peacefulness. Though I know He *created* this diversity, still when I am around some who are very different from me in temperament, I am so inspired by them that I am tempted to want to shuck *everything* I am and do in order to become one of *these* people.

I am thinking of a friend whose desire to learn the Word of God and her hunger to know the Author of Life fall somewhere just this side of a John the Baptist-style fervor. Pam can't go very long without speaking of Jesus and of something new she is learning. However, unlike me, this ardent passion does not jump and twitch and shout with nervous energy; it exudes like a white-hot beacon, brilliant and unwavering. She is very Mary-ish. She quietly learns and ponders and then extends a tranquil but beckoning "Come-hither" finger that draws others to sit at her feet. Then, when we have tired of speaking, with a comeliness fashioned of godly reserve and with much thought and few words, she imparts *wisdom*. She will invite a herd of people to her house for a video Bible study which she has already finished. But rather than having to poke a sock in her mouth to keep from blurting out unnecessary and even irritating commentary about what's coming next or what parts you really don't want to miss, she sits serenely learning another layer, gracefully allowing everyone else the same chance she had to learn the first layer. She seems to have no temptation to feel as though she is ever the authority on anything just because she might have had more exposure to it than someone else. She is truly God's willing handmaiden, and I think that she might have been in the running to be Mary if Jesus were coming into our world today.

This causes me to wonder how we, as His children, are to figure out what parts of our personality we are to accept, maybe even embrace, as being useful in demonstrating this or that about the nature of God our Father and which parts need to be rejected and prayed over and allowed to be remolded. If I am a person whose energy is a little hard to bridle or one who feels the need to speak few words, probably God has His reasons for wanting this to be the case. How, then, when I am so inspired by one very *different* from me, can I incorporate more of her holiness into my God-given style of shining? I think it's a question worth asking on a regular basis and worth much listening to hear His answer.

~NOVEMBER 22~
A SHINING STAR IN THE UNIVERSE

"Do everything without complaining or arguing so that you may become blameless and pure, children of God without fault in a crooked and depraved generation, in which you shine like stars in the universe as you hold out the word of life..." Philippians 2:14-16

"Offer hospitality to one another without grumbling." 1 Peter 4:9

With all we are called to do in order to shine *on* and *in* this dark world, it might be hard to make ourselves realize that some of our brightest rays can emanate from some of the things we *don't* do. In fact, some of the things we *don't* do can be our strongest witness for Christ.

My mother-in-law is the perfect example. She is a luminous beacon to all who know her, and yet a personal profile might not indicate why this is so. She is a soft-spoken lady who never, *ever* draws attention to herself intentionally. She is not flashy or flamboyant, and yet she is adored and admired by everyone, especially those who know her *best* and spend the *most* time with her. (That in itself is something, since many if not most of us had rather almost anyone give a character analysis of us than our family members who have been privy to an up-close-and personal view of us.) She does many things right and demonstrates 1 Corinthians 13 love for all of us, but one grace in which she outshines all others I know is her control over *complaining*. Paul motivates the Philippian Christians to live with an uncomplaining spirit by explaining that thereby they might become "blameless and pure," and "children of God without fault" in an otherwise warped and corrupt world. He goes on to say that as they offer the world the Truth, their lives will shine with this very Truth they are trying to sell.

I wonder how often we do a lot of energetic evangelism only to be ineffectual because of some of the vestiges of worldliness that cling to us, giving off a terrible stench of half-hearted belief in what we are saying. On the other hand, some can say little but give off the unmistakable and irresistible aroma of Christ in telltale ways that strongly indicate that they are living by some other unworldly and supernatural code of conduct. The refusal to be a grumbler is one of those finer points of Christian living that many of us downplay. However, when someone gets a grip on it and lives it out with a good amount of consistency, everyone notices and is inspired. Even though we might think complaining will make things better, usually it only makes things worse. Doubtless, we should be honest about how we are doing, but that can be done without a complaining and bitter attitude that undermines faith in the God who is watching over us. We can speak of our hardship with a sweet and accepting spirit that gives glory and proves our faith in the One we claim to be our Deliverer. Our spirit in these times of trial could very well be the shining star that leads someone else Home.

~NOVEMBER 23~
A CORNUCOPIA OF THANKS

"Enter His gates with thanksgiving, and His courts with praise; give thanks to Him and praise His name. For the Lord is good and His love endures forever; His faithfulness continues through all generations." Psalm 100:4-5

"Thank you for the world so sweet.
Thank you for the food we eat.
Thank you for the birds that sing;
Thank you, God, for everything."
For budding life—both petal and skin—
And the courage it gives me to hope again;
The oranges and yellows of Your autumnal world,
And the pink in the cheeks of our new baby girl.
For her days ahead full of trouble but grace
That will give her the strong feet to win the long race.
For a husband who lays down his life in your care,
And forgives me unendingly and goes on from there;
For my children whose faces go with me each day,

Growing older and wiser but still loving to play—
Sons and daughters as they've always been,
But now brothers and sisters who've become my friends.
For hearts who cherish my history,
And whose knees bend in prayer for me stubbornly;
For their eyes that are tender and hearts that are strong;
Tongues that will lovingly tell me I'm wrong.
For arms that enfold me and kiss away tears;
For the blood of your son that shatters my fears;
For brown earth that blossoms beneath yellow sun;
For a spirit that sings and feet that can run;
A mind that remembers and heart that can see
Such visions in detail of all that can be.
For bright hope and warm comfort that always abounds
When I fall disheartened with my face to the ground.
You remind me of all of the times in the past
When the bleakness I feared had won didn't last.
So for seasons that change, for the thrill of surprise,
For Your Son who came near to reveal Satan's lies,
For You packed in everything above and below,
What can I say? How can I show
My thanks for this cornucopia so sweet
Sent down with your blessing and laid at my feet?

~NOVEMBER 24~
A DIFFERENT THANKSGIVING

"After this, the word of the Lord came to Abram in a vision:
'Do not be afraid, Abram.
I am your shield,
Your very great reward.'" Genesis 15:1

Oh, Lord, in this season of fruitless requests
When I'm called just to trust you to do what is best,
In reluctant thanksgiving I come; still I come—
Not with bountiful faith, but at least with some.
In sorrow I sit, but at least I just sit
And not rush around madly trying to make pieces fit.
I know you are wishing I'd just leave this alone
In your hands while I count all the blessings I own.
Oh, please see I keep trying, but I'm crippled, it seems—
Haunted by losses and fractured dreams.
Please move me along from this waiting place
To your higher ground of selfless grace

Where my own minor bruises fade from my view,
And I bow in thanksgiving for the Blessing of You.
You said just to "stand" when we've done all we know,
So I'll stand here in your armor until you say "Go,"
Praying that the mind of Christ will move in
So at last I might lose, and you finally might win.

Maybe this Thanksgiving things feel different from the other years. Perhaps the blessing you feel you need most continues and continues and continues some more to hide elusively. If the blessings you are counting seem still not to overcome the weight of the pain and disappointment, push that list aside and focus fully on the one greatest Blessing—your "shield and your very great reward." Remember, Dear One, that when we can manage to stay put before God, when we can manage to remain *standing* even though we can't make much forward progress, we are at just the right place to take the rare opportunity to bless God for being the Everlasting Arms when all others fail, the Mighty Shield when every other defense has fallen. In our dearth we find a different kind of cornucopia; in our penury, a new way to give thanks.

~NOVEMBER 25~
OBEYING THE COMMAND FOR RENEWAL

"Therefore, I urge you, brothers, in view of God's mercy, to offer your bodies as living sacrifices, holy and pleasing to God— this is your spiritual act of worship. Do not conform any longer to the pattern of this world, but be transformed by the renewing of your mind. Then you will be able to test and approve what God's will is— His good, pleasing, and perfect will." Romans 12:1-2

I know I keep coming back to this scripture, but honestly, can you think of any greater hope than that we can be— right here on this earth— *transformed?* And it all starts with our *minds!* I like that. If it all started with our hearts (or what we usually think of as our hearts), I would feel at a loss to know how to accomplish much. I know from experience that I can wish and even tell myself not to want something or like something, and I can even *act* differently from how I feel, but usually that doesn't *instantly* change the way that I really *feel*. Now, it is true that we can act ourselves into a better way of feeling much more successfully than we can feel ourselves into a better way of acting, but even then it is not just because of our actions that our feelings change. No. What changes our feelings is, indeed, something that starts in the mind. Real change begins when we *learn* something new. The reason that we can eventually act ourselves into a better way of feeling is that our minds learn something *new* from our experience. Learning new things is what renews our minds and gets us into position to be transformed.

Having said all that, now let's go back and look at the man Jesus told about who sold all he had *in joy* in order to buy the field that contained what he considered the greatest treasure of all. Maybe, in all honesty, we don't *feel* that way. Maybe after getting alone with God and asking Him to shed His light on our greatest treasures we have discovered that we are more in love with what we have and are than what Christ has for us and wants us to be. It could be that when we read this parable and the next one about the pearl of great price, when we look at the Macedonian churches that gave eagerly out of their poverty, when we look at Paul who gave up a powerful, influential future in the Jewish Sanhedrin, we feel discouraged. We might feel that we are not in the same league with these unselfish people and that they just must have had a different kind of *heart* than we do. We might feel, way down deep in our secret heart of hearts, that we are doomed to go through the remainder of our days in this life living a sort of charade about *really* loving *God* and *His* desires more than we do *ourselves* and *our* desires.

If so, there is no need to despair. Keep *desiring* to have the desire you need. Pray for the desire to do what it takes to *learn* that new something that will renew your mind and thus change your heart. Mind renewal *is* possible through Christ! We *can* be transformed! If it were not possible, it would not have been stated in *command* terms in a cause and effect statement. In fact, there is a double effect from the same cause. The action we are to take (the cause) is renewing our minds. The double effect of this is that (1.) we will be transformed, and (2.) we will be able to know God's will for us.

~NOVEMBER 26~
STRUGGLING WITH ALL HIS ENERGY

"We proclaim him, admonishing and teaching everyone with all wisdom, so that we may present everyone perfect in Christ. To this end, I labor, struggling with all His energy, which so powerfully works in me." Colossians 1:28

Who is your spiritual hero? Don't read any further until you know the answer. Probably it is someone who does well a thing or many things that you consider very hard or very undesirable. She might be obviously gifted and has won your admiration for allowing her gift to be used so freely. Or she might just be willing to do as much as she can for as many as she can in areas she is obviously gifted in as well as areas she is not. In this case, she has won your respect for being a willing and faithful vessel for God.

The hero I am thinking of is also my very good friend. I firmly believe God has placed Denise in my life and caused her heart to look upon me favorably so that I might learn to walk in her footsteps. She is a champion of the down and out. I suppose some of her good deeds might be connected somehow to a "gift," but I know that she often dives head first into many pursuits that she knows nothing whatsoever about at the time she takes the leap. She simply sees a need and starts moving in what seems to be the right direction. One step at a time she perseveres until the thing is done: a family is fed, children are clothed, the head of the house finally has a job, someone decides to give the church a chance for the first time in her life.

When my friend first introduced me to this verse, I marveled at the resemblance of these words to her very life. She had always been amazing to all of us because of her boundless energy and remarkable productivity for the Lord, and now I knew her secret. It's a safe bet that all Christians understand that we are to be vessels filled with Christ, but she had these words in her heart to remind herself when tiredness befell her that the end of her was only the beginning of Him: *"To this end I labor, struggling with all His energy, which so powerfully works within me."*

The Psalmist said in Psalm 119:11, "I have hidden your word in my heart that I might not sin against you." Hidden in Denise's heart is this resounding testimony that as Christians we have much more energy than our own. There is nothing God calls us to do that He will not enable us to do. The greatest leap we have to make is believing in what we haven't yet seen. Being creatures of this fallen world, we might be tempted to believe it is all about our energy and ability and foresight, but my friend Denise demonstrates over and over again that the Divine Dynamo is released by true faith. When we put our feet into the water, the Jordan really will part (Joshua 3:15).

It does take our *willingness* to spend our energy, for God is not a puppeteer who forcefully manipulates our strings to make us perform. Living godly lives is not easy. But we need not so quickly shrink away from hard tasks or the needs of people that seem providentially put into our paths simply because we don't think it is *in* us. Our truest heroes' greatest strength is their faith that God will supply what they lack.

"...but those who hope in the Lord will renew their strength. They will soar on wings like eagles; they will run and not grow weary; they will walk and not be faint." Isaiah 40:31

~NOVEMBER 27~
GETTING WISDOM

"Lay hold of my words with all your heart; keep my commands and you will live. Get wisdom, get understanding; do not forget my words or swerve from them. Do not forsake wisdom, and she will protect you; love her and she will watch over you. Wisdom is supreme; therefore, get wisdom. Though it cost all you have, get understanding." Proverbs 4:4-7

Supreme wisdom is, of course, God's Word, and it should be our True North on every leg of our journey. There cannot be enough said or written about the importance of studying scripture to show ourselves approved of God as workers who need not be ashamed because we correctly handle those words. We cannot overemphasize the importance of being ready to give an answer to all who ask about the reason for our hope. We also know that even "the foolishness of God is wiser than man's wisdom." However, let us not jump to the false conclusion that just because we don't read it in the Bible it is not God's wisdom.

God is the maker and author of all things true and good, and in order for us to be as "shrewd as snakes" as Jesus commands, we must be willing to apply our brains to learning. Solomon asked for wisdom that He might lead God's people well. This means that he would have had to use his mind in various and sundry ways as King of Israel. No doubt he applied his mind to learning these skills. Paul, in his great treatise on Mars Hill in Acts 17, illustrated that he knew something about the culture of those with whom he was speaking. Indeed, the more we sharpen our minds in learning, the more we are able to apply God's Word to this world and the people in it who so desperately need it. The Old and New Testaments are filled with the admonition to love God, not just with all our hearts and souls, but with all our minds.

I'm only saying all this because it seems that in these post-modern times, Christians shy away from conversations that require in-depth knowledge. Most of this is probably from fear of coming across as intolerant or inflexible. In our desire to blend in and not rock any boats, some have deliberately avoided seriously studying science and even the Bible. We'd just rather shrug our shoulders in some sort of holy ignorance. Another reason is that we have become just plain lazy. We are unmotivated to become intellectually enlightened because we misunderstand scripture. We might think that being "like children" means being unlearned rather than dependent. We might think that being smart is equivalent to being arrogant. Paul was a man of "great learning"; in fact, Festus accused him of being "mad" because of it. Because Paul developed his mind, he was able to influence other intellectual people. Some of us are put in the paths of intelligent and intellectual people who will be much more likely to listen to and respect us if we can speak to them on their level.

We have the Words of Life! We need to get all the wisdom we can about Them and around Them. If we continue to come across to the world as stupid and thus do not gain their ears, are we really loving the Lord our God with all our minds? We need not fear. There is a way to be both knowledgeable and kind, both informed and holy.

~NOVEMBER 28~
REASONABLE CHRISTIANITY
PART 1

"So [the apostle Paul] was reasoning in the synagogue with the Jews and the God-fearing Gentiles, and in the market place every day with those who happened to be present." Acts 17:17 (NASB)

"'Come now, let us reason together,' says the Lord." Isaiah 1:18

Informed and holy. These can and should be natural bedfellows, and yet somehow it seems most of Christendom considers that there should be a "yet" rather than an "and" placed between intellect and belief in Christ. *How* this has happened is for a book of history or philosophy to probe, but *that* it has is a belief that if we do not at least consider as a fact, we cannot move away from.

Are we afraid if we study our beliefs thoroughly enough to do a good job of defending them that perhaps we will study ourselves out of believing? Do we fear that our faith in Christ as the Truth, the Life, and the Way cannot bear scrutiny? Could we inwardly tremble at the thought of being challenged about our way of life because our belief is too subjective to be explained in words or even with scripture? While it is true that by the time most practicing Christians reach midlife we have walked with Christ long enough to see and know *by experience* His faithfulness, what are we to do about those younger ones without these years of testimony who are lost and searching for the true God? Do we expect them just to trust what we say? Is our only answer to them that it is just something down inside us that we *feel* we should follow? If we are honest about all this, what we might find is that we were born into this way of seeing things, and it was natural that we take the baton that was passed off to us by our parents, or at least our culture. If this is as far as we have ever questioned and delved into the reason we believe, there might be a demon of tentativeness, insecurity, or even downright denial and fear lurking just beneath the surface of our consciousness. It might just be waiting there until we are finally not so distracted by busyness, noise, activity, and chaotic and obligated life as we know it that it can emerge, get our attention and begin openly haunting us.

How do we feel about conversations with others who do not see eye to eye with us about the scriptures? If we are reluctant, is it because we are not prepared to give a reason for believing as we do? Is that okay? Is it okay to continue living a lifestyle that mirrors belief but hides a heart and mind that are not so sure? Of course this is better than abandoning all restraint and throwing ourselves recklessly into evil simply because we are not sure there will be consequences, but is this the *best* way for us to honor and glorify the God who has left us here to prepare others for Eternity? Is just habituating a certain lifestyle divorced from the person of Christ and driven only by a vague and random choice of authority really what we can call a close relationship with our Master? Wouldn't Christ be better magnified and made more attractive by minds "*prepared* to give an answer to everyone who asks the reason for the hope that [we] have"?

~NOVEMBER 29~
REASONABLE CHRISTIANITY
PART 2

"Always be prepared to give an answer to everyone who asks you to give the reason for the hope that you have." 1 Peter 3:15

"Do your best to present yourself to God as one approved, a workman who does not need to be ashamed and who correctly handles the word of truth." 2 Timothy 2:15

"...a workman that does not need to be ashamed..." Why is the metaphor of a worker chosen here, and why might this worker be ashamed? A worker is one who accomplishes a given task or produces a given product. If he does not perform his task well or if the product he makes is of poor quality, he would, or at least should be, ashamed. When we present ourselves to God, we are reporting as workers to do a certain job for Him, namely replicating Christ with such quality that others believe and want to follow and serve His, and our, Father and Master to the end that all would be redeemed from this temporary, fallen world and delivered into His presence where there is no more evil. We are given "the word of truth" as our tool. This "word," the gospel, can be both read and seen in our spirit-filled lives if we handle it correctly and skillfully. If we do not, one result will be shame.

There is more than one way we can be ashamed about this. We might be ashamed because we handle it incorrectly, wielding this Sword of the Spirit (Ephesians 6:17) not to bring hope and cut our way out of evil strongholds, but to lacerate deeply with hateful condemnation. This might be one of the things many fear who refuse to defend the gospel intelligently. They are afraid to present the countercultural ideas in scripture because some who don't agree might be offended. We must not let the enemy talk us into believing that knowledge equals arrogance. One of the deep mysteries of the universe is how we got to the point of believing that *offending* godless mindsets was wrong, but there it is. Many, many do feel this very thing. If we really believe in the goodness and light that Christ came to pass on to us to shed forth, is it not logical that His very purpose was to be *at odds with* and even want to *destroy* the *enemies* of goodness and light, i.e. evil and darkness? But somehow many have come to feel that it is "intolerant" or "judgmental" to take stands that others take issue with, even the carriers /promoters of evil and darkness, whether they are ignorant and naïve carriers or malignant and purposeful ones. However, 1 Peter 3:15b-16 qualifies the manner in which we do this work: *"But do this with gentleness and respect, keeping a clear conscience, so that those who speak maliciously against your good behavior in Christ may be ashamed of their slander."* When we know how to handle the Word of Truth correctly, we have no need to become defensive or offensive. We simply (but *thoroughly*) present the written evidence and live lives consistent with that evidence. We can and should be both knowledgeable and kind.

But another reason we might be ashamed is that we do not handle the Word of Truth at all but just ignore it and avoid all indepth conversation about it. Let's be sure we aren't throwing out the baby with the bath water and avoiding one extreme by taking the other one.

~NOVEMBER 30~
LIVING FOR RIGHTEOUSNESS

"But just as He who has called you is holy, so be holy in all you do; for it is written: 'Be holy because I am holy.'" 1 Peter 1:15-16

"He bore our sins in His body on the tree, so that we might die to sins and live for righteousness; by His wounds you have been healed." 1Peter 2:24

"Do not offer the parts of your body to sin, as instruments of wickedness, but rather offer yourselves to God as those who have been brought from death to life; and offer the parts of your body to him as instruments of righteousness." Romans 6:13

What then do we mean by living out the "word of truth"? The first two words that come to my mind when pondering the walk of the Christian are "righteous" and "holy." But these words, like so many, might have for you been blurred into abstraction by familiarity to the tongue and ear. If we are to be responsible for living lives characterized by these descriptors, we need to refresh our minds with their true meanings until they become more concrete again.

The concordance in my NIV Study Bible contains 258 references to "righteous" and "righteousness." It contains 231 references to "holy" and "holiness." "Righteous" is denoted to mean morally right or justifiable, whereas "holy" carries a definition concerned with dedication or devotion to the service of God. Although I have not yet done an exhaustive study of their use in the Bible, it seems that sometimes they are used interchangeably and other times "righteousness" seems to be a byproduct of a more sacred "holiness." It is interesting that eleven of the twenty-seven New Testament books include an exhortation to holiness in the very first chapter, indicating it as one of the identifying marks of a Christian. Probably the most accurate picture of holiness is that of being set apart for use by God. If we, like Jesus, are set apart for God's use, our lives should be characterized by righteousness. But what does righteousness look like?

What is righteousness? Sometimes our default belief is that righteousness is negatively defined by what we *don't* or *won't* do. Surely it is scriptural to pay attention to ridding ourselves of certain behaviors: *"For the grace of God that brings salvation has appeared to all men. It teaches us to say 'No' to ungodliness and worldly passions, and to live self-controlled, upright and godly lives in this present age, while we wait for the blessed hope—the glorious appearing of our great God and Savior, Jesus Christ, who gave himself for us to redeem us from all wickedness and to purify for Himself a people who are his very own, eager to do what is good"* (Titus 2:11-14). But in order for us to fulfill the last part of that scripture, *"eager to do what is good,"* we must be very careful not to adopt a "play-it-safe" idea of righteous living based upon passivity rather than activity. Jesus didn't just go about resisting sin; He went about doing good. And

Abraham's faith, which was credited to him as righteousness, wasn't just a refusal to do evil, but an active willingness to obey God in many daring ways.

Righteousness requires us to *launch* out, not *hide* out.

~DECEMBER 1~
EXAMINING OUR BELIEFS

"I urge you, therefore, brethren, by the mercies of God, to present your bodies as a living and holy sacrifice, acceptable to God, which is your spiritual service of worship. And do not be conformed to this world, but be transformed by the renewing of your mind, that you may prove what the will of God is, that which is good and acceptable and perfect." Romans 12:1-2 (NASB)

Our beliefs form the roadways of our lives. Most of what we do and how we act are a direct result of what we really *believe*. We might *say* we believe a certain thing or *desire* to believe a certain way, but the bottom line decisions we make and the places we choose to set our feet down stem directly from what we most strongly believe. I say "most strongly" because beliefs are not necessarily all-or-nothing things. There is factual information that is substantially provable that we should not classify, for these purposes, as "beliefs," such as how many degrees a right angle contains, and how many feet make up a mile, but in areas concerning empirical truth, our beliefs are, more often than not, measurable. We call what we *believe* the things that we have more reason to think are true than not to, in other words, what we are more than fifty percent convinced is true. The more we believe a thing, the more it becomes a part of the response mechanism that causes us to live in a certain way.

This is important for us to realize because we will need to be honest with ourselves and those whom we are trying to win for Christ in order for good and healthy growth to happen. Our dilemma is that we are commanded in the scriptures to cleave to certain beliefs and to disdain others, but we have learned from experience that we cannot directly, by our own efforts, change our beliefs. If we cannot change our beliefs, we cannot change our character.

The good news is that we can effect these changes *indirectly* if we desire to. This is what Paul means here by transforming our minds and in 2 Corinthians 10:4-5 by "demolish[ing] arguments and every pretension that sets itself up against the knowledge of God" and taking "every thought captive to make it obedient to Christ." It is also why he tells us this in Philippians: "...whatever is true, whatever is noble, whatever is right, whatever is pure, whatever is lovely, whatever is admirable— if anything is excellent or praiseworthy— think about such things." While it is true that these things listed are subjective matters, if we believe more than fifty percent that the Bible is true and inspired by God, studying it and thinking about it regularly and consistently positions us to strengthen our beliefs and therefore change our behavior and thus our character. 1 When Jesus said in Matthew 12:34 "Out of the overflow of the heart, the mouth speaks," He wasn't issuing a statement of eternal doom upon his hearers; He was helping them to understand their great need to get on with the business of changing their hearts by way of changing their minds.

In the same way, we should remember when evangelizing others, that what they *presently* believe is not as crucial as what they *desire* to believe. It gives us an insight to what Jesus meant when He spoke of mustard-seed faith and a little bit of yeast. A little can become a lot; small belief can be grown into huge, life-changing belief.

~DECEMBER 2~
THE VAST EXPANSE OF A LIFE

"He has filled the hungry with good things but has sent the rich away empty." Luke 1:53

"For you know that it was not with perishable things such as silver or gold that you were redeemed from the empty way of life handed down to you from your fore-fathers but with the precious blood of Christ, a lamb without blemish or defect." 1 Peter 1:18

"This day I call heaven and earth as witnesses against you, that I have set before you life and death, blessings and curses. Now choose life, so that you and your children may live and that you may love the Lord your God, listen to His voice, and hold fast to Him. For the Lord is your life, and He will give you many years in the land He swore to give to your fathers, Abraham, Isaac, and Jacob." Deuteronomy 19-20

A life is a terribly big thing to fill without allowing God to give it meaning.

A big house with a lone survivor is so sad. When one loses a spouse, a big house suddenly gets so much bigger. Where there was once quiet conversation, hearty laughter, shared meals, a head on the other pillow, now there is a deafening silence and smothering emptiness. All the insulation seems to have melted away, and life just seeps through the walls. The memories may be sweet and many, but memories aren't enough to shut out the echoes of lone footfalls on the suddenly hard, cold floors.

Lives without Christ as their focus and hope are like these big, empty, lonely houses. This life is all we have right now, and though many speak of its fleet feet, to others it is just one long, drawn-out string of empty hours after another, inter-rupted only by a few hours of sleep's unconsciousness and distracted only by some kind of livelihood that may or may not ease the soul. Even if it does, she knows that it will be there only for a season. A time is coming when whatever she has found to do with her hands and mind will come to a close, and she will have to face the winding down of her life.

Peter speaks of "this empty way of life." Doomed to the ways of this world, "empty" could be a mild way of describing life. Most tend to feel pity for those who are materially destitute. We have organizations and funds to help these who are obviously lacking the basics needed for physical survival, but the destitution of a soul is far more pitiful. Trying to maintain relationships without the salt of mercy, forbearance, and forgiveness, and frantically searching for some kind of meaning to connect the days and years that could answer the yawning questions about the afterlife eventually produces a hunger that no banquet can satisfy, a coldness and naked vulnerability that even the most palatial dwelling cannot fortify. The ever-deepening trenches of shallow routine and mind-numbing habit and the tragic dead-end roads of drug addiction and sexual promiscuity that many take in an effort to escape such are all too common in lives devoid of the deep meaning and high motivation of living for the eternal Cause that throbs with a Christian's every heartbeat.

These thoughts have been bleak, but we must never forget, lest we lose our fervor to share Christ, that there is another way of life devoid of many of the character staples Christians think of as commonplace. Let us pray for hearts sensitive to spiritual misery.

~DECEMBER 3~
DINNER BELL

"Here I am! I stand at the door and knock. If anyone hears my voice and opens the door, I will come in and eat with him and he with me." Revelation 3:20

"The kingdom of heaven is like a king who prepared a wedding banquet for his son." Matthew 22:2

"A certain man was preparing a great banquet and invited many guests. At the time of this banquet, he sent out his servant to tell those who had been invited, 'Come, for everything is now ready.'" Luke 14:16-17

"For the Lord Himself will come down from heaven, with a loud command, with the voice of the archangel and with the trumpet call of God, and the dead in Christ will rise first. After that, we who are still alive and are left will be caught up together to meet the Lord in the air. And so we will all be with the Lord forever." 1 Thessalonians 4:16-18

Glorious, outrageous anticipation
Like nothing ever before —
Like suddenly beholding from your window
A king approaching your door.
In heart-swelling, standing-on-tiptoe excitement,
I ready my eyes for the Light.

> My second wind kicks in, for I'm certain
> I'm almost done with this fight.
> A bud about to burst open;
> The sun about to rise.
> But, oh, how can such compare to This,
> Something surpassing the skies?
> So…rest up for the Celebration,
> Or just stand in the yard facing east
> All night and all day looking up to the clouds
> With my napkin tucked in for the Feast?

Our worries about tomorrow or next week will suddenly be obsolete. Whether we were able to pass the test or lose the weight will no longer matter, and the acne and cellulite will cease to threaten us with their shame. But whether we ever learned to forgive will matter more than ever and will haunt us as we stand in the revealing searchlight of the Lamb of God. Some sweet day that even Jesus doesn't know yet, it will happen. It could be ten minutes from now. "In the twinkling of an eye" we will be changed, for Jesus will have come, and our time in this place will be over.

~DECEMBER 4~
BEYOND GOOD WORKS

"Whoever believes in the Son has eternal life, but whoever rejects the Son will not see life, for God's wrath remains on him." John 3:36

Motives are so important. Let me qualify: I believe that getting people to begin attending worship services with a body of believers is worth doing, whatever the motive of reluctant worshippers. Just getting them in our midst could destroy a lot of misconceptions and allow their motives to change drastically. However, for believers desiring continual growth in the life of Christ, a failure to examine our motives closely and regularly can cripple not just ourselves, but those who are watching us and wondering if there is a real Lord behind everything we do.

Doing the right things for the wrong reasons might not be a purposeful or even a conscious thing; in fact, we could go right on living this way for years if we don't realize how powerful a tool it is of our enemy, Satan. Acts 8 tells the story of a new Christian named Simon, who for a living, performed magic. After Simon's baptism, he observed that the apostles could impart strong measures of the Holy Spirit by the laying on of their hands. In his excitement, he offered them money to buy this skill, just as he had no doubt done for years in his secular job. The apostles rebuked him sharply and prayed for his deliverance for having his heart in the wrong place. Jesus warned against disfiguring our faces when fasting and making ourselves a spectacle when praying in order to win the praise of mere mortals rather than offering devotion to God. In fact, the ones Jesus rebuked the most harshly and most often were the Pharisees, who were hyper-diligent about obeying the law but either out of touch with or indifferent to their rotting hearts hidden inside. He called them "whitewashed tombs which look beautiful on the outside but on the inside are full of dead men's bones and everything unclean" (Matthew 23:27). I am not suggesting that all misplaced motives are of such an evil degree as this, but there is a danger of escalation once we let a thing go unchecked. (We really do get better and better at those things we practice.) But it is good for us to ask ourselves if we might be interested more in directing others' attention to what good Christians *we* are than to how good and powerful our *God* is.

Another way we might be affected by this problem is with our non-Christian friends or acquaintances. We might be tempted to believe that unbelievers who are model citizens and join humanitarian forces and give generously to socially constructive causes are just as pleasing to God as Christians. This is such a dangerous error because it allows for false security. If we think someone is "good enough," we will turn our evangelistic efforts elsewhere, when in truth we may have been placed in this person's path "for such a time as this." "No one comes to the Father except through Me," Jesus assures us in John 14:6. Good works are simply not enough. They might relieve the world of some badness, but they have no effect upon the afterlife of the soul.

"When they arrived, Samuel saw Eliab and thought, 'Surely the Lord's anointed stands here before the Lord.' But the Lord said to Samuel, 'Do not consider his appearance or height, for I have rejected him. The Lord does not look at the things man looks at. Man looks at the outward appearance, but the Lord looks at the heart.'" 1 Samuel 16:6-7

~DECEMBER 5~
BEING TRAINED BY IT

"God disciplines us for our good, that we may share in his holiness. No discipline seems pleasant at the time, but painful. Later on, however, it produces a harvest of righteousness and peace for those who have been trained by it." Hebrews 12:12-11

Joni Eareckson Tada is one of my favorite devotional writers. This lady became a quadriplegic after a diving accident as a teenager. After a bout with depression and some hard struggles with God, she turned her life over to Him utterly and as a result has encouraged millions with her testimonies about His goodness.

In telling about some of the terrible pain that comes to her neck and shoulders as a result of so much of the rest of her body's paralysis, she described how her physical therapist works to stretch and knead her muscles, sometimes using what she calls "the torture tool."

> "When she first started using the torture tool, I hated it. It felt as though my muscles were being ripped away from their tendons. After many sessions, however, I have learned that it was that very tool that made the biggest difference in my pain. It hurts a lot, but it hurts real good." [2]

There are torture tools in our lives too, and if we think back, we probably can remember responding to them in various ways. When we were spiritually unaware, we might have seen them as accidents of fate or as someone else's fault. As a consequence, we learned nothing valuable from them, aside from, perhaps, not to touch the same hot stove again or stay up too late on the night before an exam. When we were spiritually immature, we might have viewed times of suffering as a way a spiteful God could get back at us for something we thought we had gotten away with. As a result, we might have been angry at Him, believing Him to be narrow-minded and heartless. Or we might have been scared of Him because we felt no way of appeasing Him. We might have wanted to ignore or deny His existence, believing He was not the type to give second chances. But now that we have gone further down the road with Him, we know better. Now we know that the way to better days is *to be trained* by our suffering.

Our "torture tools" may indeed be directly from God, or they might be of our own making, in spite of God. But either way, when we lay ourselves and our pain at His feet, taking up His Word and praying with the aid of His Spirit, we can arise and move forward knowing with confidence that He can use these hurts to bring a brighter, even delightful, relief that we would never have known without them.

Joni has leaned to give thanks for her infirmities because she knows that God has used her in uniquely wonderful ways. (Wonderful: full of wonder!) She knows that what some people need most of all is someone with skin on to *show them how* to do this hard thing.

Offer your pain to God's glory. Yield yourself up into His hands. He who delivered His Son from the cross to glory has promised to do the same for us.

"Those who suffer according to God's will should commit themselves to their faithful Creator and continue to do good." 1 Peter 4:19

~DECEMBER 6~
THE FRUIT THAT EATS US

"And the Lord God commanded the man, 'You are free to eat from any tree in the garden, but you must not eat from the tree of the knowledge of good and evil, for when you eat of it, you will surely die." Genesis 2:15-17

From such a distant perspective, both geographically and historically, it doesn't seem like such a difficult thing to do—eat everything in the garden but this *one* thing. But the serpent was crafty, and they succumbed to curiosity and/or greed. The death they died—that of their innocence, of their blissful walking with God "in the cool of the day"—has been visited upon us all. We lost our Garden, at least for the space of our lifetimes on this earth. As a result of that transgression brought on by their alliance with Satan, everything is a lot harder than it had to be. We walk through a minefield knowing that it is only a matter of time until something else blows up in our faces. Oh, we are spared the worst of it, for sure. God saw to it that we don't have to live this way forever. He has paid a huge price to ensure us the availability of Reunion with Him when we finish the race that is marked out for us.

It is my hope that today's thoughts will not hit you right between the eyes, but sadly, some of us know all too well that the apple doesn't fall too far from the tree. Certainly it is true that "if anyone is in Christ is a new creation; the old has gone, the new has come!" (2 Corinthians 5:17) However, just as Christ did, all of us who follow Him must suffer through temptations, and Satan finds most of his ammunition in what he knows of our life before Christ. The Bible never pulls any punches about Satan's ravenous appetite.

As I recently shared some stories from my past with a friend, I realized that some of the things I learned at a very early age have found ways to haunt me even in the thick of my craving to be a true follower of Jesus. Woven throughout the fabric of my victories and growth in the Lord, I can trace strands of that old, familiar color and texture mixed in. Granted, these few do not significantly define the overall pattern, and those without a trained eye might never even notice what the Lord and I know to be a defect in the garment. But once upon a time, I ate of the knowledge of good and evil, and as a result of learning some things God didn't plan for me to learn, there are some recurring struggles, some lingering trials that I shouldn't have. Way back there, I decided I needed to know some things about which God wanted me to remain ignorant. I traded off some innocence for some emotional experiences— a mess of pottage, thirty pieces of silver. Certainly God can use my mistakes for His glory and bless me in a myriad of other ways, but I know that I have missed some of the fullness of this life He would like for me to have had. Just as Eve's eating hurled tragic ramifications upon the whole world, ours can cast terrible shadows over our whole lives.

Beware of entering into situations God has plainly forbidden. Do not be fooled by believing there are extenuating circumstances that make your case the exception to the rule. There is some dangerous knowledge you can never unlearn.

~DECEMBER 7~
SURPRISE VISITS

"For the Lord himself will come down from heaven with a loud command, with the voice of the archangel and with the trumpet call of God, and the dead in

Christ will rise first. After that, we who are still alive and are left will be caught up together with them in the clouds to meet the Lord in the air." 1 Thessalonians 4:16-17

"Listen, I tell you a mystery: We will not all sleep, but we will all be changed— in a flash, in the twinkling of an eye, at the last trumpet. For the trumpet will sound, the dead will be raised imperishable, and we will be changed." 1 Corinthians 15:51-52

Hardly an American can go through this day without recalling what happened that Sunday morning at Pearl Harbor back in 1941. In the midst of a time when Americans on both sides of the sea were buying Christmas trees and preparing another year to welcome the Christ child, some unfriendly visitors showed up unexpectedly in the skies above Pearl Harbor. Taken by surprise, many Americans were killed in a matter of a few hours. The problem was not that our Armed Forces didn't know we had enemies; it wasn't even that we were militarily inferior. We had the knowledge we needed, and we had the potential of saving ourselves; we were just *unprepared* for such a cataclysmic attack that particular day. *We were simply, but tragically, caught off guard.*

Recently 82% of the Americans polled in a George Barna survey professed to believe that the Bible is the Word of God. That sounds like wonderful news until you hear the second half: only 41% could name even *one* of the four gospels. Saying we believe when we do nothing to act upon those beliefs reveals one of two problems: (1.) We have become accustomed to thinking and saying that we believe without introspection or study. Since we almost always act upon our strongest beliefs, it could be that some other belief has sneaked in to eclipse what we thought was strong enough to last with no tending; (2.) or, we have forgotten that we are accountable not just for believing *in* God, but actually *believing* God so that we take Him at His Word. It's a safe bet that those who couldn't name more than one of the gospels probably couldn't tell you what the Bible says about what will happen at the second coming of Christ either.

Jesus knew that the waiting would take its toll on us, so he taught several parables of warning. He told about a successful farmer who, because his focus became his wealth, determined to build a big barn and rest securely in his plenty for many years. But an unexpected visitor showed up at his house that very night. The visitor was death. He described some good servants who stayed up to wait for their master to return from a wedding banquet, an owner of a house who was not watching when a thief broke in, a wicked servant who, because he thought his master would be a long time returning, beat the other servants and got drunk, only to get caught. He also used images of ten virgins and their oil lamps, three servants left in charge of their master's money, and the dividing of the sheep and the goats to point out the necessity of readiness for that Final Day.

Let us live with a sense of urgency. Let us start early and stay up late to be sure our bags are packed. Let us strive to see and to love others as Christ does. Let us throw out life lines and store up treasures in Heaven. A Visitor is due anytime now.

~DECEMBER 8~
YOUNG RESCUERS

Don't let anyone look down on you because you are young, but set an example for the believers in speech, in life, in love, in faith, and in purity." 1 Timothy 4:12

I couldn't fully grasp it then, but the human paradox and heavenly providence of our friendship is clear to me now from this distance. Though plagued with the conflicts and dysfunction that accompany bitter divorces, I was somewhat financially privileged growing up in junior high school. From kindergarten, I easily fit in with other spoiled kids of privilege in my small town and learned (and taught) habits of fickleness, snobbery, even cruelty in peer relationships. I shudder at the thought that I could have so easily continued down this evil path, venturing further and further into the darkness. If it hadn't been for Paula, there's no telling what might have become of me.

She was a bit of an oddity to me and my group. She was unlike us in so many ways: she was a country girl, her daddy was dead, and her mother worked hard to raise her and her five siblings in a small house way out in the country. She even rode a school bus. She was pretty, so she was not a total outcast, and if we were allowed to invite more than a few to our birthday parties, she got to be high on the list of "extras." She was quiet and smart, always had her homework, never cheated in school, was kind to everyone, and unlike others who didn't "qualify," Paula never seemed to mind being kept out of the inner circle. *All of us* went to church, but she also studied her Bible regularly and seriously. Sometimes, in fourth grade, I would see it among her schoolbooks or on her desk during study hall.

As a result of some hard wake-up calls, I made the decision as a freshman in high school to step out of the circle. With the divorce of my parents and the marriage of my sister, I knew I needed a friend, and so, recalling all her admirable traits, I pursued Paula. And lo, the most unexpected thing happened! God created in us the sweetest and tightest of friendship bonds that took us not only through high school but through college, as roommates, as well. Because of life-long tendencies and a young and immature spirituality, I led Paula into a few shady areas, but because of her tender conscience and unflagging dedication to her Lord, whom she had known intimately from a very early age, the girl that I was— worldly, selfish, and spoiled— became acquainted with a Hope and Life and Light that I had never even imagined existed. There was an important moment a few years into our friendship when she had to speak some very hard truths to me, but because her confrontation was bathed in much study, prayer, and love, and because her track record had won my trust, this crucial guidance changed the very dangerous direction of my life. I am grateful beyond words for the holiness of her youth.

Paul wrote these words to his young friend Timothy, but they are words of wisdom for all of us. When God gives you the chance to influence the young, I hope that you will have a chance to introduce a Paula to a Jan (and pray very hard for the Paula!). I pray that if your idea of youth is that they are all shallow and selfish, you will be blessed with a mind and heart open to the possibilities of the power of God Almighty to raise up kids like Timothy and Paula.

~DECEMBER 9~
WINTER FIRE

"For God so loved the world that He gave His one and only Son that whoever believes in Him shall not perish but have eternal life." John 3:16

The shadows of winter swallow the sun that adorned the bright head of June.
December's demons dance their darkness and cape the harvest moon.
But you are with me even so; my hands in yours stay warm.
Alive in my soul burns the passionate hope of the Christmas Child who calmed the storm.

A sheet of ice looms ghostly ahead; the road is black with its danger,
Trying to hide its treacherous scheme to cloak our memory of the manger.
The winds keep howling their winter moan, then gust into a cry,
Hoping with their plaintive dirge to drown the lullaby.
But you are with me even so; my hands in yours stay warm.
Aglow in my heart burns the hot, constant spark of the Christmas Child who defies my storm.

Ice is forming on my windows; deadly crystals entice.
Sometimes the chill lures my tired will to be glazed by the hard, cold ice.
Then I remember Bethlehem's manger and the infant Messiah's first cries,
And the thaw that came over the world that night forms a warm-flowing joy in my eyes.
For, oh, you are with us even so! Immanuel strong and warm.
Born to be claimed, reborn to be named our undying peace through the storm.

Once long ago on some obscure calendar date Jesus Christ was born in Bethlehem, but He is reborn every day somewhere in hearts that were dark and afraid. Could He be waiting to return for us because some cold hearts we encounter each day are awaiting the spark of His Life that we carry but do not offer? Let's hasten His return by telling them!

~DECEMBER 10~
GRACE ON A DONKEY

"He was in the world and though the world was made through Him, the world did not recognize Him. He came to that which was His own, but His own did not receive Him. Yet to all who did receive Him, to those who believed in His name, He gave the right to become children of God..." John 1:10-12

I'm thinking about what Christmas means
On this tinseled December day,
Past the shepherds and wise men and mangery things;
Past the Baby who lay in the hay.
Our helpless hearts were so crowded with sin,
With a desperate need to be right
That though there was no room in Bethlehem's inn,
Earth still received Heaven that night.
And as precious as the thought of that infant might be,
There's something more rapturous still:
The Man who grew up to set us all free
From our stiff-necked, hell-bent will.
We can serve as one Body and not myriad factions—
Eyes for eyes and teeth for teeth—
Unchained from rash words and knee-jerk reactions,
Since He taught us of mercy's release.
Since He came on a donkey in the womb of a woman
To bleed out the Life God adored,
Unspeakable luxuries too costly for flesh,
Now flesh and blood can afford:
Receiving rejection and returning a smile;
Not always needing to win;
Turning cheeks and walking extra miles;
Letting others start over again.
Because He consented to be humble and poor
And came down to love face to face,
Humanity can know what our hearts were made for;
We, too, can appropriate grace.
Now the Baby has gone back to His Father
To prepare us a Home free from sin.
No manger but a mansion! We need not be bothered
Like He was in Bethlehem.

~DECEMBER 11~
FAITH ENCOURAGING FAITH

"These things I remember as I pour out my soul: how I used to go with the multitude, leading the procession to the House of God, with shouts of joy and thanksgiving among the festive throng. Why are you so downcast, O my soul? Why so disturbed within me? Put your hope in God, for I will yet praise him, my Savior and my God." Psalm 42:4- 5, 11; 43: 5

Almost everyone I talk to these days is waiting for something. My husband and I are waiting for our house to sell. We need out of this one and into a smaller, simpler one, but we can't go buying until we sell. Once we made the decision to sell, we spent a couple of bone-breaking weeks getting the house in condition to sell, put it into the hands of a capable realtor- friend, and now all we can do is wait. We have done all we can.

I have spent a lot of time praying during this waiting. But it struck me a few days ago that if *this* kind of waiting feels hard, how much harder must be the waiting many have endured and are enduring still. I have dear friends who are waiting for their children to return to God's path. Every morning they pray that this will be the day their prayers will be answered as they strain their eyes to catch in the distance a glimpse of their child making her way back home. Others I know are waiting for a good report from the doctor that the tumor is benign or the cancer is in remission. Still others are waiting, as they have done for years, for the blessed conception of a longed-for baby.

And then there are those I have known who waited silently but desperately for things to get better: for their income to exceed their output for just a few consecutive months so that they could get caught up with their creditors; for an anger-plagued loved one to *mean* it this time so that the violence could finally subside in her home; for the pain at last to abate; for the love at last to begin; for the demon of addiction to cease its gnawing, persistent demands for more and more at greater and greater expense to body and soul. Most of us have known some who *were* waiting but are waiting no more. Hope grew smaller and smaller on the horizon until finally one day they could see it no longer, and so they chose not to go on living this life. If only their horizon had not been drawn so close to the earth! If only their memories could have been stirred up and their vision extended beyond this place and these mortals into another place where real Hope lives!

The psalmists knew about waiting. Things looked bleak and cheerless to them, too, as they ran for their lives against all odds and waited for a word from the Lord. But they knew the secret of waiting well: to keep their hope kindled so that it wouldn't die out before help arrived. Psalm after psalm shows us the pattern; they would resolutely recall the faithfulness of God, recite in specific detail times when God had delivered them, times when they had met Him in the sanctuary, had heard His voice clearly, had seen Him at work beyond the shadow of a doubt, thus confirming His omnipotence. They knew that if He was omnipotent then, He was omnipotent still. They had more reason to believe He was watching and would rescue in due time than not to believe it. And when I set my mind and heart to it, I know the same thing. As you wait, count your blessings. Honor Him who desires and deserves your trust with a calm and confident hope.

"I am still confident of this: I will see the goodness of the Lord in the land of the living. Wait for the Lord; be strong and take heart and wait for the Lord." Psalm 27:13-14

~DECEMBER 12~
CHRISTMAS APPLES

"Then they opened their treasures and presented Him with gifts of gold and of incense and of myrrh." Matthew 2:11

I've always thought the greatest gift is words. You can quit eating macaroni and cheese four times a week in order to save for an extravagant something for everyone on your list. I really *do* believe in extravagant giving, but I know that the things bought with the big dollar often fail to afford the desired heart-result without first having established what we're trying to *say* in giving them.

Proverbs 25:11 says, "A word aptly spoken is like apples of gold in settings of silver." If words are the deepest, most definitive messengers, this Proverb provokes some pretty deep thought: Someone might argue that if words are so foundational, why do writers strive for the perfect metaphor to turn the abstract into the concrete, the words into pictures? Why do they take a bland statement of fact and embellish it with imagery until it, like a caterpillar to a butterfly, is transformed into a poetic work of art? Good points, but finish the thought. When a student of the poem discovers the pictures, the teacher then asks him to communicate his discoveries in *words*. When the beloved reads the sonnet, her mind takes the pictures and translates them back into *words* of her own: "How thrilling that he loves me this much!"— which was the author's truest and most basic motivation for writing the sonnet. He has succeeded in communicating the feelings in his heart via word pictures to his beloved. He didn't really want to give her the ocean's constancy or the rose's fragrance; they were just the means to an end, a way to communicate the eternal and delightful aspects of his love so that she could *get* it and say, "How thrilling that he loves me this much!"

The goods we find inside the festively decorated boxes at Christmas were carefully chosen and paid for at the behest of some sentiment inside the buyer's heart that took her through the stores searching, finding, touching, inspecting, cocking her head in a visionary way to find out if it would send the right *message*. What we pull out of the packages and stockings at Christmas are no more and no less than tangible *messages*, reminders when seen, touched, smelled, worn, driven, or eaten, of someone's love, esteem, or appreciation for us. This is why we say, usually a little too casually and more, I fear, as a cliché than a conviction, "It's the thought that counts."

So, okay, even more basic than the words are the thoughts, the feelings. Yes, they are the real bottom line, but since none of us can read minds, God gave us a means of communicating them to others: words— *"words aptly spoken."*

~DECEMBER 13~
BEFORE IT'S TOO LATE

"...but let us encourage one another, and all the more as you see the Day approaching." Hebrews 10:25

This year is almost at an end. It has likely been dominated by a hectic cycle of working, eating, sleeping, and trying to grab some much needed rest and play in between. Before you say goodbye to this year, have you plainly and unmistakably honored those whose lives you thank God for each day?

Every one of us knows that the old saying, "Sticks and stones may break my bones, but words can never hurt me" is a fallacy. However, it is equally important for us to remember that *needed* words *never* spoken can be just as deadly. It's odd, but most of us are less conscientious about writing and speaking words of gratitude to those in our own households than to anyone else. Maybe because they've seen and heard us at our worst, as well as at our Sunday, premeditated best, we fear that praising them would sound hypocritical. We might fear that they wouldn't believe we could really mean the kind, loving words when they have often heard our harsh, impatient ones. But communicating our appreciation for specific qualities of our loved ones is crucial. *Any* attempt is better than silence.

Ask God to help you focus in on those dear aspects that you would so painfully miss if these precious ones were lost to you, and then, if you feel less than adequately adept at communicating, pray for the right words.

Giving the words *in writing* is special for three good reasons: (1.) A letter is evidence that you were thinking of them when they were not right there in your face; it says "Out of sight is *not* out of mind!" (2.) Unlike words that spontaneously spew from your mouth and cannot be effectively taken back or amended, these words are deliberate and can be changed before they are given; therefore, the recipient can feel confident that they are not empty or spoken from some sort of undue pressure; (3.) These words are theirs to keep and read over and over again—the gift that keeps on giving.

If you must speak instead—if eyes and voice are crucial—make a special time and place for this *deliberate* message to be delivered so that your loved one knows that these are not casual words, but rather, like the offering you bring each Sunday, *this* is a *special* gift that you have purposed ahead of time in your heart.

~DECEMBER 14~
THE CRUCIAL ART OF GENTLE INQUISITION

"What do you think, Simon?" Matthew 17:25

"What do you think?" Matthew 21:28

Unfortunately, many who believe in the value of the gift of words and want to give them to those they love have no idea how. Words are the key that unlock a burdened soul, but sadly, many are still looking for that key or are fumbling madly at the lock. Sometimes that most valuable gift we can give to another is not our words but their own, and one of the best ways to help them to crack open a window and lend us a view inside is to become curious enough to ask them questions.

Curiosity teeters on the brink of nosiness, I suppose, but it springs from a refreshingly different and purer motivation. Asking questions of those we love and desire to know better is no more necessarily nosy than praying in public is necessarily Pharisaical. There can certainly be pure motives to both of these actions. The refusal to probe due to the fear of being misconstrued has stunted many potentially vibrant relationships.

We should *let* ourselves wonder about each other! What better way could there be to take our focus off ourselves than to look deeply at another and give the blessing of our curiosity? Isn't it gratifying when someone asks you a question personal enough that you *alone* know its answer? The person has had you on his mind; you were worth the trouble and time to be *pondered*.

Try giving your undivided attention to another, asking questions such as her favorite things—authors (and why?), memories (and why?), songs, movies, dreams, scriptures, people, (and why? Why? Why? Why?). These questions open the door to what makes a person tick, lifts her sails, puts spring in her step, or punctures his balloon.

Suddenly the cool discomfort of exhausting small talk learned by rote is behind us, and we are *inside* where warm conversation flows naturally between kindred spirits. The next time we talk, our starting place will be so much closer to the heart, for we have been entrusted with an inside view.

Jesus asked many questions of those He encountered. A surprising number of times, especially for One who already knew the answer, He asked, "What do you think?"

He wanted *inside*, and each of His questions was a knock on a door. We want inside too, and questioning words can prove that we care.

Go ahead and buy the gifts. Save up again next year to lavish those you love with things they would never allow themselves to buy. But don't think *these* replace what they *really* want. Plainly communicate your heart to those you love; then the material extravagances will be so much more than consolation prizes.

~DECEMBER 15~
EVERGREEN THROUGHOUT THE YEAR

"The people walking in darkness have seen a great light; on those living in the land of the shadow of death a light has dawned. You have enlarged the nation and increased their joy; they rejoice before you as people rejoice at the harvest...You have shattered the yoke that burdens them, the bar across their shoulders, the rod of their oppressor...For to us a child is born, to us a son is given." Isaiah 9:2-6

> *Tonight the year's red carpet rolls beneath the evergreen,*
> *And little eyes are savoring what older ones have seen*
> *Of the star above the stable tied on limbs with golden strings;*
> *Of dancing flashes of color in the snow-white angels' wings.*
> *The magic inextinguishable in spite of age or care*
> *Or troubles that without this season permeate the air*
> *Still fill the chamber so reserved for frolic and frost and bells*
> *And flaunts the dream before us, 'til we're caught within its spell,*
> *Finding bright, new selves within, beribboned by the season,*
> *With tinsel of good cheer and comfort, transcending any reason;*
> *Forgetting for the moment confining earthly chains,*
> *But kept aloft and soaring on the carolers' refrains.*
> *Despair is dead, and the awful haunts are for awhile unseen,*
> *Encircled yet another year by wreaths of evergreen.*

Christians are the ones whose job it is to show a dark, lost world that Christmas is not just for one season. We are to be the evergreen message that wafts its fragrance in mid-May. We are the tinsel that shines in July and September, the candles that glow with hope's lovely warmth in February and the Fourth of July just as certainly as in December.

If it's never occurred to you that it's your job, take hold of the notion and claim it as truth. If you've never been able to do it before, believe that next year you can. A world is dying from our lack of awareness. Let us pay attention and stay evergreen throughout the year with the message of the Child that was born to shatter our yokes.

~DECEMBER 16~
SOOTHING DOUBTFUL MINDS:
THE INTERNAL EVIDENCE

"If your law had not been my delight, I would have perished in my affliction." Psalm 119:92

Is the Bible really the Word of God? There is much internal evidence that it is, and believers take comfort in coming across from time to time or even memorizing scriptures like these:

- "All Scripture is God-breathed and is useful for teaching, rebuking, correcting and training in righteousness, so that the man of God may be thoroughly equipped for every good work." 2 Timothy 3:16
- "Above all you must understand that no prophecy of Scripture came about by the prophet's own interpretation. For prophecy never had its origin in the will of man, but men spoke from God as they were carried along by the Holy Spirit." 2 Peter 1:20-21
- "For the Word of God is living and active. Sharper than any double-edged sword, it penetrates even to dividing soul and spirit, joints and marrow; it judges the thoughts and attitudes of the heart." Hebrews 4:12
- "Do your best to present yourself to God as one approved, a workman who does not need to be ashamed and who correctly handles the word of truth." 2 Timothy 2:15

In fact, the Old Testament alone claims 3008 times to be the Word of God.

However, to someone who does not yet believe, using the Bible's own words to prove that it is inspired is circular logic. If this is all we can offer to the world, we have little hope in making a case for them to learn about and become followers of our Lord and Savior. Try to take a good, objective look at this book that Americans make our best seller year after year in comparison with all other books. There is a bounty of external evidence we should make ourselves familiar with if we are to "contend for the faith" as Jude encourages us to do.

~DECEMBER 17~
SOOTHING DOUBTFUL MINDS:
THE EXTERNAL EVIDENCE

"I felt I had to write and urge you to contend for the faith that was once and for all entrusted to the saints...Be merciful to those who doubt; snatch others from the fire and save them." Jude 3, 23

There is much external evidence that the Bible is God's inspired Word. Here is a small sampling.

- **There is an inexplicable and undeniable *unity* in the scriptures.**
40 different people on 3 different continents wrote 66 different books spanning over 1500 years in 3 different languages. And this book is not an anthology, or collection of random and disconnected stories; all of these writings came together to be one united story. It is unified in *structure*; the Old Testament is the New Testament concealed, and the New Testament is the Old Testament revealed. (The

Bible calls the Old Testament a "schoolmaster" for the New.) There is also a phenomenal unity of *focus*: everything centers on Jesus Christ. It is either pointing forward to Him, following His life, death, and resurrection, or again looking forward to His final return.

- **Nothing less than divine inspiration could have been so perfectly** *prophetic.*

In order for prophecy to be authentic, it must fit several criteria: The prophecy must be made far enough ahead of the actual fulfillment so as not to have been humanly possible to be able to reasonably predict or manipulate; the prophecies must be specific; the fulfillment must be exact.

Here are just a few fulfilled prophecies that will whet your appetite to start your own research:

1. *Genesis 15 predicted long before it happened that Israel would go into captivity in Egypt for four hundred years.*
2. *Zephaniah predicted that Israel would go into Babylonian captivity for seventy years.*
3. *Zephaniah also predicted the destruction of Nineveh.*
4. *Isaiah predicted the destruction of Babylon.*
5. *Isaiah and Zechariah predicted that the Messiah would enter Jerusalem on a donkey.*
6. *Micah (chapter 5), sometime between 750 and 686 B.C., predicted that the Messiah would come out of Bethlehem.*
7. *Isaiah (chapter 9) foretold that the Messiah would come from the house of David and minister to Galilee.*
8. *In 615 B.C., Nahum (3:17) predicted that Nineveh officials, because of their unending cruelty, would disappear without a trace. Only as late as 1845 were archaeologists finally able to uncover any trace of that entire buried city.*

We are not powerless. God has not abandoned us to weakness. Rather than slink away in defeat and leave a soul without hope of a sure anchor, we should open our mouths and help them find the Answer their hearts desire and their souls require.

~DECEMBER 18~
TELLING THE TRUTH AT CHRISTMAS

"I bring you good news of great joy that will be for all the people. Today in the town of David a Savior has been born to you; He is Christ the Lord. This will be a sign to you: you will find the baby wrapped in cloths and lying in a manger. Suddenly a company of the heavenly host appeared with the angel, praising God

and saying, 'Glory to God in the highest and on earth peace to men on whom his favor rests." Luke 2:10-14

Angel hair and peppermint and dreams of snowy wonder
Frolic through December's frosty air.
Mistletoe entreats a kiss, and windows mirror amber
From the candles that are melting into Christmas.
A fire crackles in the den and draws us all together.
Boys of gingerbread adorn the tree.
Anxious fingers fashion treasures that heap beneath the boughs,
And Baby Jesus slumbers on the mantle.
Eager eyes of every age and hearts of all persuasions
Ignite and shine like downtown's celebration.
Silent night, holy night; the moon and stars are magic.
The darkness can't survive the season's glory.

Deuteronomy 6 reminded the Jews of how crucial it was to tell their children the stories about God's deliverance of their forefathers. They were to impress upon them the Truth of Truths: "Your God is the Real God, the Only God. He is the almighty and everlasting Deliverer and Judge. Hear ye Him above all others, above all else." They were to tell them when they walked and sat at home; they were to write it on the doorposts and on their foreheads. God knew that otherwise, lies would sneak in— fads of the day and mores of the culture— that would clamor noisily above the long ago, faraway Truth, and their children would believe these lies and lose their way. It wouldn't take many generations until they were completely lost again, as their forefathers, in yet another wilderness.

Is our story any less crucial? Can we afford to let the materialism and the myths of this season outshout Jesus? Heaven forbid that we waste this wonderful opportunity to tell them what all this holiday hubbub is *really* all about.

~DECEMBER 19~
FAMILY HEIRLOOM

"He who fears the Lord has a secure fortress, and for his children it will be a refuge...
The righteous man leads a blameless life; blessed are his children after him."
Proverbs 14:26; 20:7

"Do as I say, not as I do!" Depending on the circumstance, this admonition from a parent to a child can be either humorous or seriously destructive. Wise and loving parents realize that we do not need to have done *everything* right in order to teach our kids to do right. Love demands that we teach them not only what we *correctly and consistently* model but also what, due to our foolishness or weakness, we have *failed* to model. Some might call this hypocrisy, but hypocrisy requires that the one doing the preaching has no desire or intention of practicing the same. The very nature and foundation of hypocrisy is deceit. Allowing our children to fall into the same pit we fell into just because of our own poor record would be the height of folly. On the contrary, we must be even more careful to teach from our mistakes, lest they fail to bring about the growth they have the power to and thus fall into the devil's hands to wreak destruction, rather than wisdom, upon yet another generation.

However, the best case scenario is that we model well what we hope for our children. They learn more from the sermons they both hear and see than they do from those they hear only. Thereby, we pass down the benefit of both our deeds and our words— a double testimony. Solomon says the fear of the Lord provides not only a "secure fortress" for its possessor, but a "refuge" for his children, that the righteousness of the parents will bless his children. Maybe this is as simplistic as meaning that they will be good parents to their children, but perhaps the "after him" means that even after the parents are gone, the children will continue the life that was modeled for them and thus be blessed.

All this makes me think of what I hear every time I fly on a commercial airplane. "If you are with a child, be sure that you affix your own oxygen mask before you help your child with his." This is in no way judging the parent as a higher priority than the child. It's just plain horse sense: if you run out of air before you can get your child's mask on, you could likely kill both yourself and your child. A misplaced sense of selflessness here could be deadly.

And so it is with the way we pass on our Christian discipleship. We have so much more to give than words alone. Often, if our actions blatantly contradict our words, the words are destructively empty, falling on not just deaf ears, but sometimes rebellious ones. Whether you are a parent or not, someone is or will be watching you and wondering if you could be one she could follow in order to find the footsteps of Jesus.

Study diligently to grow wise, then, not just to be secure in your own fortress, not just to receive blessed heavenly oxygen, but for the safe haven and the life-giving air someone traveling behind you will need.

~DECEMBER 20~
GIFT BY STARLIGHT

"After Jesus was born in Bethlehem in Judea, during the time of King Herod, Magi from the east came to Jerusalem and asked, "Where is the one who has been born king of the Jews? We saw His star in the east and have come to worship Him...Then they opened their treasures and presented Him with gifts of gold and of incense and of myrrh..." Matthew 2:1-2, 11

If I were a wise man when you were a baby, I want you to know,
dearest Lord of my soul,

*I would have found a way to the town 'neath that star of silver to your
manger of gold.*
*As the others packed up their camels with spices and gold all befitting
Immanuel, the King,*
*My mind would be spinning the words just beginning to capture the
art I would fashion to bring.*
*Oh, lyrics melodious, celestial I'd choose each night 'neath the Star
by a flickering flame—*
*Unsurpassed flowing of imagery glowing for the longed-after infant
bearing Heaven's own Name.*
*Not even a minute would it take me to choose the gift I would wrap up
to give you back then,*
*For even now I suppose every phrase I compose and entrust with
trembling into substitute hands*
*Is a wish of a foolish and misguided plan of a blind and aimless
schemer.*
*For how could they know how deep these words go? Like a dream
only real to the dreamer.*
*Tonight as my soul spun its best similes and my phrases danced
glorious rhythms to you,*
*I finally discovered you alone are the lover with the heart my lyrics
relentlessly pursue.*
*I am no wise man, and You are no baby, and I can't hold you yet,
though I follow your Star.*
*Every day brings me nearer to that moment so dear when at last I
extol you for all that you are.*
*So since Heaven is too holy for these trappings of earth, and we can't
take these mortal things on it,*
*I'll give up fantasizing and begin memorizing my heart laden down
with love sonnets.*

However you do it best, *worship* Him this Christmas! Do it with singing, do it with poetry, do it with cooking, do it with rolling on the floor with your kids and grandkids. Most of all, do it with *heart*. Throw all you have and are behind what you do. Worship the Gift that is Jesus!

~DECEMBER 21~
COUNTING THE COST:
THE SLEEPING DOGS HE WON'T LET LIE

"Be perfect, therefore, as your heavenly Father is perfect." Matthew 6:18

These words end a description Jesus is giving on how to love perfectly, or supernaturally, rather than imperfectly, or naturally. He makes no bones about expecting His listeners to aim for a heart to love their enemies and pray for their persecutors, to love those who do not love them and to *wait* for the reward for loving rather than to have to have it now.

Jesus seems to want us to know from the outset what being his disciple really will mean, so He comes right out and tells us. It will mean being perfect. Of course alone we can never do it, but alone He never expects us to be if we are His. His high calling does not mean that He will not help us unless we do this thing right, but rather that being perfect is the only thing He *will* help us to be. He will consent to give us nothing less than this. Anything else we decide to become other than this will have to be done by our own means. His scholarship fund covers only that concerning itself with becoming perfect.

As children, when we got sick, we might have wished for nothing more than to be left alone in our beds to watch TV or read, but we usually got more than that. We got our throats swabbed and were given bad-tasting medicine and sometimes even shots. That was because our parents who loved us knew that in order for us to get well, more than watching television was called for. They knew that even though we wanted to swallow only ice cream, we must swallow medicine as well, if we were to get up and be healthy again. They could have "let sleeping dogs lie" and saved their money and the trouble of forcing us to swallow the bitter medicine and hold still to take the shot, but because they loved us and knew what was *best* for us, they gave us *more* than we asked for.

Unlike with our parents when we were sick, we don't *have* to take this medicine or give into the full treatment; we *can* walk away from Jesus, rejecting His prescription. But as long as we stay *with* Him, He will push us toward perfection. He will knock on different doors and want inside different rooms until He is allowed inside our entire house. He is kind and gracious and will not knock on every door at the same time, or else our houses would all collapse. But He will not move into one room and stay either.

This is good news for us. Just as we would not want to stay sick in bed forever as children, we don't want to be stunted in our growth now. Just as our parents visualized how we would feel when our health returned and so went to the trouble to give us the full treatment, Jesus can see what we cannot see— He visualizes what we are to *become*. He sees the beauty we cannot imagine from our vantage point, so He bids us to trust Him to lead us there. I don't just mean Heaven; I mean here in this life. We may not trip through this life lightly and gleefully, but if we continue to place ourselves in His care, we will be healthy in a way we could never imagine when we were trying to kick the needle out of His hand or pursing our lips tightly against the medicine. Let us ask Him to help us desire to be perfect in Him, even if the job is not finished until we reach Heaven.

~DECEMBER 22~
GRACE WARRIORS

"When [Saul] came to Jerusalem, he tried to join the disciples, but they were all afraid of him, not believing that he really was a disciple. But Barnabas took him and brought him to the apostles." Acts 9:26-27

Barnabas was so called by the disciples because of his quality of abounding encouragement. Although everybody else was skeptical about Saul, known far and wide for his history of executing Christians, Barnabas was willing to take a chance on his sincerity. Because one of such honorable reputation was willing to stand up and vouch for Saul's authenticity, he was able to become Paul, the apostle and great missionary who evangelized much of Europe and Asia Minor, as well as giving us so much of the New Testament.

Our newest grandson, Eli, reminds me very much of Barnabas, the "Son of Encouragement." When anyone speaks to this baby, his face lights up like a Christmas tree. With no background check whatsoever, each and every stranger who reaches to take him from his mother's arms is immediately endorsed by Eli's welcoming countenance. He has an unusually trusting spirit which is willing to give everyone the benefit of the doubt. As he grows, we will have to teach him at least a little bit of discretionary judgment, of course, but I pray that he will never outgrow the ability to give folks the benefit of the doubt.

Our easy access to so much disturbing news, with the mass media at our fingertips, makes us easy targets for skepticism. And with such widespread disregard for God, there is good reason to be wary about evil; certainly everything that looks and sounds like a sheep is not a sheep. But we must pray for the wisdom not to allow skepticism to *drive* our lives and to cause us to go through our days negatively motivated. God knows our limitations in the judgment of character, and He expects us to be reasonable about our assumptions. Just because some have proved to be charlatans and hypocrites, that is no excuse for making wholesale judgments and hasty generalizations. This is playing it *too* safe, and it should sound an alarm that perhaps we are more concerned about never again looking like a fool than about reaching everyone we possibly can for Christ.

Nourished and fertilized skepticism grows deadly fruits. It behooves each of us who tend toward skepticism to comb our brains for memories of times we so desperately needed someone to take a chance on *us*. Maybe our family name had preceded us infamously, or maybe we, ourselves, had strayed and come back. It takes honesty about our tendencies and much prayer to overcome these tendencies, but if we commit them to Him, the God of peace will be faithful to sanctify us "through and through" (1 Thessalonians 5:23-24).

Rather than automatically assuming someone is going to be a waste of our time and money or break our heart, next time let us approach God's throne for wisdom and courage to be a grace warrior. None of us wants to discourage a Saul from growing into a Paul. Ask God to open your eyes this very day to an opportunity to reach out like Eli and be somebody's Barnabas.

~DECEMBER 23~
CHRISTMAS MEMORIES

"I thank my God every time I remember you." Philippians 1:3

My Dear Sister Judy,

Looking back, it was only a handful of seasons; in the scope of our lives, it was only a few, but it seemed like scores of Christmases then, whose comings and goings would never end, when Mother would bring the Christmas tree in in colors no tree ever grew. Like cotton candy, more than a tree, flocked in blue, even pink-tinted snow, we'd deck it in fashionable "ice"covered lights, and when our picture window would fog up just right, 303 Tenaha would extinguish the night, and our proud eyes and hearts would glow.

I remember my Betsy-Wetsy doll; I remember your Tiny Tears. There were red and yellow cowboy boots, chemistry sets, and stocking loot, Roman candles, almonds, and Juicy Fruit, dependable, year after year.

And we could always depend on Mother to run from the pictures Daddy would click. Cousins came over, or we went there, anxious to see how each other fared, still in pajamas, but nobody cared— and there were log-sized peppermint sticks!

You played your piano or accordion, and Daddy made all of us sing. For this one day, at least, a ceasefire was called; no bombs could be dropped, no axes could fall. It was all for one, and one for all— a miracle only Christmas could bring.

It was magic for sure, and we couldn't wait for the season to work its charm. Duke Ellen and Janis would appear with their things; you'd play your records and compare diamond rings while we'd cuss and bust my new trampoline. Life was happy and safe and warm.

The family weather was unstable; in a flash it could turn ice-cold. And its fabric was fickle— burlap or cashmere—it was anyone's guess all the rest of the year. But when we pulled out the tinsel, we packed up the tears, and fashioned a tapestry of gold.

Some logs in that hearth we've resigned to the ages; some better as ashes than embers. But the way our parents made Christmas- oh man! Weren't they something? Wasn't it grand? Just Mother and Daddy, Judy, and Jan, and those precious Parker Decembers.

(To my little big sister, who alone can share these rare memories)

Remember these days?

Quick—before you get up and are swept into the season's bustle today—grab a pen and write some shared memories of a Christmas Past to someone you love!

~DECEMBER 24~
IN SKIN CALLED JESUS

"He was in the world, and though the world was made through Him, the world did not recognize Him. He came to that which was His own, but His own did not receive Him. Yet to all who received Him He gave the right to become children of God...The Word became flesh and lived for a while among us. We have seen His glory, the glory of the one and only Son who came from the Father, full of grace and glory...From the fullness of His grace we have all received one blessing after another." John 1:10-12, 14, 16

One day in skin called Jesus, the God of Heaven stepped out of the Book
To walk and talk and eat among us,
And let us feel His breath upon us—
To let us touch Him with our fingers of flesh,
And give us a closer look.

For He was the Word loosed from the pages, laughing and sweating, with dusty feet—
Wisely passionate and meekly glad,
The pride of His Father in humility clad,
From His seat in the Throne Room to the Place of the Skull
So that agony and ecstasy could meet.

Gritting His teeth, God withheld His hand from His Son now covered in sin—
And the man in skin called Jesus died—
And with Him the shame God could not abide.
His humanity had bought us eternity;
God lost so that we could win.

Think of it! What must it have been like for God to watch His perfect Son growing from year to year "in wisdom and stature" knowing that each day brought Him closer to the agonizing death which was the purpose of His life? No one but the Omniscient could have fathomed such foreboding agony; no one but the Omnipotent could have borne it. Ponder such love and live out your deep gratitude this Christmas and in the new year.

~DECEMBER 25~
JOHN 3:16: A MANGER SCENE

"While they were there the time came for the baby to be born, and she gave birth to her firstborn, a son. She wrapped Him in cloths and placed Him in a manger, because there was no room for them in the inn. And there were shepherds living out in the fields nearby, keeping watch over their flocks at night, An angel of the Lord appeared to them, and the glory of the Lord shone around them, and they were terrified. But the angel said to them, 'Do not be afraid. I bring you good news of great joy that will be for all the people. Today in the town of David a Savior has been born to you; He is Christ the Lord. This will be a sign to you: You will find a baby wrapped in cloths and lying in a manger." Luke 2:6-12

Humanity strutted in the shadow of Death
Pleased to be charmed and beguiled,
But the fragrance that mesmerized flesh reached Heaven
As the stench of creation defiled.

Out of the portals of purity
From a realm bathed in radiant light—
From out of the very heart of the Father
Into the bowels of night—

Was sent a Beacon to show us
A light that our spirits were losing;
Was cast as a Buoy to save us
From a torment of man's own choosing.

For God in His mercy so loved man in his sin
So foolishly dying in need—
Who doused each flicker of His image in us
With the chilling disgust of our greed

That He sent down His own Son to die at our hands,
A King from the pure Halls of Joy,
At unutterable cost—Oh, unthinkable loss!
To be Mary and Joseph's boy.

~DECEMBER 26~
GENERATIONAL SIN: THE CURSE AND THE RESCUE

"Therefore, just as sin entered the world through one man, and death through sin, and in this way death came to all men, and because all men sinned..." Romans 5:12

Thus begins one of the most frustrating sentences in the Bible to an English teacher who can find no peace within the confines of most sentence fragments. I suppose there was just no simple way to phrase such a historically-encompassing concept as Adam's bringing man's condemnation and Christ's bringing man's reconciliation.

Even though God makes abundantly clear (see Ezekiel 18) that He does not inflict upon us the punishment for our forefathers' sins, still we can be influenced *greatly* by the sin we "soak" in as we grow up in its midst. Generational sin can soak so deeply into our fabric that we might not even know that everyone *doesn't* think this way or act that way until we have already been stained by it for many years.

It was man, not God, who stepped out of the relationship God had planned. Because Adam and Eve ruined the perfect relationship God desired, we, too, are affected by sin's power.

"But God demonstrates His own love for us in this: While we were still sinners, Christ died for us. Since we have now been justified by His blood, how much more shall we be saved from God's wrath through Him? For if, while we were God's enemies, we were reconciled to Him through the death of His Son, how much more, having been reconciled, shall we be saved through His life! Not only is this so, but we also rejoice in God through our Lord Jesus Christ, through whom we have now received reconciliation." Romans 5:8-11

Even though we are the ones who stepped out of the relationship, God took the initiative to resolve the ruined relationship. He did this by bringing to us a new Adam who, though He could have chosen to be disobedient, "...humbled himself and became obedient to death—even death on a cross" (Philippians 2:8). In the next chapter of Romans, we see the result of our rescue: "But now that you have been set free from sin, and have become slaves to God, the benefit you reap leads to holiness, and the result is eternal life" (Romans 6:22).

Becoming "slaves to God" turns us into rescuers also! Now we follow our Rabbi in throwing out the lifeline. And first we throw it to our children and, as a result, to our grandchildren and their grandchildren. Just as it was with Christ's life, how much *more* will they be saved through our reconciled lives? Generational sin loses its power when we are rescued to become rescuers!

~DECEMBER 27~
SPIRITUAL BAIT

"When a man's ways are pleasing to the Lord, He makes even his enemies live at peace with him." Proverbs 16:7

Obviously there will be times when we will come upon against the forces of evil and must speak and act in defense of Truth in such a way that might offend others. At those crossroads we are bound to "obey God rather than men" as the apostles did. Some of their actions, like some of Jesus,' irked their opponents to the point of getting them thrown into jail and crucified. This is why Paul wrote in Romans 12:18, "*If it is possible,* as far as it depends upon you, live at peace with everyone." He knew that sometimes it would *not* be possible; it was not a whole-sale, unqualified command.

But this proverb speaks of God's desire for us to add light to areas of darkness, not just to areas that are already light. As appealing as it might sound sometimes, we cannot live our lives in monasteries; we were left here to minister to others, and for such we must be equipped. The Christian life is to be lived enthusiastically and articulately not just inside the walls of churches, where we blend with family, but out in the world's darkness. I must always endeavor to remember that, truly, the universe and all God's desires for it are not built around me. Psalm 139 convinces me that yes, He *knows* me and you intimately and wants to do a customized work in us for which we were "fearfully and wonderfully made." However, this work He is doing *in* us is not just *for* us but for those whose paths we will cross. God wants to work not just *in* us but *through* us.

One way we can equip ourselves to allow Him to do His work through us is to keep our prayer life and our penitence current. A slipshod prayer-life that waits for times of convenience or the right mood to befall us will not keep us up to date. We will not walk through our every day ready for His use. This randomness of devotion will effect in us a sense of insecurity about how to proceed when we encounter a lost soul on our path. What we need is confidence, not insecurity; we desperately need spiritual discernment, not worldly timidity that comes from unpreparedness. If we allow our penitence to lag, we hinder our prayers and limit our usefulness to our Master who left us here, not just to play but to be *used*, as we wait to be taken to Glory.

We are told in Hebrews 4:16 to "approach the throne of grace with confidence," and Philippians 4:6 encourages us in the same way: "...in everything, by prayer and petition, with thanksgiving, present your requests to God." Beth Moore, in a video I watched recently challenged my thinking in this area.[3] When you pray, do you ask God for favor in the hearts you will meet this day? Does this sound like a strange request? The scriptures back it up; we can and should ask this with confidence. Let's not be shy about asking Him to give us favor so that we can ultimately bring Him glory. If bringing eminence to Him rather than to ourselves is our motivation, we can pray with confidence that God will cause people to *like* us! In this way, we become spiritual bait. Paul did this on many occasions. Read Acts 17 to see him at his best.

Jesus tells us in John 15:8 to "bear much fruit." When we gain the trust and respect of others, we can more easily gain their ears and their hearts.

"Make every effort to live in peace with all men and to be holy; without holiness no one will see the Lord." Hebrews 12:14

~DECEMBER 28~
RAISING OUR EBENEZERS

"Then Samuel took a stone and set it up between Mizpah and Shen. He named it Ebenezer, saying, 'Thus far has the LORD helped us.'" 1 Samuel 7:12

Here Samuel, Israel's prophet, intervenes for his nation who is about to undergo an attack by the powerful Philistines. Samuel sets up an Ebenezer to honor and commemorate the Lord for all He has done thus far to deliver them.

Years ago, my friend Candy took me with her to a family retreat in Oregon where I came to know and love the women in her family. One of the unforgettable lessons I learned there from these sisters was the blessed importance of the ancient practice of erecting Ebenezers. The word "Ebenezer" means *"stone of help."* These ladies were in the habit of setting up these stones of help to thank God for bringing them to and through passages of their lives. They were wise enough to know that it wasn't by their own cleverness or skill that they had traversed the turbulent waters and tumultuous storms of their lives, and so they stopped before moving forward into dangerous forgetfulness long enough to ceremoniously and worshipfully honor *El Roi, the One who sees me, Jehovah Jireh, the Lord who provides.*

Since that time, I have, alone and with others, adopted this ritual of marking a spot of deliverance, completion, and momentous occasion with this ceremonious setting up of a *stone of help.* After I have erected my Ebenezer, I usually sing these verses of an old favorite:

> *Here I raise my Ebenezer;*
> *Hither by Thy help I've come;*
> *And I hope by Thy good pleasure,*
> *Safely to arrive at Home.*
> *Jesus sought me as a stranger,*
> *Wandering from the fold of God;*
> *He to rescue me from danger*
> *Interposed His precious blood.*
>
> *O to grace, how great a debtor*
> *Daily I'm constrained to be!*
> *Let Thy goodness, like a fetter,*
> *Bind my wandering heart to Thee.*
> *Never let me wander from Thee,*
> *Never leave the God I love;*
> *Here's my heart, O take and seal it,*
> *Seal it for Thy courts above.* [4]

Oh, let us take special care not to take for granted the blessing of God's help and mercy! Let us never be blasé about His blessings! Before this year gets away, take someone with you and raise to Him an Ebenezer for delivering you safely to this point.

~DECEMBER 29~
THE LOVELY PROMISE OF LATER ON

Unfortunately, sometimes life's storms hit us with great, heaving gusts. The winds are so brutal and the rain is so constant that not only can we find no *fun* under the sun; we cannot even find any *comfort* here. But there is comfort *above* the sun. Here is a collection of "Later On" scriptures that serve us as a blessed balm.

- *"Those who sow in tears will reap with songs of joy. He who goes out weeping carrying seeds to sow will return with songs of joy, carrying sheaves with him." Psalm 126:5-6*
- *"I consider that our present sufferings are not worth comparing with the glory that will be revealed in us." Romans 8:18*
- *"Weeping may endure for the night, but joy comes in the morning." Psalm 30:5*
- *"For our light and momentary troubles are achieving for us an eternal glory that far outweighs them all. So we fix our eyes not on what is seen but on what is unseen, for what is seen is temporary, but what is unseen is eternal." 2 Corinthians 4:17-18*
- *"Therefore, since we are surrounded by such a great cloud of witnesses, let us throw off everything that hinders and the sin that so easily entangles, and let us run with perseverance the race marked out for us. Let us fix our eyes on Jesus, the author and perfecter of our faith, who for the joy set before Him endured the cross, scorning its shame, and sat down at the right hand of the throne of God. Consider Him who endured such opposition from sinful men, so that you will not grow weary and lose heart." Hebrews 12:2-3*
- *"Be patient, then, brothers, until the Lord's coming. See how the farmer waits for the land to yield its valuable crop and how patient he is for the autumn and spring rains. You, too, be patient and stand firm, because the Lord's coming is near" James 5:7-8*
- *"Since, then, you have been raised with Christ, set your hearts on things above, where Christ is seated at the right hand of God. Set your minds on things above, not on earthly things. For you died, and your life is now hidden with Christ in God. When Christ, who is your life, appears, then you also will appear with him in glory." Colossians 3:1-4*

- *"Whatever you do, work at it with all your heart, as working for the Lord, not for men, since you know that you will receive an inheritance from the Lord as a reward." Colossians 3:23-24*
- *"But store up for yourselves treasures in Heaven where moth and rust do not destroy, and where thieves do not break in and steal." Matthew 6:20*
- *"In my Father's house are many rooms...I am going there to prepare a place for you. And if I go and prepare a place for you, I will come back and take you to be with me that you also may be where I am." John 14:2-3*
- *"For the Lord Himself will come down from Heaven with a loud command and the voice of the archangel, and with the trumpet call of God, and the dead in Christ will rise first. After that we who are still alive and are left will be caught up together with them in the clouds to meet the Lord in the air. And so we will be with the Lord forever." 1 Thessalonians 4:17*

~DECEMBER 30~
HEART ROCKS:
SETTING OUR HEARTS UPON PILGRIMAGE

"Blessed are those whose strength is in you, who have set their hearts upon pilgrimage...They go from strength to strength till each appears before God in Zion." Psalm 84:5, 7

This beautiful psalm begins with these words: *"How lovely is your dwelling place, O LORD Almighty! My soul yearns, even faints, for the courts of the LORD; my heart and my flesh cry out for the living God."* Such lovely words! They embody a sort of *haunting* quality that beckons to and links up with some homesickness in my heart that grows more and more poignant with every year that passes. We are about to end another one—one more year of growth. If we were trees, we would have manufactured one more ring to be numbered in our trunks. I pray that since we are something more than trees, we are marked with one more road, a concentric level higher than last years', that we have accomplished on our way to being a blessing to the God who created us for the very purpose of growth.

In a couple of days, we will embark upon a brand new year. However you feel about New Year's resolutions, I pray that you will take to heart Psalm 84 and let it inspire you to move on from where you are up to yet another higher road. Some of us might have an idea of what lies ahead on that road that awaits us. We might be straining at the bit to get to that bright place, or we might apprehensively turn our faces away from the specter ahead that we are tempted to fear deep in the pit of our core. Some of us have no idea what to expect as we move on, so we might just wish we could stay right here.

But we dare not stay. We must go on. Our whole life is just a series of camping spots until we arrive at Home, and each year is a microcosm of our whole life of pilgrimage. Hopefully at each of our campgrounds we have picked up a heart rock or two to carry in our pockets— a treasure of wisdom, a memory of grace and deliverance, rock-solid assurance that God is on the trail and has strewn before us more evidence of His love and presence.

If you are a little *overly-eager* about leaving this place for the next, maybe some prayer of examination is in order. Are you running away from unfinished business, eager to get around the next bend so you won't have to look at what you don't want to finish or give up to God? Unforgiveness, a need for confrontation, confession? If you are *frightened* to go on, maybe you are depending too much on sight and self while knowing that you are growing older, wearier, and your vision growing dimmer and duller. A prayer for stronger faith and more dependence upon God is in order. If you are *reluctant* to go, not because of a future you dread but a present you love, a prayer for courage and vision is in order. Ask God to help you believe that He has more in mind for you than just a series of encores.

Let's get our praying done, and pack up. It's time to go.

"No eye has seen, no ear has heard, no mind has conceived what God has prepared for those who love Him." 2 Corinthians 2:9

~DECEMBER 31~
A DELIGHTFUL SHATTERING

"Let us fix our eyes on Jesus, the author and perfecter of our faith, who for the glory set before Him endured the cross, scorning its shame, and sat down at the right hand of the throne of God." Hebrews 12:2

"Know that the Lord is God. It is He who made us, and we are His. We are His people, the sheep of His pasture." Psalm 100:3

"So we fix our eyes not on what is seen, but on what is unseen. For what is seen is temporary, but what is unseen is eternal." 2 Corinthians 4:18

It is hard to fret when you are looking into the face of Jesus. Refuse to look away from Him. Keep reminding yourself that this world is not real. Reality is being prepared for us, and we must wait patiently and accept no substitutes. In all you do, keep your mind fixed on Him, remembering that it was He who made you and not you yourself. No matter how long and hard you stare at the things that confound, regardless of how much effort you exert to fix the things that frustrate, the effort will never completely suffice.

I am convinced that first things will never be first until in *all* things we can see *Him*, until our imaginations belong totally to *Him*. Then, and only then, can we offer Him the very dregs of our jars in gratitude. When we assign things to their proper places, first things first, then the second things will bring us far more joy and far less pain than they did when they were out of their proper order on top of the stack where *God* belongs.

Someday, maybe today or tomorrow, the skies will split, and there will stand *Jesus* who will have come to take us Home finally. God our Father will welcome us into a time and place where all the superlatives will in the twinkling of an eye blossom gloriously into nouns. Eternal will become *Eternity*; glorious will suddenly be *Glory*; and that sprout, heavenly, will bloom into *Heaven*. The foretaste will give way to the Feast, and even though we may never have to worry about hunger in Heaven, I believe that somehow our taste buds will receive this Feast eagerly. Everything that confounded us on earth will dissolve in a long sigh of relief, acceptance, and maybe even understanding. Luxury will become commonplace, but because our Spirits will shed their fearful and defensive natures, we will not fall into the grievous heresy of taking the luxury for granted.

A resounding thunder will shake the pillars of Heaven as the jars that were His vessels on this dim earth shatter delightfully at His Holy feet.

ACKNOWLEDGMENTS

I am grateful beyond words for all those who have encouraged me as I have written. Thank you to my dear children and grandchildren, Emily, Ben, Jeremy, Leslie, Allison, Bryson, Callie, Joel, and Eli for generously allowing me many valuable spaces of loneliness and for your hearts full of belief that I could, against all odds, overcome my personality long enough to sit still and see this project through. Thanks to my faithful partner in prayer for sixteen years, Sharon Ritchie. Thanks to all those who spent hours helping me edit out the roughness and wisely advising me: my sister, Judy Brownlow, my sister-in-law Cynthia Taylor; my daughter, Emily Gillmore; Paula Thurmond, Candy Hanson, Andrea Lee, Pamela Horn, Wylene Williams, Genell Permenter, Ellen Agan; and to my faithful Larry for your many hours of tedious and exhausting technical work and your ever-ready listening and discerning ear. Your patience and calm spirit are my greatest earthly comfort.

And mostly, I thank you, Holy Spirit, for reminding me over and over of these words from Philippians 1:6: "Being confident of this that He who began a good work in you will carry it on to completion until the day of Christ Jesus."

ENDNOTES

February

1. Thomas Carlyle, *The Collected Works of Thomas Carlyle* (London Chapman and Hall, 1858).

2. George Orwell, *Animal Farm* (New York, NY: Signet Classics, 1945), 4.

3. Karl Marx, *A Contribution to Critique of Hegel's Philosophy of Right* (Cambridge: Cambridge University Press, 1970).

4. Johnson Oatman, Jr., "Higher Ground," *Praise for the Lord* (Nashville, TN: Praise Press, 1997), 234.

5. William H. Danforth, *I Dare You* (New York, NY: Cosimo, Inc, 2006), 8.

6. Author unknown

March

1. Oswald Chambers, *My Utmost for His Highest* (Barbour and Company, Inc., 1993), 341.

2. Twila Paris, "A Heart That Knows You," *A Heart That Knows You* (Nashville, TN: Star Song, 1992).

3. Thomas Ken, "Praise God from Whom All Blessings," *Great Songs of the Church, Revised* (Abilene, TX: ACU Press, 1986), 73.

4. William Wordsworth, "The World Is Too Much With Us," *Adventures in English Literature* (New York: Harcourt Brace Jovanovich, 1979), 454.

April

1. Rear Admiral Grace Murray Hopper as quoted by John Shedd, *Salt from My Attic* (Portland, ME: The Mosher Press, 1928).

2. Michael Card, "Job Suite, *The Way of Wisdom* (Chatsworth, CA: Sparrow Corporation, 1990).

May

1. Robert Browning, "Pippa Passes," *Bells and Pomegranates* (1841)

2. Wordsworth, 454.

3. C.S. Lewis, *Mere Christianity* (New York, NY: Touchstone, 1996), 171.

4. John Wesley, "Sermon 113," London, December 30, 1788.

5. C.S. Lewis, The *Weight of Glory* (New York, NY: Touchstone, 1996), 159.

June

1. Malcolm Muggeridge, *The Green Stick* (New York, NY: William Morrow and Co., 1973), 81-82.

2. Browning, "Pippa Passes."

3. Douglas Groothius, *Confronting the New Age* (Downers Grove, IL: InterVarsity Press, 1988), 85.

July

1. William Shakespeare, *As You Like It (Act II, Scene VII).*

2. Beth Moore, *The Patriarchs: Encountering the God of Abraham, Isaac, and Jacob* (Nashville, TN: LifeWay Press, 2005), 233.

3. Gary Thomas, *Sacred Influence* (Grand Rapids, MI: Zondervan, 2006), 152.

September

   1.   Lewis, *Mere Christianity*, 163.

   2.   Dr. Bruce H. Wilkinson, *Old Testament Keyword Learning System* (Atlanta, GA: Walk Thru the Bible Ministries, 1989), 15.

   3.   Lewis, *Mere Christianity*, 177.

   4.   Reginald Heber, "Holy, Holy, Holy" (w. 1826), *Sacred Selections for the Church*, Ellis Crum, ed. (Kendallville, IN, 1971), 59.

   5.   Ibid.

October

   1.   Michael Masser and Gerry Goffin, "Saving All My Love for You," (WhitneyHouston, Artist), Arista Records, 1985.

   2.   Twila Paris, "Sweet Victory," (Twila Paris, Artist), Star Song, 1992.

   3. Lewis, *Mere Christianity*, 182.

December

   1.   J.P. Moreland, *Love Your God with All Your Mind* (Colorado Springs, CO: Navpress, 1997), 74-75.

   2.   Joni Erickson Tada, *Pearls of Great Price* (Grand Rapids, MI: Zondervan, 2006), May 16.

   3.   Beth Moore, *The Patriarchs: Encountering the God of Abraham, Isaac, and Jacob* (Nashville, TN: LifeWay Press, 2005), Video Session Eight, 195.

   4.   Robert Robinson (lyrics based on 1 Samuel 7:12), Nettleton (Traditional American Melody) "Come Thou Fount of Every Blessing," *Great Songs of the Church*, Revised Edition (Abilene,TX: ACU Press, 1986), 595.

LaVergne, TN USA
14 September 2009
157798LV00001B/156/P